D1443053

The Search for Peace
in the Middle East

The Search for Peace in the Middle East

The Story of President Bourguiba's Campaign for a Negotiated Peace Between Israel and the Arab States

Samuel Merlin

Thomas Yoseloff

South Brunswick • New York • London

© 1968 by A. S. Barnes & Co., Inc.

Library of Congress Catalogue Card Number: 68-27264

Thomas Yoseloff, Publisher
Cranbury, New Jersey 08512

Thomas Yoseloff Ltd
18 Charing Cross Road
London W.C. 2, England

6878
Printed in the United States of America

Preface

MR. GEORGE BALL, THE NEW UNITED STATES AMBASSADOR TO THE United Nations, has on several recent occasions expressed the opinion that the crisis in the Middle East is potentially a greater danger to world peace than Vietnam. He is not the only man in the know who thinks so. The reasons for this somber view are varied, but the most ominous one is the fact that in the Middle East, both the United States and the Soviet Union are there on the spot, armed with the most sophisticated and deadly instruments of destruction. The danger is that the two giant nuclear powers may be drawn into a confrontation by a combination of circumstances not necessarily of their own making.

It is to President Bourguiba's historic credit that he alone, among Arab leaders, realizes the full implication of such a danger and undertook an initiative—at the risk of his career and his very life—to remove the time-bomb of the explosive Middle East. The specter of a confrontation between the super-powers was not, however, the only motivation for launching his campaign for a negotiated settlement of the Israel-Arab conflict. He acted out of self-interest in trying to stem the aggressive and expansionist drive of President Nasser's pan-Arabism, which he considers the ultimate danger to the independence of each and all of the Arab States.

This book attempts to tell the story of this peace initiative—its background and dramatic repercussions in the Arab world, in Israel and in the West. It also attempts a close scrutiny of the whole web of inter-Arab power relationships, the understanding of which is imperative for any apprehension of the complexities and confusions of the Israeli-Arab conflict. In the light of all this, the author tried to discern the trends—if any—which may lead to a peaceful settlement of the Palestine problem and tentatively to adumbrate the basis upon which such a settlement may eventually take shape.

5

The author felt that in order to grasp the full significance of President Bourguiba's campaign one should also get a closer look at the man who created the storm—his life, his career, his philosophy and his aspirations both as a leader of his own people and as a statesman in the international arena.

Chronologically speaking, this book tells the story of the campaign which President Bourguiba launched in the Old City of Jerusalem on March 6, 1965 and which he continued in a sustained manner till the end of September of that year—for about seven months. (All dates mentioned in the book, unless otherwise indicated, refer to 1965). This is not to say that after that he dropped the matter. Far from it. Whenever an occasion arose he came back to it, though only intermittently. And in the wake of the military disaster which befell Egypt, Jordan and Syria as a result of their defeat in June 1967 at the hands of the Israelis, he picked up the initiative and sustained it till this very day with ever increasing vigor. But what he had to say on the subject since September 1965 were mostly variations and elaborations of the theme he fully developed before that.

Critics will, perhaps, point out that the story of these seven months of inter-Arab relationships and Israel-Arab attitudes as they came into relief during President Bourguiba's campaign, is told in too great detail. They will perhaps ask why was it necessary to write such an exhaustive report about what may be considered a mere episode on the margin of history. The answer is that in the view of this writer it is not an episode but an event of great historic magnitude. When in our day and age a leader of a state tries to break away from a totalitarian and fanatical constellation—and pan-Arabism is such a system—it is a matter of transcendent international significance. Bourguiba considers himself the Tito of the Arab world, and rightly so. For an Arab leader to proclaim his independence from pan-Arab tutelage and to leave the Arab league is, within the given geo-political context, as important as is for a Communist head-of-state to declare his independence from Moscow.

Tito's rebellion was not a mere episode but a beginning of a process which sooner or later may well bring about the disintegration of the pan-Communist monolith. All the subsequent upheavals in Poland, Hungary and Czechoslovakia are to one degree or another traceable to this first rebellion. What happened in Czechoslovakia in the first part of 1968 is both a continuation and logical development of Tito's challenge to the Kremlin.

For an Arab statesman to proclaim the imperative of peace with Israel is the equivalent of a Communist leader in Eastern Europe embarking upon a policy of democratization and humanism. Both are anathema. In each case the challenge constitutes a real danger to the survival of the totalitarian regime in their respective orbits. The Kremlin cannot tolerate such a heresy in Eastern Europe nor can Nasser permit it in the Middle East. In the long run pan-Communist totalitarianism probably cannot survive the exercise of freedom in any country within their sphere, nor can totalitarian pan-Arabism survive peace with Israel. Both have quite frankly confessed it being the case.

That's why Bourguiba's campaign for a negotiated peace between Israel and the Arabs deserves detailed reporting, close scrutiny and analysis in depth.

This writer also hopes that whoever reads this chronicle will not only become acquainted with the events which took place during that short period of time, but will also get a thorough idea of what the conflicts and tensions in the Middle East are all about: the nature and pattern of inter-Arab relations, the role and manifestations of pan-Arabism, the essence of the Israel-Arab conflict; the claims, counter-claims, contentions and aspirations of all the parties concerned. An attempt to depict all this on a larger canvas and over a much longer period of time would neither substantially alter the picture nor add any new basic elements. What happened during the several months in 1965 when Bourguiba launched and developed his initiative is, in a sense, a synopsis of the whole drama of the Arab world as centered on Palestine.

*   *   *

No "expert" can be expected to write about the contemporary scene in the Middle East with any certainty that subsequent events will not outmode the narrative, at least to some extent, even before it sees the light of day. The present volume, except for the beginning of the introductory chapter, Chapter XXVI and L'Envoi, was written in 1966. Since then many things have changed in the area, mainly though not exclusively, as a result of the Six-Day-War. The immediate events which led to the outbreak of hostilities and those which followed in their aftermath, had a traumatic effect upon both the Arabs and Israel. No doubt, some of the events which are described and analyzed in this narrative may seem somewhat remote, in the light of later developments. Yet in the opinion of this writer, the changes which took place are more apparent than real; more on the surface than in depth; more fleeting in nature than basic. Despite the changed frontiers resulting from Israel's spectacular victory and some significant revisions in the tune and style of Arab diplomatic and propaganda utterances, the basic issues of the Israel-Arab conflict remain in 1968 what they were in 1965, and for that matter in 1956 and even in 1948. More than that, some of the portentous events which took place after this book was written not only don't, in the opinion of this writer, make the narrative obsolete, but on the contrary, illuminate it and add to its poignancy.

At all events, until a final solution is found to the Palestine drama, the French maxim, that the more things change, the more they are the same, holds good, as far as the Middle Eastern scene is concerned. In view of these reflections I felt that it was not necessary to rewrite the manuscript in order to adjust it to the latest newspaper headlines. I am not even sure that what in the manuscript may seem today out of date will not become topical again on publication day. Therefore, I thought that under the circumstances the best approach would be to leave things as narrated and analyzed originally rather than to revise them. To apply a method of hindsight would be to tamper with history rather than to rectify it. Thus, with only minor adjustments, I leave this essay to stand on its merits or demerits as it was originally written.

* * *

Yet perhaps a few qualifying remarks are called for. Though I believe that were I to write this book now, I would not have produced an essay basically different from the one I prepared a couple of years ago, some minor parts would have been brought up-to-date. In view of the fact that certain of the *dramatis personae* have in the meantime been removed from the scene I should have, of course, referred to them in the past tense, like in the case of Mr. Ahmed Shukairy, who is no longer the head of the Palestine Liberation Organization. In certain instances I would have an opportunity explicitly to exemplify conjectures with events which have taken place since 1966.

As to General de Gaulle whom I so greatly admired in 1966 I still continue to regard him as a towering statesman of our time. Yet, I would probably have treated him with greater skepticism and perhaps even with some misgivings. Because his attitudes, policies and acts became somewhat tarnished lately due to his excesses, extremism, and plain opportunism. In a word, I didn't, when I wrote the book discern as I do now, his sin of pride—what the

Greeks called Hubris—which made him overstep the invisible line of what is permissible to mortals, regardless how great.

Nasser, despite or perhaps because of his disastrous miscalculations and adventurism of May 1967 would have remained the same. And, so also the Israelis, despite their military triumph in June. They have proven once more that they can make war and take care of themselves militarily more brilliantly and with greater dedication than any other nation in modern history, but they still haven't learned the art of peace.

As to Bourguiba, he is still fascinating and perplexing as he was two years ago, only more so.

*　　*　　*

The composition of the Arab governments often change in such swift succession that it was difficult in each case to indicate the shift or removal. Therefore, whenever referring to a personality holding a certain office in an Arab Government, it has to be understood that he did so at the time, that is, in 1965, though at the present he may no longer hold the same position.

The excerpts of most of President Bourguiba's speeches quoted in this volume were reproduced from official transcripts published in French by the State Secretariat for Information and Orientation of the Tunisian Government. The translation of these as well as of his interviews and other source material used in this book, whether from the French, German or Hebrew, were done by the author. References to Arab sources were used from translations.

Acknowledgment

THE SEARCH FOR PEACE IN THE MIDDLE EAST IS PUBLISHED UNDER
the auspices of the Institute for Mediterranean Affairs. An independent, non-profit, educational organization the Institute was
established for the purpose of investigating the basic problems of
the Mediterranean area—many parts of which are beset by strife
and upheaval—with a view to formulating tentative options for
peaceful solutions to some of the explosive situations of that
region.

The Institute takes no stand, expressed or implied, on any issues
dealt with in the studies it publishes directly or through commercial publishers. Its reports and studies when produced by a panel
of experts reflect the consensus of the members who made up the
particular study group. When a study is prepared by one person
it reflects the ideas and philosophy of the author who is responsible
both for the statements of fact and expressions of opinion. The
Institute is responsible only for determining whether such studies
and reports should be presented to the public.

The Institute considers that President Habib Bourguiba's initiative for a negotiated settlement of the Israel-Arab conflict deserves
a comprehensive report and a thorough analysis of its implications.
This volume is, therefore, presented to the public as a contribution
to the discussion of the crisis in the Middle East and as material for
a better understanding of the issues and background of the Palestine conflict.

* * *

The author takes pleasure in expressing his gratitude to the
Institute for the generous and patient assistance in providing him
with the means and the time to prepare this book.

Contents

14   Contents

Part Three
THE MAN
His Life and Philosophy

The Search for Peace
in the Middle East

We could defeat the Arabs a dozen times and they would still remain in existence. If we lose once, we are finished.

> David Ben Gurion

A victory is the greatest tragedy in the world, except a defeat.

> Duke of Wellington

No tribunal has ever had the luck of trying a case where all the justice was on the side of one party and the other party had no case whatsoever. Usually in human affairs any tribunal . . . has to concede that both sides have a case on their side and, in order to do justice, they must take into consideration what should constitute the basic justification of all human demands, individual or mass demands—the decisive terrible balance of Need.

> Vladimir Jabotinsky

In what is truly tragic there must be valid moral powers on both sides which come into collision. . . . Both suffer loss and yet both are mutually justified.

> Hegel

Things do not get better by being left alone. Unless they are adjusted, they explode with a shattering detonation.

> Winston Churchill

Part One

The Story

1

Introduction

THE MIDDLE EAST IS THE REGION PAR EXCELLENCE OF RUMORS.
Alarms which seemed false suddenly astound everyone by proving
true. Surprises are not an exception to the rule of life but a constant pattern: endless revolutions, coups, countercoups, assassina-
tions. Alliances are concluded and alliances are reversed. Alignments and partnerships shift. Yesterday's implacable and sworn
enemy is proclaimed today's best friend. The Middle East is a
region where one heartily embraces yesterday's plotters against
one's life and subverters of one's regime. Those who were yesterday declared assassins are today proclaimed devoted and loyal
brothers; the renewed friendship is sworn to remain eternal. With
luck it may last a week or a few months.

Amidst this restlessness and inconstancy one factor has remained
static: the Israel-Arab conflict. Yet it, too, is part of the pattern:
for years one expects it to simmer in the limbo of no-war and no-
peace, and then suddenly it erupts into a world-shaking explosion.
When it erupts one is surprised both at its magnitude and at its
fantastic results. Then almost everybody agrees that there is
nothing to be surprised about.

The Israel-Arab war of June 1967 is part of that pattern. In May
and in the first days of June of that year the skies became dark and
stormy when the State of Israel with its two-and-a-half million
people found itself confronted by a formidable alliance of all its
Arab neighbors; an alliance, supported by all 13 members of the
Arab League, and representing a combined population of more
than one hundred million.

Egypt, the leader of the coalition, was in possession of a tremendous army equipped with the most modern weapons, including
missiles, provided and installed by the Soviet Union. In swift and

dramatic moves President Nasser galvanized the whole of the Arab world. His mechanized divisions moved to the frontier of Israel; the United Nations Emergency Peacekeeping Force was ordered to withdraw; the Strait of Tiran at the entrance of the Gulf of Aqaba was blockaded and announced to be mined; the armies of Syria to the North and of Jordan to the East were put under a unified command headed by Egyptian generals.

The Arab leadership, the press, the radio, the TV networks, celebrated in advance the obliteration of the State of Israel and the annihilation of her population. Dread and anxiety at the prospect of the mighty Arab war machine overrunning Israel and exterminating its people swept public opinion in all of Western Europe and in the United States and in many other countries. The concentration of Arab forces on Israel's frontiers, the encirclement and the threats looked so overwhelming that Israel, among other measures, hastily converted public parks and football fields in the major cities into emergency cemeteries and large factories into emergency morgues with the expectation of handling 50,000 or more dead. The spectre of mass genocide loomed ominously on the horizon.

For days and weeks the Israelis seem to have been overawed by the prospect of an apocalyptic showdown and paralyzed into agonizing vacillation and inaction.

Then, unexpectedly, the Israelis took the offensive and in a few hours smashed the Egyptian air power and singlehandedly won one of the greatest victories in the annals of history. It then took them only five more days to conquer the whole of the Sinai peninsula; to station their troops all along the east bank of the Suez Canal; to reopen the Strait of Tiran; to occupy the whole of the west bank of Jordan and the old city of Jerusalem; and to crown all their military objectives with the scaling and conquest of the heights of Golan in Syria. Thus, at the end of these lightning operations, Israel had quadrupled its territory; and if it were not for the cease fire orders by the U.N. Security Council, the Israeli armies could have reached Cairo, Damascus and Amman. The Arabs suffered more than 50,000 casualties. The Israeli casualties were 679 soldiers killed and 2,563 wounded, 255 of them seriously.

After it was all over, specialists and people generally in the know —in Israel, in Europe, in America and even in the Arab countries —claimed that the defeat was no surprise to them. They had known all along, so they asserted, that were there to be a military showdown the Israelis would have no difficulties in scoring a decisive victory. It was a foregone conclusion, these observers pointed out. Hadn't the Israelis done the same thing twice in the past: in 1948 and 1956? Didn't the Israelis show during the last 19 years that they could, if they so wished, penetrate with impunity into neighboring Arab territory—to retaliate for acts of infiltration and sabotage? In retrospect and with the necessary hindsight, these arguments seem quite plausible. *In fine*—there was no surprise.

But this is, perhaps, only the most dramatic example of the nature of the Middle Eastern scene where events are frequently expected and surprising at the same time.

*   *   *

This restless, feverish Middle Eastern scene has been emotionally and politically dominated for the last 20 years—since the establishment of the Jewish state—by the Israel-Arab conflict. And though the war in June changed many things on the map and in the life of the region, the essence and the elements of the conflict remain the same. What happened in June 1967 could have happened almost any previous year. The story we are about to tell in this book took place two years earlier—in 1965. The Israel-Arab conflict was then as acute and seething as ever.

As in 1967, that year also began under especially clouded skies. An early spring produced threats and counter-threats, nasty rumors and alarms. Not since the Suez crisis in 1956 were the prospects of peace gloomier or the predictions more pessimistic. Many spoke of 1965 as the year of a new—perhaps, final—confrontation between Israel and her Arab neighbors. It started ominously with serious Israeli border clashes with both Syria and Jordan. The heavy exchange of gunfire on December 31, 1964, resulted in casualties on both sides.

The Olive Tree Incident

The eerie, Kafkaesque atmosphere of the Middle Eastern political climate is illustrated by an incident that took place a week earlier, on December 23. In the Mount Scopus area—then an isolated Israel enclave* in the Jordanian sector of Jerusalem—stand some olive trees. The Chairman of the Israel-Jordan Mixed Armistice Commission asked the Israel representative to permit a few women from the Jordanian village Issavia to pick the olives. The

---

* This enclave was demilitarized and consisted of the original campus of the Hebrew University, its library, and Hadassah Hospital.

Israelis agreed, on condition that three of their armed police watch the picking. By arrangement, the policemen were to be stationed at an agreed upon topographical location. Around noon on the appointed day, six Arab women appeared and began picking; three Israeli policemen also appeared and watched. The women worked for only about three-quarters of an hour and left. The policemen remained, waiting for the women to return. They did not. Instead, Jordanian troops suddenly opened fire and wounded all three policemen. For more than three hours the policemen lay under fire while U.N. officials tried in vain to reach them with medical aid. Finally the firing ceased, the men were picked up and carried through Mandelbaum Gate to an Israeli hospital.

U.N. officers were extremely embarrassed because the responsibility was theirs. Israelis were sure the incident was intended as provocation. But after several days of investigation, the truth was revealed. By the agreement, the policemen were to be stationed at a spot on the map indicated as 13311. On the copy given the Israelis, the U.N. typist had carelessly made it 13331. The Jordanians, as soon as they realized the Israelis were stationed a few meters away from the spot where they expected them, promptly opened fire. This incident typifies the weird atmosphere prevailing in Israel-Arab relations, even when the two sides attempt peaceful, humanitarian action.

"The Summer of the Third Round"

This was not a major incident. It merely symbolizes the climate. Such minor incidents multiplied. On both sides of the borders as well as in the capitals of the world, qualified observers saw serious deterioration. Colonel Nasser was described as in a "pre-Suez" (1956) mood and Israel in a "pre-Sinai" (1956) mood. In the Arab capitals, especially Cairo, March was frequently mentioned as the month for the crisis to come to a head.

Rumors of impending war swept Cairo. President Nasser's most influential spokesman, Hassanein Heikal, editor of Cairo's *Al Ahram,* warned the Egyptians of "a dangerous summer." On February 21, President Nasser himself declared that 1965 was a year of danger for the Arabs because "imperialism and Israel are all out to wage their last battle against Arab unity."

King Hussein of Jordan thought that more than at any time since the Israel-Arab war 17 years before, there was the danger that 1965 might well be the year of a decisive confrontation between Israel and the Arabs. He declared that Israel's attack was to be expected imminently. Israel's Premier Eshkol at a press conference in London admitted that "the chances for peace are not very promising." Border incidents, multiplying with increasing fury, brought serious casualties on both sides.

March was indeed a month of crisis with portentous signs of impending disaster. The Arab hate factories were working overtime, pouring out threats of conquest and annihilation. A unified command of the Arab armies, though still mostly theoretical, was reportedly making plans to protect the work of diverting the headwaters of the Jordan River. The Chief of Staff of the Egyptian Army ordered military leaves cancelled. Some forces were put on modified alert. Reserves were called up and large scale maneuvers were reported in various parts of the country including the Gaza strip. The strip itself was said to have been declared off-limits to foreigners.* Egyptian planes were reported in Israeli skies, while Cairo accused Israel of intruding into Egyptian air. Spy rings were discovered by both sides. Eli Cohen, Israel's legendary arch-spy who succeeded in infiltrating into the highest echelons of the Syrian hierarchy, was tried and executed.

The arms race hurtled on. Each side published horrendous tales about the other's military preparations for imminent attack. The Egyptians reported that Israel had carried out a test mobilization of reserves. The Arabs tried to implement their plans to divert the Jordan headwaters, and the Israelis bombarded the sites of the operations. On several occasions Arab guerrillas infiltrated Israel and carried out acts of sabotage. Four border battles at the beginning of March involved heavy artillery and tanks.

Israel Threatens Preventive War

In Israel, voices were raised for some drastic action in the form of a preventive war. Chief among these was that of Moshe Dayan, commander and hero of the 1956 Sinai expeditionary force. Even Premier Eshkol and Foreign Minister Golda Meir proclaimed in unmistakable terms that Israel would use force to prevent the diversionary project from being undertaken. In January Prime Minister Eshkol had warned that Arab plans to divert the Jordan headwaters in Syria and Lebanon would be regarded as "an encroachment on our soil"; hence, "a military confrontation would become inevitable."

* (Cairo later denied this.)

On March 6 Mr. Eshkol also voiced a warning that if terrorist raids continued, Israel would take energetic action against the countries from which the terrorists infiltrated. The Israel press also sounded grave warnings in connection with the increase in armaments in Arab countries, especially Jordan. King Hussein was reported planning to double the strength of his army, mainly through weapons acquired from the West. Israel Chief of Staff Itzhak Rabin declared that if this increase really materialized, Israel would have no choice but to reappraise some of its basic policies toward Jordan.

In March President Johnson sent a special envoy, Under Secretary of State Averell Harriman, to Israel, and another representative, Assistant Secretary of State, Phillips Talbot, to Cairo. Their mission: to prevail on Egypt and Israel to avert a head-on collision. King Hussein thought Harriman's mission had been successful and that the immediate danger of an Israel military offensive had been prevented. But the correspondent of the London Daily Express learned that Harriman had not received from the Israel Government a firm commitment not to attack.

The press in the major Western capitals reported an ever-deteriorating situation that could ignite at any moment. Some correspondents saw alarming signs pointing to an unavoidable cataclysm. The London Daily Telegraph averred that the arms buildups and plans to divert the Jordan headwaters were "leading step by step to an inevitable collision involving missiles and possibly nuclear weapons."

The London Daily Express published a comprehensive report based on on-the-spot investigations by its correspondents in all Arab countries and Israel. Their conclusion was that in the opinion of American and British diplomats, Israel and the Arab States were nearer to open warfare than they had ever been since Suez in 1956.

The German Arms Deal

The first part of 1965 was indeed a mad season. The Middle East had become a phantasmagoria where everyone played a weird part—the Arabs, Israel, West and East Germany, the United States, Russia, China, even Spain.

Israel, the "remnant" of the Nazi holocaust, was booming, thanks to West German "repatriations," and looked to Bonn for protection and military assistance through a secret arms deal.

At the same time, Egypt was basing its plans to settle accounts with Israel upon West German scientists who were working over-time to build up powerful weapons, including missiles, for the destruction of the Jewish State. Now the Israelis did not know whether to bless or curse Germany. The Government in Jerusalem was sharply divided. However, it tried to exert pressure upon Bonn to recall its scientists from Cairo. The Germans insisted that theirs was a democratic country; and anyone was free to go where he wanted and do as he liked.

Then the "sensation" exploded: the Egyptians "discovered" an arms deal—a "discovery" that for months had been circulating in the German as well as in the world press. The Germans had been sending hardware, mainly tanks, to Israel. Bonn, however, then disclosed that its arms deal had not been exactly a bilateral arrange-ment, but a tripartite one. The United States, following a policy of not supplying arms directly to the Middle East, (probably to avoid annoying Nasser) permitted the Germans to ship to *Israel* American armaments which the United States had previously sent to Germany. But the Germans were not just a secret broker: they footed the bill. The State Department confirmed Bonn's version.

Nasser went into a frenzy that forced the Germans to lose their perspective. They panicked and cancelled their commitment to Israel; more, they sent to Socialist Nasser a Spanish Fascist, Mar-quis de Nerva as emissary to inform Cairo about Bonn's surrender and ask for terms of conciliating the Egyptian leader. President Nasser was of course, elated; and at the same time he felt that he was given a unique opportunity to kick the Germans while they were down. So he hinted at recognition of East Germany by in-viting that satellite's Chief of State, Herr Walter Ulbricht, to visit Cairo. This was too much for Bonn, and Chancellor Erhard an-nounced that the Federal Republic would recognize Israel and establish diplomatic relations with her. With this, the crisis did not end; on the contrary, President Nasser considered it opportune to widen and intensify it.

A Fit of Frenzy

Colonial Nasser personifies, perhaps, more than anybody else in the reawakened nations, what is often called the "charismatic" leader. His appeal to the masses is tremendous. His charm in dealing with heads of state and representatives of foreign govern-ments, both of East and West, is often irresistible. That he became the most articulate leader of the Arab world is due not only to the size, history and cultural tradition of Egypt, but also to his own talents, which are considerable, and to his intelligence and shrewdness.

The trouble with charismatic leaders is that when they are suddenly removed, they leave barely a ripple and are soon forgotten, as was the case with General Abdul Karim el-Kassem of Iraq ("The Only True Leader"), and more recently with Ben Bella of Algeria and Nkrumah of Ghana. But in February 1965 President Nasser still enjoyed tremendous prestige and popularity. After a strenuous "electioneering" campaign, he was reelected to a new six year term as President. He received 99.999% of the vote. (98.5% of the electorate participated in the balloting).

Granting all his talents and superiority, the Egyptian President at times exhibits irrational behavior bordering on hysteria, if not paranoia. Some observers think it may be simulated. His outbursts of rage, his cursing, insulting his opponents or those whom he considers at a particular moment his enemies (often the United States) are disconcerting. He tells the Americans to choke or explode, or drink themselves to death in the Mediterranean.

This irrationality became especially obvious during the German-Egyptian crisis which had developed out of the secret arms deal between Bonn and Israel. Each day his utterances became more violent and illogical, almost delirious. He threatened West Germany. He extended the threats to other great powers as well. He asserted that a showdown with Germany was the first step to the liberation of Palestine. He made gestures of seizing West German assets in Egypt; of expropriating German property*; of cancelling payment of debts to the Federal Republic. Nasser demanded "unconditional surrender."

When Bonn did surrender and abruptly cancelled the arms deal, Nasser increased his abuse and began to threaten the whole of the Western world. He wanted, he explained, to teach a lesson not only to West Germany but to all imperialist powers, especially the United States. He warned the great powers not to sell arms to Israel—rejecting the concept of an arms balance between Israel and the Arabs. What balance can there be, he demanded, between 50 million people and 2 million? He hinted that unless the Western powers stopped helping Israel, he would stop dealing with them; he would organize a pan-Arab boycott; he would deny them Arab

---

* Trade unions controlled by the Government moved to confiscate all German ships anchored in Egyptian ports.

oil and passage through the Suez Canal. He boasted of having in the past (1956) defeated France, England and Israel, and now, in 1965, Germany, with his mighty arm still outstretched for greater deeds. He was going full speed ahead, he declared, with rockets and atomic weapons. He promised the Arabs he would lead them back to Palestine through fields drenched with blood; that for this purpose he was building up an army of three million men.

Observers thought Nasser's mood was caused, partly at least, by the tremendous difficulties converging upon him and his country at that moment: the frustration in the Yemen, where 50,000 of his soldiers were bogged down; his economic difficulties—lack of food, commodities and hard currency. At the beginning of the year, Egypt was already on the verge of bankruptcy. In order to meet the most pressing financial commitments, Cairo had, according to press reports, sold thirty tons of gold to Zurich. In addition, activities of subversive groups inside the country began to be discovered, largely, probably, as a result of the Yemen adventure. As a diversion from these near crises, these observers pointed out, the more extreme of Nasser's aides, and perhaps he, himself, might have contemplated a leap into a military adventure against Israel. By such means Nasser might at long last unite the Arab world, not the least result of which might be the bailing out of Egypt by those Arab countries rich in resources and economic potentialities.

In the Middle East Everything Is Possible

Of course, such a grandiose scheme to challenge singlehandedly the major Western powers as well as Israel, should have been considered sheer nonsense. Realistically speaking, Egypt under Nasser presented no menace as a mighty power. Nasser had as yet defeated nobody on the field of battle—not even the primitive tribes in the Yemen. His threats would not be mere braggadocio, but pure megalomania—unless intended as a calculated ploy to befuddle the Western powers and, above all, the United States, and to keep Egyptian morale at the highest possible pitch.

The threat to withhold oil from Western Europe and the United States would prove ineffective. The Arabs are in greater need to sell than the West to buy it. The threat to close the Suez Canal to international traffic is equally absurd. It would deprive Egypt of vitally needed income in foreign currency. The Western powers would adjust the shipping problems to the necessity of going around the Cape, with some inconvenience, but without serious disruption in oil supplies. The threat to attack Israel might prove more dangerous to Egypt than to the Jewish state.

But in the Middle East anything can happen, as epitomized in that story so often told and repeated about the scorpion asking a frog to ferry him over the Nile. When the frog expressed reticence out of fear that the scorpion might sting him to death while crossing, the latter explained the absurdity of such an apprehension: "After all, if I sting you, I'll go under together with you. Isn't this logic of things the best guarantee for your safety?" The frog agreed and in midstream, the scorpion did sting the frog and they both started to drown. The frog asked "How could you do it, knowing quite well that you will go under with me?" Tho which the scorpion answered: "It seems that you forget that this is the Middle East." Characteristically, this joke is extremely popular with the Egyptians themselves.

The Spell Is Broken

In that atmosphere of unreason, mutual hate, fear and whipped-up frenzy, President Bourguiba appeared on the scene with an olive branch. He saw it as an historic imperative to act without delay to check this mad course, which if not reversed, would inescapably lead to disaster. He launched a campaign of common sense and moderation, hoping that he might propel along with him anyone brave enough to swim against the powerful current of irrationality.

His was a mighty and courageous act. Of course, being a lone and vilified prophet in the Arab world, he did not succeed in averting disaster but only in postponing it for two years. Yet he deserves credit for at least temporarily having broken the spell of hysteria. And now that the Arabs have paid the bitter price of defeat and humiliation, because they ignored his advice, he emerges not only as a Cassandra whose warnings came true but also as a leader whose words are listened to with greater attention and respect than ever before.

The Six-Day War has demonstrated dramatically how right Bourguiba was. Three years ago his was a voice crying in the wilderness. Today the Arab world, though slowly and clumsily, edges towards acceptance of his philosophy. In this sense his peace campaign is only beginning.

2

A Tour That Made History

ON FEBRUARY 15, 1965 PRESIDENT HABIB BOURGUIBA LEFT TUNISIA to begin a "pilgrimage" through the Arab Middle East, Iran, Turkey, Greece and Yugoslavia. His departure did not create a ripple anywhere outside Tunisia. When his tour ended, he had made history in grand style. During his two-month journey, his name and utterances were reported almost daily by the communications media of all the continents. World opinion hailed him as a wise, imaginative, and courageous statesman of international magnitude. In Paris, De Gaulle reportedly likened him to himself—they both, he said, had a rendezvous with history. American and European editors proposed that Bourguiba be given the Nobel Peace Prize.

From the Arab world, however, came no lasting acclaim. This, even though the Tunisian President had started his tour as a champion of the cause of Arab nationalism and unity. True, he received a hero's welcome in Cairo and most of the other capitals of his itinerary. But by the time he had finished, he was being attacked as a traitor to the Arab cause and a saboteur of Arab unity. Arab mobs burned him in effigy in the streets. Violent demonstrations were staged against him and his country in a score of cities. "Death to Bourguiba!" reverberated through the Middle East, from Baghdad to Cairo. Of the Arab League nations, only his own country gave him a triumphal reception—the greatest of his career—when he returned.

Bourguiba's words and actions during those eight weeks and the weeks and months that followed are of more than transient interest. They enormously affected inter-Arab relationships. They exposed cracks in the "solid" front of pan-Arabism. shifted alignments in the Middle Eastern power struggles, even affected the course of international politics beyond the Arab world.

What Habib Bourguiba did was to explode a "peace bomb" in the Old City of Jerusalem, then still in Jordan's hands. Never before since Israel's birth had *any* Arab dared hint at what the President of Tunisia openly suggested on that March day in 1965.

Accompanied by his wife and a group of some sixty high Tunisian dignitaries and journalists, President Bourguiba completed somewhat uneventful visits to Egypt and Saudi Arabia. For the next leg of his tour King Hussein sent Jordanian Air Force planes to escort the distinguished visitor to Amman. He landed to a twenty-one gun salvo, attended a lavish banquet in his honor, and received Hussein's highest decoration. In return, Bourguiba in his speech of thanks pledged to continue to help the Palestianian Arabs as he had in the past.

The published schedule for Bourguiba's visit to Jordan included an extensive tour along the Jordan–Israel armistice lines, especially in the Jerusalem area, with visits to some of the refugee camps and the Old City itself. It also indicated that the two heads of state would undertake serious discussions about problems of first-rate importance.

Jordanian daily newspapers reported on Bourguiba's visits to the Dome of the Rock, Al Aksa Mosque, and a children's school. The Old City newspaper *Al Manar* wrote on Monday, March 2: "We tell you now that on the next visit we want to receive you in Jaffa, Haifa, Acre, and Nazareth" (once predominantly Arab cities now in Israel).

The next day Bourguiba appeared before a huge rally of Arab refugees in the Akbat Jather camp near Jericho. According to the report of the Old City daily *Falastin,* he told the assembled refugees:

> Emotions is not enough, neither is willingness to sacrifice. To regain the plundered fatherland you need patience—lots of patience, and preparedness.
>
> Nothing is easier than to compete in speech-making and stirring up the masses. But no battle has ever been won in this way. What is important is steadfastness in labor, truth in speech, straight-forwardness in action, and a winning perseverance in the hearts of the people. [sic]

Such a summary of a long speech of rather convoluted logic

and acrobatic rhetoric is not only bad reporting but probably
intentional distortion. For if this were the gist of his remarks,
there is nothing sensational in his words. There is in them no
obvious deviation from the general Arab line. The objective of
"regaining the plundered fatherland" is still there; it is difficult
to see what steadfastness in work, truth in speech, and straight-
forwardness in action—all fine virtues—have to do with the liberation of Palestine.

What we do know now is that neither the *Falastin* nor any other
newspaper did *not* report faithfully what had happened. For Bourguiba had said a lot more than the few vague and ambiguous
phrases reproduced out of context.

Having now before us the full text of the speech we cannot but
marvel at the political boldness and the psychological skill of the
man who dared risking to appear before the most embittered
people in the world, whose only spiritual nourishment consist of
wild promises of speedy liberation, revenge and regaining their
homes and fields left behind (or which they never had but in their
imagination) and to tell them that they live in a world of illusion
and delusion.

Bourguiba told the refugees that their leaders misled them and
that their politicians were guilty of intransigeance and inflexibility: ". . . the policy of 'all or nothing' brought us only defeat in
Palestine and to the sad situation in which we find ourselves
today." It was a great mistake to reject any compromise solutions.
The Arab leaders rejected such solutions as offered by the British
in the White Paper of 1939 or by the United Nations which offered
Partition of Palestine. Each time they regretted having rejected a
previous compromise.

He warned his listeners that if the policy of intransigeance continued the refugees would be condemned to live in the conditions
of misery "for centuries to come." To act only out of emotions
leads only to an impasse.

What he proposed was to adopt in the Middle East the same
policy of "stages" he pursued so successfully in the fight for Tunisia's independence. And he indulged in an exposition of a super-
machiavellian philosophy of achieving one's ends "by detours, in
phases and ruse", until final victory is assured.

How sincere he is in his convictions when expostulating such a
machiavellian method is difficult to judge. This writer believes
that throughout his campaign Bourguiba used it rather "to sugar
the pill" he was administering to desperately embittered people,

in order to see his message come across at all. We will return to this puzzle time and again during the course of our narrative.

Machiavellism notwithstanding, what he *did* say was new, startling, revolutionary, and, to Arab ears, anathema. He took a grave risk in saying such things to—of all people—the refugees. But they did not stone him; they applauded. A student from the city of Nablus said afterward that President Bourguiba was "the only chief of state to have defined the true dimensions of the problem."

The trigger that was to explode the long echoing chain reaction was pulled during a press conference in the Old City on Saturday, March 6, 1965, at the end of Bourguiba's visit in Jordan.

At that press conference he staggered an audience of journalists, government officials, and representatives of the refugees with an unambiguous assertion that the Arab leaders had misled them with irresponsible and demagogic promises to throw the Jews into the sea. The time had come, he declared, to abandon these illusions, return to realism and common sense, and think about a peaceful settlement with the Jews.

The news conference was taped—both the statement and the questions and answers—and broadcast *once* on Amman Radio. Two Old City dailies—the *Jerusalem Times* (In English) and *Falastin*—published extensive accounts on March 7. Other papers in Jordan published only fragmentary reports, from which the main point of Bourguiba's message was omitted or obscured beyond recognition. Hence, those of his remarks which were reported did not make much sense. Apart from that, a fairly comprehensive account appeared in a dispatch from United Press International, filed in the Old City of Jerusalem on March 6, 1965.

Nevertheless, the story was rather slow to reach the world press. Its explosive contents and far-reaching implications became apparent only a few days after the event when it began to provoke stormy repercussions in several Arab capitals and a heated controversy in Israel. Thus, the prestigious *Le Monde* of Paris, usually excellently informed concerning the Middle East, knew nothing about it until March 8. It learned of Bourguiba's sensational statement only after the Tunisian President had arrived in Beirut, where the controversy among the Arabs began in earnest. *Le Monde* had no direct information from Jordan and had had no representative at the press conference. Only on March 9, did it publish the main points of his statement, as carried on the UPI wire several days earlier.

The New York Times fared even worse. It, too, had had no representative at the press conference in the Old City and it did not use the UPI story. It never actually caught up with the Jerusalem story itself. On March 8, it printed a short and inconspicuous Cairo dispatch about the uneasiness Bourguiba's statement had created in Lebanon; it capsuled Bourguiba's Jerusalem views in two short paragraphs. Later it was to report subsequent developments at some length.

What did Bourguiba say that was so sensational? Many things never before uttered by an Arab leader, certainly not with such bluntness, and in such a context. He had just concluded a tour of the refugee camps and witnessed the ravages of the war connected with the establishment of the State of Israel.

> I wished to see for myself the situation in Jordan . . . which has many and strong ties with us, and so I accepted King Hussein's invitation to visit [here], and during the short time I have spent [here], I was given an opportunity to see for myself the results of the greatest tragedy which has occurred in this century of tragedies, wars, blood, and destruction.

"Who is responsible for it?" he asked, and went on to answer:

> I shall not here go into the many reasons for this [tragedy], but I may say that the main reason is that the leaders in most States do not measure up to their full responsibilities. . . . It is regrettable that those in responsible positions in the Near and Middle Eastern countries instead of working for the benefit of their peoples, work instead for their own benefit. . .

What is wrong with the Arab leaders? In what sense did they fail in their responsibility? Bourguiba thinks they are guilty of many things, but above all of insincerity:

> The rulers must not deceive their peoples, but should be frank with them and should refrain from being driven by sheer sentiments. . .

How did the leaders deceive the people? In many ways. For

instance, promising "tomorrow we will return to Palestine" is deceiving the people. "Where will they return?" he asked.

The chief deception, however, is their insistence that they will solve the Palestine problem by war.

> There are those who believe that war and bloodshed solve problems. But war and bloodshed have never solved a single problem. . .
> 'To throw the Jews into the sea' is an empty slogan and I don't believe in it.

If the Palestine tragedy should lead to war in the Middle East and then spread and assume world proportions, it would be mainly the result of Arab leaders' irresponsibility. True, the dangers of war are not only in the Middle East. But wherever there is such a danger it is the fault of irresponsible leadership:

> So toward the end of the twentieth century, we see a world wrecked by instability and feel that it is [once more] on the brink of war which might break out at any time. We expect it to break out in the Middle East, the Far East, or Africa.

One should not indulge in erroneous clichés when dealing with a tragedy of such magnitude as that of the people of Palestine, Bourguiba warned. To say that the only ones responsible for this tragedy are the Zionists or the Jews is a naïve, ignorant, or simplistic approach to historical facts. Many more factors were involved. The efforts of the Zionists were only one, or perhaps a result of many others.

> My tour along the armistice lines was a saddening experience, and gave me an insight into the tragedy of the loyal people of Palestine, which throughout its entire existence has been subjugated by others. Internal conditions, world wars, the efforts of the Jews, and the mistakes of the Arabs over the last 23 years, as well as their tragedy in fighting—these were the factors that created these saddening sights.*

In these few sentences, President Bourguiba struck two important notes: 1) the Jews are *not* the exclusive cause of the

---

* In the UPI version, Bourguiba added lack of a strategy on the part of the Arab leadership. (*Le Monde,* March 9, 1965.)

refugees' misfortune; and 2) the Arabs of Palestine were never in the course of history an independent people; they had always been subjugated.

As to the Arabs of Palestine they were, indeed, victims of events beyond their control—such as the two world wars, which brought about respectively the Balfour Declaration and the Partition. But in addition, he implies that the Arabs have themselves to blame for what happened. Here his chronology provides the illumination—"the mistakes of the Arabs over the last 23 years," which brings us back to the early nineteen-forties. We may guess, but only guess, he was referring to, perhaps, Hitler's atrocities against the Jews, with the added implication that it was wrong for the Arabs to be intransigent in the face of the Jewish tragedy. If this conjecture is correct, Bourguiba meant to point out that here was a moral wrong and a tactical mistake which alienated world public opinion and gave impetus to the Hebrew underground.

Arab intransigence was an error then and subsequently right up to the present. Their "tragedy in fighting," that is, their defeats in their confrontations with the armies of Israel was both a demonstration of this intransigence and its tragic result.

At the Jerusalem press conference, responding to a question on the United Nations action in 1947, Bourguiba said that partition was not such a bad solution of the Palestine problem. In any case, under the circumstances it should be viewed as the lesser evil.

> Had the Arabs accepted previous solutions and continued to demand their implementation, this tragedy would not have come about.

And, he added with grim humor, he was glad the Arab League had not dealt with the problem of Tunisia as it had with the Palestinian situation.

What does he propose instead?

> All I would wish is that we learn a lesson from the tragedies in the past and return to common sense. . . . We know that country [Palestine] in which blood flowed in the past and where the Crusaders fought their battles. The Franks stormed Jerusalem and blood flowed like rivers. Today I saw Christians, laymen and clergymen, living in peace and brotherhood with Moslems here in Jordan. This proves that when inferiority complexes and lust

for power disappear, there is room for all sects to live together. . . .
But if they could have lived like that in the past, the Crusades
need not have taken place at all. . . . It, therefore, occurred to me
that perhaps such coexistence can also be achieved with the Jews.
. . . *The day will yet come when it will become evident to all that
these tragedies are meaningless.* . . .

The religions are linked with one another and offer a wide
sphere of cooperation on the basis of respect for our freedom and
our honor. . . . Such a thing is possible. . . . It is possible to cooperate with the Jews on the basis of mutual respect. Our hands
are joined with theirs since they are a 'People of the Book'. . . .
In this land there is wide scope for all ethnic and religious communities to live in harmony and cooperation. . . . [if only] they
will reject hatred and free themselves from their complexes and
their extremists. . . . Cooperation and understanding serve as a
strong basis for a real peace. . . .

What we want is a true peace based on love and brotherhood.
(Italics added.)

The Tunisian President insisted he was not a mere visionary,
and that what he suggested was not Utopia. He is a pragmatist,
and his is a hardboiled, realistic policy. What he suggests is dis-
carding methods which have proven worthless in the past and
adopting his way, which has worked. "What we have done in Tunis
should serve as an example to the rest of the [subjugated]
peoples."

From the beginning of his Middle East tour and in the months
that followed, he never ceased to expound his theory of gradualism,
and to exhort the Arabs to adopt this Tunisian way of achieving
a political aim. Since it worked so successfully in liberating Tunisia
from the French, it should serve as well for others.

Bourguiba did not suggest that the Arabs should renounce their
rights or their hope of regaining them.

I am convinced that the future will lead to freedom. . . . so long
as the oppressed people do not lose heart. . . .

Now it remains for us to act to find a solution to this tragedy
[which is considered a result of] British-Zionist imperialism; and
that is similar to French colonialism in seeking to gain control
over the resources of a state and resettle a different nation in that
country.

How is this aim to be achieved? he was asked at his news conference. And what is the Tunisian way? How is it to be applied to Palestine?

"The rights which have been taken away [from Palestianians] can be restored gradually, by stages," he replied. But this task requires a new and realistic approach. It is complex. It demands perseverance. There are several prerequisites, including an honest appraisal of the historical factors and a realistic approach to present-day conditions. This, in turn, requires freeing oneself from fanaticism, demagoguery, and the passion for war and bloodshed. But nothing can be achieved unless the Arabs develop a new and more qualified leadership, endowed with a sense of realism.

> First there should be leaders well qualified and capable of taking action after making an accurate appraisal of the situation through a full study of all the circumstances. They should not act unilaterally, and should be aware of events around them.
>
> It is the task of the leader—and this is what happened in Tunisia—to raise the awareness of the people so that they may understand all the conditions of their struggle—but he must not be fanatic and not pander to their emotions. I have never encouraged the Tunisian people to spill blood. I have frequently come into conflict with my people—but in perspective subsequent events have proved my views were right and farsighted.

What he holds against the Arab leaders is their inability to face facts. They live in a world of emotions and fancies; when faced with realities, they usually meet disaster, or at the least, humiliation and disappointment.

We should not, Bourguiba urged, confuse a whole nation with the official policies and actions of its government. And when the struggle is over, not only is it wrong to hate the people of the erstwhile enemy, we should not even hate their government.

> In Tunis we fought against the imperialists—fought without hatred, but also without compromise; and in the end, conditions emerged for fair cooperation with the state which had subjugated us. We fought imperialism, but from the moment that imperialism withdrew, we extended a hand in cooperation, friendship, and fraternity to the people which had subjugated us. The blood that was shed over thirty years was the price we paid for liberty and honor. We turned over a new leaf in our relations with France, which are now based on mutual respect among human beings. . . .

Nor must the aim of a struggle for liberation be to humiliate the antagonist.

> I succeeded in liberating myself from France, without having beaten the French Army—it is thus that I triumphed over imperialism. It is thus that France did not feel that it lost completely. The end of imperialism has thus been in the interest of France as it has been in the interest of Tunisia. That is what I call a constructive fight.

The best peace, he said, is one which results in neither victors nor victims. In the Palestine situation the same pattern should be followed; indeed, there is even more justification for peace and cooperation between the present antagonists: "Are we not all believers in The Book? . . . One must therefore envisage a true cooperation toward peace." Arabs and Jews had lived peaceably for hundreds of years "since the time of the Patriarchs Abraham, Jacob, and Joseph (sic) ," and there are still strong links between them.

"I am not afraid," he told his hearers in perhaps the most dramatic moment of his sensational declaration, "to appease imperialism, or to make concessions to it. I am not afraid, even though this may expose me to murder, since conditions offer alternatives."

There is also the need to be realistic in evaluating the relative forces which the antagonist and one's own country can muster for the confrontation. Essential to this is a valid appraisal of the worth, mentality, and thought pattern of the antagonist. In fighting the French, he said, "what was needed was not only the correct tactics but also an understanding of the enemy and his thoughts." There is nothing to be gained in visualizing the antagonist as the devil incarnate, under every condition. Such an attitude leads only to erroneous policy and hence to disappointment and humiliation.

The Arabs must also realize that their conflict with Israel is not a *tête-à-tête*, occurring, as it were, in an international vacuum. No single situation in our time is isolated from the rest of the world. "Around and beyond the Arabs there are two giants, and in their struggle [the Arabs] must take into account world conditions."

In answer to a question, he added that the Arabs in their calculations must also consider who are the supporters of their enemy. In the months ahead he was to stress repeatedly that regardless of the immediate temptation to align themselves with the Communist bloc, in the long run it would be a grave mistake, if not actually disastrous, for the Arabs to alienate themselves from the West—its traditions and its culture. He considered the Arab leaders' contemplation of a Soviet alignment as one of the manifestations of their reckless irresponsibility.

Since war does not solve problems, an exclusive preoccupation with armaments is not only meaningless, but dangerous. Far from strengthening the Arabs, it only weakens them further. Concentration on armaments diverts their economic and human resources from the constructive planning necessary to raise the standards of living and to build up a stronger, more wholesome society, he said.

A journalist asked how Jordan could protect the security of its 360-kilometer-long border with Israel. What did Bourguiba consider to be the obligations of other Arab states to aid Jordan, and to help the refugees return to their homes? In his answer Bourguiba pursued his indictment of pan-Arab leadership. The security situation, he said, is difficult because pan-Arabism, far from leading to unified strength, leads to isolation. Pan-Arabism tries to impose itself through terror. But fear deepens the divisions among the Arab states, and makes each an isolated unit confronted with the power of Israel.

> Every Arab state bordering on Israel feels that in case of war, it will be left to stand against her on its own; every state feels it necessary therefore to devote 70 per cent of its budget for military purposes. This is a danger, since power lies not in armaments. Only part of this budget should be devoted to armaments, with other funds devoted to industrialization, science and the future; only thus will we grow stronger than the enemy. To concentrate on armaments alone means undermining the strength of the Arabs, and that would be a catastrophe.
>
> It is time the air was cleared in connection with the Palestine problem and an end put to the divisions, to the imposition of leadership and unity through terror. . . . A logical plan must be drawn up, while the standard of living of the people is systematically raised. . . . Time is needed for this . . . let us not go back to the past. . . . Let us leave the arms and tanks aside and call upon our politicians to look far and high. . . .

In their endeavor to raise the standard of living and to achieve economic and technological progress, the Arabs should not be inhibited from learning from others or from accepting assistance from other nations at a more advanced stage of development.

The Tunisian President, reported the *Jerusalem Times,* "stressed the need for winning supporters for the strengthening of Arab relations with all peace-loving nations and peoples 'who are ahead of us in civilization, science and industry' in order to catch up with them. 'We can only catch up if we can get rid of all inferiority complexes.'"

Bourguiba's statement at the Old City press conference reflects the political philosophy that has come to be known as Bourguibism, or gradualism. He succeeded there in expressing in capsule form all his ideas of the statesman's imperatives: to appraise a situation realistically, and to base his policies and actions on historic realities rather than on wishful thinking.

At the end of the eight-day visit, Hussein and Bourguiba simultaneously issued a joint communiqué in Amman and Tunis. In it, King and President expressed their belief that Arab unity is the final national aim of the Arab people, and that it would be achieved by coordination of efforts, cultivation of friendship, and cooperation among the people.

In the light of the previous day's peace bomb, the communiqué was, if not a *non sequitur,* in any event, an anti-climax. It asserted that the Arab summit conferences represent important stages in the struggle of the Arab people, and that every effort must be made to implement the "plan of action" on the Palestine issue approved at those conferences. The two heads of state noted Jordan's need for full support in its special responsibility to protect the Arab homeland against Zionist aggression.

As the statement was broadcast over Amman Radio, no reference was heard to either "the liberation of Palestine" or the diversion of the Jordan tributaries, though these are clearly implied in the statement's reference to implementing the resolutions of the summit conferences.

According to Reuters, the communiqué stated that King Hussein and President Bourguiba agreed to work for the internal progress of their countries, and to develop them economically and socially in a democratic way. The report added that the visitor signed agreements concerning economic development projects, tourism, and education.

When Bourguiba arrived in Beirut from Jordan on March 7, the day after his Old City press conference, he received a hero's welcome.

He was greeted by President Charles Helou, Mme. Helou, and Prime Minister Hussein Oweini, accompanied by members of the cabinet and the chiefs of Arab diplomatic missions in the Lebanon.

Tens of thousands of cheering people lined the road from the airport to Beirut. Several times the open limousine had to stop to receive wreaths of flowers from delirious donors. "All Beirut newspapers welcomed the visitor," Reuters reported. The daily *As-Safa* referred to him as "the founder of a new school of reasoning in politics and goodwill in international relations."

In his welcoming speech, President Helou addressed his guest as "brother" and extolled his virtues and talents, praising him as an intrepid fighter and a great tribune who had struggled many years for his country's independence, progress, and prosperity.

But the next day at the official dinner, Helou declared that his government was determined "to fulfill its obligations toward the Arab sister nations" concerning "the Palestine problem."

Was this a mild dissociation from Bourguiba's declaration in Jerusalem? According to the *New York Times* correspondent in Beirut, President Bourguiba's espousal of moderation and reason in dealing with "the Jews" cast a pall of uneasiness on the festive atmosphere. It soon became clear that Reuters' report of a unanimously friendly Lebanese press was perhaps overstated. A reservation appared in the pro-Nasser daily *Al-Nahar*:

> We welcome President Bourguiba and Bourguibism, which he will in all probability expound during his visit in the Lebanon. But . . . we hope the distinguished guest will avoid calling once more for peaceful coexistence with the enemy. . . . We know his creed is moderation and his principle is "Take what is offered and ask for more later." It seems that his statements yesterday [in Jerusalem] derived from this principle which, however, can apply to all questions except Palestine.

On the other hand, the moderate newspaper *Al Khayat* commented:

> What Bourguiba said publicly in the Old City of Jerusalem, many of the other Arab rulers are saynig privately when talking in their inner circle.

None of them, *Al Khayat* continued, had the courage to tell the people the whole truth. This has led to a situation in which the Arabs have to prepare themselves to defend Syria and the Lebanon from Israeli aggression, instead of concentrating on the main thing —the liberation of Palestine.

Another newspaper, *Al Jaryda,* speculated about a connection between Bourguiba's statement and the plan for a Jewish-Arab Federation which might have been inspired by De Gaulle. "Though such a plan," it wrote, "is not particularly attractive, some Arab countries may choose not to reject it outright." But, speculated the paper, let us imagine that Bourguiba succeeds in persauding the Arab countries to his principle of taking what is offered and demanding more later. Would the Palestinians themselves agree to such a solution? And would Israel be ready to sign an agreement in this spirit? And, would international Zionism agree to the idea of transforming Israel into a neutral Jewish-Arab State? Perhaps the Western Powers might pressure Israel into accepting such a plan. But had not these same powers failed so far in their endeavors to bring Israel to implement the United Nations resolutions? The Arabs, concluded the article, though they must be realists, cannot afford to make further concessions. "They have conceded too much already."

At all events, the Lebanese government felt constrained to take extraordinary precautions to protect the visitor. Foreign journalists and photographers were not permitted near the plane when it landed at Beirut. The route which the two presidents traversed from the air port to the capital was guarded by uniformed and plainclothes police. A Lebanese Air Force helicopter flew over Bourguiba's plane during the landing and then accompanied the procession all the way to town.

Bourguiba delivered two addresses in Beirut. One on March 8 expounded his political philosophy—Bourguibism—and the policies of his Socialist Destour party.

The second, made March 10 at the University of Beirut where he accepted an honorary doctorate, was a philosophical address on a very high level. He discussed the need for the Arab world to awaken to new values if it was to emerge fully from centuries of decadence. He said that the challenge to the Arabs was not merely political, economic, and social—it was total, involving the most fundamental attitudes. The Arabs, he said, cannot meet these challenges in a spirit of isolation, but only in the process of a permanent, creative dialogue with other cultures and civilizations.

In the originality of its thoughts, breadth of its concepts, lofti-
ness of its sentiments, boldness of its challengess, and exquisiteness
of its style, this address stands out as an unusual performance in a
generation whose statesmen usually are known for their banality.

On March 11, Bourguiba held a press conference which turned
out to be one of the most dramatic held by a chief of state in
modern times. The tension and interest were heightened by a
forty-eight-hour postponement, probably caused by Bourguiba's
need for more time to clarify the position of the Lebanese President and Prime Minister, and to consult with his own advisers.

In postponing the press conference to the last minute, he seems
to have used the same technique as in Jordan, and for the same
sound reason. The sooner he could leave after exploding his bomb,
the easier his hosts would feel.

This time he was to elaborate even more forcefully upon the
ideas he had expressed in Jerusalem. His indictment of the Arab
leadership for its failure to solve the Palestine problem was to be
more devastating.

Before an audience of more than three hundred correspondents
—Arab and foreign—he began by analyzing the Tunisian experience in its fight for independence. The gradual achievement,
phase after phase, should, in his opinion, serve as a pattern for
the fight for Palestine. The present all-or-nothing policy would
not advance the cause of the Palestinians. The Arab leaders, he
said, knew quite well that war against Israel was impossible; otherwise they would have tried it before during the past seventeen
years. He added:

> Were the Arab states to decide to go forth to battle, I would
> join, and would dispatch the Tunisian army to fight against
> Israel. But what am I to do? The Arab states have not yet taken
> such a decision. Since this is the situation, perhaps it might be
> wiser if we were to substitute common sense for emotionalism
> and let rationality guide our steps. All my life I have been a man
> of political action, and not of words. Words alone will not bring
> us nearer our goal and will only hurt our most vital interests. It is
> time that the Arabs recover their sense of reality and begin to
> look at world problems as they are.

The press conference became a debate. Some journalists were
vociferously hostile. They hurled not questions, but provocations.
Under the animosity, the tension, the affronts, Bourguiba's initial

calm gave way to spirited rejoinder. "You cannot conquer the Israelis! What do you propose to do?"

"A hundred years' war!" retorted a journalist.

Eyes flashing, Bourguiba replied:

> Do you mean we are to pass responsibility over to posterity? And then who knows what sort of leaders the Arabs will have by 2065?
>
> You can continue to drug the masses with provocative slogans and unfulfilled promises. As things have been drifting for the last seventeen years, the Arabs have not made an inch of headway. The fact is that Israel could not be defeated in the past, and there is no chance of it in the future. War with Israel is impossible. The great powers, guarantors of the Jewish State, would stop us. It is time to abandon demagogy. . . . Hence, realism should lead us to look for another way than war. . . . There is no use butting one's head against the wall. It would be better to try to circumvent it or scale it.

A journalist asked whether he really had said in Jerusalem that in the Arab–Jewish conflict there must be neither victors nor vanquished. Bourguiba responded with something he seems later to have decided never to mention again:

> I propose a solution without either winners or losers, for—and let us not forget this—we are at present in the position of losers. . . . I prefer to begin by putting myself in a neutral position, unless, of course, you have another solution.

Foreign correspondents reported afterward that Bourguiba's statements were received by the Arab journalists and in the Lebanese capital with shock and surprise.

The conference lasted more than an hour. At the end, he was both confident and defiant. During his visit in Jordan, he said, the Palestine refugees welcomed his proposal to solve their problem gradually, in stages; but there seemed to be some Lebanese journalists "who are more Palestinian than the refugees," and some Arab rulers "more Nasserite than Nasser himself."* In the further course of his campaign he was to insist that the Arab press which

---

* Censorship or rather "orientation" seems to have been applied to the Lebanese press and radio concerning Bourguiba's statements, and as a result a few passages seem to have been omitted.

"raises a hue and cry against me does not reflect the sentiments and opinions of all the Arabs."

At the end of the visit, host and guest again issued a joint communiqué. In it the two Presidents expressed their unshakable determination to work together to defend Arab–Palestine interests, and to advance Arab unity. They agreed to cooperate in the implementation of the resolutions which were adopted at the two summit conferences and in cultivating the two countries' economic relations.

The Lebanese press is quite free, but some of it is financed by Cairo. Reaction in the Arab world had once more raised its head, wrote one paper, thanks to an ambitious Arab leader. He was an agent of imperialism, said a second. Another forecast an imminent secret meeting between Bourguiba and Golda Meir.

So savage were the attacks that Bourguiba (as the daily *Al Khayat* revealed later) threatened to leave after the second day. The Lebanese government acted to avoid an open scandal by mobilizing its best people in the field to mollify the Nasserite newspapers, at least for the remaining few days of the visit.

The attacks were renewed after he left. On March 16, 10,000 students demonstrated in Beirut against West Germany and Bourguiba. In Lebanese Tripoli rioting students clashed with police, and 23 persons were hospitalized. Demonstrations also broke out in Sidon.

Bourguiba's Jerusalem and Beirut declarations gave many of the world's newspapers the impression that he had told the Arabs to make peace with Israel and coexist with her on the basis of mutual respect. Yet, though Bourguiba spoke of peace, cooperation, harmony, brotherhood, love, and mutual respect, he did not explicitly propose peace with Israel. Actually, a careful reading of what he said shows his statements to have been ambiguous, if not openly contradictory.

With some justification one could read his words as an appeal for peace. But with no less justification one could also interpret his aims as no different from those of Nasser or other Arab leaders —namely, that Israel must disappear from the political map—but that that end should be achieved not by war but by peaceful means.

The Tunisian leader did not once say that the Israelis had any justice on their side, or that they had a point of view which should

be, if not agreed to, at least appreciated. He never explicitly mentioned Israel as a political reality with which one must come to
terms. When he referred to her, it was by implication and always
in an inimical sense, as the enemy against whose aggression the
Arabs must protect themselves. Like the other Arab leaders, he
characterized Israel as created by "British Zionist imperialism."

Of Jews in general he spoke as a rule in complimentary terms.
Whenever he spoke of the necessity of a peacful solution, it was
with "the Jews" that peace should be concluded—perhaps implying that if the Jews of Palestine were reduced to the status of
just another ethnic community within the frame of an independent
Palestine, a peaceful solution might be possible.

Though he would soon substantially qualify his stand, it remained ambiguous and contradictory all through his tour and for
many months afterward. He used ambiguity and contradiction as
instruments of communication and persuasion—adapted always to
place, country, and audience—an old technique of being all things
to all men, yet never going far enough to disqualify himself either
as Arab patriot, or as Arab statesman seeking a new, peaceful
solution to the Palestine problem.

We shall trace these consecutive manifestations with a view to
discerning the underlying thoughts and motivations of Bourguiba's
peace offensive, and to determine, of course, whether it *was* a
peace offensive at all.

Did Bourguiba's Jordanian and Lebanese hosts know what he
was going to say? Did Bourguiba face them, or at least Hussein,
with an embarrassing *fait accompli*? Neither the Jordanian King
nor the Lebanese President has ever chosen to throw any light
upon this question.

Bourguiba asserts unequivocally that he discussed his ideas and
proposals with all the rulers whose countries he visited and they
agreed—privately, that is. In fact, he asserts, it is *they* who discussed
it with him. In an interview with the British quarterly *Views*
(Autumn, 1965) he relates that the leaders of the states he visited
in the Middle East "spoke to me about their troubles, their problems" related to Palestine. And he expressed his views frankly
and boldly:

> I said to them: It is all very well—emotion, passion—we have
> gone through all of it. We need emotion to further great causes,
> as a motor within man. But this is not enough. We have to cal-

culate, we need intelligence, reason, we must see the difficulties, the obstacles, we must try and overcome them, one by one. It cannot be done all at once. We have to work with tact and strategy. The Arab chiefs are wholly ignorant of these problems. We cannot just cry over injustice and colonialism. I said to them, we have been through all of this before the (foundation of our) movement—the Neo Destour. For fifty years all our crying, our complaining about French injustice and colonialism led us nowhere. A head is needed to lead and orient all this energy, this passion and this strength toward reasonable and practical solutions. . . . We must have enough courage to dominate our passions if we want to reach our goal honestly and sincerely.

This, of course, does not mean that he actually told Hussein and Helou he was going to say these things at the press conferences. Yet it would be hard to believe that they were not informed of his intention. It stands more to reason that Bourguiba told his hosts what he would say, at least in general terms, especially since he had already spoken in a similar vein in the refugee camps.

One must also consider that Jordan's King and Lebanon's President, though they did not publicly identify themselves with Bourguiba's views, nonetheless consistently refrained from taking a stand against him:* What is more, the Jordanian and Lebanese papers published detailed accounts of Bourguiba's views. In Jordan, at least, the press is not free to do as it likes. The non-Nasserite Lebanese papers were generally sympathetic. One Jordanian newspaper, *Al Manar*, came out on March 7, the day after the press conference, in praise of his ideas:

> The Arabs should learn a lesson from what Bourguiba said. They must understand that in dealing with the Palestine problem one has to be realistic and not be swept away by emotions. After all, Bourguiba fought for the independence of his country and he accumulated a lot of experience.

Some observers in Israel suggested that perhaps King Hussein himself had prompted Bourguiba's campaign—that it was born during one of the conversations at the beginning of the visit. Hussein may have expressed concern over the threatening mood in Israel as a result of the *Fedayin* (commando) raids and of Jor-

* However some of their officials, including the prime ministers, made statements sounding as if they were intended to dissociate themselves from Bourguiba's views.

dan's decision to double the strength of its army. The two Arab statesmen may have thought it worthwhile for the Tunisian President to voice on the Israel frontier the reassurance that the conflict need not result in war; that, on the contrary, some Arab statesmen were seeking a peaceful solution, of which there was a good possibility.*

Others thought Hussein was interested in such an initiative because of conditions in Jordan itself. The hopeless-appearing situation of the refugees was being exploited by Arab rulers; but some of the refugees, especially the restless younger generation, were seeking action that would improve their plight. In the weeks preceding Bourguiba's visit, tensions among the refugees had reached alarming proportions. Ahmed Shukairy, a firebrand native Palestinian, under the inspiration of Nasser (and, paradoxically, as a result of Bourguiba's own speeches at the recent Arab summit conferences) had created the Palestine Liberation Organization, to organize the refugees into a military unit. (As we shall see in later chapters, this PLO was a far greater threat to the stability and sovereignty of Jordan than to the security and survival of Israel.)

King Hussein must surely have been pleased to hear an Arab statesman attack the extremist Arab leaders as fanatics, demagogues, and irresponsible adventurers, whose policies had proven sterile. By contrast the Jordanian monarch would appear a reasonable ruler who could solve the Palestine problem by more realistic, hence more efficient, means.

Bourguiba's statements would also imply that King Hussein did not need Nasser or Shukairy to do it for him. Hence, the Tunisian President's appeal (in the joint communiqué) for all possible aid to Jordan to cope with the Palestine problem in view of the "special responsibility placed on her" to defend "the Arab front line." Hence also, perhaps, Bourguiba's insistence that the Palestine problem was primarily the concern of the Palestinians themselves. A war would prove catastrophic, above all, to them. Since Jordan had been in the past an integral part of Mandated Palestine; and also because the majority of the Palestinian refugees are in Jordan and are Jordanian citizens, this may be interpreted

---

* *Davar,* in its editorial of March 8, asks: "Did he [Bourguiba] make his moderate statements in compliance with a request by King Hussein? At any rate it cannot be assumed that he made them against the will or without the knowledge of his host." This is also the opinion of *Ha'aretz* in its editorial of the same day.

as saying that Jordan is the heir, or at least the trustee, of the Palestinians. It is probably in connection with the integration of the refugees into Jordan that Bourguiba emphasized the imperatives of raising the people's social and economic standards and developing the country's technology—thus achieving a better and stronger position from which ultimately to deal with the Palestine problem.

What is more significant than mere conjecture is that Bourguiba, in some respects at least, echoed sentiments and attitudes which King Hussein had expressed in the past. As far back as January 17, 1960, in a special interview with an Associated Press correspondent, Hussein had said that the Arab leaders are demagogues who have no real interest in the plight of the refugees, but are using them only as "pawns for selfish political objectives."

> In saying this, I am not talking about the Arab people, but Arab leadership. Since 1948, Arab leaders have approached the Palestine problem in an irresponsible manner. They have not looked into the future. They have no plan or approach. They have used the Palestine people for selfish purposes. This is ridiculous and, I could say, even criminal.

What is striking about the interview is not only that its content resembles Bourguiba's declarations in Jordan, but that its wording is sometimes almost identical.

Again, at a televised press conference on April 20, 1964, in Washington, King Hussein declared that Israel–Arab peace is possible under certain conditions, such as those in relevant UN resolutions, or when "Israel ceases being a threat to the Arabs"—whatever that may mean.

Later, when the inevitable break came between King Hussein and Shukairy, the Jordanian monarch's echo of Bourguiba's ideas became more obvious. For example on June 5, 1966 when the King delivered a speech at a graduation ceremony at Ajlun College, 60 miles north of Amman, he ridiculed the idea that imperialism was the exclusive cause of the Arabs' trouble. Israel, he said, could only be confronted by emulation of the "planning, organization, determination, and preparedness for sacrifices of the Zionist movement." Like Boufguiba, he derided those "who love theatrical heroism," and pointed out that *his* "mobilization plan calls not for speeches but for sweat and work." The Arabs, he said, must make sacrifices "not only in the military field but also for the building up of a free, stable, and organized Arab homeland"; and he cited the construction of the Mukheiba Dam on the Yarmuk as an example of constructive sacrifice.

These similarities not only provide a clue as to whether Hussein (and, for that matter, Helou) agreed in advance to what Bourguiba would say; they may also answer the more important question whether Bourguiba's outburst was just a momentary spurt or whether it represents deep undercurrents in the Middle East, which, if properly encouraged and fostered, may yet affect the course of history.

Bourguiba visited nine countries (seven Moslem, five of which were Arab). For many months after his tour he continued waging his campaign in Tunisia and on a world scale by diplomatic activities and through press, television, and radio. It is amazing in retrospect that Bourguiba was able to sustain the interest of world opinion for such a long time. Dealing constantly with the same subject in much the same way, his every speech, his every interview, his every television appearance, nevertheless created a sensation. When he appeared on a program with other statesmen, as, for instance, on the French television network, he overshadowed the other participants, who were scarcely noticed in the press.* Everything he said after the first two press conferences in Jerusalem and Beirut was mostly elaboration, amplification, and to some extent qualification, of what he had pronounced earlier.

Why did the Tunisian President choose Jordan and the Lebanon for his sensational pronouncements? He chose to express them in Amman and Beirut for a variety of reasons. Because the two countries are closest and most exposed to Israel, they would have most to lose from any military encounter with her. The governments of both these countries are moderate in their attitudes, pay only lip service to pan-Arabism, and are interested chiefly in advancing the economy and social welfare of their peoples. They are jealous of their independence. They are plagued by the ten-

* April 3, 1965. On that program devoted to the dispute over the diversion of the Jordan headwaters, there also appeared Abba Eban, then Deputy Premier, and Shimon Peres, then Deputy Defense Minister, of Israel; an official representative of the Lebanese Government, and the Minister of Information of the Syrian Government. The world press extensively reported Bourguiba's statement. The presence of the others was scarcely mentioned.

sions engendered by the activities of the extremists—in Jordan by Shukairy's PLO and in both Jordan and the Lebanon by the guerrilla organization "Al Fatah" ("the Conquest") ** which carries out intermittent raids on Israel territory and subjects both countries to Israeli retaliation.

Paradoxically, the independence of both countries depends to a great extent upon the existence of Israel. Nasser has made no secret of his design to swallow up the comparatively small and militarily weak countries in the Middle East. As long as Israel exists, she provides a powerful buffer against Egypt's encroachments. Israel is content so long as her small neighbors maintain their moderate stance.

By breaking the spell of war hysteria at a critical juncture, Bourguiba rendered both a great service. It was not a thankful task. Hussein and Helou did not dare associate themselves openly with him when the storm broke. More than that: eventually they felt compelled to let subordinate spokesmen join the general stream of condemnation. In a televised interview in Paris (relayed from Yugoslavia where he was the guest of Marshal Tito) Bourguiba was to say that some of the leaders who had castigated him after he had had private talks with them "showed greater understanding in our conversations than when facing the mob." This he was to repeat time and again in the course of the following months, more in melancholy than in anger.

We now resume the story of Bourguiba's tour in its chronological sequence. It began with Egypt, where he arrived on February 16. Everything augured well, and the signs were that this trip would put a period to a long train of Tunisian–Egyptian recriminations. Bourguiba told Arab journalists who interviewed him before his departure that he was leaving on a pilgrimage to thank the Arabs of the Middle East, and especially of Egypt, for the aid they had extended to Tunisia in its march toward independence (Escaping from French authorities in Tunis in 1945, Bourguiba spent a number of years in Cairo after the Second World War. Otherwise, however, Tunisia got no discernible help from the Arabs in its fight for independence.)

President Nasser prepared a triumphant entry for Bourguiba into Cairo. He decided to treat his guest with maximum pomp, honor, and cordiality; he put on his warmest smile when he met Bourguiba at the airport. (King Hussein, also then visiting Cairo,

** Al Fatah's military arms is "Al Assifa" ("the Storm").

accompanied the Egyptian President.) They drove back in an open car, Nasser standing all the way, waving to the cheering crowds, and beaming perfect harmony. Bourguiba, for his part, was exuberant.

Bourguiba accompanied Nasser to the presidential palace (where a few days later the Communist leader of East Germany, Walter Ulbricht, was to stay as official guest of the Egyptian Government). According to Radio Cairo, Bourguiba received one of the most enthusiastic welcomes ever given a foreign chief of state by the Egyptian people. *Le Monde* interpreted the welcome as a new step in the reconciliation betwen Nasser and Bourguiba, dating from the 1961 Conference of Non-Aligned Nations held in Belgrade.

On the morrow of his arrival, the University of Cairo gave the illustrious guest an honorary degree. On February 21 he addressed the Egyptian National Assembly for an hour and a half. Then Nasser took his guest on a tour (which was part hospitality and part compaigning for reelection as President).

Despite all these amenities, it soon became clear that the romance had gone sour.

Observers are in almost unanimous agreement that the falling out was precipitated by the German issue. The Egyptian–West German crisis over the arms deal with Israel was just then developing at a quick pace. At the first of the meetings on the joint tour, held in the huge tent at Aswan on February 18, Nasser delivered a fierce attack against the West German Government for its recently disclosed secret arms deal with Israel. He praised the then Algerian President, Ahmed Ben Bella for his unstinting support of Egypt's position on the German question. He expected Bourguiba in his answering speech to express similar support and solidarity. The Tunisian President failed even to hint at it.

With each additional stop on that tour, Nasser became more violent in his talks. He presented the German issue as one of life and death for all Arabs. "Everything will be lost if the Arabs do not appear united in this crisis between Egypt and Germany." And, "the Arabs will be annihilated if they do not unite now." He warned that "if the Jews win this battle [over Germany] then the Arabs had better bury their faces in the mud." He became more and more insistent on his invitation to Bourguiba to show strong support. But to no avail.

At this juncture, Tunisia's continued good relations with Germany were extremely important to Bourguiba. France had cut off

most of its aid as a result of the Bizerte tragedy and the nationalization of the land of most of the French landlords. And the United
States was too deeply committed in its foreign aid programs to
offer much hope for substantially increased help. But West Germany, with her booming economy, showed willingness to consider
substantial investments in Tunisian enterprises.

President Bourguiba had been expecting a succession of most
important visitors from Germany: the President of the Bundestag,
the chairman of its economic and finance committee, and, above
all, Alfried Krupp, head of the still vast industrial empire. The
purpose of legislators' visits was to discuss the possibility of large-
scale German economic aid; Krupp's was concerned with conver-
sion of the famous former French naval base at Bizerte into a
commercial port and dockyard—a project vital in Tunisian eyes
to their economy and prestige.

Perhaps even more important to Tunisia than direct economic
assistance from Germany was German support for Tunisian ad-
mittance into (or association with) the European Common Market. Tunisia, indeed all of the Maghreb, looks to association with
the European trade community as one of the most promising
possibilities of economic rehabilitation. To achieve this, there was
needed not only France's goodwill (at the moment quite reserved
as far as Tunisia was concerned) but also Germany's.

A few hours before leaving Cairo, President Bourguiba told
J. Ben Brahem, the correspondent of *Le Monde*:

> Bonn has ceased sending arms to Israel. This is a considerable
> success. One should have stopped there, and not engaged in a
> provocation which cannot but thrust Germany into Israel's arms.
> Anyhow, as far as we are concerned, we see the incident as closed,
> and we are not going to budge one inch further. Why take a stand
> in a situation "in case it arrives?" Why align oneself *a priori?*
> Instead, we should, before taking any decision, consult each other.

Nasser was in no mood to indulge in the slow process of consultation with the members of the Arab League before taking a
decision on the German situation. His mind was made up and he
acted peremptorily, speaking for all the Arab states, making threats
on their behalf, pressuring their representatives to adopt resolutions dictated by Egypt. More than that, Nasser expanded the
contretemps with West Germany into a pan-Arab conflict with all
of the Western Powers. He presented it as a conspiracy of the West
to unleash Israel against the Arabs.

In a speech in Cairo on February 21 celebrating the seventh anniversary of the union between Egypt and Syria (ignoring its demise), Nasser warned that the Arabs must be on guard against "the enormous dangers facing us this year." "Israel," he said, "has got more arms from America and Britain, and various kinds of other assistance from West Germany and France, and is preparing an aggressive plan." Amid wild cheers from his audience he announced that the diversion of the Jordan headwaters had started, "and if Israel attacks now, she will meet a unified Arab force, with units from Morocco to Iraq." He extolled the Arab summit conferences which had succeeded in transcending differences of opinion and working out a unanimous blueprint for action "on behalf of Palestine."

"Israel has threatened to go to war if we divert the headwaters. Let us not forget she is not alone. She is supported by imperialism, which is capable of opening a number of fronts against us, as America has just done by using West Germany. America wanted to help Israel with arms, and it did so indirectly through Bonn."

And Nasser added: "Imperialism can help Israel at any minute to obtain whatever she wants, and we know that imperialism has plans ready for this year—plans in the Persian Gulf, in the South Arabian Peninsula and in lands everywhere else in the Middle East—in places that wouldn't even occur to the Arabs as possible." He said that 1965 was a year of danger for the Arabs because "imperialism and Israel are all out to wage their last battle against Arab unity."

In the past, he concluded, such plans of aggression were prepared by Israel and the imperialists on the basis of the deep divisions among the Arab states. But now they would have to prepare such plans in the face of unity and purpose. This unity was most effectively demonstrated by the stand of all the Arab states against West Germany.

Bourguiba was on the platform when these reckless assertions were made. When it was his turn, he did not openly challenge Nasser on all points. But he did say that there was as yet no such thing as Arab unity:

> Arabs should not commit the same mistakes as in Africa, where countries rushed into union without preparing the ground. Let us be frank and tell the truth: the Arabs have not yet achieved the social and economic pre-conditions which would make union successful.

*Jeune Afrique** reported that the Cairo audience, expecting "aggressive and grandiloquent slogans," was somewhat disappointed, and gave Bourguiba only lukewarm applause. This was one of the first times an Arab leader had spoken to them of unity in realistic terms. But the enlightened elements of the Arab world, continued *Jeune Afrique,* applauded him for "trying to restate the concept of Arab union in a new ideological context, devoid of verbal artifice."

The next day (February 22) the Egyptians stampeded a committee of representatives of Arab heads-of-state meeting in Cairo into a "unanimous" resolution supporting Egypt in its dispute with West Germany over Israel: Any measure West Germany might take against Egypt "will be considered a hostile act against all Arab states" and would meet a unified Arab position.

According to a spokesman, the Arab representatives had also decided that West German arms gifts or any military, economic, or financial aid to Israel constituted a threat to the "Palestine people" and all of the Arab countries.

On this note Bourguiba's trying visit to Egypt came to an end, and he left for Saudi Arabia. By this time he seems to have made up his mind, if he had not already done so earlier, to defy Nasser not only on the German issue but on Palestine as well. While he considered the German-Egyptian dispute a passing incident, he well knew that his decision to retain a free hand in the Arab-Israel conflict would involve him in dramatic and protracted confrontations with Arab leaders and Arab public opinion. He also understood that precisely in this challenge on the Palestine issue would come the test of his country's independence vis-à-vis Nasser's bid for dominance in the Arab world.

Bourguiba later told Jean Daniel of *Le Nouvel Observateur* (April 15) his version of events:

> When I was in Egypt the German affair exploded. You know what happened. A few weeks earlier President Nasser had invited Ulbricht, the head of the East German Democratic Republic. This was absolutely his right to do. He did not have to consult anybody on this matter. Then he discovered those famous arms shipments to Israel. When he made his speech in Aswan, I heard it; I was

---

* An Afro-Arab weekly in French, printed in Paris; edited by a prominent Tunisian Bashir Ben Yahmed, former Minister of Information.

there. Later I told President Nasser that it was not necessary to exaggerate the incident beyond proportion; that West Germany suffered from an understandable guilt complex toward the Jews, and found herself in a difficult diplomatic situation; but she is a great industrial country and can be very useful to the Arab world. And since the Arabs obtained from Erhard [the West German Chancellor] a decision to immediately stop sending further arms shipments to Israel, one should be satisfied with such success. After all, this was a decisive gesture by West Germany.

The success was admitted but the Egyptians did not consider it sufficient. The incident took on momentum and grew out of all proportion to its importance, without any of the countries of the Maghreb taking part. So much so, that one day the Foreign Ministers of all the Arab countries found themselves facing a virtual *fait accompli*: an open break with Bonn. And whoever opposed it was a traitor to the Arab nation. This, of course, was a *diktat*, forcing a decision upon others. I did not accept it. I have never accepted it. What the devil! Arab unity hasn't been achieved yet. . . . Well, I said, no! I decided that evading the issue would no longer serve any purpose and I declared publicly that West Germany would not die if we broke relations with her.

President Nasser answered me indirectly in his speech at Mansourah. It is possible, he said, that West Germany will not die because we have broken relations with her, but it is Arab unity which will die if we are divided in this determination to break with her.

In other words, Arab unity depends upon unconditional support by the Arab Governments for the United Arab Republic on a matter about which they are not even consulted. . . . Well, this is a conception which I don't share at all. . . .

. . . Certain Arab Governments, being very weak, accept the status of satellites in exchange for support on the internal plane. Tunisia, like Yugoslavia, is not going to be a satellite of anybody. This was my answer. . . . If misunderstandings have sometimes taken on the proportions of a public scandal, it is because of my determination to preserve Tunisia's independence. Some have cherished the hope that I will be disowned by public opinion in my country. You have been here to witness how the Tunisian people welcomed me after I had been away for seven weeks. . . .

And as to the problem of Israel: I believed that it was high time to say publicly what everybody in the leading circles of the Middle East thinks silently. This [my speaking aloud] will induce people [in the Middle East] to become conscious of the problem; and I can state that signs of such an awareness are already manifold. Perhaps this will bring about a thaw; perhaps we will break out of the paralysis ['*l'immobilisme*'], and perhaps the Arabs will adopt at long last a clear stand and a strategy of taking the offensive. . . .

During his seven-day state visit in Egypt, Bourguiba made several speeches at receptions and mass meetings, delivered an address at Cairo University in exchange for an honorary degree, and held a news conference on the day he left. Interviews with him appeared in several Egyptian papers. But outside Egypt, virtually nothing was reported of what he had said.

It is difficult to say whether the Egyptian newspapers correctly reported Bourguiba's thoughts and attitudes. The Egyptian press is notoriously irresponsible in its reporting. Later, after all hell had broken loose, Bourguiba declared that one of the things that had enraged him during his Cairo visit was the brazenness with which the Egyptian press had put into his mouth statements such as "The Israelis must be thrown into the sea," which he would never dream of making.

To shed some light on the controversy as to whether Bourguiba had discussed with Nasser the declarations he was to make in Jordan and the Lebanon, it is important to know what Bourguiba said in Cairo, and how he said it. Certain records are available. The speech he delivered at Cairo University was later published by the Tunisian Government. The contents of this address, scholarly in tone, are interesting not so much for what is said as for what is left unsaid.

There are, of course, sensational utterances. There are also sensational silences. An almost inconceivable thing occurred. A leader of Arab nationalism, visiting the capital and center of that nationalism, delivered a long address about Arab nationalism without even obliquely referring to the Palestine problem.

Instead he delivered an academic lecture on the subject of "Destourian Socialism." He spoke of the imperative of economic development taking precedence over everything else. He explained why pragmatic socialism is best suited to achieving this task; why dogmatic socialism (Marxism) is both irrelevant and harmful if applied to underdeveloped countries. He argued the absurdity of introducing a doctrine of class struggle in countries where there are no classes; the importance of the individual as having moral and dignified worth. There was no hint of the political problems that agitate the Arab world, no mention of Arab unity. He did refer to the heritage of Islam as a factor helping to mold the new pragmatic socialism. But he did not so much as tip his hat to the "Palestine problem."

Yet, though he did not openly indulge in polemic, Bourguiba's speech was structured in such a way that almost every paragraph was, or could be construed as, a criticism of Nasserism—the political and social regime. He spoke against any ideology of hatred; against the repression of liberty; against a policy of *"nationalisation à outrance"* and the abrogation of private property; against dictatorship in any shape or form, regardless of its aim, rationalization, justification, or pretext.

Instead, he stressed the importance of educating the masses to think rationally and to view events (and aspirations) realistically. He strongly advised weaning the people away from emotionalism and fanaticism and seeking conciliation, instead of spreading division.

> It is our conviction that the revolution [of the post-colonial peoples] is nothing but a means to achieve happiness for man, who remains the final and supreme value [in himself]. . . .
>
> It is our duty to try to help man to better himself, first and above all by the use of the language of reason. We consider the revolution as a means to bring about the liberation of man, of all men, without any distinction. . . . Hence, we do not believe that the revolution must necessarily have recourse to violence, or use "strong methods," or raise extremism to a principle. . . .
>
> We, for our part, refuse in principle the shedding of blood whenever it is possible to avoid it, and we prefer to see our revolution advance resolutely toward prosperity and in a climate of the joy of living. . . .
>
> We assert that the "policy of stages" has the advantage of helping the people accept the necessary evolutionary changes and is, therefore, most efficacious in the achievement of revolutionary objectives. . . . We hold that this procedure is [also] more efficacious than extreme agrarian reforms which nationalize with one coup all the land, and thus are unable to exploit it under the best conditions. . . .
>
> The building of socialism remains an eminently human enterprise . . . and also a continuous creation. In it man plays the most important part. Upon his courage and his creative imagination essentially depends its success. . . .

At the end of his visit, before taking off for Saudi Arabia, Bour-

guiba held a press conference in Cairo that lasted an hour and a half. The following day, Egyptian headlines (as well as those in Israel) suggested full agreement with President Nasser on all issues, including the policy toward West Germany. But the text does not match. The reports, though apparently omitting any direct polemical tone, indicated clearly that Bourguiba had expressed reservations.

On relations with Germany, he called attention to a statement issued by the Tunisian Political Bureau shortly before his departure, which committed Tunisia to supporting the Egyptian position. But it was a limited commitment: "We are all united and stand up as one man against providing arms for your enemy." But by now it was no longer the issue, since Germany had already stopped sending arms to Israel.

According to the Egyptian press, he was also in full agreement with President Nasser on Ulbricht's visit. Yet it quoted Bourguiba's remark that the crisis between Cairo and Bonn was almost over, and that the threat would not be carried out. The crisis, he said, stemmed not from this visit but from the sending of weapons to Israel. Perhaps this part of the statement, too, includes those words which, Bourguiba had declared, were put in his mouth.

When asked by a journalist about his views concerning Arab unity, he said it could best be achieved if the advances are gradual. For the time being, the relationships between the Arab states must be based on mutual consultation.

In his speeches on Egyptian soil about pan-Arabism and extreme forms of socialism, he spoke freely, albeit cautiously, and with extreme courtesy. He said he was against *forced* inter-Arab unity just as he was opposed to extreme measures to introduce socialism. He strongly emphasized the foolhardiness of indulging in grandiose pan-Arab enterprises in the international arena, and radical socialism and forced industrialization internally. Instead, he said, the Arabs in general and Egypt in particular should solve the most urgent problems facing all of them: extreme economic underdevelopment, and spiritual-cultural ignorance and fanaticism.

Only when the Arab states have given their people a higher standard of living, and a greater self-awareness, could discussions about unity become meaningful. Unity, which is proclaimed artificially and prematurely, is "suspicious." Of course, a generation or more may pass before true unity is realized, but there is no urgency unless one is animated by ulterior motives. Indeed, it is necessary to educate a new generation of Arabs and liberate them from all the psychological handicaps they now suffer. What these handicaps are Bourguiba would describe in detail in the next few months to whoever was ready to listen.

On the Palestine problem, Bourguiba declared his support of the resolutions of the Arab summit conferences. But in elaborating upon his position he also qualified it. Instead of all the Arab states undertaking common military action against Israel, the Palestinians should make their own fight (as the Tunisians and Algerians had done) for independence.

He also answered questions about the other countries he would visit. The fact that the governments of Turkey and Iran were unwilling to support the Arab position on the Palestine problem did not affect the friendship between Tunisia and those Moslem states. Bourguiba was later to avail himself of the friendly disposition in Teheran and Ankara to argue for the cause of Palestine.

Asked his opinion concerning the Yemen conflict, he replied that he would like to serve as mediator in the dispute between Egypt and Saudi Arabia. This conflict should be brought to a speedy end; it was detrimental to Arab interests in general.

The conclusion of his visit brought a customary joint communiqué by Bourguiba and Nasser. It proclaimed their full agreement that supply of weapons to Israel encouraged Israel's aggressive policy and constituted a serious threat to all Arab states. It declared their adherence to the idea of Arab unity, their support of "the Palestine Liberation Organization," and their willingness to help the PLO "restore to the Palestinian people their rights in full." They also declared their accord on the necessity of liquidating all foreign bases in Arab states.

The communiqué reiterated established Arab positions on neutralism and anti-colonialism, citing the examples of Vietnam, Southern Rhodesia, and Portuguese Africa. (*Le Monde* noted that their call for neutralism in Vietnam, unlike the usual Egyptian practice, was not weighted against the United States.) They reaffirmed their commitment to the United Nations.

The comuniqué expressed "an identity of views" regarding the building of socialism and a common determination to increase commercial and cultural exchanges. At the same time, the Cultural Affairs Ministers of the two countries signed a Tunisian-Egyptian cultural accord, providing for an exchange of scholarships and radio-television programs, and increased cooperation in the areas of film-making, journalism, tourism, and archeological research.

The two heads of state agreed that upon completion of Bourguiba's tour he would return to Egypt for an additional three days of consultations.

It sounded as if Bourguiba had fallen completely into line with Nasser's views. All the main points of pan-Arabism were there: Arab unity; socialism; support of Shukeiri; and by implication, liquidation or dissolution of the State of Israel and the abolition of foreign bases in the Middle East.

But he never came back. After his visits to Jordan and the Lebanon, it was not likely that he would.

Bourguiba and his party arrived in the Saudi Arabian city of Jiddah on February 22, the same day he left Egypt. King Feisal set a precedent by going to the airport to meet a foreign dignitary. Besides attending the usual receptions, dinners, and discussions, the Tunisian President visited the holy city of Mecca. At a banquet given by the King, Bourguiba appeared, not in his usual European garb, but in the Tunisian national costume of white robes. Toasts were exchanged and brotherly amity vowed.

Observers, however, believe that the visit consisted not merely of pomp and protocol but also of serious business. They suggest that the Tunisian President discussed with the Saudi Arabian monarch the need to create a bloc of moderate, Western-oriented Arab states that could stem both the tide of Nasser's ascendency and the deepening penetration of the Soviet Union as a result of Nasser's bid to dominate the Arab world. It is also probable that at their meetings the two heads of state broached the enlargement of such a bloc into a Moslem front to include Iran, Turkey, and perhaps Pakistan. A year later this idea became a burning issue in the Arab world, and King Feisal emerged as the avowed protagonist of a Moslem Front.

Before leaving Jiddah, Bourguiba held a press conference and discussed the results of his efforts to find a solution to the Yemen problem: "The points of view still remain very divergent. I have tried to bring them together. Time will do the rest."

At the end, both leaders pledged themselves in the usual communiqué to uphold the resolution adopted at the Arab summit conferences, especially with regard to the "restoration of usurped Palestine to the Arab nation."

3

Reactions in the Arab World

WHILE HE WAS STILL IN EGYPT, CAIRO NEWSPAPERS HAD BOURGUIBA declaiming that it was necessary "to throw the Jews into the sea," one of their favorite clichés. We may picture the confusion of the Egyptian propaganda-makers, therefore, when the bombshell exploded in Jerusalem.

Reaction was of two kinds. The first was to deny that anything had occurred which altered the course of the "drown the Jews" campaign. Fabricated denials by Bourguiba were used to spread the notion that the whole thing was a hoax by some Western journalists. Such "denials" appeared not only in Egyptian papers but in Jordanian and Lebanese as well. Other journalists in those countries stopped short of fabrication by printing conjectures that Bourguiba's words had been misunderstood. The more earnest of these apologists generally agreed that in view of Bourguiba's patriotic record, his words were *probably* distorted. They therefore asked him to state his views without ambiguity.

We must remember that there *was* ambiguity, and Bourguiba's statements *do* lend themselves to contradictory interpretations. Thus, for instance, the president of the Lebanese Press Association, after a conversation of more than an hour with Bourguiba in Beirut, could honestly declare that the references to the possibility of Arabs living in peace and mutual respect with Jews were a distortion. Several members of Bourguiba's entourage, out of embarrassment, timidity, or conviction, supported the distortion claims.

The denials struck receptive ears. It is just inconceivable, wrote the Beirut *Al Yaum,* that the celebrated Arab patriot should have said such things, especially in view of the opinions he expressed on the same subject at the Arab summits and at the Conference for African Unity. Simultaneously the Egyptian press tried another tack. It implied that Bourguiba was not completely himself: "He is not well," "He is tired."

But Bourguiba did not recover from his "temporary aberration"; he was not shamed into a reversal. On the contrary, he seemed determined that Jerusalem and Beirut should constitute not an isolated episode, but the beginning of a sustained campaign.

When his plan became clear beyond a doubt, how did the Arab world react?

A distinction must be made between two phases in Arab reaction. In the first period, following Bourguiba's statement in the Old City on March 6, Egypt showed some reticence and much confusion. One reason for the relative lack of response (we shall discuss others in later chapters) was the ambiguity of the Jerusalem declaration, which was general and vague; it did not detail his proposal.

The second phase of Arab reaction followed his speech at home on April 21, after the completion of his tour, when he spelled out his plan: to seek a peaceful solution of the Palestine conflict through direct negotiations between Palestinian Arabs and Israel. In this second phase, it was Nasser who led the campaign against Bourguiba.

One could hardly expect any kind of consensus. Although the divided Arab world generally gives the impression that on the Palestine question at least it is united, the response to Bourguiba's plan ranged from cautious praise to outright condemnation.

The most violent reactions came from the two Arab states Bourguiba avoided on his tour—Syria and Iraq.

Asked at his Old City press conference why he was not planning to visit Damascus, he replied testily that he regarded Syria as being in the throes of civil war.

> How can I visit a country where private property is being expropriated, where the shops are broken into and its citizens hanged? The situation there is similar to that in the Sudan and in Yemen.

Then, in more restrained terms, he continued:

> ... I want to save the Syrian Government any trouble my visit might create. I have in fact postponed, not cancelled, my visit to Syria, and sent my Foreign Minister to Damascus to explain the situation.

The vehemence of the reactions in Syria may therefore be explained first by that country's unyieldingly extreme policy toward Israel; second, by its snub from Bourguiba; and third, by his offensive explanations about the omission. The Damascus press called Bourguiba a man suffering from a superiority complex, "ready to sell out the vital interest of the Arabs, at the service of imperialism, for a mess of pottage."

At a press conference at Aleppo, General Amin El Khafez, the Syrian ruler of that time, warned that Bourguiba's "regime will be overthrown by his own people." In answer to a question by a journalist, Khafez said: "The Arab masses who in the past liquidated regimes whose leaders acted against the interests of the Arab cause, will do it again against the new deviationists." The only solution to the Palestine problem, he added, "is to reconquer that country by force of arms and give it back to its rightful owners. The Jews must go back where they came from."

Khafez was to modify his extremist views somewhat at the Arab summit conference in Casablanca that September. It is interesting to note that while the Arab leaders he denounced are still very much in control of affairs in their respective countries, *his* whereabouts are unknown. He was overthrown and arrested by one of his rivals in his own Ba'ath party the night of February 22-23, 1966.)

A Damascus crowd denounced Bourguiba as a traitor and marched to the Tunisian Embassy, but was dispersed in front of the building. Demonstrations also broke out in the Syrian port city of Latakia.

The reactions in Iraq to Bourguiba's declarations were so violent that on March 12 the Iraqi Minister of the Interior informed Bourguiba that the government could not guarantee his safety. Bourguiba therefore decided to cancel his Iraqi visit, which had been scheduled to begin March 20. The cancellation was ascribed by the Tunisian delegation to "the confused situation reigning in Baghdad," implying that, as in Syria, there was a reign of anarchy in Iraq as well. He probably referred to the anti-Bourguiba and anti-German demonstrations which broke a day earlier in the Iraqi capital. Mobs in Baghdad attacked West German properties, and Bonn's Embassy was set afire.

Later, Marshal Abdul Salam Aref, President of Iraq, sent a personal note to Bourguiba which was delivered by the Iraqi Ambassador in Tunis. The contents were kept secret by both sender and receiver, but next day there appeared in the Cairo *Al Ahram* an interview with the Iraqi President in which he gave expression to his opinion about the Bourguiba initiative.

> Lately we have been hearing strange ideas concerning the Palestine problem. They were voiced exactly at a time when we were waging our battle against West Germany. These statements reveal the error of those who wish to minimize the importance of the Arab interest in the cause of Palestine. Those who make the declarations have no part in the struggle.

Reaction in the Arab world was adverse in practically all countries and on all levels.* Lebanese officials accused Bourguiba of "preaching abandonment of Palestine to Zionism." Students and mobs demonstrated in the major cities of the Arab world. With significant exceptions: Hussein and Helou, of course, remained silent. Pierre Gemayel, leader of the strongest political party in the Lebanon (the Phalangists) and a member of the Cabinet, came out unequivocally in favor of Bourguiba's proposals. In an interview with Edouard H. Saab of *Le Monde,* Gemayel elaborated his own proposals for a peaceful solution to the Palestine problem, and suggested a plan for a binational state on the pattern of Lebanon.

The Lebanese press was not uniform in its reactions. It reflected not only the divided feelings of the two major contending religious communities—the Christian and the Moslem—but the divided political sympathies with (and often actual allegiance to) foreign

---

* Bourguiba was denounced at an international symposium on Palestine, held in March 1965 in Cairo under the auspices of the Palestine Student Association and in which delegates from all Arab countries, as well as prominent guests from both East and West, participated. It proclaimed that since the Arabs have no quarrel with the Jews as such, there is no Arab-Jewish problem, and no solution necessary. But what Bourguiba was advocating was a *modus vivendi* with Israel, which is not acceptable because Israel must be obliterated by force.

regimes: the Nasserites on the one hand and the Ba'athists on the other. The government itself seems to have been divided into three factions. One—represented by the then Prime Minister Hussein Oweini—declined to denounce Bourguiba, declaring only that Lebanon would abide by the decisions of the Arab summits; the second, represented by the Christian Phalangist party, endorsed Bourguiba's proposals on the ground that they were not different from what Nasser himself had proposed; the third, represented by the then Minister of the Interior, *Takieddine Solh,* demanded outright denunciation of Bourguiba.

The pro-Nasser crowds in the Lebanese capital staged tumultuous demonstrations. Ten thousand rioters attacked the *Société Tunisienne de Banques* to protest Bourguiba's "lack of firmness" on both the West German and Israel issues. They broke bank windows and tore down pictures of Bourguiba.

Of course, the most intriguing question is Nasser's attitude towards Bourguiba's campaign.

The Egyptian President seemed for many weeks unable to make up his mind on how to react. Aware that the Tunisian leader had dared openly to challenge his leadership with scorn, he nonetheless apparently chose to avoid a showdown. His visible early reactions were cautious. He slackened his drive for pan-Arab centralism but he tried to preserve appearances until the furor should blow over. "I shall not insult Mr. Bourguiba, for I set great store by Arab unity," he declared on several occasions.

Why this reticence?

Bourguiba explains it simply by pointing out that basically his proposals are not much different from those periodically advanced by Nasser. But since Nasser is afraid of the masses, he has chosen to express these proposals in private, or in the foreign press, or before foreign visitors; these words and ideas never reach his own people. Such behavior Bourguiba considers cowardly.

He told his press conference in Beirut that when he was in Egypt, only a few days earlier, Nasser had agreed with his approach and philosophy. More than that, he said, the Egyptian President had complimented him on his approach, and expressed regret that he had not known him personally and intimately before. But, added Bourguiba, Nasser was too busy with his electioneering to give these ideas thoughtful consideration.

But Jean Daniel, the editor of the French weekly *Nouvel Observateur,* (April 15, 1965) got from Bourguiba a somewhat qualified version of his visit to Egypt and his discussions with Nasser:

I was given a marvelous reception in Cairo not only by the leader of the U.A.R. and his government, but also by the Egyptian masses. All this made me happy indeed. It was a satisfaction for me to experience this show of Arab brotherhood. What made me even more happy was my feeling that at long last the Egyptians were doing justice to Tunis, her fight [for liberty] and her experience.

I was sincerely happy, and if you ask me why I didn't content myself with this reception [instead of looking for trouble], I would say that you misunderstand my sentiments. On the contrary, the purpose of my tour in the Middle East was to prove that all the clouds were dissipated. Fundamentally there remained few problems between us.

For a year or so things had moved ahead with the Arab leaders, and each time I developed my point of view, I was listened to with attention and respect. I said to President Nasser that one cannot endlessly remain on the defensive, that such a position only strengthens Israel, that many friends of the Arabs are embarrassed by our incapability of solving the Palestinian problem. I said to him: The problem is frozen; we will never be able to get out of this impasse. For eighteen years all the efforts of the Arabs have been in vain. Why don't you consider using my methods? The results cannot be worse. I told him that Tunisia has proven how successful a policy of "phases" can be, and that the Israeli affair is a typical problem which should be solved gradually, stage by stage.

Everyone knows that war is impossible, that it will be stopped by the great powers as soon as it breaks out; that the United States is committed to intervene with equal firmness against any aggression, whether by Israel or by the Arabs. Apart from that, the Arab states have been engaged for some time in a study of the best way to entrust the task of liberation to the Palestinians themselves. This task involves formulating a program and alerting international public opinion, both Arab and non-Arab.

Finally, in Cairo I told them that one day I will make public my proposals, but on condition that I should not immediately be treated as a perjurer, or a traitor to the cause of the Arab nation. Everyone was in agreement. True, there might have been some difference of conception, but there was no grave disagreement.

As if to clinch the argument, President Bourguiba indicated that in an interview published in *Réalitiés*, (May 1965, English edition) Nasser had expressed basically the same point of view.

Perhaps this is not a completely reliable appraisal; it would certainly contradict his previous statement that Nasser was too busy with his election campaign to listen to him attentively. The discussion, then, could not have been very thorough. Even in the account Bourguiba gave *Nouvel Observateur,* there are certain imprecisions. The single sentence. "There might have been some differences of conception, but no grave disagreement," poses the possibility of genuine misunderstanding. And Bourguiba's "One day I will make public my proposals" does not necessarily ensure that Nasser understood that "one day" might actually come the next week.

Yet the spirit of the account is probably correct: Nasser, however busy, must have listened to Bourguiba expounding his views. Bourguiba said "Everyone was in agreement," implying that Nasser was not alone, and that some of his close associates participated in the discussion. And in these conversations Bourguiba received the impression that Nasser, too, did not consider war the only solution to the Palestine problem.

Perhaps Bourguiba himself thought that "one day" meant the indeterminate future; but then the German complication arose and Bourguiba was annoyed by Nasser's peremptory handling of it. This is what most observers, including those of his own entourage, believe.

Did Nasser give his tacit blessing to Bourguiba's peace offensive? Some observers thought that he did and moreover, they discerned a tripartite deal among Nasser, Bourguiba, and King Hussein. It would be unlikely, they argued, that Bourguiba would make such a statement during an official visit without informing his host beforehand; and since King Hussein at that time was attempting to get on the best possible terms with President Nasser, it must be assumed that Hussein could have consented only if he believed that Nasser had agreed.

But why should Nasser have concurred? For a number of reasons, say these commentators. For one: Just as in having Bourguiba speak out against the sterility of the policy of such demagogues as Shukeiri, so Nasser might have been interested in a similar attack on the leaders of the Syrian Ba'ath who were clamoring for an immediate war against Israel. King Hussein was in Cairo for a time during Bourguiba's visit in Egypt; the three might have held a "little summit" and decided to give the Tunisian President a green light. That subsequent events made the actual concurrence embarrassing to Nasser might explain his reluctance immediately to take a stand against Bourguiba.

The Egyptians denied all this vehemently. They did not deny

that Bourguiba had extensive conversations with Nasser both in private and in the presence (and perhaps with the active participation) of King Hussein. But they insisted that in these conversations, Bourguiba did *not* succeed in persuading Nasser to his view. The editor of *Al Ahram,* which usually serves as a mouthpiece for the Egyptian President, wrote in an article entitled "Dialogue with Mr. Habib":

> No Arab, whoever he may be, can envision the possibility of peaceful coexistence between the Arab peoples and Israel. . . . The Palestine problem cannot be solved around the conference table and on a basis of mutual respect, when the two parties to the conflict do not represent equal rights. The Zionists robbed the people of Palestine of their fatherland. Now they have to give it back to them. . . . Even if Bourguiba had in mind coexistence between the Arabs and a Jewish minority after Israel has been liquidated, this could only be discussed after that liquidation has been achieved.

The editor of *Al Ahram* then analyzed the meaning of "Bourguibism." In substance, he said, it is synonymous with a policy of concessions. That despite these, Bourguiba achieved great success in his own country was, he implied, sheer chance. He placed the blame for much of Bourguiba's "wrong decision" on his foreign advisers, particularly Cecil Hourani.

But the most revealing point in the *Al Ahram* article is its admission that "the problem of Israel is not necessarily the one which we should be perturbed about, especially since Bourguiba claims that his statements were misunderstood, and there is no reason to doubt the correctness of his explanation. . . ."

If "the problem of Israel" is not the issue, what *is* the issue? Is it that no Arab leader may express an independent opinion? Is it that Bourguiba dared to criticize the pan-Arab leadership—or, more precisely, Nasser? This is probably what *Al Ahram's* editor had in mind.

With Bourguiba, too, Israel was a secondary issue—or perhaps only a means to an end, as Bourguiba has repeatedly said it is with Nasser. What Bourguiba was fighting for, and he never tired of saying it, was the right to have independent ideas about everything and to express them openly and publicly. If Palestine were truly his first concern, he could readily have made affirmative statements of policy for a solution, and refrained from fierce attacks on Arab leaders whose only effect could be to insure that they must oppose what he proposed.

Nasser himself, though he refrained from explicitly referring to Bourguiba, declared that "under the present circumstances there is no room now in the Arab world for talk about compromises. We are still in a stage where we have first to overcome the various challenges by taking offensive action. Compromises of any kind would only serve the interests of the enemy."

Nasser's opponents exploited his failure to make a forthright attack on Bourguiba. The Ba'athist daily in Beirut, *Al Ahrar,* wrote on April 17, that Bourguiba's campaign "cast a shadow" upon Nasser. It demanded the minutes of the conversations between the two Presidents.

For their part, the Tunisians took dual advantage of Nasser's reticence. First, they took it as proof that the Egyptian leader agreed with the Tunisian President. Second, they pointed out that Bourguiba had the courage to state his convictions publicly, while Nasser did not. Thus, the Tunisian Ambassador to Paris in a radio interview congratulated Nasser for his tacit support while the Tunisian press was criticizing Nasser for not coming out openly in support of Bourguiba's initiative.

Strangely enough, Nasser eventually did come into the open. In his interview with the French magazine *Réalitiés,* he declared that he favored solving the Palestine problem by peaceful means on the basis of the United Nations resolutions. This is in essence Bourguiba's thesis.

When this interview appeared, the Tunisian newspaper *Al Sabah* published an extremely critical editorial accusing Nasser (though not by name) of cowardice. The editorial first expressed satisfaction that "a celebrated head of an Arab state said in an interview with a foreign newspaper that he was willing to accept the United Nation resolutions concerning Palestine, though these resolutions are not perfect." It went on to deplore the publication of such declarations at a time when the Egyptian press and radio continued "an extremist line which has become classic. . . . We wish that head of state were able to find enough courage to tell the truth and to free himself from the pressures of his own people, pressures which he himself engendered. Only then will he be able to act effectively for the rescue of Palestine and its people. Were he to embark upon such a cause it would prove much more fruitful than his fiery speeches and conspiratorial activities."

4

Interlude

AS WE STUDY THE STRATEGIC AND TACTICAL ASPECTS OF BOURGUIBA'S tour, we discern a well-conceived plan. Apart from his overall objective, he had a particular purpose for each state he visited. In Saudi Arabia he questioned King Feisal about Nasser's intentions in sending a large army to fight the Yemeni royalist forces (which were being supported by Feisal). In Cairo he appeared to listen attentively to Nasser's opinion of the possibilities for restoring peace among the Arabs. In Jordan and Lebanon he exploded his peace bomb. Then he apparently decided to take a breather and see what the reaction would be.

The adverse reaction, noisy as it was, did not surprise Bourguiba. A member of his entourage told J. Ben Brahem of *Le Monde* that "fundamentally the Egyptian reaction was less aggressive than one would expect." The official expressed his belief that the time was ripe for certain Arab leaders to listen to common sense and accept a policy based upon realities.

It was precisely during the time of Bourguiba's tour that the crisis in Arab-West German relations reached its climax.

Here some chronological reference will help:

Bourguiba arrived in Beirut on March 7, 1965. On that same day West Germany decided to establish diplomatic relations with Israel. Nasser retorted that if this happened the Arabs would break ties with Bonn and recognize East Germany. During an Arab League conference that was in progress at this time in Cairo, tremendous pressure was being exerted on all other Arab governments to fall in line with Nasser.

Bourguiba entertained some hope that a showdown between him and Nasser on the German issue might still be avoided—and that Israel itself might provide a comfortable way out. The latter hope was based on a report published in Bonn on March 11 that Israel's price for formal relations with Bonn was West Germany's guarantee of Israel's territorial integrity and a resumption of the suspended arms shipments; Bonn had rejected these conditions. Bourguiba felt greatly heartened by this report, and announced at his press conference in Beirut that the issue had resolved itself: Bonn was not going to recognize Israel, and the Arabs would not have to retaliate.

But events did not vindicate this hope. Bonn extended diplomatic recognition to Israel, (though without any special commitments or even promises) and on March 14 the Arab League Foreign Ministers met in Cairo to face this fact. Egypt called for a showdown. Tunisia, supported by Morocco and Libya, voted against the Egyptian proposals.

That same day Bourguiba arrived in Iran after a short stay in Kuwait, with Turkey, Yugoslavia, and Greece still ahead. It must have seemed clear to Bourguiba that he now had to play down the Palestine question to avoid fighting, in effect, on two fronts: the issue of West Germany on the one, Palestine on the other. He did not want to dilute his challenge to Nasser by involving it with the German issue. His immediate objective, therefore, was to induce as many Arab governments as possible to resist Egypt's insistence on breaking relations with Bonn and recognizing East Germany. He lost—and he won. A majority voted to break relations with Bonn but not to recognize East Germany. And those who voted against the severance announced that they would not abide by the majority decision.

Bourguiba saw the crisis over Germany as a fleeting incident; the Palestine problem he viewed as a fundamental issue requiring time for a solution. He must weigh its complexity against the sensitivity of Arab opinion. For the rest of his tour he refrained from making provocative declarations, hoping thereby to impress Arabs as the voice of reason speaking for Arab patriotism and nationalism. He even took pains to send his chief troubleshooter, Secretary of State Mongi Slim, to Cairo to reassure Nasser.

In an interview with the Cairo *Al Ahram*, Slim explained that his President had been misquoted, that he had said, in fact, that it was possible and necessary to achieve peaceful coexistence with Jews, but not with Israel. (This was true as far as his Jerusalem statement is concerned. But Bourguiba subsequently moved forward from that point of view.) But even from the distorted reports in the Egyptian press it was clear that Mongi Slim was sent not to deny, or to apologize, but to clarify and in a sense to confirm, the basic ideas of the Tunisian President.

After he saw Nasser, Slim told the press he was "very satisfied" with the results of the meeting. He then left for Teheran to report to Bourguiba. Elsewhere in Bourguiba's entourage, however, there seems to have been some confusion and embarrassment. One member tried to deny that Bourguiba had actually said in Jerusalem what was ascribed to him. "All these reports," this man told a correspondent of *Le Monde* in Beirut on March 9, 1965, "are extremely false" both as to the content and the spirit of his declaration. The most that can be attributed to his President, he continued, was advice of caution and "an exact evaluation of the situation and the circumstances before undertaking any rash action."

Le Monde remarked editorially: "The fact is that all the representatives of the great press agencies that were present at the news conference emphasized in their dispatches the appeasing declarations of the Tunisian chief-of-state."

After his stormy visit to the Lebanon, Bourguiba went to Kuwait. Here, in the view of some observers, he took a step backward. If the reports in the Arab newspapers are correct, the Tunisian President said in a radio address in Kuwait that "we will get back the conquered parts of the Arab world. And we will achieve this by a coordinated effort among all our forces, and by the strengthening of military power and preparedness. . . . We will try to activate the economic and technological forces of the Arab states." He extolled the Arab nation and its struggles, and ended with the words: "The future is ours."

At the end of his three-day visit in Kuwait, Bourguiba and the Emir said in a joint communiqué that they were determined to work for the restoration of Palestine to its rightful owners and to carry out the resolutions adopted at the Arab summit conferences.

It is difficult to say whether Bourguiba's zigzags were the result of contradictory trends of thought which he could not yet reconcile, or to a design to make ambiguous statements so that his ideas might be more readily acceptable to the Arab rulers and people. Some observers, including French journalists in Bourguiba's entourage, suggested that Bourguiba was following the celebrated method, once expounded by Lenin, of taking two steps forward and one step backward.

It is worth keeping in mind that Bourguiba's tour of the Arab countries was to end in Kuwait, a little sheikdom of no major political significance. He may not have considered it a worthwhile platform for his non-conformist ideas and decided to treat his visit there in routine fashion, voicing the usual clichés of Arab nationalism.

The remaining countries in his itinerary—Iran, Turkey, Yugoslavia, and Greece—are outside the sphere of pan-Arab influence. Because his audiences in those lands were quite different, his objectives would not be expected to be the same.

In Cairo he told the news conference (February 21) that he would use the occasion of his forthcoming visits to Iran and Turkey to argue for the cause of Palestine, and would try to influence a change in their policy toward Israel. He considered, he said, the main source of Arab complaints in their relations with Turkey and Iran to be the unwillingness of these two non-Arab Moslem countries to support the Palestinians.*

He kept his promise faithfully. However, as we shall see, his declared intention was not the exclusive—perhaps not even the main—purpose of his visit to the two countries. In Teheran his chief thought was not so much to create an anti-Israel front as an anti-pan-Arab front; his words were directed not so much against Tel Aviv as against Cairo.

Of all the countries Bourguiba visited, he received the most cordial and enthusiastic reception in Iran and for good reason. Here the two heads of state found themselves on the same side of the fence: strong opponents of pan-Arabism and of Nasser's bid for ascendancy in the Middle East and beyond. But while the same apprehensions of Nasser's aspirations might have been latent in the other countries he visited, in Teheran these sentiments could be expressed without inhibition.

Days in advance of his visit, Bourguiba was hailed in the Persian press as an outstanding statesman of great vision. His statements on the Palestine problem were favorably heard and widely quoted. In the capital his political courage and wisdom were universally hailed.

---

* The day Bourguiba arrived in Teheran, the official organ of the Tunisian Neo-Destour Party (al Amal) published an article predicting that the meetings between Bourguiba and the Shah might result in a change in Iran's attitude toward Israel and the Palestine problem. The article appealed to Iran to support the "Palestine Nation—which fell victim to the most flagrant injustice of the 20th century."

"Here at long last is a Chief of State with whom we can act in concert because like us he speaks the language of common sense," declared a member of the Iranian cabinet.

The Shah sent a special plane to Kuwait with a delegation of notables to accompany Bourguiba to Teheran. He was received at the airport by the Shah, the Empress, the Prime Minister, the whole Cabinet, the chiefs of staff, members of the diplomatic corps, and celebrities of all sorts. Planes of the Iranian air force flew overhead; a 21-gun salute greeted the visitor.

At the intended end of the visit, seven days later, President and Shah issued a long communiqué. Bourguiba said that he viewed with grave concern the future of Palestine and the plight of the Palestine refugees. Both governments pledged to "continue to demand in all international bodies that the recommendations of the United Nations should be observed in a spirit of justice and faithfulness to the principles of the UN Charter," by all parties involved in the Palestine conflict. In essence it was a very moderate statement and contains nothing essentially detrimental to Israel.

It was also announced that the Shah had accepted an invitation to come to Tunisia on a state visit. Because of the sudden cancellation of his visit to Iraq, Bourguiba prolonged his stay in Iran four days longer—to March 24.

The significance of Bourguiba's visit to Iran was much greater than appeared when it took place. The Arab world may be stirred for a long time by the impetus given there to the creation of a federation of Moslem states—Arab and non-Arab—in the Middle East and beyond.

The idea may not have originated with Bourguiba; it may have been broached in general terms by his Persian hosts. Though he did not discourage it, Bourguiba took a cautious attitude, in keeping with his philosophy about such matters: to go slowly, and to separate general aspiration from immediate action. When at a later date, King Faisal of Saudi Arabia made the idea of a pan-Moslem federation a central theme of his own policy, if not of his career, Bourguiba still took the same attitude of caution.

Bourguiba arrived in Ankara on March 24 for a seven-day visit. He was met at the airport by President Cemâl Gürsel, Prime Minister Ürgüplü, members of the Cabinet, and the presidents of both Houses of Parliament.

That evening General Gürsel gave a dinner in his honor. Bourguiba made a speech studded with historic references to the cordial relations between the Turks and the Tunisians. To the pleased surprise of his audience he referred to Turkish rule of Tunisia not as a regime of occupation (the usual description in standard texts) but as a "liberation" from the Spanish yoke.

He repeated this line in his address to the Turkish Parliament when he performed one of the most acrobatic feats of rhetoric in his long tour. What had until then been referred to as Turkish domination, was now called cooperation between peoples in one tremendous political structure in what might be called a commonwealth of nations. He glorified Ataturk as one of the great leaders in modern history, whose triumphs made other small nations take heart. He recalled that when he was 20 years old, his own imagination had been fired by the example of the Turkish hero; Kemal Pasha (Ataturk) had become the young Bourguiba's model. He praised Turkey's diplomacy during World War II as the greatest achievement in the history of that art, adding that in essence it had laid the foundations of what is now called "positive neutralism."

But interspersed with these encomiums were criticisms of some aspects of the Turkish experience. He expressed doubts about the wisdom of Kemal's extreme secularization of the State in a Moslem land. "It was, indisputably, a troubling innovation for most Moslems," and it alienated the Arabs. He reminded the Deputies and Senators that "Islam preceded the State." He seemed untroubled, in this address, that he himself had been trying, as much as possible under prevailing conditions, to secularize Tunisia. (We shall have more to say of this.)

He told the by now somewhat restive lawmakers that the Turks' lack of popularity among the Arabs was not due to historic Ottoman domination—but to reasons rooted in their modern history. He cited Turkey's "bad" record at the United Nations. He reminded his listeners, by way of example, that when Tunisia tried in March 1952 to bring her problem of her independence before the Security Council, Turkey ranged herself on the side of France, Great Britain, and the United States, while a distant Moslem country, Pakistan, supported Tunisia with great force and eloquence. To him, who had then been in exile in Southern Sahara, it was a grievous disappointment.

But these remarks were only a prelude. He was well aware, he went on, that the main reason for the present strained relationship between Turkey and the Arabs was Turkey's attitude toward the Palestine problem. But to lead up to his main theme, Bourguiba first referred to a problem much closer to home: Cyprus. The Turks could justifiably expect to hear some discussion from their guest about this problem of such tremendous emotional importance to them. But he gave very little satisfaction to their expectations. He offered no hint of any solution for this problem; he merely used it to introduce what he was going to say about Palestine.

His speech was a strong indictment of Israel, pronounced in forceful terms:

> Many are those, and on all levels, who appreciate the deep concern you entertain as to the eventual fate of the Turkish community in Cyprus. Believe me, it is our wish that this painful problem be solved without mutilation, without irreparable rifts, and above all that this community should not remain with the feeling that it has been the victim of an injustice. I take the liberty of insisting on this point, because it is perhaps the most important. We live at a time when popular sensibilities are so acute that individuals are willing to bear a great deal of private misery, but are moved to rise to oppose an arbitrary decision inflicted upon their brothers or others near to them. We live at a time when the least encroachment upon the ingenuity and the rights of a community becomes an offense to each individual personally.
>
> And since we are invoking here the vicissitudes of communities dear to us, I hope you will not hold it against me if I remind you that we, the Arabs, care (and we consider it our duty to care) about a whole people that refuses to resign itself to a global injustice of which it found itself a victim. Deprived and expelled from their homeland, banished by international institutions from which they were justified in expecting protection, the people of Palestine pose to all of us a question which we cannot dodge. Is it possible to accept, to ratify, a *'fait accompli'*, when this represents a reward for violence and the theft of a fatherland? I imagine some would like to relegate the Palestine tragedy to the archives of causes which have already been pleaded too long. But in this case we are not able to, nor can we allow ourselves to, become tired, indifferent or to forget.
>
> As far as the Arabs and true Moslems are concerned, the State of Israel, cut out from a usurped land, came into being out of colonial logic. Gentlemen, please keep well in mind that 1948 was the last date, the end-line of this kind of enterprise. It was a demarcation between two currents of history. Had a few more years passed, the conquest of Palestine would no longer have been realizable.

It is a distortion of this conflict, and it is to indulge in a grave moral prejudice against the Arabs, to interpret their hostility toward Israel in terms of racial or religious antagonism. No such consideration plays any part, and nothing is further from our thinking. What happened in Palestine can be defined in a very few words: it is a matter of expropriation by force.

In various circles one wonders why the wound didn't heal. How could it? Colonialism had a long history of horror and cruelty; if, however, some peoples who were its victims did dress their wounds and establish more confident links with their former oppressors, it is because decolonization set up a social and human order which made a dialogue possible. But this did not happen in Palestine. There, the perpetrators of the iniquity, far from seeking to repair the evil, exert themselves to aggravate its effects. Eight years after the brutal partition of Palestine and the formation of the State of Israel, we witnessed the Israeli aggression of 1956 against Egypt. Eight years after Suez, we witnessed the diversion of the water from the Jordan. From where, then, is one to expect peace and justice when usurpation is followed by defiance, and when new threats are grafted upon old encroachments?

It would be easy for you to recover and expand your radiance in the Arab world, not by the classic means of onerous propaganda, but by certain gestures, by the sympathy and interest you witness in regard to the Arabs, to their trials, to their problems.

He then spoke of the road Tunisia had traversed since independence, and of its ardent desire to establish close cooperation between the two countries. To offset the resentment he could naturally expect, he reverted to the theme of his past inspiration by the Turkish example, and spoke of his "pilgrimage" to Turkey, where he had found fortitude in the decisive period of his fight for Tunisia's independence. Now he had reached the end of his prepared speech, but momentum carried him along and he cried out: "Long live the recovered friendship between the Turkish and Tunisian peoples!" Apparently this saved the day. The Parliament gave him a standing ovation.

Bourguiba's public speech and certainly his private talks with Turkey's officials were not entirely without results. In the joint communiqué published at the end of the visit on March 30, the Turkish President and Prime Minister assured Mr. Bourguiba that their government regarded the grave Palestine problem with appreciation and sympathy, and agreed that it should be solved equitably. Turkey sincerely desired to strengthen the ties of friendship with all Arab countries. The newly appointed Turkish Foreign Minister, Hasan Esat Isik, at a news conference with a group of Tunisian journalists who accompanied their President on the tour, said that Turkey's relations with Israel were kept at "a normal level." But, he added, his government would "not develop her relations with Israel in a way contrary to the interests of the Arabs."

Although this statement would appear to be an achievement of sorts for Bourguiba, it must be seen within the context of prevailing events. Ankara had just signed a new trade agreement with Israel, which specified an increased trade ceiling of $30 million— $5 million more than the previous agreement. A Foreign Ministry spokesman tried to minimize the importance of the agreement by calling the ceiling theoretical, since last year's trade had run well below this figure. But the Minister of Commerce later told a news correspondent that Turkey did not discriminate in her foreign trade and would develop her commercial relations with any country as it suited her interests.

Why did Bourguiba make these extreme anti-Israel remarks in the Turkish Parliament? They provided support to the Israeli official line which says that deep in his mind and heart he is no different from other Arab leaders: he views Israel with hatred and looks forward to its disappearance from the face of the earth. It saddened those marginal groups in Israel which thought Bourguiba's initiative was the opening of a new age of mutual understanding.

Taken at their face value his remarks should not have occasioned surprise. The Tunisian press and some newspapers in other Arab countries announced in advance that one of the purposes of Bourguiba's visits to Turkey and Iran would be to influence those governments toward more sympathy and understanding for the cause of the Palestinian Arabs, and less friendly relations with Israel. This is what he *had* said in his press conference in Cairo. Bourguiba, though a moderate, is no traitor to the Arab cause, which is near to his heart. He does not recognize Israel. Despite the naïve expectations of some Israelis, including leaders and journalists, it is preposterous to expect an Arab leader to be converted to Zionism, or even to adopt to any degree the Israeli point of view. The Israelis will have to realize that there is a genuine clash of basic opinions and of emotional attitudes between the Arab states and Israel. The problem is not how to convert each, but how on the basis of historic realities to arrive at a *modus vivendi*. Neither side can be expected to forget or renounce its appraisal of historic events. But despite these contradictory opinions, they must strive for an accommodation in a spirit of compromise.

Careful reading of his Turkish speech shows that though Bourguiba was inimical to Israel in appraising historic events, his speech did not contain any call for violence. On the contrary, we may perhaps even read constructive implications. For example, there is the inference that if Israel had not indulged in the Suez Campaign of 1966, and later in the diversion of the Jordan waters, there might still have been a possibility of healing the wounds.

We must also keep in mind that Bourguiba speaks several kinds of languages and says different things to different audiences. To the Arabs he says that they must be realistic and look for a compromise solution. To non-Arab Moslems he says that by entertaining normal and friendly relations with Israel, they hurt Arab feelings and relieve the pressure upon Israel to mend her ways.

We shall see that after his visit with Tito, Bourguiba became even more moderate in his appraisal of historic events and the emergence of the State of Israel. He was later to tell Jean Daniel of *Nouvel Observateur* that he found Tito opposed to the oversimplified Arab formula which Bourguiba had until then espoused, namely, that Israel is merely a colonial territory like any other. He was given to understand by his Yugoslav host, himself a great friend of the Arabs and on intimate terms with Nasser, that such a qualification of Israel is silly.

What is more puzzling is why he raised the problem of Turkish secularization. It is known that Bourguiba does hold Kemal Ataturk in great esteem precisely because he succeeded in freeing Turkey from the frozen religious tradition that kept the country immobilized for centuries. He tries in his own country (as we shall see) to follow in the footsteps of the celebrated Turk. There is no easy explanation, but it is difficult to believe his remarks were gratuitous, or that they represented extemporaneous *gaffe*. He prepared the speech long in advance, and its text was carefully discussed with collaborators in the Tunisian political hierarchy. We should also remember that the Turks, though comprising a secular state, are still Moslems; and he can better build their concern for the Moslems of Palestine by playing on their religious ties.

Bourguiba may also have been trying to assemble a grouping of Moslem states as a counterbalance to Nasser's pan-Arabism. Bourguiba sees in pan-Arabism the gravest danger to the independence of each Arab country, and he strongly resents Nasser's peremptory way of dealing with individual Arab governments. He therefore tried to sell the Turks on the formation of some kind of loose Moslem bloc; but this could happen only if Turkey still considered itself a Moslem country and believed that Islam still has meaning in modern political and international history.

The day before he left Turkey Bourguiba held a press conference in Istanbul. Turkish and foreign correspondents were asked to prepare their questions in writing in advance. The correspondent of the Tel Aviv afternoon newspaper *Ma'ariv* submitted a series of questions which the Tunisian President answered in detail and quite frankly. To the question about his opinion on the violent reaction of the Arab press to his statements in Jerusalem and Beirut, he answered:

> My statements may not have pleased some Arab journalists, but I am confident that many Arabs and Palestinians did not think my proposals treasonable, and rather welcomed them.

To the question on what solution he has in mind, he answered:

> It is not my duty or that of any other Arab leader to determine how to solve the Palestine problem. It is the duty of the Palestinians themselves. We should propose, but not impose, methods and solutions.

A dig at Nasser, of course.

Asked by the same Israeli journalist what he had in mind when he said the Palestine problem must be solved "by stages," he said frankly he did not know. "What is imperative is that the Palestinians themselves first accept this method."

He also repeated his contention, expressed on many other occasions, that Nasser did not have the right to impose his personal policy toward Bonn upon all the Arab governments. "We joined the Arab League but this does not mean that we surrendered our sovereignty."

Bourguiba arrived in Belgrade on March 30, 1965 for a seven-day state visit. He was met at the airport by Marshal Tito, members

of the Yugoslav Government, and the Central Committee of the
Communist Party. In Bourguiba's entourage were Mongi Slim,
other Tunisian officials, and leading members of the Socialist
Destour Party.

The next day he was given a large reception in the town hall
of Belgrade and proclaimed an honorary citizen of the city. In his
speech he not only omitted reference to the Middle East or Palestine, he did not mention the word Arab. He had the highest praise
for Marshal Tito, who, he said, by defying Stalin had made Communism respectable in many parts of the world. Tito's courageous
defiance of the "mighty," he continued, served as an example for
all other Communist parties to follow. Probably hinting at his
own quarrels with Nasser and the insults hurled at him by many
Arab patriots in the Middle East for defying Nasser's impositions,
he declared:

> Yes, your courage has really stupefied us. Not only because you
> have said 'No!' but because having placed above everything else
> your (national) personality and dignity, you have exposed your-
> self to being misunderstood and insulted by those of your com-
> rades whose own thoughts you have shared. You have accepted all
> this, but by a *tour de force* you have succeeded in preserving your
> own political line which alone could assure the happiness, bal-
> ance, and progress of the republic of Yugoslavia.

Again, without referring explicitly to the Middle East or Palestine, he praised the Yugoslavs for their successful experiment of
having various ethnic and religious communities live in the same
political framework.

> And finally we have been impressed by the political structure
> you have erected which permits the [various] human communi-
> ties not only to preserve but also to develop their specific values
> and their religions. Thus, an equilibrium has been assured which
> seems to us to constitute a model capable of inspiring and profiting
> other states who should also favor coexistence of different ethnic,
> religious, and traditional communities in the same framework.
> This model seems to me to be especially valuable these days . . .

This statement may have carried some implication for Palestine,
i.e., that Bourguiba prefers some sort of unitary state in Palestine,
perhaps on the Yugoslav pattern, with a framework flexible enough
for various ethnic and religious communities, formerly antagonistic

to each other, to live in comparative peace. One cannot truly say that the Yugoslav state distinguishes itself by being too flexible. But it probably was not so much Bourguiba's intention to inspire Israel and the Arabs with Yugoslavia's example, as to flatter Tito by suggesting that other states should imitate the Yugoslav structure.

He was to take up the same theme several days later during his visit in Greece, the last country of his protracted tour. But there, comparing the Cyprus situation with that of Palestine, he wavered between partition and a unitary state, reflecting his perplexity in seeking a solution to the Palestine problem.

On April 3, Bourguiba visited the capital city of Slavonia, where thousands of its residents gave him a tumultous reception. Then, after conferring with Marshal Tito in Belgrade, Bourguiba was invited to join the Yugoslav leader at Brioni, Tito's secluded island residence in the northern Adriatic. On the deck of a luxury liner, the two continued their political talks against the breathtaking backdrop of the north Adriatic Sea.

In a joint communiqué the two Presidents expressed their concern over the sharp deterioration of the international situation. They appealed to all peace-loving nations to increase their efforts to prevent the aggravation of conflicts in various parts of the world, including the Middle East. They renewed with great emphasis their support of the policy of coexistence and peace among nations, and deplored colonialism in all its forms. They declared their support of "the rights of the people of Palestine"—a formula adopted at the last conference of neutralist countries in Cairo. This joint statement does not contradict Bourguiba's assertion that Tito refused to include Israel as one of the colonial countries or bases that must be liquidated.

The length of his visit, the composition of Bourguiba's entourage, his long talks with Tito in Belgrade and Brioni, the moderate text of the joint comuniqué, tempt the interpreter to speculate that the Tunisian attached special importance to this visit. It gave him the opportunity to present to Tito his views on pan-Arabism, Nasser's personality and strategy, and the Israeli–Arab conflict. Aware of the close relationship between Nasser and Tito, and of the influence and prestige the Egyptian leader derived from this friendship, Bourguiba might have been trying to shed a different light upon the complex situation in the Arab world. Perhaps he even hoped to wean Tito from Nasser. The Tunisian President's interview with Jean Daniel in *Nouvel Observateur* appeared to admit as much.*

Since Bourguiba also intimated in this interview that he suspected Tito of harboring hidden sympathies for Israel, observers were curious to know what Tito would say in Cairo during his forthcoming visit at the end of April. Would he deny the suggestions made by the Tunisian President? Neither from his speeches nor from the joint communiqué as reported in the press could one arrive at any clear conclusion.

The communiqué published simultaneously in Cairo and Belgrade is an extremely long and comprehensive document. The reference to Palestine, however, was worded more or less like the one published less than a month earlier in Belgrade at the end of Bourguiba's visit there. It, too, fell back on that resolution of the neutralist summit concerning the "rights of the Palestinian people." This seems a roundabout way of taking a direct stand.

But Tito also made a public speech at a dinner given by President Nasser in his honor. Nasser spoke first, and was relatively restrained. His theme was peace. Everything must be done, no effort should be spared, to preserve peace. He criticized Peking for demanding the creation of another organization parallel to the United Nations. In spite of its present crisis and the requirements of adjustment in its procedures, declared the Egyptian President, the United Nations has nonetheless succeeded in avoiding chaos in some countries. His complaint against militant extremism was even stronger: "We must state that in several regions of the world there are those who prefer military action to negotiations. . ." Inevitably he spoke of Israel—"the main base of aggression directed against the whole of the Arab world," and rebuked the great powers for supporting Israel.

Then Tito spoke. He agreed fully with his host in berating attempts to solve international problems by force of arms. He also denounced the dangerous activities of the imperialist powers which seek to sow dissensions among the Arab states to preserve their positions in the Middle East, and to hinder the progress of

* April 15, 1965. At the time this interview was published, Marshal Tito was on a visit in Algeria. He addressed, together with the former Algerian President, a mass rally in Algiers. The *New York Times* correspondent noted that Tito did not echo his host's condemnation of Israel. (*New York Times*, April 17, 1965).

the Arab countries. He also referred to "the dangers" incurred by "certain countries" in assisting Israel militarily.

Were these remarks meant to rebut Bourguiba? They are too general and too stereotyped to provide an answer. In fact, one wonders whether Nasser's moderation was a result of Tito's influence, or vice versa. Were Tito's remarks about the Middle East intended to make obeisance to Nasser? Remember, the Nasser–Tito dinner coincided with the controversy then raging in the Middle East—with its background of violent demonstrations against Bourguiba. It was the very time when the Tunisian Embassy in Cairo was attacked by crowds seemingly out of control, and when the Tunisian Arbassador's residence was burned.*

Bourguiba arrived in Athens on April 5 for a six-day State visit as guest of the King and Queen. He was met at the airport by King Constantine and his Cabinet. A surprisingly large number of Athenians came out to greet him and cheer him loudly. Foreign correspondents were somewhat puzzled as to the reason for his popularity.

Bourguiba, who sees bridges rather than abysses, used the occasion to try to build a bridge between the eastern and western Mediterranean. The speech he made at the dinner given in his honor (on April 5) by the King was dedicated to the proposition of "A Mediterranean Cooperation":

> Everything invites us to cooperate fraternally from one end to the other of that Mediterranean in which, like a mirror, each of us can see his own identity, while at the same time he discovers the image of all his neighbors—all of whom are a part of very ancient history. Yet, all are ready for a new start.

---

* A few days later Tito was on an official visit to Oslo, Norway. According to a dispatch by Reuters, the Marshal drew the attention of his hosts to the explosive situation in the Middle East, and used it as an argument for strengthening the United Nations and renewing the Geneva talks on disarmament. He asserted that Europe cannot live in isolation; it is futile to think it would not be affected by conflicts elsewhere, such as the Middle East and Southeast Asia.

At a still later date, during the debate in the United Nations General Assembly on the Palestine problem, the Yugoslav delegate took a somewhat stronger pro-Arab stand than usual. This was explained by some observers as a wish to give support to Nasser at a time when his fortunes were at a rather low ebb. Others interpreted it as being inspired by a more selfish motivation: Yugoslavia's own prestige having been on the wane, she must cultivate Arab friendship.

He could not bypass the Cyprus problem, but his words were so cautious as to sound obscure. His opinions on this topic are of double interest, since he compared the Cyprus problem to that of Palestine:

> We fully understand your deep concern with the future of the Cypriot Greeks. Nothing is more difficult than to straighten out a situation which has become deformed by false solutions. In Cyprus as in Palestine, and other points on the globe, the mistakes of an erroneous diplomacy have created painful dilemmas. It is not enough to establish an artificial entity and to expect it to serve as a durable framework for the growth and development of an ethnically divided population. What is surprising in this case is not that the Zurich agreements proved impractical, but that they lasted so long. Reality sooner or later, gets the upper hand over those too subtle combinations presuming to tame her. The institutions which are promulgated in Cyprus are those of a laboratory and not of life. Out of two communities they wished to make one state. It was wrong even to try. It would be imprudent to try to preserve it. These two communities need a rational and supple system of guarantees which would enable them to live together in a new climate. It is not for me to formulate suggestions on this subject, but I am convinced that the worst storms are over. From now on in a more peaceful Mediterranean, a settlement is in the offing, without useless passion and unfortunate precipitation.

A few analytical remarks may be attempted.

1. There is a contradiction, or at least an inconsistency, in linking Palestine and Cyprus as if "an erroneous diplomacy" had offered the same solution for both. Whereas the United Nations proposed partition for Palestine, the Zurich agreements planned a *bi-national* state for Cyprus.

2. He criticized the Zurich agreements, yet he offered no other guideline for a solution, unless we infer a hint at partition, which is preferred by the Turks and anathema to the Greeks.

3. He said that though "an erroneous diplomacy" decreed making of "two communities one State," sooner or later life would sweep it away; but on other occasions he had proposed just such a solution for Palestine. It is true that he usually sanctified partition for Palestine, asking Israel to go back to the original United Nations frontiers, thus ceding room for the refugees to be resettled in the evacuated territories. But sometimes he speculated about some kind of unitary state, perhaps to be later drawn into a

larger Middle East federation. On such occasions he even expressed regret that the million Europeans had left Algeria; if they had stayed there too, a new experiment might have evolved.

4. In one respect Bourguiba is consistent: we should act without useless passion in order to arrive at a healthier psychological climate.

Otherwise, he barely mentioned the Palestine problem while in Greece. Before he left it was announced that the King and Queen had accepted Bourguiba's invitation to visit Tunisia sometime in the future.

Greece was the last stop of Bourguiba's long tour—54 days, the longest he had undertaken since taking over the affairs of his country more than 10 years earlier.

Before leaving he held a press conference during which he had a parting shot at Nasser and pan-Arabism. Asked whether he aspired to replace Nasser as the leader of the Arab world, he quoted Clause 8 of the charter of the Arab League, which stipulates that all Member States are sovereign and equal in their right. "One cannot talk about a 'leader of the Arabs'," he declared. "Each country has its own leaders."

By daring to state this simple fact, he gave himself a stature larger than just that of a leader of his own country.

5

For a Negotiated Peace

BOURGUIBA HAD REMARKED, AT HIS PRESS CONFERENCE IN THE
Old City, that he should not because of his views be considered a
traitor, or marked for assassination. Most of the Arab press and
radio, and many public figures in the Arab countries, disagreed
vigorously. Bourguiba became the most reviled Arab leader since
Nuri al-Said was assassinated in 1958: "traitor number one to the
Arab cause," "stabber in the back of the Arab Nation while it
was engaged in a life-and-death struggle against imperialism and
Zionism," "the Tshombe of the Arabs," "a stinking tool of the
Zionists," "Ben Gurion's man," "a lackey of imperialism," "a can-
nibal feeding on the flesh of his fellow Arabs," "a Judas selling
out his brothers for thirty pieces of silver," "a dangerous madman,"
"an arch-spy who cannot be trusted with the military secrets of
the Arab conclaves."

Did Bourguiba really expose himself to assassination? There is
sufficient reason to believe his life was in danger. Among the several reports of attempts upon his life, the first appeared upon his
arrival in Beirut immediately after his press conference in Jerusalem. As usual in the plot-ridden Middle East, the rumors were
obscure and contradictory.

According to the Beirut newspaper *Al Khayat*, two Syrians
crossed the frontier in a private car for the purpose of assassinating
Bourguiba. Though the secret police were tipped off in time, they
did not succeed in intercepting the men at the border, and a reward of $3,000 was promised for information of their whereabouts.
Several suspects were arrested. A few days later the Lebanese Government denied that such an assassination attempt had been discovered.

In the latter part of May, the world press reported another attempt, this time supposedly to be carried out in Tunisia itself. According to the London correspondent of the *New York Herald-Tribune* (May 24, 1965), who attributed his information to "reliable sources," a unit of six men, notorious in terrorist activities of several countries, had left Cairo for Tunis. They were supposed to operate in three groups of two men each. They were described as experienced shots, experts in explosives and the dagger. They had been furnished with a variety of passports from several Arab countries, and with money. Tunisian security forces were taking appropriate measures.

The usually well-informed Israeli and French correspondent in Washington, Philip Ben, said he had received confirmation of this story from an American source. According to this source the State Department on the basis of "exact information on this matter," asserted that it was Ahmed Shukairy who had instigated the plot, and that Nasser was not involved. For the leader of the Palestine Liberation Organization, the liquidation of Bourguiba was "a matter of life and death," according to the opinion quoted by Mr. Ben.

A team of outstanding reporters who interviewed Bourguiba at home after his tour found Tunis quiet. "The only sign of concern that the President's quarrel with other Arabs might lead to a violent attack on his person, is seen in the careful guarding of his residence at Carthage, where the interview took place."

Similar unconfirmed reports were also current during his visits to Istanbul and Teheran. Some credence should be lent to these reports since in both countries it was officially announced that Bourguiba was somewhat indisposed—variously attributed to a cold, the flu, or throat inflammation—forcing him to limit his appearances to public receptions and dinners; he did not do any sight-seeing. Most of the conferences with the Shah of Iran and the Turkish statesmen seem to have taken place in the private suites in which he stayed.

The danger in Iraq must have been quite real since Baghdad authorities informed Bourguiba that they could not guarantee his safety, and he canceled his visit there.

Whether these reports were factual or not, they reflect the atmosphere of passion and hatred which Bourguiba engendered in the Arab world. He himself had the feeling that he had endangered his life. As we have seen, he had at the very outset of his campaign in Jerusalem voiced his apprehension that by expressing his heretical views he may be exposed to an assassin's attack.

When Bourguiba returned to Tunisia after his long and dramatic tour of the Middle East, he was given a triumphal welcome by the people who, in spite of bad weather, flocked by the tens of thousands from all parts of the country to cheer him.

He was carried shoulder-high from the airport building to his car. The five-mile road into Tunis was lined with cheering young people—schoolchildren in national costume, boy and girl scouts, and youths in sports-club uniforms. Every shop or business displayed photographs of the President and Mrs. Bourguiba. Accustomed though he was to cheering crowds, he seemed nonetheless exceptionally moved by this manifestation of loyalty and devotion. He thanked the crowd for having come "to bring me comfort." He did not try to hide his elation from the foreign correspondent who came to interview him.

Yet, gratified and comforted as he was by this show of popular affection, Bourguiba nevertheless felt he owed his people a thorough explanation of the meaning and purpose of his peace initiative. He tried to give this on several occasions, chief of which was his address before an audience of the National Federation of Destourian Students, delivered in Carthage on April 21.

This speech had been heralded as an event of great significance; the French-language newspapers in Tunisia judged it so important that they delayed their deadlines five hours to print a full translation from the Arabic. It was long, rambling, and, to one not present to be carried away by Bourguiba's oratorical talents, imperfect in structure and discursive quality. But he was not speaking to us; he was addressing Tunisian students of his own party, some of whom might one day find themselves at Tunisia's helm.

Though the official title of the address was "For a Negotiated Solution of the Palestine Problem," half of it did not deal with that subject at all, even indirectly. The impression is that before actually tackling this hot issue Bourguiba felt he had to speak of other things—of youth and its duties toward the state; of students who should follow a twofold course simultaneously: of studying in order to acquire professional or technological skills, and of learning how best to convert these skills to the benefit of the nation.

He spoke a great deal about himself: his glories and triumphs, his devotion and sacrifice, his vision and brilliance. He often referred to himself in the third person as de Gaulle is often reproached by his opponents for doing. And then he modestly "wished them all to become Bourguibas." The only element in this first part of the speech that may have had some relevance to the topic was his explanation of the virtues of "Bourguibism."

Finally, and without transition, he came to the point: "I should like also that you become acquainted with the essence of my thoughts concerning the Palestine problem." Most of these views he had expressed on previous occasions and would continue to expound. But an apologetic tone appeared in this presentation, as if he felt it necessary to explain to his own people that, far from being a traitor, he was a greater patriot than those other leaders who cry war but do nothing to bring Arab problems nearer solution. He went on:

> During my tour in the Middle East I found myself face-to-face with the problem of the Palestinian refugees whose lot has moved me. Being by temperament a serious and straightforward man, I could not but state that they are still being lulled by illusions. If this is continued, in twenty years they will still be in the same situation as they are now. I have already had occasion to advise the Arabs that when one sees one has made a mistake, he should try to rectify it. But instead of admitting error, they look for an escape. I therfore addressed myself directly to the refugees in order to tell them that passion and nostalgia to return are perfectly understandable sentiments, but the power of emotion should play the part of a motor which, by itself, can run blindly if it is not directed by a brain capable of chanelling the generated energies toward a goal. . . . This is what the leaders in charge do not understand. It is unheard of! The very notion of tactics and efficiency eludes them. I told them there is perhaps a way to embarrass Israel, but they prefer instead to insult her. I told them that for seventeen years they have been doing just that without result. When I speak to them about methods and tactics—they answer me with talk about principles, justice, colonialism. . . . Who denies that an injustice has been committed?
>
> In Tunisia, too, the French occupation had been an injustice. But had we adopted a similar method, had we refused internal autonomy (which contained a large dose of injustice) and insisted that before anything else France first withdraw, the French would never have left. After fifty years of the French Protectorate it

would have been madness to imprison ourselves in a purely negative attitude, simply saying No. That's why we followed more
sophisticated tactics. . . .

As far as Palestine is concerned, just the opposite happened. It
seems that some leaders do not think seriously about the liberation
of Palestine and would gladly do without my advice. This is the
crux of the debate. The spirit that prevails among them is the
same as we knew in Tunisia in the old Destourian circles thirty
years ago. They [the Arabs in the Middle East] did not find anybody who would propose a solution which would bring about a
change. Yet the road which was followed for the last seventeen
years ended in a blind alley.

By contrast we put into practice our method for only ten years,
and the results we know. Yet, at the time, Palestine was in a much
better position than was Tunisia. At that time [when the British
decided to evacuate] Palestine was possibly on the threshold of
independence. The armies of seven Arab states moved to liberate
that country. What the results were you also know. By contrast, in
the Maghreb, we could liberate ourselves completely without the
help of anybody. If you have anything of a concrete proposal, I
told them [the Arab leaders in the Middle East], we are ready to
help you. Whenever I said this, they answered that I am a friend
of Israel and an enemy of Palestine! That is their mentality. It
does not differ from the mentality of the old Destourians who accused us of having sold ourselves to France by accepting co-sovereignty [with France]. . . . These accusations were not devoid of
comical aspects. . . . The French settlers, in a secret report recently published, characterized the old Destour who claimed complete independence and denounced Bourguiba's treason as: "Not
very dangerous; nothing of importance." By contrast, in the same
report they denounced the Neo-Destour as a movement particularly dangerous to the regime of the French Protectorate. . . .

I have no responsibilities for the Palestine problem. For years
I said: In view of the geographic position of Tunisia, it is impossible for me to assume responsibility in the Palestinian affair,
though the Palestinians are our brothers. I thought to help them
only by advice which they are free not to follow. . . . If I have now
decided to express my point of view on a solution to the problem,
it is not that I was motivated by the least desire to make myself
the spokesman of the people of Palestine. I did it because I am
an Arab and it pains me to see what has been done to the refugees. Were I guided by selfish considerations I, too, would
shout the same slogans which they love so much and assure them
that we are ready to die for Palestine. But I don't feel myself

capable of such cynicism. I think it is a tragic error to make one's brothers, who are in distress, believe that we commit ourselves to assure their return when no Arab country has any offensive strategy for the liberation of Palestine.

Here, Bourguiba reiterated the absurdity of a war policy on the part of the Arabs; it has no chance of success.

By contrast, we demand respect for the resolutions of the United Nations. And this cannot but serve the interests of our cause even if Israel refuses to [yield]. We would then have legality on our side, and we would be in a more favorable position in case of armed conflict. There is no doubt that the political positions [of the parties to the conflict] will contribute to the success of an armed conflict at the same time that they lend to it a justification or legitimacy in the eyes of international opinion. One must beware of having the whole world against oneself.

[By contrast, the present] attitude of the Arabs to the Palestine problem suits only the interests of Israel, which exploits the threats and insults of the Arab radio networks to obtain ever more arms and money, under the pretext that she is threatened by all the Arab countries. She [Israel] would appreciate much less a more reasonable attitude, susceptible of gaining for us the sympathy of international opinion. This situation reminds us of how similar our own situation was when we were engaged in our fight for liberation. Then the French preferred the Old-Destourians, despite their verbal extremism, as against a Bourguiba who was nonetheless disposed to accept internal autonomy in the frame of his seven-point program [of April 1950].

The apologetic character of this speech is evident in almost every paragraph. Furthermore, Bourguiba felt that he had to spell out for his audience of Tunisian students what he meant by a return to the legality of the United Nations resolutions. He felt the need to explain the rumors that were rife about his meeting with Israelis—in Israel, in Tunis, anywhere. If Bourguiba was tempted to hold such meetings—and he may well have been—he abandoned the idea. A great deal of the second half of his speech, then, was devoted to these two subjects—the meaning of "back to the legality of the United Nations resolution" and his part as a potential mediator—and he wrapped them up together.

It is true that information emanating from Tel Aviv and broadcast abroad with the purpose, I am sure, of poisoning the atmosphere, insinuates that a Tunisian-Israeli meeting is considered. To this I answer that I am not a Palestinian leader. Were I one I would not object to such a meeting. I agreed to meet with Frenchmen when Tunisia was still under the protectorate of France. Our discussions were sometimes fruitful, sometimes sterile. What damage could they do?

But I am not responsible for the Palestinian affair. It is with the Palestinians that one will have to negotiate—that is, if there are negotiations—and not with me. Apart from that it will be necessary for Israel to declare clearly that she agrees to negotiate on the basis that I suggested. What I proposed is the application of the United Nations resolutions; that is, the one about partition which would permit restoring to an Arab Palestinian State an important part of the territories now occupied by her, and the one concerning the return of the refugees—these two resolutions being closely linked for the sake of balance. If the Israelis are sincerely willing to accept such a compromise they must declare that they agree at least to negotiate on this basis. But, so far, they have not said they accept this as a basis for discussions. They limit themselves to saying they are ready to negotiate with Bourguiba. On what basis will Bourguiba be invited to come to Israel or to receive Israeli negotiators? Bourguiba has made precise suggestions. If they are accepted by Israel, it is with the Palestinians and the Arabs [?] that the dialogue will have to be engaged. . . .

For my part, I could put the problem in all its clarity before the next summit conference of the Arab heads-of-state which will take place in Rabat* It will be difficult to escape or to hide any longer, once Israel agrees to negotiate on the basis I have indicated. If such negotiations actually take place they would make it possible not only to restore a vast portion of the Palestinian territory and bring the refugees back to their homes but also to diminish the present atmosphere of war, allay the hatreds, and reduce tensions. Everyone will then be able to breathe more freely and find himself in a plainly better situation than now. Things will not just stop there, but will take a turn in which both the Arabs and the Jews will modify their respective ways of seeing things, and a climate of cooperation will be established for the mutual benefit of both parties. It is certain that the situation which could thus evolve would be far preferable to the present one, in which the two parties go on staring at each other like two China dogs while

---

* The conference was held in Casablanca.

deliberately ignoring each other and Israel's influence gains in Africa and Asia. . . .

This is my position. . . My point of view I expressed clearly. Now, let me wait and see what Israel has to say. If she accepts the basis I have proposed, she will have to negotiate with the Palestinians, who are the most directly concerned. In such a case the situation would be perfectly clear.

If she rejects my proposals, on what other basis can there be a dialogue? What is the use then to go to Tel Aviv or to receive emissaries here to expose myself to accusations of treason? It is out of the question that I should lend myself to this kind of misunderstanding.

I do not say that if I were the spokesman for the Palestinians I would not agree to discuss with the Israelis as I talked with the French each time I found them inclined to start a dialogue. . . .

Finally, if we possess proof that Israel takes the thing seriously, we will be disposed to contact the Arab countries and clarify their views concerning the position one should adopt. But as long as Israel does not accept the basis for negotiations I have indicated, I have nothing to submit to the Arab leaders. Besides, I am aware they find it difficult to withstand temptations of demagoguery or to appear lacking in patriotism nad ardor to defend Palestine. That's why I do not entertain much illusion as to the chances of success of this kind of attempt. Yet it should be done on solid ground, not on vague rumors aimed at making people believe the possibility of contacts with Bourguiba in Tel Aviv or Tunis. Such rumors are, of course, devoid of foundation; Bourguiba has no intention of becoming a mediator in this affair.

If Israel agrees with our suggestions, it is up to her to contact our brothers, the Arabs, to find out their views. Such contacts can be arranged in Rome or any other country abroad, between the representatives of the parties concerned. We could facilitate such a getting together, and in agreement with President Nasser, try to arrive at results which would change the physiognomy of the Middle East.

But this does not seem to me a possibility in the near future. The Israelis do not want to yield a single inch of territory in Jaffa, Acre, Nazareth, or elsewhere. The Arabs for their part distrust each other to a point where today it is difficult for them to move from their present positions. . . .

Here is confusion and contradiction. In speaking to the Palestinian refugees he had derided the Arab leaders' promise that they would return to their homes, asking sarcastically: "Where will they return?" Yet in his Carthage speech he said his proposals would "make it possible to restore a vast portion of the Palestinian territory and bring the refugees back to their homes"—that is, to both truncate Palestine *and* take back the refugees. This is the more confusing since he also says that the two different resolutions of the United Nations—one concerning the partition frontiers and the other concerning the right of the refugees to return—must be linked together for the sake of balance. The meaning is that if Israel should relinquish territory, she would not have to accept the refugees within her own borders.

But there is still another perplexing element. Bourguiba is known to cultivate his friendship with the moderate Arab leaders —among them King Hussein—with a view to creating a bulwark against Nasser's expansionist policies. It has been suggested that Bourguiba made his declaration at the Old City of Jerusalem to strengthen King Hussein's hand against the encroachments upon Jordanian sovereignty by Shukairy's Palestine Liberation Organization. But the PLO—a front for Nasser—has the avowed aim of setting up an independent Palestine comprising the territories that had been under the British Palestine Mandate. These would include both the west bank and Transjordan, and would mean liquidation of the present Kingdom of Jordan. In his Carthage speech Bourguiba suggested that the application of the United Nations resolutions "would permit the restoration to an Arab Palestinian State of an important part of Israeli territory." It would be interesting to know Hussein's reaction to this.

But the confusion and contradictions are of secondary importance, and can be attributed to the defensive nature of his speech. He cared less about logic and consistency than about demonstrating that he was not betraying the Arab cause by suggesting a negotiated peace with Israel. To this end, he chose to use all the clichés current among the Arabs, intimating that his aim was no different from theirs; only his method was more realistic.

Bourguiba's choice of audience—the Neo-Destourian students— was as unorthodox as some of his other acts. In the Arab countries (as in the Asian, African, and Latin American) it is the students who are most violently addicted to extreme nationalistic (read pan-Arabic) slogans. They are the standard-bearers of the nationalistic and pan-Arab movements. It is they who demonstrate, attack foreign embassies, burn opponents in effigy, strike, and indulge in orgies of violence.

In contrast to other Arab leaders, Bourguiba came to the students not to arouse them with extremist slogans, but to explain himself, to justify a political philosophy and its consequent political course. And in view of the students' particular sensibilities on the Palestine issue it is significant that he chose them as his audience rather than some other forum. Here for a change the students came not to demonstrate against Israel or some other foreign power, but to express their approval of a peaceful policy and their loyalty to a leader who was dedicated to such a policy.

Of course, it is possible to see this as an oblique demonstration— in this case against Nasser. But it *did* seem different from demonstrations in other Arab or African countries. The human elements here are probably politically and spiritually more mature and wholesome than anywhere else in the "Third World."

A few days later Bourguiba made another important speech to his people, this time in Sfax. The theme was the same: not only was he no traitor to the Arab cause but he was a better nationalist than Nasser, whom he accused of duplicity. The Egyptian leader, he declared, cut the figure of an extremist when speaking to the Arabs who hate Israel—but posed as a moderate in the eyes of the African nations who entertain friendly relations with Israel.

President Bourguiba reminded his listeners that he was the first head of state to bring up at a conference of the Organization for African Unity the problem of African countries that recognize Israel. The Palestine situation, he recalls having told that conference, "is a colonial affair and should be treated as such."

> President Nasser while recognizing that it was a colonial problem, did not want to embarrass the African chiefs-of-state and did not ask them to take a stand, though they recognize Israel and maintain increasingly properous relations with her. And this, because he has ambitions to play the role of leader in Africa and he was obviously careful not to embarrass them.
>
> But when it comes to talking to the Arabs, he is all extremism. Which is to prove that Nasser actually has not the cause of Palestine at heart but only his personal ambitions to become the uncontested leader of both the Arab world and Africa as well.

He also accused Nasser of having distorted his position:

> The starting point of the campaign against Tunisia and the

Tunis-Cairo crisis was [Nasser's] speech in which he said the suggestion of negotiations [with Israel] was bargaining. That is fundamentally erroneous.

We would not accept any bargaining on the rights of the Palestinian people. But for seventeen years people have been talking about these rights without any results. No one would take us seriously if we were to talk about war against Israel. On the other hand, our international position would be very strong were we to demand the application of the United Nations resolutions. And if we had to go to war to defend these resolutions we would have the whole world on our side.

Bourguiba's preoccupation with public opinion began with the people of his own country. But he also knew from the outset that his tour would provoke passionate controversy which might lead to serious international consequences. He realized that his peace campaign might affect relations between his country and the Arab leaders of the Middle East. Therefore, Tunisian leadership at the highest level was put, as it were, in a state of emergency.

Bourguiba kept in constant touch with his chief colleagues, with whom he held urgent and dramatic deliberations. He was accompanied on the tour by an unusually large team of high-level advisers; he also invited his key Ambassadors to join him in Beirut for consultations. When the first wave of anti-Tunisian demonstrations reached disturbing proportions, the fifty members of the Central Committee of the governing Socialist–Destour Party met in emergency session. During the long hours of the meeting, reports were examined, issues discussed, and options analyzed. The decision appears to have been: stand firm, defend the new policy and be as tough as necessary toward the pan-Arabists. Above all, make it most uncomfortable for those responsible for the anti-Bourguiba demonstrations.

When he returned from the tour, Bourguiba held intensive conferences with his top aides. Because he thought it important to have his policy and initiative formally approved by the governing Neo-Destour Party and the Tunisian legislature, he convened a special meeting of Parliament on April 15 to pass a resolution endorsing his policy on Palestine. This move may have been undertaken merely to manifest a show of national unity, in answer to the urging of the Arab press and radio for Tunisians to overthrow him.

On April 24, the Central Committee of the Neo-Destour Party "welcomed President Bourguiba's proposals for a compromise solution of the Palestine question." This was not simply a formality: the meeting lasted four hours. The significance of such a resolution may be manifold. Bourguiba may have wanted, first, the leadership of his party to take collective responsibility for his views and initiative, thus preventing any unwarranted polemics from the back benches. After such a resolution he might reasonably expect that members of his Cabinet would not take a different public view from his as some, like the Interior Minister, seemed inclined to do. Second, he wanted to demonstrate to the Arab rulers that both the people and the government were behind him; third, he sought to lend additional importance to his proposals before world public opinion, elevating his initiative from a personal adventure to the official policy of his party and government.

A few days later he received the Grand Mufti of Tunisia for a long audience. The highest religious authority in the country had just returned from a Pan-Moslem conference in Mecca. Bourguiba expressed his confidence that before long the whole of the Arab world would become convinced that "the hypocritical policy, which dodges responsibility and opiates the people with sterile hatred to make them forget the real problems facing them in their lives—this policy cannot endure."

The Tunisian press and radio seem to have been cued to take up the President's cause loudly and with as few inhibitions as possible. On the eve of the meeting of the Central Committee of the Neo-Destour Party which officially approved his initiative, *L'Action*, the French-language official organ of the party, wrote editorially that Tunisia had both the duty and the right to say what she thought about the Palestine problem. The only way, the paper said, to solve the problem was "stage by stage," through a dialogue between the Israelis and the Palestine Arabs. It also indicated that under certain conditions Tunisia might even be instrumental in bringing the two parties together. And it lauded Bourguiba's campaign as one of the most realistic initiatives ever attempted to move the Israeli–Arab problem from dead center.

Tunisian officials also took pains to explain in those days of self-justification that if Israel rejected Bourguiba's proposals, the effect would be to demonstrate the Arabs' desire for peace with a consequent strengthening of their diplomatic position in the international arena. At the same time, it would embarrass Israel.

Are there differences of opinion in Tunisia as to Bourguiba's present views on the Palestine problem? Are there doubts among some of his collaborators about the wisdom of his initiative, which virtually isolated Tunisia in the Arab world?

There was certainly some opposition. It is not easy to ascertain its scope and depth. Nasser's pan-Arabism meets with strong opposition and resentment in almost every Arab country, but it also has a strong appeal everywhere. Some observers believe it has supporters even in Bourguiba's own Cabinet. As far back as January 22, 1958 the excellently informed Swiss *Neue Zuricher Zeitung* wrote:

> In Tunisia, even in the government itself, two conflicting currents become more and more noticeable: a liberal one . . . pro-French and pro-Western led by Bourguiba; and a pan-Arab one led by Mehiri, Minister of the Interior, which is . . . against France and looks toward Egypt and the [Arab] East.

In this campaign, Bourguiba clearly had both the intellectuals and the masses solidly behind him. *Jeune Afrique,* generally reliable, published an unofficial poll at the beginning of April which found a large majority in agreement with their President on the Palestine issue. The well-known reporter and specialist on Arabic affairs, J. Ben Brahem (also the correspondent of *Le Monde*) , summarized the state of opinion in Tunis:

> The responsible personalities, the politicians, intellectuals, younger generation—in a nutshell, the most political-minded and mature groups of the Tunisian population—agree with the thesis that realism is essential, war is an impossibility, and a negotiated settlement is essential. The Neo-Destour Party launched a campaign urging the sending of telegrams of support (which is, of course, a sign of the existence of certain reservations) . But it is also decernible that the support transcends the usual camp of Bourguiba's followers within the party. A young professor I have known on some occasions to be a nonconformist taking an extreme anti-Bourguiba stand, declared to me: 'On the problem of Palestine I am in perfect agreement, though I am not a Destourist and no Bourguiba enthusiast. We Tunisians are realists in politics and not fanatics; we try to judge problems and situations by means of cold logic and we seek common-sense answers. We arrive at constructive solutions and concrete results testable in reality, while the Arabs, if we are to judge by the way they steer their ship, risk—because of their intransigence and fanaticism—another mili-

tary catastrophe in Palestine.' Let us put it clearly: even those who have reservations as to the timing [of Bourgiba's initiative] realize they must appreciate Bourguiba's political courage and take a personal pride in it. War is unpopular. . . . A student told me: 'I confess frankly that I don't want to be sent to fight in Palestine. First of all because I am not interested in this kind of war; I have no sentiment for it, and nobody believes in it, not even the Egyptians, so why should one wage it?'

Concurrently Bourguiba was trying to prove to the Arabs of the *Machreck* (the East—the Middle East) that he did not intend to put himself and Tunisia outside the pale of the Arab world. He offered to meet Nasser and clear up the misunderstandings. He sent special envoys to various Arab countries to clarify his position and his intentions—which are those of a good and loyal Arab patriot having only the cause of the Palestinians at heart.

But this is not a simple task. To reconcile standard Arab nationalism with Bourguibism is almost an impossibility. And because the Tunisian President determined to try, his campaign became extremely complex and ridden with contradictions. It engendered such confusion that some observers despaired of determining what he really had in mind.

There is no doubt Bourguiba undertook his 1965 tour with his peace initiative as its prime objective. Paradoxically, as a background to this tour, the official newspaper of his party, *L'Action,* republished on March 4, 1965 his violently anti-Israel speech delivered fourteen months earlier at the first Arab summit in Cairo.* The republication took place the very day he exhorted an audience of Arab refugees that Arabs and Jews should learn to "live in peace and harmony together after having gotten rid of their complexes and their extremists."

A fortnight later (March 16) when the first violent reactions erupted in the Middle East against his statements in Jerusalem and Beirut, President Bourguiba sent his astute troubleshooter, Mongi Slim to Cairo "to smooth things over" with Nasser. And then again, at the end of April when all hell broke loose as a result of his proposal about "a negotiated settlement" of the Palestine conflict, he sent through his Egyptophile ambassador in Cairo,

---

* The reason for this is obscure. Perhaps it was intended as credentials, presenting Bourguiba to the Middle East as a veteran fighter for the cause of Palestine.

Mohamed Badra, a written message of "explanation" for the Egyptian President.

Some papers in Israel and other countries published a summary and excerpts of this message, which seemed to amount to a complete disavowal of everything he supposedly had said during his excursion. In the message, the Tunisian President suggested a meeting with Nasser to dispel any misunderstanding arising from his recent declarations, with a view to "preserving Arab unity and strengthening our common aspirations for dignity, independence, and strength."

Bourguiba pointed out:

> There is no difference in our objective, which is to give back to our Palestinian brothers the means to reconquer their usurped homeland. My plan is designed to get the question of Palestine released from stagnation, to harass Israel, to embarrass her politically, and to win support of world public opinion for our cause.

The message went on to assure President Nasser that Bourguiba had not changed his position since the first Arab summit conference in Cairo, and proceeded to quote the most extreme passage from the address he delivered at that conference.

Yet it was not so simple as that, and such excerpts or a summary out of context are a misrepresentation of Bourguiba's thought. The message contained all the twists and convolutions reflecting the complex nature of the Israeli–Arab conflict and the subtleties of Bourguiba's own thought processes. He dealt at length with himself as an Arab patriot who has dedicated his life to the struggle for the Arab cause, and the independence of Tunisia in particular. With such a background to his credit, he pointed out, he was willing to undertake additional risks, despite "the emotional campaign and scurrilous attacks against [me] which are intended to grossly mislead Arab public opinion." What the Arabs need, he went on, is not that kind of emotional excess, but rather "a quiet and businesslike dialogue." Hence he was ready to meet Nasser to clarify his position and amplify his proposal.

His declarations on Palestine were not intended to breach the wall of Arab unity, he explained in the message, but on the contrary to reinforce it. "I have done everything to preserve unity in the Arab world." But this unity can be solid and grow in strength only if it is based on truth. "It was absolutely imperative to let the voice of truth be heard."

And then, to explain what the truth is: "We are all in agreement that the Arab countries are in no position to launch a war against Israel to liberate Palestine and give it back to its rightful owners." As to activating guerrillas to be dispatched into Israeli territory, it is too risky. The Arab states bordering Israel would be unwilling to adopt such an idea, not only for fear of retaliation but also because the great powers—both East and West—wish to preserve peace in the world. They are, therefore, ready to punish anybody trying to change the *status quo* in the Middle East by violent means. In this connection Bourguiba once more indicated that the arms race in the Arab countries curtails the possibilities of developing their economies and sabotages their potential to achieve "practical results" in this vital field.

Bourguiba suggested that his proposals concerning the application of the United Nations resolutions were essentially no different from those Nasser himself advanced as far back as 1955. Their aim was to launch a political offensive on behalf of Palestine, and move away from dead center in the Israeli–Arab conflict. If Israel would abide by the original United Nations resolutions—the return of the refugees and cession of territory—the fundamental factors of the Palestine problem would be changed in favor of the Arabs, and then "new possibilities will be opened for a permanent solution."

At the same time Bourguiba thought Israel would reject his proposals, and this would strengthen the bargaining power of the Arabs even if war should break out. In any event, his plan could embarrass Israel and mobilize world public opinion in favor of the Arabs. The long missive, "written in classical Arabic," wound up with the assurance that Tunisia's government would always be ready to come to the assistance of its "sister states" in case of war with Israel.*

There is one particularly fascinating sentence in this message which lends itself to several interpretations. "The Arab leaders," said Bourguiba, "were too hasty in voicing their reactions [to his proposals] in order to stand well with Cairo." It is both a

* The contents of Bourguiba's message to Nasser were made public in the Tunisian press on April 29, 1965 and were repeated on the Tunisian radio network several times until May 2, 1965. Nasser refused even to receive the message. On May 9, 1965, Tunisia's Ambassador to Paris stated that if the Arab states actually declared war on Israel, thousands of Tunisians would leave for the front to participate in the reconquest of Palestine. Events did not support this promise.

compliment and a reproach to Nasser. It also is a sardonic remark reflecting his views about the small worth of those Arab leaders, and implying the supreme importance of an understanding (or at least a *modus vivendi*) between the two serious and responsible leaders—himself and Nasser. One condition, however: they must deal with each other on an equal footing.

Bourguiba's able colleague, Ambassador to Paris Masmoudi, summed up in an interview with the French-language Beirut daily, *Le Jour,* (May 10) the desires of his President to be considered part of the Arab world:

> If the Arabs of the Middle East suspect us and really believe we are a fifth column in the midst of the Arab League; if they are afraid to divulge their military secrets in the presence of a Tunisian delegate at conferences dedicated to Palestine and the Jordan waters, then it means they renounce completely and irrevocably engaging in any dialogue. . . .
>
> Now, one must act fast. . . . I personally have always counseled against any Tunisian isolationism which would cut us off from the *Machreck*. Our vocation is authentically Arab. Yet, they must respect our freedom of opinion, recognize our right to speak out and not necessarily to think like everyone else. The climate of suspicion has become so systematized in the Arab world that one winds up doubting oneself.

6

Nasser's Counterattack

THE EGYPTIAN PRESIDENT'S INITIAL RESPONSE TO THE TOUR HAD combined reticence, perplexity, and embarrassment. He seems to have hesitated to launch a counterattack and back-track on his six-teen-month-old policy of pursuing Arab harmony and cooperation. Finally, however, Egypt could no longer remain on the defensive.

Nasser's passive attitude had all along seemed paradoxical be-cause it came at a time when he was in a rather violent mood. It had been a period of reckless irritability—authentic or feigned. Possibly Bourguiba's uninhibited frontal challenge had caught Nasser by surprise and had at first the sobering effect of shock.

In any case, from the day of Bourguiba's peace explosion in the Old City of Jerusalem, March 6, to the middle of April, not only Nasser but most Egyptian spokesmen took a cautious attitude toward the Tunisian President. Nasser himself said that he was "not going to insult Mr. Bourguiba, for I set great store by Arab unity."

Even the Egyptian press, known for its vehemence and virul-ence, seems to have received instructions to use some of the same restraint. It published excerpts and summaries of Bourguiba's various statements made during the previous six weeks "with notable lack of criticism," according to Hedrick Smith in *The New York Times,* who also wrote that "the Egyptian press was generally restrained toward Libya and Morocco on the German question considering the paramount importance of the issue to the Arab world." The *Times* correspondent also wrote that "some experts believed that Mr. Nasser had been hesitant to take the initiative in abandoning the policy of Arab harmony he nurtured at two meetings of Arab leaders last year."

There are, of course, deeper and more weighty reasons for Nasser's initial reticence and his subsequent abandonment of restraint. In truth there is no irreconcilable difference of opinion between Nasser and Bourguiba on the basic question of Palestine, though there are divergences over strategy and tactics. Nasser agrees that under certain conditions the Arabs should come to terms with Israel. Since 1954 Nasser has been known about twice a year to express opinions about a peaceful settlement of the Palestine problem along lines similar to those Bourguiba now advocates.

The Tunisian President describes with a chuckle the puzzlement of some Arab journalists outside Egypt at Nasser's hesitancy to attack him. He claims that he "was really astonished at the outcry which followed" his own statements, since the Colonel expressed opinions on Israel "basically" similar to his own, especially in the interview with *Réalités,* which we shall discuss later. He claimed that not only does Nasser share his views, but that when he was in Egypt he told the Egyptian President of his intentions to make them public, and that Nasser did not oppose the plan.

One of Bourguiba's most capable and trusted colleagues, Ambassador Masmoudi, told an interviewer of the French-language daily, *Le Jour,* in Beirut:

> What Bourguiba said on the Palestine question was nothing but a result of painstaking discussions he previously had with various Arab leaders. . . . Ahmed Shukeiri and President Nasser each confessed to him that the refusal of the Arabs to accept the application of the United Nations resolutions was a grave error. The Tunisian chief of state even informed Nasser that he would come out publicly in favor of the Resolutions. . . .

A noted Arab journalist, Tewfiq Mokdissi. remarked quite pertinently in his column for the Beirut newspaper, *Al Jarida:*

> A question mark is raised over the protests voiced by certain quarters against Bourguiba, who has after all not actually introduced any new element into the Arab stand on Palestine. All he wanted was to get the Palestine question moving again at the level of the United Nations.

There were even indications that Egypt might adopt a more moderate line toward Israel in her own press. In fact, at the beginning of April, editor Heikal declared in his celebrated weekly column in *Al Ahram* that Israel's Jordan water diversion did not constitute a danger to the Arabs. This is, of course, a departure from the previous line that it constitutes, in fact, a *casus belli.*

And then, of course, there was the quasi-sensational interview with the correspondent of the French magazine, *Réalités,* in which Nasser expressed views on the Palestine problem strikingly similar to those of Bourguiba.

The Egyptian President's hesitation aroused suspicions that he was an accomplice in the foul deed. The Ba'athists in Syria and their supporters elsewhere were particularly outspoken in their suggestions that Nasser was privy to Bourguiba's plot.

The anti-Nasser utterances were direct results of Bourguiba's assertion in his interview with Jean Daniel of the *Nouvel Observateur* that Nasser not only agreed with him, but did not oppose the idea that Bourguiba should make his views public. Many newspapers throughout the Middle East reprinted this statement prominently, some under streamer headlines on the front page.

For weeks a rival Arab leader had suddenly stolen all the limelight with top billing and unanimous acclaim in the world press. Nasser, if mentioned at all, appeared only as the target, or in some cases the defendant trying to justify himself. Even in Arab countries, for instance the Lebanon, some widely circulated papers kept Bourguiba on their front pages.

To a leader as publicity-conscious as Nasser, this was disturbing indeed, for Nasser realizes that in modern times the most powerful weapon is not the cannon, the jet, or even the missile, but propaganda. It was not his army that saved him at Suez, but his microphone. He had built up one of the most powerful propaganda apparatuses in the world, presided over by a man who actually was coached by the Nazi Goebbels' propaganda ministry. (Nasser has been using not only German missile scientists, but also German propaganda experts.)

Now in the face of the Bourguiba onslaught, Nasser surveyed his Palestine position in all its weakness. Indeed there was little substance with which to stage a counterattack. The Egyptian leader knew that his rebuttal could be neither skillful nor convincing.

But above all Nasser knew that the Palestine problem was only a smokescreen behind which Bourguiba could most effectively challenge his bid to leadership of all the Arabs. To Nasser at least it was clear that the Tunisian President's opposition was not centered on Palestine, but on pan-Arabism. And even beyond that—on leadership itself.

There was no argument on the basic merits of the Palestine problem, only on who would give the tone to the Arab campaign for Palestine, who would decide the tactics to be applied—when to blow hot and when cold, when to be intransigent and when to appear moderate. Who would choose the best front for fighting political battles against Israel, in the case of such a problem as the West German arms incident? Nasser believed that these decisions had to be centralized, with no freewheeling permitted. There should be only one authority—Nasser. The other Arab leaders would have to comply.

Bourguiba was not alone in his desire to challenge this view. But other leaders, though even more concerned than he, did not dare, for one reason or another, to speak out openly. Bourguiba dared. And with what aplomb!

Aware as he was of the weakness of his position, Nasser had to wait for a proper and popular excuse to counterattack. The opportune moment was provided by Bourguiba in his speech in Carthage, when he suggested that the Palestine problem could be solved through direct negotiations between the Palestine Arabs and Israel.

Thus, after several weeks of hesitation, Nasser now had sufficient excuse to pick up the gauntlet. After this, to continue on the defensive would be the worst possible tactic. He therefore ordered the counterattack. Although his propaganda weapons may have been ineffectual against Israel, they might serve in an internecine fight.

What was the purpose of the counterattack? What did it hope to achieve? Nasser could not believe there was any danger that negotiations with Israel would take place in any foreseeable future. What must be forestalled was Bourguiba's challenge for Arab leadership. Other moderate Arabs must also be discouraged. For if they joined Bourguiba, the danger of a negotiated peace with Israel could become real.

The campaign was thus aimed at intimidating the moderates and isolating the Tunisian President. Its success was modest: Nasser could still coerce some of the Arab rulers, but only enough to prevent them from coming out *openly* for Bourguiba; he could not force them to come out *against* him.

One who was in no way intimidated was Bourguiba himself. Not only was he not frightened into recanting, he was to retaliate on a scale and with enough vehemence to shake the Arab world and cause a major crisis in inter-Arab relations.

No previous Bourguiba statement infuriated Arab leaders as much as that apologetic speech in Carthage. Why? What was so provocative as to bring the Arab League to a dramatic break with him?

The speech contained a mortal heresy: the suggestion (even though on limited conditions) of direct negotiations between the Palestine Arabs and Israel, and the offer by Bourguiba of his good services to bring them about. This is such a sensitive point with the Arabs that the very suggestion is almost a blasphemy. King Abdullah was assassinated because he secretly entertained contacts with Israelis. The Arab intransigeance on this subject often expresses itself in such ridiculous obstructionism as refusing to participate in international conferences and causing embarrassment to uninvolved hosts.

The Arabs refuse any direct negotiations because they would imply *a priori* recognition of Israel, regardless how limited, casual, or temporary the occasion. A possible reason for Israel's unhesitating willingness to meet the Arabs at any place and at any time to talk peace is that such meetings would signal an *a priori* recognition.

A central figure of the Egyptian establishment, Khaled Mohieddine,* one of the original group of officers who overthrew King Farouk, and a member of Parliament in charge of the Socialist Union's (the only legal Egyptian party) Department of Press Orientation, defined this point of view quite honestly and clearly in an article in the Cairo *Akhbar El-Yom.*

> Our dispute with Bourguiba does not stem from the fact that he advocates a peaceful solution to the Palestine problem. We have always wished to see all [international] problems resolved by peaceful means. . . . The whole question is, however, how we are going to achieve such a solution to this problem. According to Bourguiba we should sit down with the Israelis at the same table. Does Bourguiba think that Israel will reonounce a single inch of

---

* Not to be confused with Zakarya Mohyeddine, the Egyptian *Vice President.*
Vice President.

territory? Of course not. And *what Bourguiba preaches is not peace but Arab capitulation.* (Italics added.)

President Nasser and his aides concluded that the proposal of direct negotiation, however logically and apologetically tendered, was precisely the thing to attack. They should also prove that Bourguiba, far from being motivated by concern for the plight of the Palestinian Arabs, was in fact a traitor to their cause.

On April 23, the Egyptian press and radio launched the counter-attack. The period of hesitation and restraint was at an end.

The main theme was the rejection of any thought of ever recognizing Israel or entering into any negotiations with "an imperialist marionette, which will never achieve the status of a legal and orderly state."

The man entrusted with the campaign against Bourguiba was Nasser's friend and intimate propaganda adviser, Mohammed Hassenein Heikal, editor-in-chief of the most influential *Al Ahram.* In his weekly column, Heikal first of all denied Bourguiba's assertion that he discussed his views with President Nasser. This is, of course, of cardinal importance.

Then the editor termed Bourguiba's Carthage speech the most dangerous statement ever made on the Palestine issue. He accused Bourguiba of "moving within the lines of a plan laid down by the Western imperialist powers in a conspiracy against the entire Arab destiny." He indicated, quoting "responsible sources," that the Egyptians intended to force the Arab states to choose between Cairo and Tunis at the meeting of the Arab Prime Ministers to be held in May. And unless Bourguiba recanted and Tunisia retreated publicly from its present stand, Cairo's participation in the scheduled Arab summit scheduled for September in Morocco "would be of no value."

He suggested that in the presence of such a man as Bourguiba, the military secrets of the Arab high command would not be safe. The position the Tunisian had chosen, Heikal contended, "does not permit the UAR to join him in any political consultations concerning the Arab present and future."

The same theme was taken up a few days later by another government-controlled newspaper, the Cairo *Al Goumhouria.* It justified the exclusion of President Bourguiba from all pan-Arab deliberations on the ground that Tunisia was no part of the Unified Military Command of the Arab League and did not in any way participate in the Jordan headwater diversion plans. At the same time the writer assured his readers that Bourguiba's declarations would pass with the wind, and nothing would remain of them except the tragic memory within Bourguiba himself. (As it turned out, it was Bourguiba who refused to attend the forthcoming "Summit" conference at Casablanca. Nasser's attitude at that conference will be surprisingly meek and mild.)

Al Ahram, continuing its campaign against Bourguiba, accused him a few days later of choosing to launch his campaign precisely at a time when many Asian and African countries had "begun to realize that Israel serves as an instrument in the hands of imperialism and had consequently started to express their support of the rights of the Palestinian people."

Another influential Cairo newspaper, *Akhbar El-Yom,* was even more vehement. It bade him: "Shut up, Bourguiba!" It charged him with "a stab in the back of the people of Palestine." Bourguiba, it said, "has become raving mad."

Heikal also propounded the same theme, that Bourguiba was insane. The Tunisian President's attitude, he wrote in his weekly column, could be explained only by one of two possibilities: either his health was such that he did not realize what he was saying, and therefore was not responsible; or he had sold himself completely [to the U.S.] and without hope of return.

This propaganda barrage was not without confusion and embarrassment. On the one hand the papers had promised no longer to print Bourguiba's statements, since he was either mad or had sold out to the imperialists; on the other, Bourguiba's pronouncements were being published prominently in the press of other Arab countries. So the Egyptian papers continued to publish them —on the front page, with red banners, to boot.

Arab newspapers throughout the Middle East, some of them subsidized by Cairo, picked up the tune, and even tried to outdo the Egyptians. The day the Egyptians gave the sign for the counterattack, the Beirut *Al Moharrer* editorially demanded that Bourguiba be "ostracized without mercy." It termed Bourguiba's proposals "high treason" and exclaimed: "A man who is executed by law for having sold a military secret deserves more mercy than the man who sells an entire people and the cause of a nation to the enemy." Accompanying the editorial was a cartoon showing a Judas Bourguiba walking away with thirty pieces of silver while Palestine dies on the cross. (About half the Lebanese population is Christian.) Another Lebanese newspaper, *Al Ahrar,* also called

Bourguiba "the Judas of the Arabs." It demanded that he be "liquidated."

In Damascus *Al-Ba'ath* said: "The Arab people from the ocean to the gulf today hear the voice of treason; and the Arabs will regard the Tunisian President as an alien spokesman." The strongest reaction came from the Executive Committee of the ruling Ba'ath party in Damascus; it passed a resolution denouncing Bourguiba, and appealed to the Tunisian people to overthrow the regime as the only way to purge themselves and prove their dissociation from their President. Observers considered the resolution an appeal to the Tunisians to assassinate their leader.

The then ruler of Syria, Amin el-Khafez, declared a few days later in a speech at Homs that his government would "never agree to deal with the present Tunisian regime." He intimated that his government would break relations with Tunis. The same day he recalled the chief-of-mission in Tunis for consultations "in view of the recent declarations of President Bourguiba concerning the solution to the Palestine problem, which constitute a deviation from the unanimous position of the Arabs."

Some Arab governments fell in line; others thought it the wiser course to stay out of the fray and keep silent. Marshal Sallal, President of republican Yemen, declared that "Bourguiba's statements constitute the worst stab in the back of the Arab nation. Such a stab we have never gotten even from our enemies."

Iraq supported Nasser. The Premier, General Tahir Yahya, declared that "the united will of the Arab nation rejects absolutely any bargaining over the Palestine affair. . . . The Iraqi army will consider it a great honor to be given the privilege of serving as the *avant-guard* of the Arab forces that will liberate sacred Palestine."

Lebanon and Jordan were not wholly aloof. The Lebanese Premier, Hussein Oweini, said his government was against "half measures and partial solutions. Zionist aggression has to be extirpated."* The Jordanian newspaper *Al Jihad* described the Tunisian President as "an agent of the Western powers to whom the task has been assigned of destroying Arab unity." Another Jordanian paper asserted that though Bourguiba was the voice, his declarations emanated from Tel Aviv, Washington, and London.

---

* Yet, almost at the same time, the Lebanese Ambassador to Washington, Ibrahim El Akhdab, declared at an international symposium at the Naval Academy in Annapolis that Lebanon had always been against solving international problems by war. That symposium included the Tunisian Ambassador, Rashid Dris, who expounded Bourguiba's thesis.

The Mayor of the Old City of Jerusalem annulled the decision of the municipality to call one of its streets "Bourguiba." The Jordanian Premier, Wasfi El Tal, refuted Bourguiba on the point that the Palestine problem was a matter for Palestinians, insisting it was of concern to all Arab countries.

A Moslem Conference in Mecca passed a resolution censuring Bourguiba's proposals and called upon all Moslem countries to strengthen the Arab countries bordering Israel.

Shukairy, head of the "Palestine Liberation Organization," announced he had decided to give up the notion of opening offices in Tunisia (as he had planned to do in all Arabic countries). He did not think the Palestinians could now expect any help from that country.

There were demonstrations. In Cairo some 200 Palestinian students rioted before the Tunisian Embassy. The police dispersed the demonstrators, arrested five of the leaders, and reinforced the guard around the building. The students being led away by the police shouted toward the assembled foreign correspondents that Bourguiba was worse than Eshkol, and that he was mad. They called on the Tunisian people to kill him. Demonstrations also took place in the Old City of Jerusalem, Ramallah, and in several refugee camps.

The governments in several Arab countries found it necessary to protect the Tunisian embassies from possible violence. In the demonstrations that erupted in Beirut, Baghdad, and Damascus, the governments sent police and troops to guard the embassy buildings as well as some companies in which Tunisian ownership was involved. Two score Arab students broke into the Tunisian Embassy in Madrid and demolished the furniture; the police arrested most of them. Thirty Arab students demonstrated in New Delhi when Bourguiba's special representative, Mongi Slim, arrived there on an official visit. There were no arrests.

Nasser, though presiding over the counterattack, was still careful in his denunciations; he said very little. When he did speak he avoided reference to Bourguiba directly. In his speech delivered on April 23 in Cairo at an official dinner in honor of King Yang di-Pertuan Agong of Malaysia, Nasser said that "the cause of Palestine is now confronted with an enormous challenge betraying the bad faith of the enemies of the Arab nation on the one hand, and a false appraisal of the situation on the other"; never did he speak Bourguiba's name. In the face of these dangers, the President of the UAR continued, it is the duty of all Arabs to close their ranks and, with all means at their disposal, to meet these challenges.

Voices in the Maghreb were more moderate. Exercising extreme prudence in its stand on the Palestine issue, the Moroccan government kept silent. So did Libya and Saudi Arabia—in fact the Cairo press accused them of supporting Bourguiba's proposal for direct negotiations with Israel.

A spokesman for the Algerian Foreign Ministry said that his government would refrain from taking any "independent initiatives" in the Palestine problem and would rather act in accordance with the policy formulated at the last two Arab summit conferences.

The Tunisian press stood firmly behind Bourguiba. All Tunisian newspapers strongly condemned the anti-Bourguiba campaign. The official organ of the Socialist Destour Party hit back at Nasser himself; it pointed out that before foreign audiences he expressed the same ideas as Bourguiba; before an Arabic audience he dubbed these same ideas "an imperialist plot."

"Unfortunately," it wrote, "this is not the first time that Arab leaders are smitten by lack of rationalism and consistency, and this is the least of the causes for the decline of their standing in the Arab world."

7

The Break

THE CRITICISM, THOUGH IRRITATING, WAS ON A COMPARATIVELY small scale. The demonstrations were initial skirmishes. Though the moderate Arab governments, including Lebanon, Morocco, Saudi Arabia, and Jordan, paid some lip service to the general condemnation, they tried through diplomatic contacts to persuade Nasser not to press for extreme action at the Arab League Conference (of personal envoys of heads-of-state) due to begin April 28. According to reliable reports, the Lebanese government appealed to the Secretary General of the League to commit himself to preventing a rift in the League. The Beirut daily *Al Khayat*, reported on April 25 that President Helou would take up the matter in person with Nasser during a stopoff at Cairo en route to Paris.

Moderate Arab rulers were able to prevent the Arab League from expelling Tunisia, or from taking other punitive measures against Bourguiba, since such decisions must be adopted unanimously. They were acting primarily in their own interests—the expulsion of Tunisia from the League would have created a dangerous precedent for any Arab state which did not blindly follow the Cairo line. But they did not succeed in preventing a violent crisis from developing between Bourguiba and Nasser.

When the envoys assembled in session of the Arab League on that April 28, events were already out of control. In Tunis the day before, demonstrators had attacked and stoned the embassies of Egypt, Iraq, and Syria in protest against the anti-Tunisian demonstrations in those countries a few days earlier. The North Africa correspondent of the British Broadcasting Company estimated crowds as large as 100,000. Other correspondents gave the figure of 20,000; Ben Brahem of *Le Monde* spoke of "more than 10,000";

Reuters mentioned "tens of thousands." This was the *first* of such demonstrations in Tunisia against any foreign legation since the attack on the French several years earlier, and the *first ever* against any other Arab state.

Long columns bearing posters and Tunisian flags had marched on the three heavily guarded embassies. The main demonstration took place in front of the Egyptian Embassy, which was cordoned off by policemen carrying submachine guns, supported by several hundred national guardsmen in full battle dress with fixed bayonets. The demonstrators nevertheless broke through the police lines and hurled rocks and inkpots at the embassy. Then they broke in, smashed windows, and climbed to the front balcony, where they put up a huge portrait of Bourguiba. After violent clashes which lasted several hours, the crowd was finally dispersed by the guardsmen, who had made no use of their guns or tear-gas grenades; but two fire engines that went into action with water hoses were stoned.

Some of the Tunisians carried a coffin containing an effigy of Abdel Gamal Nasser. Others carried a huge painting of a camel ("Gamal" is camel in Arabic) with the head of Nasser. Many carried posters in English and French which reviled Nasser and extolled Bourguiba. One said: "Stop lying, stop talking, think!" Another read: "We had enough speeches for seventeen years. It's time to do something constructive for Palestine." Many demonstrators shouted: "Death to Nasser!" "Shukairy is a coward!" "Bourguiba is a realist!" Students had such slogans chalked on briefcases which they waved over their heads while marching.

A similar but smaller-scaled onslaught was carried out against the Syrian embassy. A huge group surrounded the Syrian Legation, stopping all Syrians leaving or entering; the angry crowd was, however, prevented by the security forces from breaking through. There was also a demonstration in front of the Jordanian Embassy.

In addition, the demonstrators sent delegations in to the embassies of Egypt, Iraq, and Syria, with a formal resolution strongly protesting the propaganda inimical to their President. The resolution expressed unqualified support for his proposals.

Sporadic demonstrations, mainly by students, continued for most of the day. The Tunisian capital, according to Reuters, resembled a besieged city. Ambulances carried off wounded demonstrators and policemen. Heavily armed steel-helmeted guards and police were stationed in the city's main squares, while lorries packed with guardsmen and police waited in side streets.

Demonstrations also took place in outlying towns throughout Tunisia. Trade unions, other organizations, and individuals from all over the country sent telegrams to Bourguiba expressing their support.

Tunisian movie houses that day showed no Egyptian films, although these were customary fare. Instead, they ran French, American, and British pictures.

Various reports, including that of *Le Monde's* correspondent, confirmed that the demonstrations were well planned, but that the Destourian organizers themselves were surprised by their magnitude and vehemence. It was generally agreed, however, that they expressed grass roots Tunisian indignation at the attacks against their President.

They also reflected deep-seated attitudes peculiar to the Tunisians. If Bourguiba is a tremendous success in his own country, it is because he expresses articulately what his people feel and think—though at times they themselves may be unaware.

The demonstrations also showed that Bourguiba, far from being overwhelmed by Cairo's intimidation, had decided to retaliate with weapons so successfully used by Nasser that they had become, in the words of a Tunisian newspaper, classic. The Neo-Destour Party official organ *Al Amal* wrote editorially the morning after the demonstrations that "Tunisia has decided that from now on it will be an eye for an eye."

Bourguiba told his colleagues he was determined to carry out his design as revealed in his Middle East tour, whatever the consequences might be. He was convinced his ideas were the correct and only ones with a chance of success.

Although the demonstrations exceeded original anticipations, and aroused violent reactions in Cairo (as well as other Middle Eastern capitals) , Bourguiba and his colleagues were relaxed about the new crisis. "Tunisia is not going to die," Bourguiba is reported to have remarked.

Tunis asked its Ambassador in Cairo to come home, for urgent consultations. As a precautionary measure, the Tunisian Ambassador to Iraq and the Chargé d'Affaires in Syria were instructed to go to Beirut.

Actually, Bourguiba's show of toughness was evident from the very beginning of his campaign. He snubbed Syria. He threatened to cut short his visit in the Lebanon unless the government restrained the press. He cancelled his visit to Iraq upon the outbreak of demonstrations there. And in his own country he called off a banquet he had planned to give participants at a convention of the pan-Arab Medical Association because a delegate from Egypt and another from Jordan had criticized him in their speeches. In his Carthage speech he called such criticism not only absurd, but characteristic of a psychological sickness in Arab society.

Nasser acted swiftly; he withdrew his Ambassador from Tunis. The Cairo radio network "The Voice of the Arabs" attributed this action to the "disgraceful attitude and suspicious trends of the Tunisian authorities toward the United Arab Republic and the Palestine issue." That evening the National Assembly was called into extraordinary session. The first speaker was Ahmed Said, who was in charge of "The Voice of the Arabs" and a leader in inter-Arab propaganda. He accused the Tunisian President of profiteering on the Palestine problem and demanded his expulsion from the Arab League and future Arab summit conferences.

Another deputy, Khilmi Gandon, termed Bourguiba's declarations about Egypt even more dangerous than the "triple aggression during the Suez and Sinai crisis." He accused the Tunisian President of being "a spy and an agent of imperialism in the midst of the Arab world" and called upon the parliaments of all other Arab countries to proclaim an all-Arab excommunication of the man who had stuck a dagger into the heart of the Arab nation. The Egyptian Foreign Minister, Mahmoud Riad, rose and declared:

> The Tunisian President wants to play the role of a mediator in the struggle in which the Arab nation is engaged against imperialism, reaction, and racism. Yet he is not unaware that the Arab cause does not brook either mediation or negotiation. The UAR rejects this mediation as especially dangerous since it is assumed by a head of an Arab state.
>
> These declarations of Bourguiba have profoundly shaken the Arab world which today traverses a decisive period . . . . They coincide, on the one hand, with the pact Imperialism and Zionism have concluded to liquidate the Palestine problem and thwart by force the Arab plans to divert the headwaters of the Jordan River—by supplying Western weapons to Israel. On the other hand they came at a time when "the world began to realize the justice of an independent Palestine" and that the Palestine prob-

lem is the result of an Imperialist deal and of Zionist racialism.
. . . They are dangerous because they correspond to the Zionist
objectives of which the main one is to break Arab unity, the fruit
of two Arab summits. . . .

Riad reminded Bourguiba that this had been the latter's own
thesis expounded in the past, and asked whether he now ruled it
out as no longer useful. Then, Mr. Riad continued, even if Bourguiba had come to such a conclusion, why did he not wait until
the third Arab summit to expound his new ideas? Failing that,
why didn't he wait at least till the next conference of heads of governments only a few weeks away, where he could have developed
his plan for ending the Israeli-Arab conflict? The fact that Bourguiba did not so choose was proof that he truly intended to bring
about the collapse of the institutions which the Arab summits had
set up (the Unified Arab Command to defend the diversion of the
headwaters of Jordan, and the Palestine Liberation Organization) .
All in all, said the Foreign Minister, Bourguiba has provided
Israel "with a new and sharp weapon" which it will now brandish
at the United Nations and in all other international forums. Riad
argued that Bourguiba's proposals constitute a well-crystallized
plan which paves the way for the recognition of Israel and the
establishment of economic ties with her. This last element is the
greatest danger of all.
At the end of the session a unanimous resolution was voted,
asking President Nasser to act swiftly to induce all the members
of the Arab League to adopt a firm stand toward the President of
Tunisia and all other "deviationists." The resolution also demanded immediate and unequivocal action to deal with the situation which might well cause international opinion to range itself
behind Bourguiba. The time had come, it said, for the Arab governments to prove the reality of their solidarity.
On the morning of April 28, the Cairo press printed the demand
for an all-Arab tribunal before which the Tunisian President
should be tried for treason. But they were unwilling to wait for the
outcome of such a hypothetical tribunal; they had the verdict
ready—death. The next day a Cairo student association published
a proclamation demanding that Bourguiba be brought to trial
before a "Revolutionary High Court."
The government intimated it would break diplomatic relations
with Tunisia unless her President made a public confession and
recanted.

So much for the mutual verbal bombardment. The next morning, twenty-four hours after the demonstrations in Tunisia, it was the Egyptians' turn.

Outbreaks, which began around ten in the morning, were led by a group of Palestinian students soon joined by several thousand Egyptians. They assembled at the University of Cairo where, only a few weeks earlier, Bourguiba had been given an honorary degree and been hailed by the same students as a hero of Arab nationalism. Now they shouted "Death to Bourguiba!" "Bourguiba to the gallows!" "Bourguiba to the guillotine!" "Bourguiba, you sold yourself to the dollar!" African and Asian students taking courses at the University of El-Azhar joined.

The situation did not look ominous, however. They marched for about a mile and encountered a police cordon, which they easily broke through. Emboldened, they raced toward the Tunisian embassy; then the riots started in ernest.

Wave after wave of students tried to take the Tunisian embassy by storm, but they encountered stiff, and at times violent police resistance. Several times the rioters, brandishing rocks, bricks, and tree limbs, forced the security guards to within 400 yards of the Tunisian embassy. Helmeted riot policemen battled the demonstrators for nearly two hours; at one time mounted constabulary charged the crowd and furiously whacked the students with wooden staves and rifle butts. When other police flung tear-gas grenades, the students retaliated with stones.

The demonstrators finally broke through, smashed doors and windows of the Tunisian embassy and attempted to set the building afire. (There were no embassy personnel inside.) Repulsed there, they turned to the private residence of the Tunisian Ambassador, Mohamed Badra, and took the villa by storm. They overwhelmed the security forces and broke through the iron grille gates, sacked everything they could lay hands on, burned the furniture, and set the building ablaze. The fire brigade was on hand and extinguished the fire with a single engine.

The riot squad chased the students down narrow streets and collared some thirty students (according to some reports more than a hundred), who shouted insults at Bourguiba as they were led away by police, blood streaming down their faces and their shirts ripped. Half a dozen policemen were wounded and many more were bruised. The fashionable residential district of Zamleck looked like a besieged area and tear gas hung in the air for a long time.

While this was going on, a delegation of four students—a Jordanian, an Egyptian, a Tunisian, and a Senegalese—was escorted by the police to the Tunisian chancery where it handed over a resolution protesting "the savage assault against the UAR Embassy in Tunis."

The Tunisian Government immediately recalled Ambassador Badra, who had expected to take part in the conference of the envoys of the Arab League heads-of-state, and also to bring a letter from Bourguiba to hand to Nasser. He later told correspondents that the demonstrators aimed to assassinate him and it was a miracle that saved his life.

For good measure the Egyptian Government the same day expelled the President of the Tunisian Student Association in Cairo, Amor Sehimi. In a strong statement issued immediately thereafter, the General Student Association of Tunis protested that "the French authorities never permitted such insults even to Tunisian students in France during the Bizerte crisis."

After the expressions of mutual indignation, both governments took stern measures to prevent repetition of the riots. In Cairo and Tunis, armed policemen in steel helmets mounted guard outside the antagonist's embassy for several days; in Tunis, the Iraqi and Syrian embassy buildings were also strongly guarded.

Sporadic demonstrations still flared in various towns and cities in both Tunisia and Egypt, but there was no further violence. In Alexandria, where several thousand people demonstrated, security forces barred their entry to the Tunisian consulate.

The Tunisian press which thus far had reacted moderately to Arab diatribes against its President and had on the whole preserved a tone of courtesy, that day launched a vigorous counterattack. The official Tunisian news agency declared that the Tunisian people went out into the streets to demonstrate that it would no longer tolerate "the impudent insults, vilifications, deceit, conspiracies and acts of treason of the Egyptian rulers and their lackeys in Iraq and other countries."

"Let this demonstration serve as a warning," declared the commentator, adding that it "was also an expression of the wrath of the Tunisian people which for too long has been the victim of a sustained campaign of atrocity and hate-propaganda, of lies and calumny."

Under the headline "Patience Has Its Limits," *Al Amal,* the official Neo-Destour organ, apostrophized the governments of Egypt, Syria, and Iraq:

> You cashed in dollars and rubles for your own profit, and you made of the Palestine problem a flourishing business on an international scale. That is why you are so embarrassed each time a voice is raised to make the cause of the Palestine triumph.

The paper laid the responsibility for the crisis at the door of Nasser who, it said, practices a policy of subverting the regimes of legitimate governments. But if Nasser thinks for a moment that such tactics will prove successful against Tunisia, he is badly mistaken. There are limits to everything and patience can be exhausted. "Tunisia," continued the editorial, "is not going to accept any orders from Egypt, which is still protected from Israel by the United Nations peace-keeping force; or from Syria which massacred the faithful in mosques; and not even from Iraq, which sold herself out to Nasser."

The press campaign continued the next day with unabated vehemence. The newspapers declared: "200,000 demonstrators denounce Nasser's treason and say 'yes' to reason and 'no' to demagogy."

Popular support continued to pour in by wire and by letter. Meetings were held in various parts of Tunisia and resolutions were adopted. By now demonstrations had taken place in all thirteen administrative districts of the country.

Especially significant is the success of the moderate Arab governments during those dramatic days in controlling their own extremists. No excesses, no demonstrations took place in Jordan or the Lebanon. Especially remarkable was the firm hand King Hussein showed in Jordan, where the majority of the population is Palestinian. It is reported that as a "patriotic duty" he ordered his Cabinet to take all necessary measures to prevent absolutely all violence. It did.

Against the background of violence, the conference of the personal representatives of the Arab League heads-of-state opened in Cairo on April 28, to discuss joint action on Bourguiba's proposals for a compromise solution to the Palestine conflict. Also on the agenda was the perennial question of what action to take against

Israel. But the main question was: What are we going to do with Bourguiba?

Bourguiba has a consistent policy: never slam the door—either behind him, or in his own face; and he is always for talks with everybody at all times. He decided to send a personal letter to Nasser, suggesting a meeting to clarify his position, and to dispel any misunderstanding. The bearer of the message was to be his Ambassador in Cairo, Mohamed Badra. Badra was also told, in the absence of a special Tunisian representative, to participate in the conference in Cairo. The day the Ambassador set off with the letter was the day the anti-Egyptian demonstrations took place in Tunis. The morning after he arrived, his embassy was sacked and his home set afire.

Before taking off, Badra declared that though the text of the message was unknown to him, he thought it constituted "the last attempt to clarify the Tunisian position and to try to find a constructive solution to the painful Palestine problem." He added:

> There isn't a shadow of a doubt that in the long run Tunisia's voice of reason will win out and will find an attentive ear. Tunisia's position will finally be understood, and everybody will follow the road her leader paved, not only to save the peace in that stormy and agitated part of the Middle East, but also to give back to our Palestinian brothers their lands, their homes, and their dignity.
>
> Between Tunisia and Egypt there are no quarrels as to personalities, principles, or purposes. The divergence of opinion is only about tactics.

He reiterated the argument that the Tunisian approach is the only logical and possible way to rescue the Palestine problem from its long immobile position in dead center.

In Cairo, Ambassador Badra insisted Bourguiba's declarations were unofficial proposals designed to embarrass Israel by forcing her publicly to reject the United Nations resolutions on the return of the refugees. "What Bourguiba says is just one solution," Badra pointed out. "If the Arabs accept, well and good. If not, we stand with the Arabs." He also repeated that Tunisia upheld the decisions of the Arab summit conference, but that President Bourguiba "believes Israel cannot be destroyed with arms alone, but with reason and maneuvers."

The Assistant Secretary of State for Foreign Affairs who received Badra conveyed Nasser's attitude and mood: the President refused to see Badra, and did not care to receive Bourguiba's personal message or to hear his "explanations." Before he left the Foreign Ministry, Badra received an urgent telephone call from the Secretary General of the Arab League, Abdel-Khalek Hassouna, asking to see him immediately. A few hours later he received instructions to leave Cairo with his staff. In Tunis he declared that there had been a plot to assassinate him when the demonstrators attacked his home; a Moroccan student, "a criminal and a traitor," had been recruited for the task. Badra had been saved by a miracle—the call to meet Hassouna in connection with the Conference. It was during this meeting that his residence was set on fire.

There is some irony in the fortunes of this diplomat. He had been known for years as a staunch and consistent Egyptophile. He is credited with having influenced his President to patch up his quarrel with Nasser during the Bizerte crisis, and was instrumental in bringing Tunisia back to the Arab League. He is reported to have persuaded the Egyptians to stop their propaganda attacks on President Bourguiba, and his own government to make gestures of friendship towards the Egyptians. Now the godfather of Tunisian-Egyptian reconciliation saw himself forced to flee for his life from Egypt.

The Tunisian diplomats who had left Baghdad and Damascus a day earlier to find safety in Beirut were told not to return to their posts, but to come home. Simultaneously Tunis ordered its consulate in Alexandria to close. Later in May, Tunis was to close its embassy in the Sudan "for reasons of economy."

The Egyptian diplomats had already left Tunis, arguing that their lives, too, were in danger in Bourguiba's capital. The Iraqi Ambassador to Tunis was also recalled on that stormy day of April 28, as was the Syrian Chargé d'Affaires.

In Tunis, Bourguiba convoked his Cabinet in a special session to discuss the break with Cairo, and conferred with the Ambassadors he had recalled from the Middle East. He also called back Mongi Slim, who had gone to the Far East to explain Tunisia's position to New Delhi and Karachi, carrying personal letters from Bourguiba.

Reportedly Bourguiba told his colleagues that he intended to pursue the campaign regardless of the consequences. He began developing intensive diplomatic activities of his own, with a view to isolating Egypt. He sent personal messages to the heads-of-state of most of the Arab League members, including Ben Bella of Algeria. He also ordered his Ambassadors to seek audiences with the Foreign Ministers in the Arab countries to explain the Tunisian position, along the lines developed in his letter to Nasser.

The meeting of the thirteen-member Arab League opened that afternoon of April 28 with only twelve participants. After a short address, Secretary General Hassouna gave the floor to Palestine Liberation Organization leader Shukairy, who delivered a long and violent speech. The proceedings were closed, but they were nevertheless reported in the press. Bourguiba must be banned from future Arab summit meetings, and the Arab League Council should be convened in a special session in May to consider the ouster of Tunisia. It would be intolerable, Shukairy asserted, to have Bourguiba or any Tunisian representative participate in the future work of the Arab League's institutions and committees, especially those which deal with military matters concerning the liberation of Palestine.

He accused Bourguiba of causing a breach in Arab unity. To prove it, he quoted at length from statements by Israeli leaders— Levi Eshkol, Mrs. Golda Meir, Abba Eban—who though they rejected the essence of Bourguiba's proposals to withdraw to the partition boundaries, nonetheless saw them as a breach in the Arab wall.

As is his wont, he spoke at great length, beginning with the events of 1948, the outcome of which "constitutes the greatest disaster that has befallen the Arab nation for the last 100 years." He asserted that after the Arab defeat of that year, the Arabs should have instituted an investigating committee to bring to trial those responsible for the defeat.

> Though such a tribunal has never been instituted, the traitors of that time nevertheless received their just desserts. Some of them were assassinated by the indignant masses and others were dismissed from office. At the present we should not permit other traitors to bring on our heads a new catastrophe, and it is imperative to take vigorous action to punish them without hesitation or mercy. . . . I therefore demand punishment for the Tunisian President according to the gravity of his crime against the people of Palestine.

He demanded that the proceedings of the present sessions be public so that the people would have a chance to become acquainted with Bourguiba's treasonable behavior.

Political observers noted the peculiarity of letting Shukairy deliver the key address at a meeting of personal representatives of the Arab League heads-of-state revolving around a dispute between Tunisia and Egypt. He is not a member of the Arab League and he does not represent any state. To these observers, it appeared to be Nasser's response to the unwillingness of several Arab League members to take side in this quarrel, and their exertion of behind-the-scenes pressure against extreme or public action toward Bourguiba. These moderate leaders regarded it as unwise to take any irreparable steps that would make the crisis a permanent rift.

Cairo remembered what had happened in the Arab League conclaves in the preceding few months, when the Egyptian line on the German issue was largely rejected, and the majority decision adopted only under concentrated pressure. After the first flurry of emotionalism, and some strong suggestions for the treatment of Bourguiba, the Egyptians withdrew and put Shukairy in their place on the agenda. Thus it became primarily a Palestinian-Tunisian rather than an Egyptian-Tunisian confrontation, with the calculation that if no strong measures were adopted against the Tunisian President, it would not seem to be open defiance of Nasser by some Arab League members, but rather an unwillingness to support Shukairy.

The gambit failed. The moderate Arab governments, which do not view favorably either the man or his activities, and know him as a Nasser stooge, not only refused to heed his proposals but were to use them in time as an argument for withholding support from his organization.

In the meantime, the Egyptian government engaged in feverish inter-Arab diplomatic activities to try to win over the League's member-nations. So far Nasser could only count upon the support of Iraq, Syria, Kuwait, and the Republican part of the Yemen. During the night of April 28, he sent a personal message to Ben Bella asking for his support, but it was not enough to carry the day. The representative of King Hussein arrived that night explicitly instructed to exert all his influence to prevent an open rift within the League, and to try to restore the unity which had been achieved at the summits. The Lebanese representative carried similar instructions.

The opposition to Nasser had stiffened considerably since the last Arab League Conference a few weeks earlier on the German crisis. At that time only three States said no to Nasser: Tunisia, Morocco, and Libya. Now the nay-sayers included Lebanon, Jordan, and Saudi Arabia, with Algeria and the Sudan straddling the fence. *Al Ahram* complained that even "the representatives of Iraq and Kuwait spoke very mildly." At that earlier conference Nasser was able to muster at least a formal majority; this time he had no majority.

As time went by, Nasser's supporters were to dwindle further. Especially painful to Nasser was the ambiguous attitude of his vociferous friend, Ben Bella. In the past the Algerian President had distinguished himself on all and sundry occasions by extreme diatribes on the Palestine question. At this critical juncture, however, when Cairo's ears were straining to hear the voice of support and encouragement from Algeria, that voice was silent. They were to hear from him later, but it was too late to affect the outcome of the conference.

Paradoxically the meeting which had been convened to deal with the banishment of Tunisia, now under the influence of the moderate delegates embarked on an opposite course: to try to bring the Tunisian delegate back to the conference table. To an invitation to return to participate in the deliberations, Badra is reported to have declared that after the slander campaign organized by Cairo against his President, he could not sit at the same table with an Egyptian. He rejected even an appeal by Secretary General Hassouna to show up for the closing session of the Conference. Hassouna is an Egyptian whom Bourguiba could distinguish as the agent through whom Nasser had converted the Arab League into an instrument of Egyptian expansionism.

The conference, as is not unusual in pan-Arab conclaves, divided against itself, 'their ranks in serious disarray," as Hedrick Smith reported in *The New York Times*. Discussions came to a dead halt.

First there had been a procedural wrangle about the legality of Shukairy's participation and his assignment as the leading speaker; *Al Ahram* characterized it as "one of the stormiest exchanges to have taken place in the Arab League conference hall in Cairo."

The Moroccan representative spoke for those who objected to Shukairy's presentation of a draft resolution, "because he attends only in an advisory capacity and is not a full member of the heads-of-states' personal representatives' follow-up committee." This objection precipitated a battle of insults between Shukairy and the Moroccan.

A second procedural point was more basic: how can subordinate delegates sit in judgment on their superiors—heads-of-state? After all, this was only a conference of their representatives and not of the chiefs themselves. The prerogatives of such a conference, some delegates argued, are by nature limited. It can examine reports, and deal with problems already discussed and resolutions passed, but it cannot tackle new problems.

If there is a basic disagreement, the confrontation must take place on the highest level—at a summit conference. King Hussein had adumbrated this argument when he told a group of Syrian journalists in Amman that the summit scheduled for September should be advanced. "It is necessary to have such contacts to deal with current situations in the Arab world at the highest level," he said, adding that many other Arab heads-of-state shared his view.

Some of the delegates argued, therefore, that this conference had to limit itself to preparing the agenda for the two forthcoming meetings—one of the Arab heads-of-government scheduled for May 24 in Cairo, the other for the summit (heads-of-state) to take place in September. They explained that precisely because of the present crisis in inter-Arab relations, these preparations needed to be made with all caution if the irreparable was to be avoided.

As to Shukairy's suggestion, most of the delegates considered it so far-fetched that they refused to discuss it. It was as if someone were to suggest banishing an Arab from his own fatherland. Isn't the Arab League the spiritual and political fatherland of the whole Arab nation?

Some delegates argued that for the last seventeen years Colonel Nasser and other Arab leaders had expressed views not basically different from Bourguiba's present ones—so why the hue and cry? Had not Nasser, only recently in an interview with *Réalités,* said that he was for a settlement of the Palestine problem on the basis of the United Nations resolution? How did this differ so fundamentally from what Bourguiba was now advocating?

In view of the deadlock resulting from the irreconcilable positions of opposing delegates, it was decided to transfer the whole complex of problems—including the question of the purpose and

prerogatives of the conference—to a subcommittee under Hassouna, which would formulate recommendations and resolutions
for the conference.

What the subcommittee came up with was a compromise. It
would reject Bourguiba's proposals, but without criticizing him
personally. Certainly it would not ostracize him.

The resolution, therefore, adopted unanimously, refuted any
proposal for "recognition, reconciliation, or coexistence with
Israel." Such a proposal, said the resolution, constitutes a deviation from Arab unanimity concerning the Palestine problem, a
transgression against the pact of the Arab League, and a departure
from the plans agreed upon at the previous Arab summits.

Neither in the resolution nor in the lengthy statement published
at the end of the conference was there any criticism of Bourguiba.
His name was not, in fact, mentioned. The statement contained
the usual arguments against Israel "which in league with Imperialism robbed a part of the Arab fatherland, chased out its sons and
daughters, and serves as an instrument for the aggressive aspirations of foreign powers which threaten the Arab states and prevent
them from developing and growing strong." Therefore, the conference reiterated its unshakable loyalty to the policies adopted at
the Arab summits; the delegates pledged themselves to act in the
spirit of those policies and bring about their realization.

"The Arab Governments," declared the communiqué, "are
determined to consolidate the Unified Arab Command, to
strengthen the Palestine Liberation Organization and its army,
to carry out the plans for diverting the headwaters of the river
Jordan, to be ready for all eventualities and for all sacrifices required to reconquer the plundered Arab fatherland." All this, of
course, was a rehash of previous Arab conferences and had little,
if anything, to do with the problem at hand.

One new element emerged at the Cairo parley. It was decided
that the Palestine Liberation Organization should open political
headquarters in Peking.

It was also decided to have a conference of the Arab Prime Ministers in less than a month—on May 24—to analyze the latest developments and take decisions necessary to strengthen Arab unity
concerning Palestine.

No mention of Bourguiba, no criticism, certainly no hint of
excommunication. Nasser's acquiescence was attributed to Egyp-

tian reluctance to risk a split between Arab moderates and hard-liners.

Shukairy was furious; spleenfully, he walked out of the conference hall. Once outside, he tried to extemporize a news conference to announce his resignation as head of the Palestine Liberation Organization. But the Secretary General ran out and physically pulled him back into the conference hall. Journalists overheard other delegates urging him not to contribute to the deepening rift in the Arab ranks.

The next morning's Cairo press expressed its disappointment with the results of the conference, and at the same time tried to minimize its importance. Later editions dropped the text of the resolutions and the final communiqué; instead, they devoted much attention to Tito's visit in Cairo then taking place.

The pro-Nasserite press outside Egypt reacted, as is often the case, in much stronger terms. Several newspapers in the Lebanon declared that the conference had shirked its responsibility by refusing to brand the Tunisian President a traitor. The Beirut newspaper *Al-Moharrer* declared that the results of the conference were tantamount to a coup de grâce to future Arab summits.

Significantly, one of the two Communist newspapers in the Middle East, the Beirut *Nida* joined the chorus of disappointment and criticism of both Bourguiba and the conference.

Shukairy published a statement rejecting the resolutions, declaring them inadequate and not commensurate with the gravity of the hour. A few days later he warned that he would take his Palestine Liberation Organization out of the Arab summit conferences, if he did not get fuller support from all Arab League member states. According to the Organization's radio station ("The Voice of Palestine") Shukairy told a delegation of 150 notables who called on him at his Cairo home:

> I must tell you the sorry truth: there are several Arab League member-states who fail to cooperate with the Palestine Liberation Organization.
> If all the member countries do not work with us in sincerity for the sake of Palestine, we will cut our ties with the summit conferences and work only with those who support us. It is better to have a few supporters who are loyal than many who go backward instead of forward.

In Tunis, by contrast, the prevailing mood was one of success. Newspaper headlines shouted "It Was a Great Victory for Us!" and "We Scored a Great Diplomatic Success."

The French-language *L'Action* stated that Egypt's failure to win a resolution to expel Tunisia was a victory, but feared the efforts to isolate her would continue. Spokesmen for the leading political circles in the Tunisian capital took pains in conversations with foreign correspondents, to point out the obvious: that the Cairo conference refused to stigmatize Bourguiba, refused to accept Nasser's proposals, and mentioned neither Tunisia nor Bourguiba in the resolutions.

The official Tunisian news agency recalled that this was Nasser's second defeat in the Arab League in only a few weeks, the first having been on the issue of breaking relations with Bonn. But this time the defeat was more evident. In the case of the German issue, the majority of the Arab states had accepted a compromise. That resolution had only suggested by a majority vote breaking diplomatic relations with Bonn; it had rejected recognition of East Germany. "This was the first time," wrote the Tunisian news agency, "that the Arab states refused to follow Nasser's lead, and stood up against him. Bourguiba's example has proven useful."

The Tunisian press continued its attacks upon Nasser, more vigorously and vehemently than ever. The newspaper *Es-Sabah* wrote on May 2, "Nasser is a sworn enemy of the truth; he strives for nothing but the promotion of his personal interests and the realization of his selfish ambitions." It accused Nasser of having used threats and pressure to frighten other Arab states.

> Slander and demagogy will not deter us from our chosen road. Nasser agreed with Bourguiba as to the essentials of our President's plan, but demagogy and spinelessness prevented him from following through.

The official organ of the Neo-Destour Party, *Al Amal*, wrote in the same vein: "Egypt does not hesitate to use a wide variety of weapons in its campaign of vilification and insults against any Arab who expresses genuine concern with the Palestine problem. . . . The proper reckoning is not far off. . . ."

The official Tunisian news agency, commenting on Nasser's May 1st speech, accused the Egyptian leader of hypocrisy, of telling lies and half-truths: "Nasser is willing to say one thing at conferences and in interviews [with foreign correspondents] on the

Palestine issue, but he does not think the same things should be told to the Arab masses."

After the hectic months of relentless activities Bourguiba felt entitled to a vacation. He left the day after the League conference (May 1) for a ten-day rest in the seaport city of Sfax. It turned out to be as much a victory celebration as a vacation. He received a tumultuous welcome from the inhabitants.

On May 2, he delivered a speech in which he hailed his victory over Nasser. He recalled that "seven years ago, during the first Tunisian-Egyptian crisis, when Nasser led a similar campaign against us, Tunisia was alone in the field to oppose similar attempts. Today, the Arab states from both the East and West are on our side and strengthen our position."

He congratulated his stubborn if timid supporters in the Arab League. In spite of the violent demonstrations against him, he said, and all the vociferous denunciations, he took some comfort from the proceedings of the Cairo Conference which offered hope that his proposals would, with time, catch on. He regretted that his campaign, which had started out with good auguries in Jordan, where the refugees received his proposals with appreciation, was later sabotaged by those who did not have the refugee cause at heart.

The chief culprit responsible for both the present crisis and the plight of the Palestinians is none other than Nasser.

> It seems that at the bottom is Nasser's will to exercise exclusive leadership in the Arab world so as to appear in the world's eyes as the uncontested master of its destinies, with all the advantages that would bring [to Egypt]. It happens that Tunisia is in no way disposed to sacrifice its sovereignty to any [foreign] leadership whatever. . . . It is unthinkable that a man like me, who fought for thirty years to achieve Tunisia's independence from France, should now agree to abdicate that independence into the hands of Nasser. . . . As a great nation Egypt has a right to our consideration. But that is no reason for it to try to impose its laws on everyone.

But he implied that he would not like to exacerbate the present crisis. Government circles also indicated that Tunisia would take no further action to aggravate the situation. Though she had recalled her Ambassadors and missions from Cairo, Damascus, and Iraq, she would not officially break diplomatic relations.

The fever began to subside and, as *Jeune Afrique* put it, "violent street demonstrations and press campaigns are not in the temperament of the country. Tunis has recollected itself, and the keynote is: 'We will not Egyptianize ourselves.'"

Nasser reverted to his cautiousness. Although he had recalled his Ambassador and most other personnel from Tunis, he did not close down the embassy altogether. He permitted two members of the staff to remain.

It seemed at the moment that neither Bourguiba nor Nasser had mortgaged the future, and the dialogue might one day be usefully resumed.

Now at long last Ben Bella let himself be heard. When the conference was over and the dust had settled, the President of Algeria, in a speech at a May Day rally, declared that though he would not lend a hand to anything that might deepen the rift among the Arabs, Algeria's silence did not mean that "we approve certain recently expressed theses" (an obvious allusion to Bourguiba's campaign). He said that he, too, was in favor of a "peaceful solution" to the Palestine issue, provided such a solution "means the disappearance of Israel." Referring to an article in a French newspaper, that so far Ben Bella had taken a reasonable stand in the dispute, he declared: "I am never reasonable when Israel is concerned. Israel stinks."

Some Parisian newspapers referred to Ben Bella's tactics as "acrobatics." So they were; since the beginning of the Bourguiba rebellion against Nasser, Ben Bella had blown hot and cold alternately and then simultaneously, indulging in mental twists and convolutions. He is for a peaceful solution, but Israel must disappear. How?

Also, as an afterthought and a perfunctory one at that, came a statement from the Prime Minister of Libya, Hussain Mazik, in which he took issue with Bourguiba's proposals, though he did not mention Bourguiba by name. The tone was mild.

Nasser finally decided to speak openly and, for the first time in two months, to refer to his challenger by name.

As an aftermath to the Cairo Conference, he thought the time had come to define the issues dividing the two leaders, to clarify Egypt's position, and to respond to Bourguiba's challenge.

The occasion was the May 1st mass rally in Cairo. Nasser delivered a long speech, the only definitive stand, so to speak, he took on Bourguiba's proposals. First of all, he said, though Bourguiba was looking for a quarrel with him he, Nasser, would not be provoked. Though he had refused to accept Bourguiba's letter, he would answer it now.

He had refused to accept it because it was intended as propaganda and was circulated by the Tunisian press and radio before it was delievered to him. (In truth, the Tunisians published it two days *after* Nasser rejected it and refused to receive the Tunisian Ambassador). He did not react to Bourguiba's statements earlier because at first they merely sounded strange, but as the Tunisian President continued to elaborate, he came to see that "the man was just talking nonsense." And he declared:

> Bourguiba argues that his proposals have already brought some results, since the Arab world has begun to think. Thus there is hope that the Palestine problem will move from dead center. Bourguiba also argues that I, too, advocated similar ideas at the Bandung Conference and even tried to have these ideas put on the agenda of the United Nations Assembly in 1960. He also asserts that he is making these proposals now, so that Israel will be compelled to reject them while the West will exert pressure upon her to accept them. To this I would like to answer: Where has the West been since Bandung? Why did not the United States exert pressure upon Israel to withdraw to the original partition boundaries and to take back the refugees? The reason is that in the United States the Zionists have strong influence, and the Arabs have nothing to compare with it. As to the repercussions his proposals may create, does Mr. Bourguiba not recall that Israel rejected these proposals as far back as 1949, during the Lausanne Conference organized by the Palestine Conciliation Committee?
>
> Now, Bourguiba claims there are already repercussions to his proposals. What are they? They are of a kind which are detrimental to Arab rights. Israel has accepted the idea of direct negotiations and rejected the proposals about the partition boundaries. Bourguiba has thus adopted the conceptions of the former Israeli Premier, David Ben Gurion, who called for direct negotiations without any preliminary conditions. Ben Gurion succeeded in pressuring some African countries into raising this proposal at the United Nations, but this initiative has been defeated in the past. Now Bourguiba has provided Israel with new ammunition, for she can come to her friends in Asia and Africa and tell them: You see, your past efforts have not been in vain; since Bourguiba accepts your views, you should again propose direct negotiations at the United Nations. This time it may receive much greater support.

In a somewhat apologetic tone he declared that if he was making Palestine a central issue, it was not merely "for internal consumption" or for the sake of "games and maneuvers or deceptions" in the international arena, but because it is a matter of life and death for the whole Arab nation.

> If in 1948 only Palestine fell as a result of aggression; now the danger is to all Arab states. Israel's policy is one of expansionism, and this is apt to bring disaster upon the whole Arab nation.

Hence, in the Egyptian President's view, the solution was the liquidation of the State of Israel. This solution was accepted by all thirteen Arab states at the last summit conferences of the Arab League; it is not vain talk, as Bourguiba claims. The Arab summits decided the instruments by which this solution would be achieved. These instruments are three: 1) a unified Arab Military Command; 2) the diversion of the headwaters of the Jordan River, and 3) the building up of the Palestine Liberation Organization. But apart from this, Egypt was preparing herself to implement her avowed aim of liquidating Israel. She would greatly increase her armaments arsenal and would eventually build up all by herself an army of between two and three million men.

Then, using a rhetorical technique reminiscent somewhat of the Sermon on the Mount, Nasser harangued:

> Bourguiba tells you he is serving the interests of the Arab cause; but I tell you he is working for the interests of Israel. . . . He claims that the plight of the Palestinian Arab is close to his heart, but I tell you he is trying to achieve the status of leadership in the Arab world at the expense of the Palestinian Arabs.

Ominously he hinted at the fate that had befallen another pro-Western Arab leader, Nuri al Said, the Iraqi Premier who was assassinated in General Kassim's revolution of July 14, 1958. He also warned that in the light of the latest developments he might have to revise the policy he had pursued at the summits and renew the revolutionary struggle for Arab unity—that is, not by unanimous agreement, persuasion, and harmony, but by an all-Arab revolution.

It was a powerful speech, and his words falling on sympathetic

Arab ears probably not only made sense, but also evoked emotional associations.

Beyond this, it was not much of an answer to Bourguiba. He distorted Bourguiba's arguments and answered the distortions. The dialogue between Bourguiba and Nasser was largely what the French call *"un dialogue des sourds"* (a conversation between the deaf).

Judged by the usual standards of Arab polemics, Nasser's was a remarkably temperate speech. He did not even hint at Bourguiba's ouster from the Arab League, nor did he threaten to refuse to participate with him in any future Arab summit. Political observers in Cairo ascribed this moderation to the Egyptian leader's determination to avoid an irreparable break in the Arab united front. The Lebanese took credit for Nasser's moderation, since the speech was made in the presence of President Helou, who had arrived that day on a state visit in Egypt on his way to Paris and de Gaulle.

At a banquet in his honor on May 1, President Helou said that the Lebanon would remain faithful to the Arab summit decisions. The destiny of all Arabs was linked to the success of the Palestinians' sacred cause.

> The main burden of this battle of destiny has been shouldered by the eldest sister, the United Arab Republic, with potentials with which God has endowed her—including your capable, wise leadership.

Though this may sound like a very strong commitment, it is in fact rather routine courtesy, for Lebanon will always remain "the second country to make peace with Israel" (a Middle East byword, which is not so much a joke as a reflection of political realities, since tiny half-Christian Lebanon, in the shadow of truculent Syria, is in no position to take bold initiatives). Significantly, Helou did not criticize Bourguiba, did not associate himself with Egyptian denunciations. And in the councils of the Arab League, he gave the Lebanese representative unequivocal instructions to oppose any censure of Bourguiba.

The New York Times' Hedrick Smith, reporting about the Cairo conference and its implications, wrote that though Nasser was at the time trying to maintain the appearance of Arab unity—without Bourguiba—it was nonetheless "widely believed here [in

Cairo] that the Arab world has reached a turning point and that President Nasser will soon have to embark in new directions."

The Cairo conference, said Smith, "has left Arab radicals suspiciously eying monarchists and moderates. There is added suspicion that Mr. Bourguiba is cleverly drawing the Maghreb . . . out of the orbit of the Arab East which feeds on hostility to Israel. . . . For President Nasser, Bourguiba has caused a dilemma. After sixteen months of promoting Arab harmony, Mr. Nasser has been brought full circle to where the Arab world stood late in 1963 with the Arabs' differences exposed in public. 'This is the toughest split in the Arab League since Iraq joined the Baghdad Pact,' said one knowledgeable supporter of President Nasser to the correspondent, 'but this is more serious because it revolves around the Palestine issue.' "

What is absolutely new if not revolutionary in this crisis is the explosion of a myth. "One of the favorite beliefs of old Middle East hands is that the one sure rallying point for Arabs is their common cause against Israel. But this spring it is the rock of Palestine on which Arab unity has smashed." (Hedrick Smith, *The New York Times,* May 3, 1965)

Thus, in this round of the confrontation, Bourguiba scored several points against Nasser, though there was no knockout. Nasser is still the acknowledged leader whose influence transcends the boundaries of his own country. The Western powers, more than the Arabs themselves, persist in considering him the leader of a region, and try if not to win his friendship, at least to mitigate his hostility. There is a serious flirtation between de Gaulle's France and Nasser. The United States provides him with considerable economic aid. Germany hopes she will be forgiven and permitted by the Egyptians to lend help. The Russians in their international gambits in that part of the world invest tremendous amounts in Nasser, mainly in armaments—not all obsolete or useless to themselves.

But this policy of both East and West is not based on a realistic appraisal of the existing situation and its potentialities. It is rather a result of intellectual inertia—a policy which keeps moving in the same old direction propelled by motives and aspirations of the past.

Bourguiba wanted to weaken those forces, and he succeeded. He wanted to expose the myth of Arab unity, and he did so. The Arab world which put up a unified facade at the first two Arab summits is exposed for what it really is: a group of states, most of them unstable, weak, reactionary, divided against each other and each against itself.

That is, in Bourguiba's view, the crucial point and the main objective. He set out to wrest from Nasser's hands the "Palestine whip" he wielded to coerce the Arabs into unity under his leadership. With the whip gone, the Arab states can begin to reflect independently, and possibly take some first steps in their halting advance on the road to independence.

One reason given by those representatives at the Cairo conference who opposed censure was that *representatives* of heads-of-state cannot deal with new problems. That would be the prerogative of a conference on a higher level. It was therefore decided that heads-of-governments should meet in Cairo on May 26.

On May 17 Tunisia dclared she would no longer participate in Arab League conferences in Egypt—ostensibly because she feared for the lives of her representatives.* Tunisia would not participate in the May 26 conference of heads-of-governments or in the Arab League Economic Council which was called to consider policy and steps against "those states which support Israel." Since he was determined to liberate the League from Egyptian tutelage, Bourguiba demanded as a first step toward that goal that League meetings cease convening in Egypt.

The next summit of the heads-of-state was scheduled to take place in Egypt again in September. Previous notions of holding it in Morocco had been discouraged by Rabat for reasons which are outside the context of this report. Now, however, with Bourguiba's boycott announced, Morocco changed her mind. Moreover, she proposed to do everything in her power to see to it that her "invitation" was accepted. It was clear to all concerned that this was a gambit to force Nasser not only to give up having the Arab League summits in Egypt, but to force him to sit at a conference table with Bourguiba. Informed circles understood that Morocco's decision was a gesture in favor of Bourguiba and had been planned in coordination with him.

Immediately after the Cairo parley, it was announced that Bourguiba would pay a state visit to Morocco in June. Moroccan sources pointed to the announcement, made at a time of acute

---

* To a panel of interviewers on CBS's Face the Nation (May 23) Bourguiba said: "One thing I can assure you: No Tunisian will in the future attend [Arab League] meetings in Cairo, because the safety of Tunisian citizens is not secure there."

internal crisis in the Arab League, as proof that the visit would transcend the usual amenities; and the letter Bourguiba sent to King Hassan covered the common position of the two countries toward the Palestine problem.

So although outwardly the Moroccan Government remained "discreet," officials in Rabat privately expressed satisfaction with Bourguiba's "realism." They recalled that they had supported him at the preceding parleys in Cairo. In addition, the Moroccan press gave prominent display to the Tunisian's repeated declarations but little space to attacks upon him. King Hassan's position was cautious and balanced, but based on loyalty to Bourguiba.

By now it was clear that Bourguiba had scored a very important point in preserving an essential minimum of unity in the whole Maghreb, even on the Palestine problem, in spite of the differences between him and Ben Bella. *Jeune Afrique* in its May 16 issue emphasized this, and suggested that all Maghrebian governments coordinate their foreign policy, to be in a position to carry out their common development plans.

For a while it looked as if Bourguiba would try to create an opposition bloc within the League, but further deliberation apparently persuaded him there was little to be gained. He was still vilified there for his stand on Palestine, and every turn of events was used by Nasser to unite the Arabs under his leadership against Israel, and against the West.

Another powerful example, the artificially provoked Arab-West German crisis, was, Bourguiba said, in press interviews* an eye-opener to him. He reflected that in such dangerous and desperate adventures, one might be able to trace the beginning, but could never predict the end. One day all the Arab states might wake up to find themselves in a situation they did not actively create, but passively encouraged by surrendering to Nasser's leadership. Yet it was they who would be the victims. Bourguiba did not relish the nightmarish prospect of one day finding himself swept along with Nasser into the Communist camp. He seems to have come to the conclusion that a conciliation with the Egyptian on any level was hardly possible.

Under the circumstances, he thought, Tunisia could not in good faith remain a part of the Arab League. Simultaneously he

* On Bourguiba's apprehension of the dangers he sees in Nasser's ever-increasing anti-Western policies, (*see* Chapter XXIX, "Bourguiba—Toward West and East.")

might also have concluded he had a better chance to influence the moderate Arab governments if he remained outside the League. Events showed that in this he was, at least partially, correct.

Tunisia's formal break with the Arab League was confirmed May 21 at a special session of the 150-member National Council of the Socialist Destour Party, which comprises all the members of the Cabinet, the governors of all the districts, senior officials, and party leaders. It wildly cheered President Bourguiba's proposal to boycott future Arab League meetings and all other pan-Arab conferences.

At this session President Bourguiba deliver what was considered by observers his most vehement attack on Nasser and pan-Arabism. He accused Nasser of conducting a smear campaign against him, unworthy of a head of state. He reiterated that when he was Nasser's guest in February, they had discussed the Palestine problem and the Egyptian leader had agreed with his proposals. He declared that attacks on his person were "resulting, unfortunately, in feelings of hostility on the part of Tunisians not only against the Egyptians, but Arabs in general."

> I refuse to go back to the meetings of the Arab states after the [vilification] campaigns and attacks against us . . . as long as the League does not apply its own charter, which stipulates respect for all member states. . . . Tunisia has lived for thousands of years without the Arab Middle East. It can once more very well live outside the Arab League and have no relations with the Arabs. . . .

He again denounced Nasser in the strongest terms for trying to impose his policies on all Arab nations.

> Nasser wishes to bring them closer into the camp of the Soviets. . . . It was all right for Nasser to align himself with the Communists if he considered this in the interests of his country and his people, or if it just pleased him. . . . It is also right of the rulers of other Arab countries to follow him . . . . but he had better not accuse me of treason if I happen not to share his policies.
> The Egyptians do not seem to have much sympathy for the Americans or the British. . . . They know better than anyone else what they want to do [for themselves], but to try to impose on us a given attitude toward the Western countries . . . who are helping us . . . is really going a bit too far. . . . I do not propose to permit anybody to draw me into an anti-American position just for

the sake of solidarity with Nasser. . . . This we will never accept [and] I told it to Nasser. . . .

As far as Tunisia is concerned, he declared, she will stay with the West, though not as a satellite, such as Nasser is coming close to becoming of the East. Tunisia will preserve her right and status of formal non-alignment.

To thunderous applause he said that the Arab League was not and could not be a monolithic super-state; but it could exist and survive only as a voluntary organization of independent sovereign nations.

He said that the last Arab League conferences revealed that pan-Arabism is a myth, which when imposed, leads not to unity but to a split among the Arab countries; that this split will grow progressively worse as Nasser tries to treat all the other Arab states as satellites. But there is no such danger anymore, he continued, since his example has shown how one can say no to the Egyptian President.

Defending his theory of gradualism in the pursuit of political goals, he asserted there was no doubt that the policy based upon this theory "placed Tunisia in the front line" of truly independent countries of Africa and the Arab world.

He said that "Nasser is panicky" because he knows that his (Bourguiba's) attitude is contagious, and may take on epidemic proportions which will eventually sweep away the whole of the Arab world.

He was sarcastic and scornful. "Since the Egyptian leaders brag constantly that their army defeated France and England during the Suez campaign, are we not justified in asking why this formidable army did not attack Israel all these years to liberate Palestine?" True, Colonel Nasser promises he will do it when he has an army of three million soldiers, and then he will "throw the Israelis into the sea. My best wishes for his success," he remarked, "except that it will not happen."

At the closing session Bourguiba delivered a second address summing up the discussions and proceedings of the conference. He again denounced the campaign of character assassination and vilification against him and his country, and expressed his hope that the Middle East would at long last "awaken from its state of torpor."

The Council then adopted the resolution breaking with the Arab League. It proclaimed that:

Tunisia has no more interest or reason to participate in any of [the League's] meetings on any level, so long as Egypt does not undertake formal commitments to respect its Charter according to which each of the participating members is a sovereign nation; and as long as Cairo will not desist from its striving for hegemony or renounce its attacks upon the dignity of all Arab states.

The resolution demanded that the League be completely and fundamentally reorganized on the basis of new principles, procedures, and directives. Also that its center and headquarters be removed from Cairo, and its meetings no longer be held in Egypt.

The Council also launched a "brotherly and sincere appeal" to all Arabs for an objective and impartial examination of Tunisia's proposals for the solution of the Palestine problem. A motion was also adopted expressing solidarity of Tunisia with "the people of Palestine" who, it said, must be primarily responsible for the liberation of their country. The Council also urged the adoption of the Tunisian thesis for a stage-by-stage political, rather than military, settlement.

On May 23 a special envoy was sent by the Tunisian Foreign Ministry to Cairo to inform the Secretary General of the Arab League of Tunisia's break with the League.

The Tunisian press reported the proceedings and the Council's resolutions and commented upon them, explaining their meaning to the people. The newspapers attacked the Arab League as an organization which had from its start failed in all of its ventures. *Al Amal,* announcing the decision of the National Council, indicated that Tunisia would no longer attend meetings of the League "as long as there persisted [in Egypt] the mentality and tendency to consider Arab states as Egyptian provinces." Tunisia would never accept this. The paper characterized Nasser as the "king of lies and crime."

L'Action said that few Arab countries had in the past been spared aggressions, plots, assassination attempts, and subversive movements conducted by Cairo. The victims were, according to the paper, the Sudan, Jordan, Syria, Iraq, the Lebanon, Tunisia, Morocco, and the Yemen.

While the Council was deliberating, Tunisian students staged anti-Egyptian demonstrations. Columns of students paraded through the streets of the capital hailing their President and shouting, "Down with Nasser." There was no violence.

The most immediate result of the break was a non-happening:

Tunisia did not participate in the meeting of the heads-of-governments a few days later in Cairo. Nor did Bourguiba appear at the summit conference of the heads-of-state in Casablanca in September. But as we shall see, even in absence, he dominated the summit. At the sessions of that autumn conference in the beautiful Moroccan city, Bourguiba would appear victorious in most of his demands and Nasser was to yield on all the major points.

The Tunisian must have been surprised and amused to observe that the more he was out of the League the greater was his influence inside its councils. He had tried it both ways: first he joined the League in October 1958 and two months later saw himself forced out. Now, by boycotting the League, he was to see his prestige and influence enhanced in the Arab world. His stature as a statesman was also to grow in the international arena.

8

"Little Summit" in Cairo

THE CONFERENCE OF THE ARAB HEADS-OF-GOVERNMENT—THE "LITTLE Summit"—opened in Cairo May 26, 1965. (The Heads-of-State Conference was due in September.) Confusion, division, disarray beset the Little Summit against a background of two major challenges to the Arab world. One had come from without: Israel's success in thwarting plans to divert the headwaters of the Jordan. The second came from within: Tunisia's decision to break with the Arab League, until it should be thoroughly purged of Egyptian hegemony.

The days preceding the conference were marked by feverish consultations among the Arab governments. How should they react to Bourguiba's campaign on Palestine and to his demands for reorganization of the League? There was some talk that Nasser and Iraqi President Aref, who had conferred in Cairo, would put forward a formal resolution to condemn Bourguiba for his heresies. What this condemnation would imply was not clear. Would they demand Bourguiba's expulsion as Shukairy proposed?

Tunisia was absent, but a letter from Foreign Minister Habib Bourguiba, Jr., to Secretary General Hassouna was distributed among the participants. It explained that Tunisia was not attending because the League had exceeded its mandate in including President Bourguiba's proposals on Palestine on the conference agenda. Bourguiba Jr. described this as a flagrant violation of the League's charter tantamount to suppression of the right of an independent and sovereign state to voice its opinions freely. The obvious intention was to discredit the head of a sovereign state for exercising that right.

144

Another reason for Tunisia's absence: "The aggression" directed against the Tunisian Embassy by the Cairo demonstrators. The Tunisian Foreign Minister asserted that the Arab League "had done nothing to safeguard the dignity of the representative of an Arab state accredited by the League, or to guarantee his safety."

In conclusion, Bourguiba Jr. declared that in any event Tunisia reaffirmed its adherence to the resolutions of the two summits concerning Palestine and the project to divert the headwaters of the Jordan.

The conference after a formal opening session, held its deliberations in secret. Hassouna made a short opening address, then Egyptian Vice President Zakaria Mohieddin delivered a lengthy speech. It contained all the stereotypes, but it betrayed none of the line Nasser would take a few days later.

Mohieddin, who was presiding, told the conference it would have "to deal firmly" with various "aggressive challenges," which included:

a) West German arms gifts to Israel (already long discontinued) ;

b) Bonn's recognition of Israel;

c) "The conspiracy aimed at liquidating the problem of the Palestine refugees";

d) Israeli aggression against the sites of Arab projects to divert the Jordan headwaters; and

e) The conspiracy of the imperialist powers supporting Israeli aggression to sabotage the Arabs' economic development.

As usual on such occasions the Egyptian delegate spoke of the historic imperative to reinstate fully the rights of the Arab refugees, and attacked the Western powers for trying to limit their economic aid to the refugees through the United Nations. He also extolled the recent achievements of Arab unity in various fields "in spite of the conspiracies of imperialism through its bases in Israel, Libya, and Aden."

Significantly Zakaria Mohieddin did not mention Bourguiba in his address. This avoidance was understood by commentators as Egypt's decision to take a moderate line, in order to preserve what was left of the "spirit of unity" of the previous summits; to avoid running counter to the wishes of the Maghreb countries and of such moderates as Lebanon and Jordan; and to isolate the Syrians who had come to the conference in a belligerent mood, as much against Nasser as against Bourguiba.

Parallel with the proceedings of the Little Summit and as a part of it, the Arab Defense Council held sessions attended by the Defense and Foreign Ministers plus the Chiefs of Staff of the member states, plus Secretary General Hassouna. Although the Palestine Liberation Organization was not a League member, the commander of the Palestine Army, General Wagi el Madani, participated in the Defense Council sessions. The Council's problem was to meet the contingencies arising from the Jordan headwaters diversion project.

The Syrians who came to the Little Summit in an ugly mood did not wish to talk so much about Bourguiba as about Nasser. To them the two were distinguishable only in that the Egyptian was worse. The Tunisian, at least, had spoken candidly and shown his defeatism and treachery; Nasser speaks, but does not perform. Where was Nasser, asked the Syrian delegate, when the Israelis attacked the diversion equipment in Syrian territory and put it out of action?

The Syrians did not even honor the conference by having their Prime Minister attend in person. Instead, they were represented by the then Deputy Premier Nureddin Atassi. They demanded an immediate decision to sabotage the Israeli National Water Carrier. According to the Middle East [Egyptian] News Agency, the Syrians demanded that the conference take a solemn decision to order the Unified Military Command forces into action on a number of fronts simultaneously "the next time Israel commits an act of aggression against the Jordan diversion project."

In the meantime they demanded evidence of what had been done to carry out earlier decisions. They criticized Nasser for his timidity and the Unified Military Command under Egyptian Lt.-General Amer for its ineffectiveness. The Command could not even move its troops into any *Arab* country, let alone Israel.

The Syrian press synchronized its reporting of the conference with a violent attack on Nasser's defeatism. On May 27, Damascus radio charged that defeatism had already crept into the conference hall, and demanded public exposure of those delegates who advocated compromises on Palestine, on the Yemen, and on Germany; but particularly those who would overlook the campaign of President Bourguiba. The radio commentator said:

> Syria calls on the Arab governments to reaffirm the principle of the full liberation of Palestine and of finding an effective Arab deterrent force to move immediately everywhere.

Everything seemed in the same (or worse) state as at the previous conference in April—but for one basic change. Some Arab leaders had stiffened their backs a bit toward Nasser. The game of unanimity that had been so successfully played at the two summit conferences began to collapse. Nasser saw himself challenged by two extremes—the physically absent but politically present Bourguiba on the one hand, and the Syrians on the other. And both challenged him on the Palestine issue.

Both challenges aimed, though by opposite means, to call his bluff—one by suggesting a negotiated settlement of the Palestine problem, the other by demanding the offensive war against Israel that had been promised since 1948. The essence of both challenges was: Fish or cut bait.

Much as he would have liked to, Nasser found it difficult to play the moderator, arbiter, and conciliator because he was not dealing with two camps opposing *each other,* but with two distinct assaults on *his own* leadership.

"Arab unity," declared the Christian daily *Al-Jaryda* of the Lebanon on the eve of the conference, "is nothing but an empty slogan destined to paper over the eternal inter-Arab conflicts."

As the conference proceeded, the Bourguiba "scandal" became almost submerged by sudden and more complicated conflicts among the various Arab governments. The chief of these arose around the plans adopted at the two previous summit conferences to divert the headwaters of the Jordan River. Quite concrete plans had been worked out and, to protect their execution, a Unified Arab Military Command was established. At the same time, another far-reaching resolution had been adopted, to create a Palestine Liberation Organization composed of Palestinians under the leadership of Ahmed Shukairy, whose bumptious aim was to "reconquer" Palestine.

Despite the obvious impracticality of these schemes the heads-of-state who met at the two summits were so eager to "do something" in reaction to Israel's completion of the National Water Carrier, the project for using the Jordan for widespread irrigation, that they adopted them nevertheless. They were also anxious to make a show of Arab unity which was desperately lacking on any other issue.

With Israel's completion of the National Water Carrier, Syria, the most bellicose of Israel's neighbors, had vociferously demanded an all-out attack. Nasser was on the spot. A war against Israel at that time would be an act of folly. It was he, therefore, who countered with the alternate scheme to divert the headwaters of the Jordan River before they reached Israel. With considerable aplomb he called it "the Master Plan of the Arabs against Israel." Diverting three tributaries which flow into the Jordan from neighboring Arab countries would reduce the volume flowing into Israel by more than 60 billion gallons of precious sweet water a year. In the long run he explained, this plan was deadly for Israel, and not less belligerent than the Syrians' proposal. From the standpoint of international public opinion, it was better not to fire the first shot in an offensive war. "It will be up to the Israelis," he said, "whether they attack us or not." This, he thought, would take him off the hook for the time being; for the rest, he hoped for the best.

But the best did not happen, though the first shot *was* fired by the Israelis. When Syrian equipment appeared and began working on the diversion site, the Israelis knocked it out with artillery fire. After several such occurrences, the Syrians stopped all work. Lebanon, which was also scheduled to begin diversion operations, cancelled their plans to do so.

Israel's resistance, therefore, created the first difficulty in implementing the summit plans. The second arose from the reluctance of other Arab states to accept Egyptian military help. The essence of the Unified Arab Military Command thus evaporated the very moment it should have begun to function.

The three countries where diversion was to take place—Lebanon, Jordan, and Syria—refused, each in its own euphemistic style, to admit foreign (i.e., Egyptian) troops. They were well aware of Nasser's ambitions. None cherished the prospect of Egyptian troops coming to help and remaining to hold. What he had failed to achieve by "Federation" with Syria, or the subversion he sponsored in Jordan and Lebanon, Nasser might now seek to achieve under pretext of protecting them against Israel. History is full of such helpful expeditions, which were of greater help to the helper than to the helped. Israel was undoubtedly a menace, but for the time being it was a passive one. Nasser had not been passive.

Each country dealt with the situation out of its own book. Small, peaceful, prosperous Lebanon had, after tragic and bloody upheavals (1957–1958) between its Moslem and Christian communities, achieved some kind of internal balance. A large part of the Moslem segment clamored for some kind of institutionalized ties with Cairo, but the administration would have none of it. Now, to avoid getting involved in a pan-Arab adventure, the Government in Beirut fell back on the armistice terms between Lebanon and Israel, reached at the end of the Israeli–Arab war of 1948–1949, which stipulate that the stationing of any foreign troops in Lebanon, even for defensive or preventive purposes, would constitute a violation.

Syria, for its part, did ask Egyptian aid. But it wanted only materiel—planes, not troops—not even pilots. Nasser replied publicly that he so mistrusted the Syrians that he would send them nothing he could not control. He would, if they wished, assist them by establishing an Egyptian air base on Syrian territory. Stalemate.

In Jordan, King Hussein had thus far withstood all pressure and successfully suppressed Egypt-based subversions. He had emerged unscathed from the assassination attempts organized by Cairo or by pro-Nasser elements inside his own country. His administration and his army had at times been involved in such plots, and Shukairy's PLO had not added to his comfort or security. The majority of the refugees are within Jordan's borders, but Hussein has not let Shukairy operate fully in his country. He was certainly not going to admit Egyptian troops to back up Shukairy's assortment of fanatics.

At the conference, the arguments were hot, the viewpoints varied. The recalcitrant countries asserted they could abide by the Summit decisions only if the foreign Arab troops were put under the command of the country in which they were stationed. This, of course, would vitiate the idea of a "unified" Arab command. Thus the Unified Command under Egyptian Lt.-General Ali Ali Amer remained a paper organization and the general a Commander-in-Chief without an army. The two major projects decided upon at the previous summit were completely deadlocked.

As if this were not enough a humiliating blow was struck by Israel at the very moment when the Arab League Defense Council was trying to find a face-saving way of dealing with the problems of the recent past. On the night of May 27, Israeli commandos attacked three targets inside Jordan in retaliation for recent raids of Al-Fatah infiltrators.

What distinguished these attacks from previous Israeli retaliations was that they were not hasty hit-and-run expeditions. This time the commandos, acting under stern instructions, evacuated all civilians from the houses in three target towns. They gave orders to the adults and candy to the children, and then with careful deliberation blew up houses and installations, including a large fuel center in Qalqilya. After carrying out these operations exactly according to plan, and as if they were on their own practice ground, the Israelis withdrew without suffering—or causing—a single casualty, except for seven Israelis who were slightly hurt by the accidental discharge of one of their own grenades on their way back.

This condescending behavior of the Israelis and the Jordanian people's helplessness was most humiliating to the Arab leaders inside the conference hall and Arab public opinion at large. In addition, Nasser was faced with the results of his own strategy: "Let the Israelis fire the first shot." They did indeed fire the first shot—in Syria—then the second, and third, and fourth, in Jordan. Nasser did not make good his promise that he "then" would take up the "battle of the Jordan."

Ugly facts now began to converge in the conference hall and demand some sort of solution. What was now to be done about the diversion plans, since Israel had put them out of action before they could even begin? Where was the Palestine Liberation Organization going to operate if it could not operate freely in Jordan?

Or should these grave problems be discussed at all? Perhaps it would be better not to talk about them? Experience at previous Arab League conferences had shown that the more troublesome problems were discussed, the more trouble ensued.

A paradox emerged. Only a few weeks earlier at the representatives conference, Lebanon and Jordan had done everything possible to prevent any censure of Bourguiba. Now they were insisting that this conference take up the problem of Bourguiba's "heresies." This, they hoped, would be the lesser evil, since such a discussion could be protracted—perhaps for the remainder of the conference. They could thus avoid the more bedeviling problems, and might be spared the embarrassing necessity of submitting a concrete program for carrying out the militant plans against Israel decided upon in January 1964. What these moderate governments wanted most was to avoid taking extreme and rash decisions, and for this the Bourguiba controversy was a welcome device. Although they were by no means ready to sacrifice him, they did want to talk, to discuss, to argue, to speculate—to temporize.

There was actually no danger now of any move to expel or even censure Bourguiba. Nasser having weighed the odds and found them meager, had abandoned the idea even before the conference

started. On the morrow of the opening of the conference, the Cairo
Al Ahram told its readers that some delegates believed a whole
Arab people should not be punished for a President's mistakes. It
added that it would not be right to expel the Tunisian people
from the Arab League although they *are* in "such a strange position." This annoyed Shukairy, and delighted the Syrians. They
could now assert that the Egyptian and Tunisian Presidents were
in league to betray the cause of the Arabs.

Some kind of resolution was passed at the beginning of the
conference—not censuring Bourguiba, but restating what had
been decided at the representatives' conference, "totally rejecting"
his proposals. It was not clear from the communiqué whether the
"rejected proposals" were explicitly attributed to Bourguiba. A
spokesman for the conference said that the Premiers had announced their intention of abiding by the decisions of last year
calling for "the liberation of Palestine by force of arms." In the
confusion of Arab dialectics this may mean many things, since
Bourguiba in his boycott-letter announced that he too abided by
these decisions.

Significantly, Shukairy this time was alone in demanding Bourguiba's expulsion. He again resigned as head of the Palestine Liberation Organization and declared that this time his decision was
final. But a few days later he withdrew his resignation. No matter;
Nasser told his (PLO) Congress there would be no liberation of
Palestine in the foreseeable future.

Though the exchanges were bitter, the recriminations implacable, these proceedings constituted only one level of the conference, and not the most important. What might have carried more
weight were a series of small caucuses of two, three, or four representatives, if only they had avoided talking at cross purposes.

The Lebanese and Algerians tried "to clear the atmosphere,"
to find a *modus vivendi* between Nasser and Bourguiba. The Egyptians wanted to know whether Jordan, the Lebanon, and Syria
were serious about carrying out the resolutions adopted at the first
summit for the Jordan diversion, and what risks they were ready
to take. Reportedly the Egyptians in the interest of precision,
carried a written questionnaire which they hoped would eliminate
future misunderstandings. They wanted mainly to know two
things: if other Arab states would permit Egyptian troops on their
territory, and if they would agree to any sanctions, or at least

censure, against Bourguiba. The Egyptians insisted that as far as they were concerned this session was to be "a test of the good will of the members of the Arab League."

The Arab press was in its best form during these days of the conference. The day the Little Summit opened, on May 26, the Cairo daily *Akhbar El-Yom* published the plan by which "the Arab forces would destroy Israel within a few hours without giving her time to sit up and take notice."

"The battle with Israel," the paper said, "was joined the moment she began pumping Arab waters away to the Negev." *Akhbar El-Yom* said that the offensive would incorporate "a surprise attack from the sea by unified Arab naval forces which will approach the Israel coast under heavy air force protection. There will be no need for subsequent lengthy withdrawal operations because the entire armada can slip within a matter of hours into the nearest Arab port for shelter."

Akhbar El-Yom also informed whoever might be interested that the air attacks would be carried out simultaneously from various bases very close to the Israel border. "Should Israel attempt to retaliate against Alexandria or Port Said, for example, she will be subjected to bombing from Beirut, or if she tries to attack Cairo she will be hit by bombers from Damascus or Baghdad, and so on. The Arab forces do not require long supply lines because they are within a couple of miles of the enemy from every attack base in the pincers move carried out by all Arab forces in combination and coordination."

This quotation is a vivid example of the world of fantasy in which the Arabs live, and against which Bourguiba was rebelling. Even more important, it may help us understand the psychological motivations behind the speech Nasser was soon to make before delegates to the First Congress of the Palestine Liberation Organization.

The Egyptian press was also true to form in covering the proceedings of the Little Summit. Day after day the newspapers reported with great enthusiasm the degree of Arab unanimity and solidarity against Bourguiba and Israel. Nasser was credited with plans, armies, pacts, unified commands—all of his own creation, all weird, all pathetic, all lacking realism on any level.

Yet in a moment of sober indignation the Egyptian leader would rebel against them, and with a great effort raise himself from this strange realm of make-believe. We shall see presently what form this extraordinary act of disengagement would take.

The conference closed without resolving any of the major difficulties and without even taking formal resolutions on problems of the Unified Arab Command or the stationing of troops. Observers considered it the greatest fiasco of panArabism in recent years. To save face it was announced that no resolutions would be made public because of their secret character. The third summit of the Arab heads-of-state, it was announced, would be held in Casablanca the following September.

The Little Summit probably represented one of the most painful disappointments of Nasser's career. He saw his fellow Arab leaders at their worst, reverting to the most sterile pattern of fragmentation, hypocrisy, and cowardice. All pretense at unity had collapsed, and what remained was mutual suspicion, recrimination, and hatred. He himself was defied on nearly all sides.

How did he face up to this ordeal and how did he react to this welter of contradictions, cross-currents, rivalries and defiances. How would he reconcile this state of affairs with the paramount and sacredly professed aim of attacking Israel and "reconquering Palestine"? Was he imprisoned in a vicious circle?

Indeed he was. But by a tremendous act of will and almost reckless daring, he was to break out of it and seem once more on top of the situation, instead of its victim. He would have a long breathing spell.

He regained control by the simple expedient of telling the truth —that Arab unity was for the time being a myth, that the Arabs were not only disunited but weak; that he could not and would not wage any war against Israel for a long time to come; that he was incapable of waging a war because he had not the men or the material.

Not only would he wage no war, he would not come to the assistance of anyone foolish and irresponsible enough to start an adventure. No one could count upon his help if in trouble with Israel; hence the best thing to do would be to leave Israel alone.

To leave Israel alone meant to lay aside the summit plans to divert the headwaters of the Jordan, he was to say in a speech regarded as one of his frankest foreign policy statements. In that same speech he grimly conceded the collapse of the policy he had undertaken seventeen months earlier to rally the Arabs against Israel.

As his antagonist, President Bourguiba, had done three months before, so Nasser, too, chose the most difficult platform to express his views. Bourguiba spoke in February and March to Palestinian refugees, leaders, and journalists in Jordan. Nasser decided to deliver himself of his oppressive burden before 400 delegates to the Palestine Liberation Congress assembled in Cairo just as the Little Summit was about to adjourn. Nasser had not been scheduled to speak at the Congress—he had not even been expected to be present. Yet, almost without notice he appeared on May 31, and received permission to address the delegates:

It was at the very last moment this afternoon that I decided to attend your meeting. The atmosphere today seems gloomy. Every one of us feels these days that the strength of Arab action has slackened.

We [just] saw the violent attacks by Syria against the conference of the heads of Arab governments, and a violent attack against the United Arab Command, and a call to launch an offensive against Israel. . . .

. . . . I am being asked: Why did you abandon Syria to her own fate when she was twice attacked by Israel? And why did not the Unified Arab Command react when Jordan was raided by the Israeli army which attacked Qalqilya, Jenin, and Shuneh? . . . We boycott companies which deal with Israel. Why was a decision not taken to boycott Bourguiba?. . . .

I felt duty bound not to let these questions pass but to come and tell you frankly and exactly where we stand. . . .

Well, we did not react because the Unified Arab Command is not yet in proper shape. This Unified Command reflects a concrete reality in the Arab world and there is no use to ignore that reality. The amazing thing is that those who clamor for an offensive war against Israel are incapable even of defending themselves.

All the Arab countries, including Egypt, are not yet capable of defending themselves. . . . If the defense of certain Arab countries is not possible, then we cannot speak of attack, and if we talk about it, and say that we will liberate Palestine, we are simply bragging and deceiving. . . .

In order to carry out the diversion of the headwaters, we would have to station troops in countries along Israel's frontiers. But political considerations and mutual suspicions have thus far prevented this, too. Egypt was ready to send an air force to Syria if she would allocate us an air base under our control. We would also have sent land forces to defend it. Had the Syrians given us the air base, without [our land forces] how could we have been sure that they would not arrest our officers, and plot against us, as they did in 1961? The Lebanon and Jordan are not ready to permit the entry of troops into their territories. . . .

If today we cannot proceed with the work of diverting the Jordan headwaters, it would be better to postpone these works until the day when political conditions are ripe, and mutual suspicions liquidated. Then it will be possible to station Arab forces in the various countries, enabling us to assure the protection of the diversion works. . . .

We must provide for Arab defense before we can carry out our ultimate goal and liberate Palestine. . . . If I cannot fight now, I am not ashamed to say that I cannot fight. . . .

But can the Arab League liberate Palestine? I say that the Arab League cannot liberate Palestine. Can the Arab League liberate the Arab South? No. Can the Arab League deliver us from the foreign bases in the Arab countries? It cannot and it will not.

This is not to say that we should liquidate the League, but only that we have to recognize its possibilities and its limitations. Let us not ask of it the impossible. . . .

But can we say now that the Arab summits will achieve the liberation of Palestine? I don't think so. . . . . There are too many contradictions among the various Arab states: between Syria and Iraq; between Syria and Egypt; between Saudi Arabia and Egypt. The Lebanon, for her part, does not want any outside Arab forces on her territory. There is even a war between the United Arab Republic and the Yemen. . . . Today the Arab countries are afraid of each other. There is a lack of confidence. . . . Everyone has his own suspicions. . . . We only delude ourselves when we pretend that everything is solved because we convene regularly. . . . If we are incapable of unity in defense, how can we talk about attack? . . .

Nevertheless these summits serve gradually to reduce the contradictions among the Arabs. . . .

We get arms, and Israel gets arms. But in facing this situation we must have the revolutionary approach. We have our manpower resources, and we can recruit two or three million soldiers. We want to return to our country, but shall we fight without preparation?

Supposing we were to attack Israel. Will I attack while I have 50,000 men in Yemen? The first thing, surely, which I would do if I decided to attack Israel would be to bring back the 50,000 soldiers who are in the Yemen so as to have them here before I attack Israel. . . .

Must we launch an assault against Israel if a Syrian tractor is hit, thus leaving Israel the initiative of choosing the time of confrontation? We surely have to be more [prudent] than that. It is we who must determine the place and the time of the showdown. . . .

We must appreciate, however, that Palestine cannot be liberated by holding conferences. When the Arab countries meet, as they met last week, some try to outbid the others; some launch [verbal] attacks against each other; some write articles and make broadcasts. . . .

No more outbidding! This can only lead us to new tragedies of the kind we have suffered enough. . . .

He concluded by declaring:

In my opinion only the Arab revolution. . . Arab revolutionary action—can solve the Palestine problem, and the United Arab Republic is the base of this revolution and of this action. . . .

Arab revolutionary action will be a violent, complicated operation, demanding that we should correctly assess the enemy so that we can overcome him.

. . . . What I am driving at is this: I want to reassure the Palestine Liberation Movement that the United Arab Republic is with you heart and soul. I appreciate our responsibility and believe we can recover Palestine for the Palestinians. But to reconquer it by force of arms, we must confront Israel and all those who are behind Israel.

This speech contains practically all the ideas and all the criticisms of pan-Arabism that Bourguiba had been propounding since February and for which he was branded a traitor. Now both Bourguiba and Nasser had exposed the Arab League as a presently worthless instrument. Both acknowledged that Arab unity was a myth, that the Arab countries were divided among and against themselves. But Nasser used even stronger and less ambiguous terms than Bourguiba's.

Both heaped scorn on the Arabs for trying constantly to defeat Israel and liberate Palestine by violent speechmaking, by conferences, by press articles, and radio broadcasts. Both demanded a stop to fervid outbiddings. Both stated that what is necessary is for Arabs to appraise realities, to assess correctly the strength and worth of the enemy. Their people must dedicate themselves to becoming economically and technologically stronger, accumulating the means and then learning to use those means to best advantage.

Both declared that war against Israel is an impossiblity and can lead only to disaster of the kind the Arabs have already experienced. Both said that if one cannot wage war, one should not talk war; and if there is talk of war while there is no ability to wage it then it is only an exercise in deluding the people.

Even the idea that only revolutionary action can achieve the desired end is not unlike Bourguiba's approach. Since the Tunisian President does not like the word "revolution" he speaks instead of *development,* of technological advancement, of raising the standards of living of the people, of bettering their lot by education and skills, of emancipation, of socialism. In essence, the meaning is probably the same.

Both addressed the Palestinians as in the last analysis the people most concerned, who will have to take their fate in their own hands. Hence both favor the organization and crystallization of a Palestinian entity.

The similarities between the two are striking enough to give the impression that Nasser studied and consciously or subconsciously made the Tunisian President's ideas his own.

Nasser's speech before the Palestinians seems almost to be a public confession of failure and an admission that his antagonist was right. We practically expect him to say: Brother Habib, we are the only two Arab leaders who possess both sense and guts. We are both genuine fighters for the Arab renaissance. Let us join hands, work together, and bring our brethren out from the wilderness.

But Nasser's speech was not meant to be a confession of guilt or failure; it was not even an apology. On the contrary, it was a broad indictment. It was an attack on the Syrians whom he accused of irresponsibility and conspiracy; on the Lebanese and Jordanians for their hypocrisy, pusillanimity, and inconsistencies. He breathed contempt, scorn, and wrath. He told the Arab leaders—both conservative and revolutionary—that if they did not meaningfully unite, and show that they meant what they said about reconquering Palestine, he would not be dragged into their irresponsible suicidal follies.

On the other hand, Nasser also settled accounts with Bourguiba. Although he identified himself with Bourguiba's ideas and approach, he vehemently attacked their author:

> Bourguiba isolated himself politically in the midst of the Arab world, and the resolutions of the Arab League cannot hide the fact.

. . . Bourguibism is a policy of compromise. Bourguiba proclaims that he has fought for thirty years—but what did he do? His country was the last to obtain the evacuation of foreign troops. Today he tries to sow defeatism among us concerning Palestine at the very moment when the Palestinians are getting ready to fight.

He stated that an abyss had opened between him and Bourguiba, and that he would deal with him appropriately outside the frame of the Arab League. He called the Tunisian names. Later (at the May Day rally, 1966) he would even call him "criminal" and "murderer," accusing him of having assassinated Salah Ben Youssef. Which only shows that in modern politics, as in ancient religion, the decisive question is not What is salvation? or How is it going to be achieved? but by whom? Who is going to be its instrument—the Messiah?

Nasser insisted that sometime in the unpredictable future the apocalyptic confrontation would take place: "As I have previously predicted, not on a field of flowers, but on a field drenched with blood."

As far as the immediate future was concerned, he of course, excluded war against Israel—postponing it *sine die*—not only because the conquest of Palestine was contingent upon an all-Arab revolution, but also because they must defeat not only Israel, but all the great powers behind Israel.

For all their parallelism, what Bourguiba advocated for the here and now—from a feasible, pragmatic point of view—and what Nasser proclaimed in vague terms were marked by a cardinal difference. Nasser succeeded in riding two horses seemingly running in opposite directions. On the one hand he could satisfy the emotionalism of the masses by continually talking of war against all the powers of evil—a war drenched with rivers of blood. On the other, he could, so far, keep from undertaking an irresponsible, irreparable, or imprudent step which might lead him into trouble, at the same time restraining other Arab hotheads and irresponsible rulers from a military adventure against Israel. And when necessary he reversed himself and canceled policies and plans which were adopted on his own advice or urging.

Of course, sheer opportunism often makes him swing from one conception to its opposite. At the Arab summits Nasser was against solving the Palestine problem by a frontal attack against Israel. Instead he offered a plan of phased and cautious action avoiding open warfare. Most typical were the plans to dig channels to divert the headwaters of the Jordan instead of shooting it out. Now, he was swinging the other way: There is no use getting involved in phased, diversionary actions—the Palestine problem will be solved only by a frontal attack upon Israel, by a huge army marching through fields drenched in blood.

Nasser's inconsistency penetrates deep, and fosters strange rationalizations. When he first developed the Jordan diversion plan, the Syrians opposed it, pointing out that such a course would be self-defeating. It would drain Palestine dry; when the Arabs reconquered it, they would find a desert. From a long-range Arab point of view the logic was certainly on the Syrians' side. But Nasser over-ruled them and the Jordan diversion became the most important aim of Arab strategy. Now, when it suited him he spoke of it with derision. He would not go to war simply because a Syrian tractor was hit by Israeli artillery.

Small wonder, then, that the Syrians were indignant. In the wake of Nasser's speech, the Ba'ath leadership and its press conducted a vigorous campaign against both the Egyptian President and the Little Summit. In a speech in Damascus, Dr. Ahmed Mounif Razzaz, then Secretary General of the Ba'ath party, spoke of "traitors other than Bourguiba," and declared that in spite of the *volte-face* of other Arab leaders, the Syrians would pursue their aim of liberating Palestine.

The Damascus government declared in a statement:

> Those who have pushed us to undertake the work of diverting the headwaters of the River Jordan, and asked us to spend enormous sums for this purpose; those who have promised us military assistance in case of aggression by the enemy against us, are those who today have renounced these same plans.

And *Al Ba'ath,* the organ of the party, asked in an editorial how Nasser could find it possible to convoke a summit conference and make it adopt the diversion plans, and then speak of "the uselessness of exploiting the Jordan headwaters, and even refuse to elaborate any other plan for the liberation of Palestine."

For its part, Tunis radio claimed that President Bourguiba's campaign had been vindicated by Nasser's rejection of Syrian extremism. The Egyptian's knees, said the broadcast, shook with fear at the lengths to which Syria wanted to push him.

Nasser, however, declined to be moved. As time went on he

pressed his position in ever stronger terms against both the Syrians and Bourguiba. He expressed doubts about the usefulness of the forthcoming summit in Casablanca if the Arab world continued to be preoccupied with Bourguiba's proposals. As to the Syrians, he told a group of Arab students in Moscow three weeks before the Casablanca conference that he would quit it if the Syrian Ba'athists persisted in their "hostile attitude toward the United Arab Republic over diversion of the Jordan River waters and the Unified Arab Military Command."

The Syrian reaction was instant. *Al Ba'ath* retorted with the charge that President Nasser was trying to "freeze the Palestine question" and "destroy the Arab summit, suspend the Unified Command, and blame the Ba'ath."

Beirut's Ba'athist newspaper *Al Ahrar* declared that Colonel Nasser and other Arab leaders who were trying "to dodge the Palestine issue" would "find themselves always face to face with it no matter how they turn."

Perhaps what is most significant about all of Nasser's double dealings is that he could get away with them. His speech before the Palestinians demonstrated more than anything else the measure of his prestige and influence among the Arab masses, who unquestioningly and uncritically accepted him as their leader. At a Damascus meeting on the Little Summit, General Amin El Khafez, then President of the Syrian Presidential Council, declared: "We witnessed how all the delegations except Syria gave the impression of submitting to a password emanating from an occult power." Bourguiba had compromised the Egyptian's leadership among the Arab rulers to a considerable extent—but among the masses, not yet to a dangerous point.

The fact that Nasser was not to have his way at all, may paradoxically be even greater proof of his prestige: the Arab leaders, though refusing to yield to Nasser where their own interests were at stake, nonetheless felt compelled to disguise their resistance in some form of submission. Except, of course, Bourguiba.

Nasser's charismatic strength appears undiminished among a large segment of Arab opinion. Of course, there is opposition to him even inside Egypt, as evidenced by the mass trials of the Moslem Brotherhood groups plotting his overthrow. And had any of these attempts succeeded, his fate might have been like that of Ben Bella or Nkrumah. But somehow his popularity has been more deeply rooted than that of any other Arab leader, which is why he can tell the Arabs the bitterest truths about their weakness, their impotence, and their need for patience; it is why he can lead them into disaster, and survive. Virtually no other leader could dare speak in such fashion without danger. (Bourguiba dared; but in establishing Tunisia's independence, he had solidified his own people behind him, which gave him a base of strength; and, although many Arabs in the Middle East also agreed with him there *were* vehement outbursts of genuine indignation that nearly cost him his life.)

Although Nasser's prestige is extremely great and his influence unrivaled, his policy is in the last account not only inconsistent, but weak. Perhaps it is weak because it is not thought out and because it is so contradictory. Bourguiba is therefore correct when he says that Nasser, instead of being a creator of policies and a leader of his people, is more and more a prisoner of both. He has created situations, institutions, and realities which, one day, he may be unable to control.

Though he may think he has postponed a showdown with Israel to a dim and distant future, he may not be able to decide the time, place, and conditions of the showdown. These may be forced upon him, if not necessarily by Israel, by a complexity of factors— some of his own creation. Some of these are generating an impetus and life of their own. For example, the more the Palestine Liberation Organization develops into an organized force and the more units it outfits and trains, the more urgent it will become for them to map a plan of action. If a plan is not formulated, action may be triggered without a plan. And such chance incidents are only one aspect of an explosive situation.

9

A Victory by Proxy

ON SEPTEMBER 13, THE THIRD SUMMIT OF THE ARAB HEADS-OF-STATE assembled for a five-day session in the colorful Moroccan city of Casablanca. In spite of its pomp and circumstance it appeared to be a repetition of the pattern of the last several Arab League conferences held in the course of the same year—but not quite. There were some surprises.

First of all, Bourguiba himself is not completely predictable, and he is never dull. He always has something to pull out of his sleeve. Even if his arguments have been propounded many times before, he usually ventures some untried aspect, or some fresh nuance. As a debater, he has a non-Arabic flair for emphasizing relevant points with forceful eloquence, and he pulls no punches. The day the third summit opened, he was at his belligerent best, undaunted. His rhetoric was vivid and devastating.

In spite of frantic efforts of all the Maghreb heads-of-state to persuade him to come to Casablanca he clung to his decision. The day the summit opened, September 13, he sent a memorandum to Secretary-General Hassouna stating he would not participate, and enumerating the reasons for his decision. Out of respect for his friend King Hassan II, host to the Conference, he sent Secretary of State Mongi Slim to Casablanca with a personal message in which he explained his position.

Five hours before the opening of the Conference, Bourguiba appeared on the Tunisian radio and made public the contents of the memorandum explaining his refusal. The speech and the memorandum were probably the most interesting if not the most sensational features of the conference.

He repeated his denunciation of "Egyptian interference in the internal affairs of all the Arab countries." There would have been nothing new in this statement if he had not spelled out with brutal frankness the character of the subversive campaigns:

> Never in the course of their history have the Arabs been more divided than they are now. Never have they slaughtered each other more ferociously than since the day Egypt took upon itself the sacred mission of unifying them. What Arab country has not found a plot against its government that originated in Cairo and was financed by Egyptian money?

He recalled in grim detail Egypt's subversive campaigns in Jordan, the Lebanon, Syria, Iraq, the Sudan, and Saudi Arabia. He added:

> Nobody is safe from Cairo's conspiracies. In the Maghreb, if it were not for the grace of God, the Egyptian intervention in the border conflict of two sister countries—Morocco and Algeria—would have precapitated us into an abyss. Cairo lost no time in fanning the flames.

In the autumn of 1963, during the Algerian-Morocco border war, he recalled, Cairo had asked Tunisia's permission to establish an airlift ("air bridge") to send men, arms, and ammunition to the Algerian Army, instead of trying to promote a reconciliation between the two countries. "Tunisia," said Mr. Bourguiba, "where the regime is solid and aware [of its responsibilities] refused this demand." Referring to Colonel Houari Boumedienne, who ultimately succeeded in getting rid of Ahmed Ben Bella, he declared:

> It is good luck that at the head of the national Algerian Army is a gallant and courageous man who knows how to distinguish between the immediate and true interests of his country, and had the courage to oppose direct participation of Egyptian elements in the operations which took place at that time on the frontier of the two [North African countries].

And this, explained Bourguiba, happened because Egypt regards the leaders of all the Arab countries as provisionals to be liquidated. Nasser is trying to recreate "the Northern Province" by absorbing its neighbors one by one. His country would never regain the confidence of the Arab countries so long as she pursued her policy of hegemony, and considered it her destiny to be the champion of Arab nationalism.

> Let her begin by changing her name. What is this United Arab Republic—which consists of Egypt alone?
> We refuse to cooperate with the Arab League as long as Egypt does not respect the member countries and the Charter stipulating that the League is an organization of sovereign countries.

The reception of Bourguiba's unequivocal declaration was, of course, mixed. The preliminary meeting of the Foreign Ministers at the summit refused the Tunisian demand that the seventeen-page memorandum be circulated officially among the delegates, or even that it be registered as an official document of the conference. On the other hand, many of the participants in the summit were pleased that somebody dared to expose Nasser's policies.

The ban on the memorandum really changed nothing. It was circulated, read avidly, and aroused exciting comment. Though they were in effect a sideshow, Bourguiba's radio address and the memorandum received more attention than the main performance. For all practical purposes, his speech outside the conference constituted the keynote at the conference itself, because in it he touched the tumor causing the Arab League's sickness.

While Bourguiba's seat at the conference table remained empty, the Tunisian flag flew with those of the other twelve nations over the green and white conference building.

Bourguiba's boycott proved salutary for all concerned, for it spared the conference an exhibition of public scandal. General el Khafez declared gratuitously that he would have walked out of the conference had "that traitor dared make an appearance in Casablanca." The Egyptians also were jubilant that Bourguiba did not show up. The absence of the man "who auctioned off the Palestine people" spared Nasser the need of a direct confrontation, and gave him a chance to concentrate on the attacks against him from the other extreme: the Syrians. In Bourguiba's absence he could assume a statesmanlike position in the middle of the road— between Bourguiba's "defeatism" and Syria's "irresponsibility." He could advance the slogan of "neither capitulation nor military adventures."

Paradoxically, the Tunisian President's supporters, though outwardly professing themselves "very disappointed," came to realize that they were better off in his absence. Before the convening—right up to the last minute—the Maghreb leaders, and chiefly King Hassan of Morocco, had tried to persuade Bourguiba to attend, promising him a united front on some of the major issues he took with Nasser, primarily the reorganization and updating of the Arab League. But Bourguiba argued he could not in good faith participate in a meeting where he might be criticized for merely daring to express an independent, nonconformist opinion. The League had first of all to purge itself, to reorganize, before he would return.

Bourguiba's trusted friend and special representative, Mongi Slim, rejected the popular belief that those who are absent lose out; it was not valid in this instance:

> Tunisia wishes by this dramatic gesture to make the members of the Arab League aware that this institution cannot function properly as long as one single power—in this case the UAR—tries to impose its hegemony over the rest of the Arab world.

His absence, Bourguiba's friends came to feel, had its advantages. He had made his points. Continuing to enlarge on them perhaps under provocation of Nasser's retorts, would needlessly exacerbate the discussions. Without him, it would be easier for them to advance and defend his theories. They could do it, so to speak, in an "objective, impersonal" way, without having to take sides on the basis of personalities. They could, and indeed did, succeed not only in defending his position (which was basically theirs) but actually in gaining a triumph.

Nasser, for his part, had nourished misgivings about the usefulness of this summit. As the date approached, he grew apprehensive lest he be caught in a crossfire between Bourguiba and Syria. He cautiously weighed the idea of not going to Casablanca at all. This was not an easy decision to make; for the summit institution was his child, and in the past he had hailed the conferences of the heads of state as his greatest achievement in search of Arab unity. Finally, at the end of August, while on his visit to Moscow, he told the meeting of Arab students he would go to Casablanca, but that he would quit the conference if it became the scene of "demagogical outbiddings." On its eve, his friend and spokesman,

Heikal, threatened in his weekly column: "It depends upon Damascus whether this summit will not be the last one."

Even in Casablanca, Nasser's doubts were with him. One of his colleagues told *Le Monde's* Eric Rouleau:

> Peaceful coexistence among the Arab states is certainly desirable and necessary. But it is justified only in the proportion as it permits attainment of well-defined objectives. It becomes harmful the moment it paralyzes all positive action, since it dooms the Arab world to immobility and impotence. If our adversaries do not exhibit a more realistic approach to the Palestine problem, we will have to regain our complete freedom of action in all fields.

Thus the third summit opened in what was characterized "a climate of uncertainties and relative pessimism."* Even before it began, it seemed already deadlocked.

Before the opening ceremonies, the foreign ministers, whose task it was to prepare the agenda for the summit, spent four days in heated debate. They never did agree on any of the major issues.

Two problems especially caused profound and dramatic disagreement: One was "rejuvenating" the League; the second concerned the essence of the Palestine issue. The delegates quarreled heatedly over how to support the Palestine "Liberation Army," and what to do about cutting off Israel from the waters of the Jordan. Who would rush help (and how?) to the Lebanon, Syria, and Jordan if Israel again thwarted the diversion works in those countries? And how could they help the revolts against British rule in South Arabia?

But every problem they faced was complicated by the first and most serious issue: the role and policies of the League's strongest member—Egypt. The Algerian delegation was reported to have submitted a draft to reorganize the League on the basis of "collective leadership"; others suggested granting wider prerogatives to

---

* The first Summit Conference of Arab heads-of-state had taken place in Cairo in January 1964; the second in September 1964 in Alexandria. At the third, eleven Arab States were represented by their heads-of-state; the twelfth by the heir apparent: Algeria, President Boumedienne; Morocco, King Hassan II; Egypt, President Nasser; Sudan, President Al Azhari; Lebanon, President Helou; Syria, President Amin El Khafez; Jordan, King Hussein; Iraq, President Abdul Salam Aref; Saudia Arabia, King Faisal; Yemen, President Sallal; Kuwait, Emir Abdallah al-Salem al-Sabah. Libya was represented by Crown Prince Al Hassan Rida as-Sanusi; King Idris was too ill to attend.

the Council of the League, thus limiting the power of the Secretary General, an Egyptian. The majority clamored for a revision of the League's charter, making its procedures more flexible.

On the Palestine issue, the divisions among the participants were as deep and stubborn as ever. Shukairy, only an "observer," demanded a follow-up of the resolutions of the first two summits with a concrete plan to enable him to build up a real army. He wanted its units recruited, trained, and outfitted in the Gaza strip, in Syria, in Iraq, and in Egypt. He wanted as well a proclamation of "obligatory military service" among the refugees in Jordan, and the establishment there of training camps for the recruits. He also demanded a "High Command" and "General Staff" of that army centered in Cairo.

The foreign ministers failed to define a specific agenda including these main issues; they left it to the heads of state to decide for themselves. The topics they did recommend were general and innocuous.

The opening ceremonies took place in Casablanca's French-built marble Prefecture. The 36-year-old King Hassan, as host, gave the inaugural address, which made immediately clear that he would take a moderate position, and that his sympathies were at least in part with the absent Bourguiba:

> Continuous dissent, conflict, and accusation have divided the Arabs and dispersed the efforts that should have been directed toward the liberation of Palestine. The Arab peoples are aware of this, and wonder if we are really serious when we claim that the "Arab atmosphere has cleared." We run the risk of losing their confidence and of deceiving them. . . .

He called upon the Arab rulers to break out of their isolation: to abandon their self-centered squabbles, and join the larger stream of world events. He appealed to them to close ranks and become a force capable of influencing the course of the world. The Arab League, he said, should live up to its "historic responsibilities" and not remain riveted to purely Arab problems.

> In order for us to play a great part in world affairs, Morocco has always proclaimed the necessity to revise the League's charter with a view to meeting the needs of the Arab nation, and achieving increased efficiency and constructive cooperation.

And, though the Arab struggle against Israel was "primordial," economic development was "no less important."

The next day another Maghrebian representative, Colonel Boumedienne of Algeria, seconded Hassan's suggestion to enlarge the agenda of the conference and include in it problems transcending Arab affairs: the Kashmir conflict, Vietnam, and racial discrimination.

Nasser, presiding over the opening session of the summit, spoke briefly. He refrained from engaging in polemics with his antagonist, Bourguiba.* He merely declared that "the task of the Arab peoples consists of the struggle against imperialism in any form." But Israel represented imperialism in its worst form for the Arabs: "The No. 1 issue is Palestine. No other issue should divert us from our goal. The Arab nations have the weapons and the will for victory."

Correspondents noticed that Nasser was not his usual self. His debonair stance and his winning smile were gone. He looked glum, and he scowled. He knew that only the shaky leaders of Republican Yemen and Iraq were firmly on his side. The others were either openly against him or suspiciously aloof.

Syria did not wait long to take the offensive; on the second day of the conference, Nasser found himself under attack by General Khafez. But he refused to be drawn into an open argument in the presence of the underlings accompanying the heads of state; he adjourned the meeting and convened a secret session limited to the chiefs, the Secretary General, General Amer (Chief of the Unified Arab Command), and Shukairy. He did the same the next day during an argument between the Egyptian Amer and King Hussein.

Thus, on the third day of the conference, the heads of state were still grappling with the Palestine problem. They wrangled and quarreled, accusing each other of bad faith, or bad judgment, or both. General Amer, in his report to the summit on military plans to insure the implementation of the diversion works, urged Jordan to permit the entry of Iraqi and Saudi Arabian troops to help protect work sites near the Israeli border.

---

* Though Nasser did not attack Bourguiba at Casablanca, Cairo radio and press launched a new series of assaults against Tunisia, the Lebanon, and Jordan for hesitating on the implementation of the diversion projects under the protection of the Unified Arab Command and its troops.

King Hussein rejected this proposal, declaring that it was "not the right time" to move troops into his kingdom. Israel would interpret such troop movement as a provocative act, and open warfare might follow. Such a prospect, he seems to have argued, would be in contradiction to Nasser's expressed views that outright struggle at this stage must be avoided.

Amer's reported reply to this was that Israel would attack anyhow as soon as work started in earnest on the water diversion project. The debate grew so heated that King Hassan urged limiting the session to top-ranking delegates, as Nasser had done the previous two days.

As the debate continued behind closed doors with restricted attendance, it became clear that the overwhelming majority of the Arab heads of state were reluctant to pursue the diversion plans. Only Egypt, Syria, and Iraq argued that the works should be resumed—Egypt, of course, on the condition that the Unified Arab Command under Egyptian Amer be permitted to move troops freely from one country to another.

The other Arab nations were reported either resisting, as were Lebanon and Jordan, or remaining aloof. Morocco argued that since in the last account this was a purely eastern affair, it would not be proper for the Maghrebian (western) governments to exert any influence.

There were also clashes concerning the form the military fight to "liberate Palestine" would take. Jordan and the Lebanon were not too happy about any form of "liberation," except perhaps in the vaguest terms. But the Algerian Boumedienne proposed that the Palestine Liberation Army be organized as guerrillas rather than as the conventionally equipped and trained force demanded by Shukairy.

Apart from that, even such rather remote problems as the Kashmir dispute between India and Pakistan encountered division of opinion. Jordan's Hussein proposed that the summit side with Pakistan, adopting a resolution recommending a solution on the basis of self-determination; but Egypt opposed it because of the close relations between Cairo and New Delhi.

For awhile the conference seemed to fall apart, with everywhere disarray and confusion. Le Monde, the best informed paper on Middle Eastern and North African affairs, was ready from the beginning to write off the summit as a complete failure. "The prevailing impression is that [the Arab League] at each new effort runs more out of breath, and that each of its meetings succeeds only in displaying its divisions rather than smoothing them over."

The Moroccan daily *L'Opinion* declared squarely that "the Arab governments have no desire to assume the risks that the [previous] summit resolutions involve."

But Nasser, who is superb in times of crisis—that is, objective crises and not those artificially created by himself—refused to yield to the general pessimism. He was determined to achieve one way or another what he called "realistic and practical agreements" on key issues, and to avoid subjects which did not lend themselves to consensus. He tried direct negotiations and discussions with other heads of state in a series of private meetings, using all his vaunted charm and power of persuasion.

It was after Nasser's secret meeting with Amin El Khafez, the Ba'athist leader of Syria, that the summit suddenly underwent a metamorphosis. From the depths of dark pessimism it suddenly shifted to the heights of dazzling euphoria as implacable enemies were transformed overnight into a team of "brothers" dedicated to eternal friendship. The two main antagonists—Nasser and Khafez—had apparently become "inseparable friends"; for, to the amazement of foreign journalists and the applause of Arab on-lookers, they were seen after the meetings of September 15 walking hand in hand. And contrary to protocol, the same car took both of them back to the hotel.

Dr. Ahmed Mounif Razzaz, head of the Syrian Ba'ath Party, and its political and ideological spokesman, now told Eric Rouleau of *Le Monde*:

> We do not think that an armed conflict with Israel is, from a short point of view, possible or even desirable. Besides, we do not know what the future has in store for us. Nor do we know whether the Palestine problem will be solved by force of arms or not, taking into consideration the changes which may occur in the meantime both in the world and in Israel itself. On the other hand, we know that we cannot accept the existence of a Zionist state. Such a state, apart from everything else, pursues a belligerent policy of expansionism. It is therefore our duty to prepare ourselves for the worst, to prepare our unified military forces for dealing with any contingency. The improvement of inter-Arab relations should now facilitate the achievement of an agreement on this subject.

In the same interview Dr. Razzaz declared he was not convinced the diversion projects were necessary or useful;

> We got at them [the projects] too late to be able to prevent Israel from approaching the waters of the Jordan River. The Zionist state is already in the process of cultivating the Negev, while out plans could not be finished before three or four years' time. Even if these works should be brought to completion, the enterprise would reduce Israel's water resources to only a very small extent. Salination, it is true, would increase. Frankly the game is not worth the candle.

What a far cry from the belligerent proclamations and repeated calls for an immediate attack upon Israel voiced only a couple of days earlier! What is almost unbelievable is that the language and trend of thought expressed by this most important personality of the Syrian delegation—next only to General Khafez—not only came close to Nasser's but in some ways even surpassed his in moderation. Nasser's usual stance was that war with Israel was inevitable, but that the showdown had to be postponed; Razzaz said that it was not certain at all that the solution would be by a military confrontation. In this he came even closer to Bourguiba than to Nasser.

He also emulated Bourguiba in his deprecation of the whole project to divert the Jordan, which might precipitate an armed conflict that the Arabs should try to avoid.

With the Syrians falling in line, Nasser felt on more solid ground; now he could try to make his own cautious position more articulate. He began to convey the idea that Palestine was not the most important problem facing the Arab world, but only one aspect of a general situation (or a grave symptom of that situation). He thought the Arabs were too much obsessed with this problem and it was unhealthy for them. A close collaborator of the Egyptian President told the same correspondent:

> The Arab world should get rid of its blinkers and widen the range of its vision. It must cease being hypnotized by the Palestine problem. In fact, this problem should be reexamined and solved in a larger frame of relationships among the international forces.

The Egyptians also began to doubt the usefulness of the Jordan diversion plans. It would take, as Razzaz pointed out, three or four years to get the projects underway and the Unified Command in shape to protect them. By that time Israel, and Egypt, too, would probably be in possession of nuclear arms. This "terror equilibrium" in the Middle East would considerably reduce the eventuality of an armed conflict, if not rule it out altogether.

This, of course, sounds less like Nasser than Bourguiba, except for this major difference: Bourguiba drew conclusions and suggested engaging in a realistic search for a negotiated settlement, while Nasser remained entangled in the impossible contradiction of liberating Palestine while avoiding war.

The partisans of Bourguiba also tried to crystallize their position more articulately. A Maghrebian delegate told Eric Rouleau:

> Our problem at present is not so much how to destroy Israel as how to contain her within her boundaries, and to dissuade her from her aggressive policies against the Arab world.

The most significant feature of the metamorphosis was, however, the courting and placating of the absent Bourguiba by most of the participants at the summit. While his adversaries—Nasser, the Syrians, and the Iraqis—did not publicly attempt to appease him, they nevertheless went along with the policy of conciliation championed by the Maghrebians and supported by the other delegations. On the initiative of King Hassan it was unanimously decided to try to bring Bourguiba back to the fold; then came the parallel decision to formulate the conference resolutions in a fashion acceptable to Bourguiba, and to submit them to him prior to formal promulgation.

More than that, the chiefs-of-state agreed to subject the Arab League to "a regime of rejuvenation," thus meeting Bourguiba's demand for revision of its fundamental character. An Ad Hoc Committee was appointed to work out the initiation of a new regime, and to examine the possibilities of adjusting the 20-year-old charter to new conditions facing the Arab world. Special emphasis was laid upon safeguarding the sovereignty of member states, and permitting the Maghreb to play its full part in the general concert of Arab international politics.

As if to prove to Bourguiba (and perhaps to themselves) that their decisions were not just pious wishes, or dim hopes for a distant future, the heads of state solemnly put their signatures on a document called a "solidarity pact." This could be considered the crown to Bourguiba's campaign to cut Nasser down to size and launch the League on a new road of emancipation from Cairo. The document, promulgated as an appendix to the Arab League's Charter, consists of six points, and stipulates:

1. Respect for existent regimes and non-interference in the internal affairs of any of the Arab League countries;
2. Non-encouragement of subversive movements regardless of whose they are or what they stand for;
3. Respect for international laws concerning the right of political asylum;
4. Revision of press laws and regulations in each of the Arab League countries, forbidding any polemics incompatible with Arab solidarity;
5. Solidarity in the service of the Arab nation and, in particular, as far as Palestine is concerned;
6. A pledge to put their press in the service of the cause of Palestine.

Another committee was appointed to revise the League Charter itself—to prepare material and proposals for discussion at the fourth summit, to be held in Algiers in September 1966.

On September 17, 1965, a final communiqué was published, containing the resolutions adopted at the conference.

After the resolutions and Solidarity Pact had been solemnly signed and the communiqué published, most of the participants thought they had witnessed an epoch-making event. They felt that the conference was a benchmark in inter-Arab relations.

Reaction in the Arab world was enthusiastic. *L'Opinion* (Rabat) called the meeting "an undeniable success that marks a new epoch in the annals of Arab League conferences." *El Moudjahid* (Algiers) said that, "for identical positions toward the great international problems . . . the declarations published at Casablanca . . . can be considered a victory of the Arab Nation. . . . This time, there were no cardinal decisions . . . no revolutionary or radical measures, but a new spirit and a realistic approach to problems."

Jeune Afrique called attention to the important role played by Morocco and Algeria at the summit. The plan outlined by King Hassan II of Morocco in his opening address, which treated the Arab Solidarity Pact and the Palestine problem, was accepted with little revision: The Moroccan success "calls attention to the growing importance of the Maghreb in the Arab world. . . . The third summit . . . was undeniably marked by the imprint of the Maghreb," and expressed the desire of the Maghreb peoples to achieve equal standing with the Arab East. Furthermore, *Jeune Afrique* attributed the realism and concern with the non-Arab world, which characterized the Casablanca conference, to the influence of the Maghreb.

Observers and participants alike regarded the promulgation of the Solidarity Pact—a document sanctified as quasi-equal with the Charter of the League and indeed in certain respects superseding it —as a complete vindication of Bourguiba and a victory in his contest with Nasser. Would he yield to the entreaties of moderate Arab leaders and sign the Pact?

Some delegates insisted he certainly should. One Foreign Minister participating in the conference exclaimed: "Times have changed. We have seen the end of the era when President Nasser could wave his magic wand of revolution and disrupt government and society in another Arab State." If that was the case, there was every reason for Bourguiba to congratulate himself upon victory.

But was it the case? How did Bourguiba view these developments? We shall deal with these questions later; at this time, it is sufficient that observers had the impression that President Nasser had actually made up his mind to mend his ways. By putting his signature on the Solidarity Pact he solemnly pledged to inaugurate a new policy *vis-à-vis* the other Arab countries—a policy of disengagement and not of interference, subversion, hegemony, and domination.

Some thought he had done it under the impact of the many disappointments his previous aggressive policy had recently brought. There was the tragedy of the Yemen, where his 50,000 troops were bogged down without any prospect of victory, or even of a face-saving retreat. Then there were the overthrow of his closest friend in the League, his disciple and admirer, Ben Bella; and the disintegration of the union with Syria which had originally created the "United Arab Republic." The regimes which he had tried to overthrow by subversion—Jordan, Saudi Arabia, and the Lebanon, not to speak of Tunisia—somehow were now stronger, more coherent, and more firmly solidified. The Sudan, which he hoped—as indeed had Farouk before him—to incorporate into Egypt through some kind of federation, not only defected the union agreement, but was now itself beset by internal secession. In addition, Egypt's economic and political situation was so troubled that Nasser had to worry about his own survival.

Some observers thought he had more to gain from the non-interference clauses of the Solidarity Pact than the other signatories. Bashir ben Yahmed, the editor of *Jeune Afrique,* suggested somewhat different reasons for the amazing change in Nasser's position:

> Imagine an Egypt which had chosen as her vocation not Arabism but Africa and the Mediterranean. The whole situation in the Middle East would have been different. Or else imagine an Egypt which had wanted to be Egyptian, preoccupied mainly with her own industrialization, and had been satisfied with flexible cooperation from the Arab world. She would then, whatever Nasser may think, probably have won more credit and evoked more response.

One thing is clear: the Pact constitutes a major concession on his part since it meant an abdication of his role as mentor of the "whole Arab nation," and its guide to socialism and unity. It indicated that he renounced all revolutionary activities in the "reactionary" Arab countries, and desisted from supporting therein opposition groups which often had Cairo as their base of operations and refuge.

Participants and observers alike believed Nasser deferred even the struggle with Israel in favor of his own country's economic and social progress, and the building of responsible Arab influence on the world scene. His new concept of the Arab world, they thought, was now the free association of states rather than of socialist governments brought into power by subversive means.

Opposition groups attached special significance to the Solidarity Pact, proclaiming it "the capitulation of Nasserite Egypt before the reactionary forces represented in the midst of the summit." Some Arab governments—Morocco, for instance—immediately used the document as a pretext to introduce or reinforce censorship of the press. And a spokesman of the opposition in one of the Arab countries declared:

> In the name of Arab solidarity and of martyrized Palestine, several Arab countries will probably not hesitate to restrict the freedom of the press in all fields of public life. Forced by the difficult situation which he faces in Egypt, Nasser unfortunately gave his sanction to political measures to be taken inside the various Arab countries against those forces which are ideologically closest to him.

These are the irreconcilable contradictions of pan-Arabism.

Signatory or not, is any leader always in a position to control the lieutenants who claim to work in his name, and for whose ideals he is the identifiable champion? The real test is whether the forces he unleashes take on a life and momntum of their own. For example, at the very moment Nasser was vowing not to interfere in the affairs of any other state, news reached the summit of a new though aborted coup to overthrow the government of Marshal Abdul Salom Aref, while the Iraqi chief was at Casablanca. The coup was attempted by the pro-Nasserite Prime Minister, General Aref Abdel Razzek, but was thwarted by General Abdul-Rahman Aref, the chief of staff who was the Marshal's brother.

Nasser was extremely embarrassed; he disclaimed any knowledge of, let alone complicity in, the plot, and in the literal and immediate sense this was probably true. But he could not escape the responsibility for having set in motion the forces of subversion and conspiracy in the name of pan-Arabism.

Ironically, the plot became known in Casablanca, exactly when Nasser and Marshal Aref were exhibiting perfect cordiality and friendship. So Brother Nasser professed his innocence of the coup; and Brother Aref, the victim, tried to minimize the whole thing. Nevertheless, the perfidious Iraqi Prime Minister and his confederates, who included the chief of national security and other high-ranking officers, escaped and made their way to Cairo. The Aref entourage announced that the plotting Prime Minister had landed there not to ask asylum but "to inform the Egyptian government about the regrettable events which had just taken place in Iraq."*

As concrete evidence of good faith immediately upon promulgation of the Solidarity Pact, all the Arab radios, press, and other propaganda organs put a sudden and complete stop to inter-Arab polemics. The incendiary fulminations so typical of the Arab radio networks and press gave place to courteous dissertations about Arab solidarity. The newspapers began to write in the tone of the Western press: matter-of-fact reporting and businesslike commentaries. The lull did not last too long.

---

* Marshal Aref died mysteriously in a helicopter crash on April 13, 1966. Many suspected at the time that it was no accident but an act of sabotage. His older brother became Chief of State on April 16, 1966. Razzak returned from asylum in Egypt and tried another coup against the new Iraqi President. He failed again.

After the third summit ended and euphoria had settled over the
Arab world, the conflict between Bourguiba and the Arab League,
some thought, had come to an end. Were not some of Bourguiba's
fundamental demands fulfilled?

Bourguiba's friends at the summit thought they had gotten for
him almost everything he had fought for. No resolution was promulgated against him or his proposals. On the contrary, the resolutions which were adopted were consistent with his philosophy
and his demands. To the charter of the Arab League was attached
the solemn Solidarity Pact which stripped Nasser of any prerogative to interfere in, let alone dictate, the policies of other Arab
states. And Nasser himself had seemingly presided over his de-
thronement. The Palestine problem was placed in a new perspective, in the light of the realities of world politics and power
relations. What more could he have been offered to make him
feel gratified with his short but intensive campaign?

Bourguiba saw the documents (in advance), and complimented
his friends at the summit, but he would not affix his signature; nor
would he consider returning to the Arab League. Why?

Many fine resolutions are an escape from the real problems
rather than a bold confrontation of them. The Solidarity Pact is
a contradiction in terms: simultaneously it proclaims solidarity
and non-interference. Can these two really coexist, especially in
the climate of inter-Arab politics? For non-interference implies
freedom of action and policy-shaping for *each* member state of the
League; full freedom is incompatible with solidarity.

When he started on his campaign, Bourguiba fought, not for
Arab solidarity, but for the right of Tunisia—and by the same
token, of any other single Arab state, including Egypt—to express
independent opinions, and when necessary to follow an independent course in its own best interests. These interests do not necessarily bring conflict between one Arab state and another, for at the
many points where their interests converge, there is natural and
true solidarity. But at every contact, independence must be explicit, and solidarity cannot be a pretext for straitjacketing the
individual states. Bourguiba saw the Pact's inherent contradiction,
and would not fall for it.

Apart from the Solidarity Pact with its built-in contradiction,
the summit remained as immobilized and impotent on the Israel-
Arab conflict as ever; it merely avoided the breaking up of the
League on that rock. Instead of bringing the conflicting plans to

some conclusion, it left them unsolved, and relegated everything to the blind and obscure future.

Bourguiba had undertaken his initiative in Jerusalem as a rebellion against this immobility, this fatalistic attitude. He had been pointing out for the last several months that the Palestine tragedy could not remain in *status quo*. It was criminal to treat human beings (the refugees) as playthings, and delude them with false hopes, while actually perpetuating their misery. Surely, he was saying, the Palestine situation will not be solved by an anonymous future; so those with the fate of the Palestinian Arabs at heart should undertake realistic steps to solve their problems and bring the tragedy to an end. But action must be undertaken now! Stop using all the verbs in Arab rhetoric in the future tense!

He had suggested a plan. That plan was totally ignored at the summit, in favor of a text which the writers intended to be all things to all men. Bourguiba reiterated his complaint: not that the text of the Arab League charter was bad, but that Nasser was continually violating the charter. Hence what he demanded was not just a revision of the charter but a change of attitude.

Mongi Slim, Tunisia's observer in Casablanca, explained:

> It is not a matter of texts, but of the spirit in which they are applied. The Arab leaders must change their mentality, which prevents any frank discussion and leads to the excommunication of anyone found guilty of expressing a non-conformist opinion— whether the opinion is well founded or not. President Bourguiba was accused by President Nasser of treason, of complicity with the imperialists, though he only expressed openly what Nasser says privately.

Is there any sign, let alone guarantee, that this mentality has changed? How many pacts of friendship and solidarity have been signed and solemnly sworn to in the past? In how many cases had the mutual recriminations and calumnies started again before the signatures were dry? From what we know of his opinions, Bourguiba would expect more than a written pact before returning to the fold. There must be authoritative pronouncements that the attacks on him were unjust, and a free public discussion of the Palestine question in the spirit of his demands. Not necessarily their acceptance; but there must be genuine debate on the merits —not name-calling.

As to the League, he demanded not so much charter revision as

practical administrative reforms. Its seat should be removed from
Cairo, and the Secretary General be a non-Egyptian, and one who
is freed from Egyptian tutelage. Short of this, no texts, no promises, no pacts or signatures would do.

Events have proven his case. The Arab leaders soon relapsed
into their old habits and "the unified nation" became once more
torn as bitterly and passionately as ever with the name-calling
supplemented by open threats of warfare and conquest. Ideology
is the supreme divisive factor; more than ever Nasser sees himself
as champion of the pan-Arab revolution against feudalists, re-
actionaries, and lackeys of neo-colonialism and imperialism. As to
Bourguiba—Nasser's latest comment is that he is a criminal and a
murderer. One month before the war in June 1967 he referred to
him as "Bourguiba the imbecile."

Victory is many things to many people. There are infinite varie-
ties of victory—as of defeat; there is often victory in defeat; and
there is Pyrrhic victory. In the contest between the two Arab
leaders, we can call Bourguiba's emergence "victorious," if our
use of the adjective is relative.

First, we must define the difference between Bourguiba's strategic objective, and his diversionary tactics. If his main purpose
was peace in the Middle East, then victory has so far eluded him
—though he scored the few local and tactical successes we have
reported.

But that was not the main objective of his campaign. His aims
were, first to challenge Nasser's leadership; second, to wreck his
fortress, which is pan-Arabism; and third, to neutralize his arsenal
of secret weapons—the Palestine issue. If we consider these three
as his composite goal, we can pinpoint distinct progress along the
road to victory. His position now seems far stronger, and his opponent's much weaker.

Bourguiba did achieve "little victories"—one might say vindica-
tions—in four successive conferences of the Arab League. First,
at the Cairo conference in March 1965, he succeeded in preventing
adoption of a resolution to recognize East Germany; he also
thwarted Nasser's attempt to have the conference unanimously
agree to break diplomatic relations with West Germany. (By the
Arab League charter, a resolution must be unanimous to be binding upon all member states.) Next, in April, the Cairo conference
of representatives of heads of state refused to censure Bourguiba
for his declarations on the Palestine issue. Then the Little Sum-

mit conference of heads of government (Cairo in May) ended with Nasser's complete reversal of policy concerning Israel; he was suddenly advocating indefinite postponement of the war against Israel whatever his true intentions were, and abandonment of the Jordan diversion scheme, as well as of commitments to aid another Arab country which might get into trouble with Israel. Finally, the summit conference of heads of state (Casablanca, September) ended with the Solidarity Pact, binding all Arab states (obviously above all Egypt) to desist from subversive or other unfriendly activities against members of the League. Simultaneously it was decided to reorganize and update the League to prevent its future use as an instrument of Egypt's aspirations.

In each of these, Nasser, for so many years the unchallenged champion and leader of the Arab world, lost ground. True, Bourguiba won each only by points and not by knockout. But Nasser was no longer the undisputed champion.

However valid the procedure may be elsewhere of making predictions based on past and present developments, in the Middle East the procedure calls for extreme caution; the usual logic of cause and effect does not necessarily apply. President Nasser has shown amazing agility in reversing the trend of events. He had frequently picked himself up with the agility of a fox.

But from Bourguiba's challenge to his authority and leadership, the Egyptian ruler emerged surprisingly shaken. Since the spring and summer of 1965 he has not been the same man; perhaps he never will be. He was plunged into a Sisyphean predicament of having pushed the great load of Arab unity nearly to the top, only to see it roll back again to the depths of turmoil and disarray. Can he push it up again? Does he still possess his youthful zest, his revolutionary determination? Will the Arab leaders fall in line again?

At that juncture—in the autumn of 1965—objective evidence showed that Nasser was still the key figure in the Middle East; he was supported by the great and otherwise unharmonious powers: U.S.S.R., the United States, and at times also France. (Their reasons are their own and have little to do with the Egyptian leader's merits or shortcomings.) Outwardly, the Egyptian people's enthusiasm remains undiminished, but to rely principally on the enthusiasm of regimented masses is a precarious business.

In the fall of 1966, Nasser seemed to have given up his ambition of uniting the Arabs by peaceful persuasion. He pronounced the end of the policy of the summits, and even of the summit conferences themselves. In his speeches celebrating the tenth anniversary of the nationalization of the Suez Canal he declared that he would not sit at the same conference tables with reactionary Arab leaders. He could not very well be alluding to Bourguiba as a reactionary; he was referring to the kings of Saudi Arabia and Jordan.

Instead, he declared, he would once more adopt what he called "revolutionary policies." This could only refer to his intention of subverting and overthrowing those reactionary regimes, as he had tried in the Yemen. This would be crass violation of the solemnly adopted "Declaration of Solidarity." It is a course full of peril. His effort in the Yemen has not been notable for its success. One thing is clear: Bourgiba's thesis that Arab unity is a myth has been amply vindicated.

10

Reactions in Israel

IN APPROACHING ISRAEL'S REACTIONS TO BOURGUIBA'S INITIATIVE,
we must keep in mind some basic considerations:

1. Bourguiba's declarations have been ambiguous and contradictory.

2. He is not a friend of Israel. If he is not an outright enemy,
he is, at all events, a protagonist of the Arab cause, and as such
sees in the very establishment of the State of Israel an injustice
to the Palestinian Arabs.

3. Israel is in a state of siege, surrounded on all land frontiers
by countries which openly proclaim their intent to liquidate it
as a state, and perhaps "throw its people into the sea."

4. All of Israel's options seem painful and risky. She is a little
country struggling for survival—and in the conviction of her
leaders and most of her people—has little if anything, to offer as
a price for peace.

Many readers will, no doubt, be more charitable than this writer
toward Israel's foreign policy and her reaction to Bourguiba's
initiative. But an effort is made here to summarize her difficulties
as objectively as possible.

Official Israeli reactions were reserved and confused. Bourguiba's statement in the Old City of Jerusalem was a surprise so
sensational that it threw the Israel government and almost all the
party leaderships off balance. Official policy had claimed there was
no possibility of an Israeli-Arab peace dialogue, because no Arab
leader would admit that the conflict might be resolved by peaceful
means. This was a comfortable attitude, because it absolved Israeli
policymakers of the need for hard thinking about a peace plan
of their own.

What is the use, ran the official Israeli argument, of offering a peaceful solution, if there is no one to offer it to? Peace can be born only through the dynamic process of dialogue; a unilaterally offered plan might be interpreted as weakness, and would in fact delay the day when a dialogue might be possible and meaningful. So each successive government of Israel has declared its willingness to negotiate for peace with Arab leaders at any time, anywhere, without preliminary conditions.

The Arabs, however, have never agreed to a peace conference. They say they would consider this tantamount to recognition of Israel, without any *quid pro quo*. It is not important here to assess the validity of the parties' attitudes; merely to summarize those attitudes.

Did Bourguiba's Old City statement change the attitude of the Israeli leaders?

An old folk song tells of a young man racking his brain as he tries to figure out what the girl meant when she said "No." The Israeli leaders, notably Foreign Minister Golda Meir, and the press, did a fantastic song and dance trying to figure out what Bourguiba meant when he said "Yes."

The Israelis had become so accustomed to hearing only abuse and threats of extermination, that when an Arab leader spoke in different terms they suspected a diabolical ruse. They were especially wary of the herald of this peace, Bourguiba.

Israelis were suspicious for good reason, if we consider Bourguiba's record. Often, in the past, he had given the impression of surpassing Nasser in anti-Israel utterances. As recently as September 1964, at the second summit of the Arab heads of state in Alexandria, he had declared:

> The Palestine problem is not only between Jews and Arabs; it is a problem of people whose fatherland has been taken by force of arms, and colonized with people from various exiles. There is no other link among all these Jews except their race and religion and their belief that what they suffered in Europe they are entitled to inflict upon the people of Palestine. Tunisia sees the Palestine problem in essence as no different from the Negro problem in South Africa. One cannot isolate it from the framework of the struggle against imperialism. Therefore we must prepare the Palestinian people for the struggle and put at its disposal all of the necessary means for its liberation. . . .

Earlier that year at the first Arab summit conference held in Cairo (January 16, 1964), he had delivered the most vehement anti-Israel speech. In it he declared, among other things:

> In solving the question of Palestine [I] would operate by constant harassment, trouble, and continuous pressure. This will develop into direct action with guerrilla warfare inside the country and political warfare from outside. These will aim at isolating Israel in the international arena and portraying her in a hateful manner before world public opinion.

Describing Bourguiba's role at that conference, the *London Economist* (March 20, 1965) summed up his ideas and attitudes:

> It was, in fact, President Bourguiba, supported by his Maghrebi neighbours, who inspired that first summit conference to treat Israel as a colonial problem—a problem to be dealt with as Tunisia and Algeria dealt with theirs. It was he who proposed a Palestinian liberation movement as the spearhead of an active struggle— an idea the Arab states seized on. . . . Thus, although he doubted the wisdom of diverting the Jordan headwaters, he has had quite a powerful influence on Arab policies over the past year.

At the same conference it was Nasser who took a moderate tone and warned the Arab leaders against acts of violence which would provoke fierce Israeli retaliation.

Several months later, in July 1964, at a summit conference of the Organization of African Unity, the Tunisian President delivered another vehement anti-Israel attack. The Arab leaders had thought that tactically and psychologically the head of a non-Middle Eastern State should expound the cause of Palestine at that conference. Bourguiba filled the bill perfectly. He was a renowned champion of national liberation, and a moderate; he accepted their request to dedicate his speech to the Palestine problem.

His was one of the strongest indictments against Israel ever delivered by an Arab spokesman. He referred to Israel as a "bandit state" and upbraided other African countries for maintaining friendly relations with it. He warned them against aiding "Israel's economic expansionism" and thus fostering growth of a state which is in essence "a phenomenon of colonialism."

Four years earlier, in New York, at a session of the United Nations Assembly, he had alleged that the plight of the Arabs in Israel was similar to that of the Jews in Nazi Germany; and **more** subtly, that the position of the Jews in Israel was paralleled by that of the French in Algeria before that country gained its independence.

In an interview in March 1964 with a representative of the Lebanese paper *Al-Yaum,* Bourguiba had attacked what he termed "Israeli colonialism" as a "cancer and scourge of that part of the world." Now that the Maghreb countries have achieved their independence, he said, they will help to free a sister-nation from the hold of of colonialism. "It is up to the Arabs, who themselves bear chief responsibility for the triumph of Israeli colonialism in Palestine, to uproot this cancer."

In likening Israeli colonialism to that of South Africa he declared that both seek to supplant the native population with a foreign minority. It is to be regretted that the majority of African nations who boycott the apartheid government in South Africa have failed to realize the identical nature of the two problems, he said.

He did not favor launching a war in the traditional sense; owing to various factors, of power relations both between Israel and the Arabs as well as between the U.S. and Russia, that would probably prove ineffectual. He would advise instead the adoption of commando tactics. Palestinians should provoke a constantly disturbed atmosphere to instill a state of insecurity in the enemy camp. Nor was this a mere pretext for evading war. "If the Arab leaders should unanimously vote in favor of war," he declared, "we would not hesitate to join them. We shall respect our engagements."

Needless to say, such utterances could be calculated to sound not only offensive but ominous to Israelis.

On Sunday, March 7, 1965, the day after President Bourguiba made his sensational statement in the Old City of Jerusalem, the Israel Cabinet held its weekly meeting. According to the Government Secretary who briefs the press after such meetings, Foreign Minister Golda Meir had declined to express her reactions, even in response to a question by a fellow Minister, until she had seen a full report of the statement.

Her answer was considered an evasion, and evoked some criticism in the Hebrew press. By the time of the meeting, Bourguiba's speech had been extensively covered on the Amman radio and in the press, and was certainly available to Mrs. Meir. The critics thought that if her answer was not an excuse for avoiding comment, she was at least strangely remiss in not familiarizing herself with it.

Yet, the *Jerusalem Post,* which usually reflected official policy of the Israel Government, printed the Cabinet meeting story along with reaction from "diplomatic sources in Jerusalem," (presumably foreign,) which described Bourguiba's speech as "very interesting, and a rare statment by an Arab leader. . . ." The sources noted that Bourguiba's remarks, considering where they were delivered, were a sign of personal courage.

A few days later in Paris, Mrs. Meir speaking to Eric Rouleau of *Le Monde,* continued her plea of ignorance. She also told him she "knows nothing at all about a peace plan formulated recently by Pierre Gemayel and published in *Le Monde.*" Yet this was in some respects a no less important event than Bourguiba's statement in the Old City of Jerusalem. In that plan, Gemayel, leader of the strongest political party in the Lebanon (the Christian Phalangist) suggested a solution to the Palestinian problem based on the principle of a binational state along the pattern of neighboring Lebanon—after the refugee problem had been solved by a free choice of the refugees, according to the resolution of the United Nations.

The Government of Israel and most political leaders were far from elated by Bourguiba's statement. With one sweep, it negated the Israeli argument that no Arab leader dared openly advocate a peaceful settlement, and it also required them to react publicly. It imposed on them an obligation to seek out the possibilities of give-and-take which might conceivably lead to peaceful settlement.

Not that the Israelis do not want peace—they do, passionately and genuinely. But they do not know what they can offer across a conference table, so they hope that somehow peace will come to them without their paying a price, or, in any event, not a very substantial one.

They are even bewildered and annoyed when told that peace *has* a price; that it is the result of a trading bout. They contend that they have nothing to give, and nothing should be asked of them. As far back as 1953 the first Israeli Foreign Minister, the late Moshe Sharett (whose political career suffered because of moderation), formulated this attitude in a Press Club speech in Washington:

We are often asked what are our peace conditions. There is but one condition—and nothing can be more simple and elementary. It is that we should be accepted and accepted *as we are*, with our territory, population, and unrestricted sovereignty. We seek no encroachment on the integrity or sovereignty of our neighbors, and are at a loss to understand how they can legitimately make such encroachments on us the condition of a settlement. . . .

Israel's policy has remained basically true to Sharett's pronouncements. The present Foreign Minister, Abba Eban, expressed the same attitude when he was Deputy Prime Minister, in an interview with the editor of the London *Quarterly Views* (Autumn 1965) : "The concept of paying a price for peace is, I think, an artificial concept. This is not something to be bought. . . ."

And in an interview with the London *Jewish Observer* (April 16, 1965), Eban remarked that of course there is danger in Bourguiba's initiative, because it may lead to misunderstanding the Israeli position:

> We want peace, of course, but our independence and integrity are prior interests. If there were a conflict between the idea of peace and the idea of Israeli independence and integrity, we should go on as we are now. . . . If Arab minds were able to make peace with Israel at all, they would be able to go a step further and make peace with Israel as it is: not with Israel as it was not and is not and will not be.

To go back to the plans formulated in the United Nations resolutions of 1947–1948, he said "would be just as feasible as to reconstruct the egg broken eighteen years ago." This metaphor became the cornerstone of Israel's reaction to Bourguiba's initiative. It was to be used by "responsible sources reflecting the official line" of the Israel government: by writers, reporters, speakers, and foreign correspondents for months to come.*

---

* When pressed very hard, Israeli official spokesmen hint at some practical offers, like a corridor through Israel between Egypt and Jordan and port facilities in Haifa. But under peaceful conditions these facilities and access would amount to little more than normal facilities granted as a matter of course by one state to another. The Arabs, rightly or wrongly, see in it a one-sided demand by Israel to be recognized by the Arab states, without solving the main problem, which in their view concerns the rights of the Palestinian Arabs.

In the ensuing debate over Bourguiba's initiative, an Israeli journalist, among many others, gave a candid and typical definition of his country's attitude:

> Whatever the world and many of our friends may think about the reasonableness of Bourguiba's proposals, as far as we are concerned the willingness of the Arabs to sit down with us at a conference table does not constitute any concession on their part. By doing this they would merely be coming to terms with reality. And for this we should not have 'to pay' anything.

The Israel Government would have liked to ignore Bourguiba's statement, but that was a luxury they could not afford. It was not just an isolated statement, but part of a well-planned, sustained campaign. The barrage continued in Beirut, in Paris, in New York, and in Tunisia itself.

The second obstacle to official disregard of Bourguiba's "peace offensive" was the sensation it created in Israel itself. The papers were full of it. Individuals and groups called special meetings in various cities and settlements to discuss and analyze its significance, and the government was asked to speak its mind. Some kind of official attitude obviously had to be formulated.

Perhaps even more compelling was the pressure which mounted in the world press, in whose headlines (often front page) Bourguiba remained for months. The newspapers and major TV networks in many countries reported his statements in detail (usually with sympathetic approval). As a result, there were even some stirrings in official American and French quarters.

The Israel government could not maintain silence.

The big problem was how to achieve the impossible: to say nothing, or nearly nothing, and make it seem like something; to appear to take a stand while avoiding taking a stand. The mental acrobatics and rhetorical legerdemain exhibited in the next few months were truly ingenious.

First the spokesmen said there was no reliable text available. Then, that the text was obscure and ambiguous, and one could not judge what Bourguiba actually had in mind. Next, that though Bourguiba's insistence that the Arabs would never solve the Palestine problem by war was a new and pleasant note, one swallow does not make a summer; it could be premature to welcome a bird which might change its plumage. Then, that Bourguiba is insincere, and really wants the obliteration of Israel; then, on the other hand that he is actually frank and accurate in proclaiming that his aims are like Nasser's, but that his methods are surer to achieve them.

Or, Bourguiba is not a major leader in the Arab world and his opinions have no weight in the Middle East. Again, he is as much Israel's sworn enemy as Nasser, but worse. He speaks not to Israel but to the Arabs. This is an Arab inner-family game and not our business. It would be dangerous for the government to speak out favorably because this might lull the Israeli public into a drowsy sense of security. After all, Bourguiba had done nothing but speak, and what value have words when the other Arabs act? Besides, what more can Israel say that she has been saying for seventeen years—that she longs for peace? Bourguiba knows all about Israel's yearning for peace, which is why he speaks only to the Arabs and not to her. Israel says nothing because she is doing things (a hint at some discreet contacts through intermediaries). The more she remains quiet, the more he will feel he must continue to talk; so let's keep our mouths shut and our ears open.

When Israeli officials finally broke their silence, they spoke out of both sides of their mouths. They were critical—even derogatory—at the same time that they admitted they could discern a positive element in Bourguiba's campaign. The press reflected this on-the-one-hand-on-the-other reasoning. "One should not forget," wrote the *Jerusalem Post,* that Bourguiba's peace offensive might be nothing but "a first step toward Israel's disappearance as an independent state. . . . One must be cautious, therefore, in treating with Bourguiba, but he is certainly a man with whom one can negotiate." (!)

Perhaps an even more telling comment is an editorial in *Lamerkhav,* the daily of the left-of-center Akhdut Avoda party, of March 8, 1965:

A Different Tune

The speech by Tunisia's president, Habib Bourguiba, in the Old City of Jerusalem, about Arab-Jewish cooperation and a possible solution to the Palestine problem, can be characterized by its vagueness rather than by its clarity, and by allusions rather than by anything definitive. Yet, what he said deserves to be listened to attentively, though it is still too early to see in his statement even a beginning of any change of attitude in the Arab world toward the State of Israel.

But the very fact that a well-known Moslem leader, the head of an Arab State, expressed his views on the Israel-Arab question in language so different from what we are accustomed to; language free from the well-known tone of hatred and sabre-rattling—constitutes in itself a positive element. One should also remember that this is not the first time a nonconformist voice has reached us from Tunisia. Not long ago the Tunisian *Jeune Afrique* published an article dealing with the problem of Israel-Arab relations in which it suggested that Israel be included in a Middle East Federation. Of course, in that article, as in Bourguiba's statement, there is not even the faintest starting-point from which to begin moving on the difficult and tortuous road toward peace, snice they do not contain even a hint of a realistic approach toward a practical solution. But they represent, even though indirectly, a recognition in principle at least of the existence of the State of Israel. . . .

The sensation of being besieged and the longing for peace are so acute in Israel that our ear is always eagerly perked to register any faint sound from the Arab camp implying a remote change from the prevailing hatred and belligerence. We must not, however, grasp prematurely (sic!) at any delusions. One swallow does not signify that spring is here, especially since we cannot yet state with any certainty that the voice we just heard is really one of a swallow. . . . Nonetheless, one must be tuned in to listen for any constructive note which is different from the usual tune, and must manifest constant willingness for a true peace, which recognizes the rights of both the Arab states and the state of Israel.

This editorial expressed a partisan attitude, but with some gradations it was a view shared by Israel's three independent nonparty dailies. Even the prestigious *Ha'aretz*, the only independent morning paper in Israel, at first exhibited the same mental convolutions and twists in its editorial of March 8. And the metaphor about the lone swallow was omnipresent. Here are two paragraphs of that editorial:

To the Israeli public, nervous as it is because of the growing tensions in the region, President Bourguiba's words about the possibility of "cooperation on the basis of mutual respect" between Arabs and Jews, were a pleasant surprise. . . . At his press conference in the Old City of Jerusalem President Bourguiba said many things which when voiced in Israel are taken for granted, but are tantamount to utter heresy when expressed publicly by Arab statesmen. We can therefore congratulate the Tunisian President not only on the wisdom contained in his statement, but also on the courage he demonstrated in addressing some unpopular truths openly and directly to Arab public opinion.

After this complimentary and appreciative opening, the editorialist analyzed the motives of President Bourguiba and Jordan's King Hussein in promulgating the statement in Jerusalem. He suggested that one motive might have been to reassure public opinion both in Israel and the United States, in order to pave the way for Jordan's forthcoming application for military assistance from America. The writer concluded:

> In this respect Bourguiba's statement at the press conference constitutes a difficulty for us. It will become harder to explain in friendly countries why Israel expects a "third round" (in the Israel-Arab war), at a time when the head of an Arab state who is the guest of another Arab state comes out with proclamations whose practical meaning is that the Israel-Arab conflict can be settled peaceably. There is, therefore, no doubt that as far as public opinion is concerned, our purpose must remain to emphasize the danger of undermining peace in our region. Unfortunately, President Bourguiba's point of view about Israel-Arab relationships is an oddity; the accepted opinions are those held by Nasser, Khafez, and Ben Bella. It is, consequently, preferable that we should not become prisoners of such delusions as the belief that summer is here because the first swallow appeared; and we'd better prevent public opinion in other countries, too, from becoming prisoner of the same delusions.

Another example typifying these mental gymnastics is an editorial from the newspaper *Davar* (March 8) officially the organ of the powerful Histadrut (trade union federation) but in fact the mouthpiece of the Mapai (Labor) party, which has thus far headed all successive governments of Israel. Minor omissions of no consequence have been made:

Bourguiba's Innovations

It would be a dangerous self-delusion to draw from the relatively moderate and very realistic pronouncement of Habib Bourguiba the conclusion that a change has come about in the attitude of the Arabs toward Israel. Even in the attitude of Bourguiba himself one should not draw such a conclusion, judging from what he has said. Nonetheless there is a positive innovation in the very fact that he found it necessary and possible to speak in a new tone concerning the relations between Jews and Arabs and the Palestine problem, especially when his words are meant to be publicized and were uttered in the Old City of Jerusalem in the presence of Arab journalists.

The analysis of the Tunisian President's statement does not justify any hope for a change in the relations. He did not say one word, gave not even a hint, which can be interpreted as accepting the sovereign existence of Israel as she is. He even referred to Israel as the enemy. . . . But the tone in which the Arab rulers speak on these matters—especially when their words are directed toward their own people and not for "export"—is usually so much more extreme that Bourguiba's negation of war and opposition to such slogans as "throwing the Jews into the sea," seems the epitome of moderation.

If in all this there were even a hint at a change in the Arab views, or even in the views of a part of the Arab leadership, the hopes for peace in the Middle East would be promising indeed. Much to our regret this is not the case. Even if Bourguiba's innovation in tone of speech were accepted [by the Arab leaders], it would constitute some progress in the desired direction. The continuous preaching of a confrontation with Israel immediately, or when the time is ripe, creates an atmosphere of hatred which in turn becomes a political factor. The leaders who incite the masses become prisoners of their own propaganda. We dare not hope that Bourguiba's boldness has created a precedent of using a new style.

These verbal twistings of Israel's initial reaction were quasi-universal—there were a few lonely exceptions. In succeeding weeks and months, however, Israeli reaction was to undergo considerable change, if not in essence, at least in style. But the changes, instead of clarifying, enhanced the confusion.

The first official reaction, short and still hesitant, came from Mrs. Golda Meir, then Foreign Minister. Appearing at the Press Club in Tel Aviv on March 12, she was asked by a journalist for her evaluation of Bourguiba's statement in Jerusalem. She said: "Certain things in the speech are impressive, and some are somewhat vague. But it is good to hear a voice that does not call for extermination. We must wait until we learn what the speaker meant."

This tendency to treat the Tunisian President's initiative lightly and with a note of sarcasm became typical of the first official line. In an interview with the editor of the *Jewish Observer* and *Middle East Review,* (April 16, 1965) Deputy Prime Minister Eban declared:

> To say that there will be no war is virtuous and accurate; but, after all, it is no more than an elementary statement of international citizenship. If someone were to say that he no longer proposes to murder me, I should react with interest but I would not recommend him for the Nobel Peace Prize.
>
> The trouble is that Arab propaganda has been so extreme that what should be a self-evident axiom becomes an act of political daring. . . .
>
> I do not think that Israelis should go overboard in their enthusiasm because Arab leaders condescend not to attempt our liquidation, which in any case they could not accomplish even if they wished.

The magazine's editor-in-chief, Jon Kimche, later wrote an editorial titled: "Thank You, Bourguiba—for Nothing!"

On another occasion, at a meeting in Tel Aviv, March 27, 1965, Eban explained to his audience that Bourguiba's statements so far were of no significance since they did not strike at the heart of the problem. The Tunisian had spoken about coexistence between people or communities, but not about states. Eban, therefore, appealed to his audience: "Let us gird ourselves with patience and see whether anything follows the first buds of wisdom; one swallow does not herald spring, especially since this swallow changes its tune daily."

Prime Minister Levi Eshkol himself was not openly sarcastic, but his first statement exemplified a certain folk wit. Speaking before the Tel Aviv Press Club on April 9, he said, in answer to a question:

> I am all ears for the somewhat refreshing note discernible in Bourguiba's statements, though one should not exaggerate in praise, "because of the evil eye." One must check and see what it is all about. It would perhaps be better not to rush out with drums and dances. Let us let him speak a few more times; perhaps he might even mention "the State of Israel" and not just "the Jews." Our too precipitate enthusiasm is also liable to do damage. He who is intelligent will understand what I mean. Yet under the surface there is also room for initiatives not necessarily of a public character.

And he concluded with the forthright statement that Bourguiba's initiative had revealed cracks in the wall of so-called pan-Arabism, which made it clear that this wall is not at all a fortress; this has great political significance, he added.

Because of the freshness of tone in Bourguiba's pronouncements, shapers of Israeli policy wanted the pleasure of hearing more and more of it without any commitment on their part. An Israeli writer explaining the reasons for Israel's reticence, wrote in all earnestness:

> His [Bourguiba's] speeches—although they have the appearance of a well thought-out campaign—may, for one, cease as suddenly as they started, leaving nothing but their memory.

As if he should keep on talking forever while the Israelis remain mute as long as it suits them!

There was also evasiveness in the Knesset. Mrs. Meir, in her address opening the important parliamentary debate over the budget of her office, (March 30, 1965) undertook an exhaustive survey of the government's foreign policy. It was a long and detailed speech touching all aspects of Israel's condition: in relation to the world, to the region, to the Arab neighbors, to Russia, to Germany, to Africa, to the Congo, to the United States, to France, etc., and to the tensions between East and West. In all that long review, she did not once refer to Bourguiba's initiative.

Mrs. Meir painted a somber picture. She warned against indulging in the illusion that any of the Arab countries had lessened the tensions or decreased their enmity toward Israel. This warning she voiced to Israelis, but even more forcefully to Israel's friends. "The Arabs' basic purpose which is the annihilation of Israel remains unchanged," she said. To the extent that there seems to be a discernible change, it is "only in tactics, not in purpose." Since the efforts to destroy Israel immediately had been frustrated, "the Arab rulers have begun long-range planning to build up [military] forces to overcome Israel at a later time. This change to long-range planning may foster the dangerous delusion among our friends outside this region that there has been some change in the basic aim of the Arabs toward Israel."

In the ensuing debate, several speakers from the left, notably Barzilay of *Mapam,* expressed amazement that Mrs. Meir did not find it important to comment on the Tunisian President's campaign.

It was only then, with the issue thrust upon her by political opponents, that the Foreign Minister gave any notice to the bombshell that was reverberating in all the world's news media. The notice she gave it was to plead ignorance once more of the meaning of what had occurred.

Israel, she said, must "still wait and see what Bourguiba really meant, and whether he has any concrete proposals. I say—and I am not ashamed of saying it—that I don't know. I also dare say there is not one member in this House who does know. . . . I challenge anyone in the Knesset to stand up and tell us what Bourguiba proposes as a solution to the Arab-Israeli conflict."

Then she repeated her statement of March 12 before the Press Club in Tel Aviv and quoted another statement she said she made on March 25:*

> The very fact that an Arab leader, and a celebrated one, said such things on the soil of an Arab state with so much courage and logic, is worthy of congratulations, and one must recognize its great importance. We have to pray that other Arab leaders follow in his footsteps and reach at least the same logical conclusion, and that they too, have the courage to tell their peoples that the time has come to adopt a constructive course instead of the one of destruction which they now follow. . . .

So far, her attitude was sober and dignified, though still avoiding any meaningful stand. But having finished quoting herself from abroad, she lapsed into domestic banter. Turning to Barzilay she said:

> Member of the Knesset Barzilay, what do you want us to do?

---

* There is no record of a statement of March 25. She may have been referring to a press conference in Paris on March 16, or to an interview with *Le Monde's* Eric Rouleau published March 17. At that time she had been in Paris to win support for Israel's request for closer relations with the European Common Market. Hence she probably felt she had to be more thoughtful in her declarations.

At the March 16 press conference in Paris she had said in answer to questions: "Bourguiba's statements served the interests of the whole region and not only of Israel. He preaches in the interests of the Arabs, and on this last aspect I cannot but express approval. Were similar voices heard more often, it would be very useful."

I shall propose to the Government that you go to see Bourguiba, or that you bring him here, or an emissary of his, or that you go and negotiate with him in his country, a peace settlement between Israel and the Arabs.

As it happened, Barzilay, in his capacity of Vice-Chairman of the Knesset, was temporarily in the chair and could not, therefore, reply. Another *Mapam* member, Victor Shem-Tov, shouted from his seat: "Why don't you propose a constructive plan to Bourguiba?" Mrs. Meir retorted: "You know what, Shem-Tov? I'll send you to Bourguiba on behalf of the Government instead of Barzilay, or you will bring him here. . . ."

Some dissidents bitterly commented that Mrs. Meir even went so far as to authorize a visa for Bourguiba, in case he should apply.

Unfortunately this informal exchange among old-timers in the Israeli parliament was taken seriously in some segments of the Western press; in the Arab world it created violent commotion. For a time there were rumors that Bourguiba had been invited to Israel, and vigorous denials of the rumors.

It is even more significant that for almost three weeks the Tunisian authorities refused to respond at all to inquiries concerning an invitation, actual or hypothetical, to come to Israel and discuss the Palestine problem. It is not that they refused to dignify such a notion by a reply, even in the negative. It was that no formula had yet been devised for even coping with the question. Only on the eve of Bourguiba's speech in Carthage (of April 21, 1965) did Tunisian officials finally declare that such a visit had never even been under consideration.

The Israeli trend of thought is clear. It encompasses three intentions: 1) to placate Israel's friends and Western public opinion by acknowledging that it was nice of an Arab leader to desist from a policy aiming at the destruction of Israel; 2) at the same time to minimize the importance of Bourguiba's initiative, and 3) to deny that in fact this initiative contained anything requiring reaction by Israel.

The peace initiative was a matter for the Arabs to discuss among themselves; when they agreed on a proposal, perhaps Israel might have something to say. The rest of Mrs. Meir's response was an elaboration of this third point. Israel could add nothing more to what it was doing to promote peace in the region. "Is it right and just and useful to preach peace to us?" Mrs. Meir asked. "Is a war on the part of Israel to be feared?" she asked. But almost in the same breath she threatened that if the Arabs should insist on the diversion of the Jordan headwaters, Israel would have no choice but to prevent it by all possible means.

On the whole the leaders of Israel were not happy about Bourguiba's undertaking. They were fearful lest Bourguiba's campaign weaken the willingness of Israel's Western friends to extend military assistance to her. It was well known that the Arab countries were growing progressively stronger militarily, and Israelis reasoned that as long as the Arabs were united in aiming at the liquidation of Israel, the Western powers could not stand idly by; they *must* help Israel retain and increase her military deterrent and defense. But if there came a real or seeming *détente,* the West might feel that the danger was no longer imminent, and lessen military aid to Israel. The United States particularly might prefer this to speeding up the arms race in the Middle East. It has always been embarrassing for the Western powers to appear in Arab eyes as the military providers for Israel.

Others sharing this fear of cutbacks in military aid advanced an additional conjecture: King Hussein had recently asked the United States to assist him in reconstructing his forces with newer types of weaponry. Israel protested strongly that this would impair her security. In view of this, so the reasoning went, Hussein was seeking to demonstrate to the Americans through Bourguiba that he had no aggressive intentions against Israel. That might temper Israeli protests and allay possible American scruples.

It was even conjectured that the scope of this conspiracy was much larger and that even the U.S.S.R. played a part in it. Bourguiba's speech came almost simultaneously with a statement by the Soviet Ambassador reflecting the desirability of improving Russian-Israeli relations. This suggested to some that Moscow had advised the Arabs to voice a desire for peace, and thus help forestall further United States penetration into the Middle East under the guise of helping Israel withstand an attack by her Arab neighbors.

Was this a Machiavellian conspiracy among Bourguiba, Nasser, Hussein, and others to place Israel on the horns of a dilemma: a) accept negotiations and test the Arabs' intentions, or b) reject Bourguiba's initiative *a priori,* and alienate world public opinion.

That the second horn—poisoning public opinion—was in Bourguiba's mind might seem implied by his own follow-up statements.

Might not an alienated or divided public opinion weaken Israel's fighting spirit? As long as the Arabs speak and act as open enemies, the nation remains united in its determination to overcome all difficulties and defend to the utmost its vital interests. But an Arab thrust toward peace might adversely affect this national *esprit*.

But above all, the Israeli government and the leading press organs were haunted by the idea that Bourguiba's intent might be solely to bring about the dissolution of Israel piecemeal—by means other than war. As Amos Ben-Vered, an Israeli writer, put it:

> Bourguiba's aim may be to obtain concessions from Israel in exchange for the Arabs' willingness to do no more than talk with her. If that is the case, every word in reply would have to be carefully weighed and every move doubly guarded so as not to fall into a trap baited with good will. (*Jewish Observer*, April 30, 1965)

Another Zionist writer expressed the same trend of thought, quoting a familiar Arab story:

> A hunter went killing sparrows one cold day. As he carried on the slaughter his eyes were streaming. Said one bird to another, "Look at that man crying." Said the second, "Never mind his tears, watch his hands." Bourguiba has made no attempt to hide his fingers on the trigger. He has made no claims that his policy would benefit Israel other than that its rump would be accepted by the Arabs and allowed to co-exist. Hence, [I do not] think it is warranted 'to fall around Bourguiba's neck and hail him. . . .'

Bourguiba's initiative had, therefore, to be regarded as a trap, his real aim as the destruction or liquidation of Israel by means other than war. This is how the *Jerusalem Post*, which reflects Israeli official policy, put it:

> One should not forget that his real aim may indeed be the implementation of the Partition Plan and the disappearance (by dismemberment) of Israel in a federated Arab-Jewish state. Ob-

viously a political offensive, based on a demand for implementation of the United Nation Resolutions, would be more effective for the realization of this aim than a war which the Arabs cannot win. . . . One should never forget that he [Bourguiba] might have come to the conclusion that a "peace offensive" . . . might be a first step toward Israel's disappearance as an independent state.

A few weeks later, on June 3, Prime Minister Eshkol declared in the Knesset that the Arab leaders (putting Bourguiba in the same category with Nasser) who take a stand against war with Israel may have some surprises in reserve:

Keep in mind my advice: Don't attach too much importance to the so-called moderate Arab leaders. It can do more harm than good, especially since we do not yet know what these so-called moderate Arabs have in store for us.

Analyses by Israeli leaders and writers suffered from their simplistic, if not mechanical, test: Is he friend or foe? Are his intentions friendly or inimical? And, since they could not find in Bourguiba's declarations any expressions of friendship, they were disappointed and apprehensive.

Of course, such a method is faulty, and produces a distorted evaluation. In order to stand for peace, one has not necessarily to be a friend; by and large friends do not need to negotiate peace settlements. It is parties who are clearly not friends who must explore peace possibilities. The Israelis were disappointed that Bourguiba did not speak like a Zionist.

Of course, he is not a Zionist. He is not even a friend of Israel, but an advocate of the Arab cause, but he expressed willingness to explore possibilities of a compromise solution of the Palestine problem. He was not converted or brainwashed; he simply arrived at the conclusion that it might serve the interests of the Arabs if they should consider coming to terms with Israel—on certain conditions.

If the Israelis had been able to clarify in their own minds this simple analysis of the Tunisian's motivations, they might have better evaluated Bourguiba's campaign and arrived at more enlightened conclusions.

Paralleling their apprehensions, Israeli political analysts and government spokesmen expressed the self-serving view that Bourguiba's campaign proved how right Israel's policy of armed strength had been all along. Bourguiba's statements had not created a new situation, asserted Deputy Defense Minister Shimon Pares; rather, the reality of Israel's military strength had brought about Bourguiba's declarations. Where previously Israel's military might deterred the Arab leaders from any reckless attack on her, now one Arab leader had taken the next step and reasoned that the Israeli-Arab conflict could be solved by mutual agreement.

Bourguiba's point of departure, these spokesmen asserted, was that "pushing the Jews into the sea" was not possible because Israel was too strong; hence he was warning the Arabs to adopt a more realistic attitude. Therefore, if Israel's armed strength continued unabated, the other Arab leaders would sooner or later recognize her as a fact of life with which they must come to terms. Mr. Peres figured that such a rapprochement would happen within ten or fifteen years. There is no better way, he claimed (and with him many political writers), to educate the Arab leaders toward reasonableness and realism than through the policy of strength.

Bourguiba's utterances, declared Deputy Prime Minister Eban, prove the success of Israel's policy of containment and deterrence over the years. We must be so manifestly strong as to make war remote from any realistic Arab mind.

In a speech in Boulder, Colorado (April 14, 1965), Michael Comay, Israel's chief delegate to the United Nations, declared that the central aim of Israel's long-range diplomacy was to convince the Arab countries that Israel is here to stay. Israel's main problem is, therefore, to avoid war through the vigilant upkeep of her military deterrent.

In a word, toughness pays; the slogan should remain: Peace through strength.

Whatever merit these arguments have in interpreting the motive or background of Bourguiba's initiative, they obviously do not constitute a stand on the substance of his proposals.

Thus, while the world news media were paying the utmost attention to the sustained campaign of the Tunisian leader and the Arab world was in turmoil, the Israel government persisted in its reluctance to express reaction. Nobody "in an official position wanted to discuss [the Bourguiba overture] publicly," cabled Granger Blair to *The New York Times* as late as April 24. A day earlier he had cabled: "The Israelis are reluctant to speak out favorably for the Bourguiba attitude for fear such a move might do more harm than good in bringing the two sides to the conference table."

To take a stand would have revealed the cornerstone of Israel's policy: Peace at no price. It would demonstrate that Israel was either unwilling or unable to concede anything, or to compromise. Yet, ignoring Bourguiba's initiative brought its own difficulties: Israel could be interpreted as cold-shouldering a proposal which friendly public opinion had approved, and as therefore not truly interested in peace. And to avoid completely taking a stand might breed the opposite danger: Silence might be misconstrued either as tacit agreement with Bourguiba's plan of entering negotiations on the basis of the UN resolutions, or as willingness to make substantial concessions to the refugees. Hence the government's conclusion: Israel must find a way of explaining away such possible suggestions and criticism, while maintaining that she was primarily interested in peace through negotiations—without positively committing herself to anything.

In this predicament Israel decided on a kind of a middle road. That was when the dialectic and political acrobatics became imperative. Both anonymous and identified officials began to issue obscure and evasive statements, usually without referring directly to Bourguiba. No single authoritative major policy statement was made by a responsible leader in a proper setting.

Instead there appeared enigmatic articles, as, for instance, the one in the widely circulated afternoon daily *Ma'ariv,* which included a so-called "statement" by the Prime Minister in answer to Bourguiba's Carthage speech. The article was signed by Yosseff Rakhif and appeared under the headline: "Eshkol Reacts to Bourguiba's Proposals: Ready to Negotiate Without Pre-conditions." Enigmatically, the story does not say when, where, to whom, and on what occasion the Premier made the statement. The text left unclear whether or not Eshkol's statements were made in an interview. There were no questions or answers. The words attributed to the Prime Minister were not in quotes, nor did they appear to be a paraphrase. It was not clear if parts of the story were from a statement by the Premier or by somebody else in the government, or were the reporter's own.

In that non-specified, half-anonymous interview-not-interview, the Prime Minister admitted that Bourguiba's initiative constituted an important contribution. He expressed satisfaction that the Neo-Destour Party supported its President officially; that Bourguiba's campaign revealed enlightened Arab circles to be sobering up to the realities; that he was ready at any time to begin negotiations with the Arabs, without any pre-conditions, except that the United Nations Resolutions do not constitute a basis for such negotiations: Bourguiba and his supporters must understand, however, that to say they recognize Israel's existence is not enough, for recognition must mean accepting Israel as it is now, and not as it was envisioned in 1947.

About the same time, *The New York Times'* Jerusalem correspondent summed up the anonymous Israel attitude in a dispatch:

> Israeli officials consider President Bourguiba's moderate pronouncements on Palestine significant, but they do not consider that . . . they constitute a break-through in the long quest for peace between Arab and Jew in the Middle East.

The only member of the government who spoke freely and frequently was the Deputy Prime Minister, Abba Eban. The Cabinet seemed to have placed him in charge of explaining the Israeli line; others were instructed to keep silent. But what he said was either negative or fundamentally irrelevant, hence discouraging. As *The New York Times* correspondent put it:

> In the only official Israel statement on the Tunisian leader's initiative, Deputy Premier Abba Eban rejected the old partition plan as "an egg broken eighteen years ago."
> And thus "whoever believes that the resolution passed eighteen years ago by the United Nations can be applied today shows a complete lack of realism."

Though each argument advanced by the Israelis had merit, the total impression was, as the Associated Press correspondent in Tel Aviv summed it up, that the Israeli reaction to Bourguiba's initiative was "frankly negative."

To get off the hook altogether, Mr. Eban used another argument: Bourguiba with his declarations and proposals was addressing himself not to Israel but to the Arabs:

> I . . . do not believe Bourguiba ever regarded himself as involved in a diplomatic dialogue with Israel. So far as we could

learn, his motives were to educate Arab opinion along a new course.*

This assumption is correct, but the conclusion that it was therefore not Israel's business to interfere in this inter-Arab dialogue is wrong. It is true that Bourguiba did not engage in an actual dialogue with Israel, but he must have expected Israeli leaders to try to accomplish among their people what he was attempting in such daring and dramatic manner among the Arabs "to educate opinion along a new course." This they dogmatically and persistently refused to do.

Another reason Israel need not feel too concerned with Bourguiba's initiative was expressed in an editorial of the *Jewish Observer* (which usually echoes and interprets Israeli official thinking) : "President Bourguiba's primary concern," we read, "is not whether the Arab countries can live in peaceful coexistence with Israel; it is whether Bourguiba, and other Arab leaders like him, can exist on equal terms with President Nasser. And Bourguiba's formulation of the questions shows clearly . . . that in his view such coexistence between Nasser and himself is no longer possible."

Such an appraisal may be perfectly legitimate. Yet why should it exclude the possibility of Bourguiba's simultaneous genuine concern with the Palestine Arabs, and his desire to see a constructive solution? It is amazing that from their largely correct analysis, the Israelis drew the incredible conclusion that Bourguiba's gambit was not their immediate concern.

Logic would dictate an opposite conclusion: Since Bourguiba's initiative was not one of sheer altruism or idealism, but deeply tied in with his own interests, its implications were more serious and its foundations more solid. Hence, there should have been points of common interest between Israel and Tunisia, with consequent concern and tolerant support of the Tunisian President's initiative.

Furthermore, a new prospect appears on the historic scene of the Middle East: if Bourguiba has demonstrated that a peaceful

---

* The same idea that Bourguiba had started a dialogue with the Arabs was expressed by Deputy Defense Minister Shimon Peres. In an address before a seminar of academicians in Tel Aviv, he declared: "Bourguiba fulfills a mission to the Arabs rather than to us, since the practical significance of his declarations is that he calls upon the Arab states to exchange for their military initiatives against Israel another initiative based upon greater political logic and upon a more moderate and sober view of the realities."

solution to the Palestine problem could serve Tunisia well, might not Nasser consider peace one of *his* options, a procedure he sometimes follows? Thus, with Israel's encouragement, new and hopeful trends might develop.

The Israeli spokesmen rationalized further. Not only was it not their business to interfere in inter-Arab polemics, but actually the less said by Israelis about Bourguiba's initiative, the better for him. Approval by an Israeli might symbolize the kiss of death for Bourguiba's campaign.

At a symposium of the daily Tel Aviv *Davar,* a member of the Knesset, Karmel, took sharp issue with this argument, and advocated an articulate, encouraging reaction by the Israeli government. The moderator of the symposium and assistant editor of *Davar,* Hannah Zemmer, interrupted him with "It may silence him [Bourguiba] altogether." Mr. Karmel retorted:

> The reasoning that a [favorable] declaration by us is liable to hurt Bourguiba is ridiculous. . . . Let us not worry about Bourguiba's welfare. What is liable to cost him his life is the words he utters, and not what we say in reaction to his statements. It was not we who prompted him to talk and it is not going to be we who will make him keep silent.

This tired old argument kept being reworked. Some Israeli writers thought that not only Israeli praise of Bourguiba's initiative would hurt him; they believed *any* approval by Western powers, especially the United States, would have the same effect. Thus, after Robert McCloskey, State Department press spokesman, commented favorably (though in the most moderate and general terms), editorials appeared in the Israel press deploring the American official's statement. They wailed that it could defeat the purpose of advancing peace in the Middle East. Such a statement, asserted Israeli writers, would vindicate the extremist Arab contention that Bourguiba was a stooge of American imperialism and that would surely have an adverse effect on Russia's relations with Israel.

> If we are to suppose [wrote Herzl Rosenblum, editor of *Yedyoth Akhronot,* in his column] that Russia still hesitates as to whom to back—Bourguiba . . . or Nasser . . . it is clear that the State Department's spokesman jumping on Bourguiba's wagon with such exhilaration is apt to push Russia even more into the

arms of Cairo; thus Washington will hurt not only us but also itself. . . .*

The argument that Bourguiba's initiative would be hurt by praising it is supposed to be a clever subtlety; it is in fact stupid and self-defeating. It is tantamount to telling the Arabs that the Israelis favor Bourguiba's proposals but prefer to keep their sympathy secret. Obviously there is no secret the moment the reason for the silence is publicly revealed; and there remains the false implication of a conspiracy, a secret cabal between the Israelis and Bourguiba to mislead the Arabs. This, of course, lends justification to the Arabs' worst fears.

Such a stupid posture, concealing one's position in important and vital international issues, is a hangover from the self-bedeviling and self-defeating diplomatic somersaults of past ages.

Though the Israeli Prime Minister and his Deputy refused to take a stand on Bourguiba's statements purportedly because he did not address himself to them, they still disputed him on every aspect of his proposals. Were those proposals, they demanded, explicit or implicit? Did they in fact involve no border changes, no refugees, no application of the United Nations resolutions, no federation, no nothing? This does not mean that Israel rejects the very idea of negotiations; on the contrary, negotiating with the Arabs is the major objective of her foreign policy. But her leaders insist that the negotiations begin with no pre-conditions, and with recognition of Israel's sovereignty and territorial integrity. Bourguiba's proposal begins with a pre-condition, and an utterly unacceptable one: application of the United Nations resolutions, which would truncate Israel, create an Arab State, establish enclaves, and return Arabs in larger numbers to present Israeli territory.

There is, of course, an inconsistency in the Israeli attitude. Their own demand for "no pre-conditions" is in effect a precondition. They define in advance what the basis should be, and what is and is not negotiable. Thus, Israel has not moved an inch from her fixed position, and the deadlock remains.

---

* Some of the most prestigious Western newspapers expressed the same view, i.e., that Israeli and American praise of Bourguiba would hurt his campaign at this stage. (*Le Monde,* April 25–26; *Manchester Guardian,* April 23.) Some political circles in Washington seem also to have shared this view.

In the first few days after the Carthage speech, the Israeli Foreign Office seems to have received numerous reports of intensive Tunisian diplomatic activity in Western Europe, the United States, North Africa, and the Far East; of the unprecedented interest Bourguiba's proposal had aroused in the world press and political circles; and of the widespread sympathy the Tunisian plan had evoked. On April 23, the U.S. State Department's spokesman "wholeheartedly welcomed" Bourguiba's initiative. That same day the major newspapers in the United States and Western Europe praised Bourguiba's initiative, his wisdom and courage, sounding like an orchestration of approval and felicitation on a broad international scale. On April 23, 24, and 25, laudatory editorials appeared in *The New York Times, The Washington Post, Manchester Guardian,* and *Le Monde,* among others.

Concurrently, unofficial news was widely circulated in Paris and abroad that de Gaulle had expressed private satisfaction with, and even admiration for Bourguiba's undertaking. (He was reported to have said the Tunisian President resembled him in that he too had a rendezvous with history.)

At precisely that time, Phillips Talbot, U.S. Assistant Secretary of State for Near Eastern and South Asian Affairs, stopped in Israel on his way to Washington from Egypt, and conferred with Premier Eshkol and Foreign Minister Meir. It was reported that in these discussions Mr. Talbot conveyed the feelings of his government about Bourguiba's initiative. It is, perhaps, reasonable to suppose that he also expressed his government's opinion that an unfavorable impression would be made by Israel's outright rejection of Bourguiba's proposals. The Israeli leaders, far from viewing Mr. Talbot's activities in the Middle Eastern capitals as helpful, on the contrary, grew apprehensive, feeling that they were facing a gathering storm.

Especially worried were Israeli diplomats abroad. In Paris where Israel has some of her best international friends, her representatives were given to understand, as tactfully as possible, that the brains back home had better come up with a constructive plan for meeting Bourguiba's peace offensive. In Paris, as in Washington, what counted first and foremost was that an Arab leader had spoken out for peace. His practical ideas were of less interest, since it is understood that an Arab patriot surely could not suggest a "Zionist" plan; this would be up to the Israelis, and thus far Israel had not done anything.

The Paris correspondent of *Ma'ariv* cabled his newspaper:

The statements by the Tunisian President concerning a solution to the Palestine problem are likely to create difficulties for the shapers of Israel's policy in Europe. No decision has yet been made setting a clear line of reaction to "the spirit of Bourguiba." That is what I have learned from well-informed circles here.

The official attitude indicated by Israeli representatives . . . is approximately the following: Bourguiba and Nasser are in essence after the same anti-Israel goal, except that Bourguiba's method is more dangerous for Israel, since, in contrast to Nasser, he hides his anti-Israeli intentions in peaceful declarations. . . .

An Israeli personality told me. 'It is not a simple thing to react to Bourguiba's statements. . . . We don't want to reject an initiative which in principle calls for peace in the region (of the Middle East). But . . . we are not going to fall for any plan, even Bourguiba's, which aims at Israel's strangulation.'

That the dilemma was not a figment, but uncomfortably real, is quite clear. Signs of it were discernible all over. The *London Economist* (May 1, 1965) pointed out, rather critically, that

the Israelis are unimaginative in affording the Bourguiba proposals no official reaction other than the old refrain that Arab refugees can be resettled only among their own people. Between taking back refugees to become a fifth column in a continuing cold war and reinstating some of them as part of a permanent settlement there is a clear distinction. If Israelis will not perceive it they could put themselves in the wrong. Already many of them believe that an Arab peace offensive could do them more harm than a military one. While the Arabs threaten war, the tide of world sympathy runs Israel's way; but if they persist in peace talk, Israel might start to look culpably intransigent in many eyes.

One of *Le Monde's* star correspondents, Jean Lacouture, competent and impartial observer of Middle Eastern affairs, remarked:

Perhaps, in fact, he (Bourguiba] is the one man for the Jewish State to dread. Certainly Israel has more cause to fear a comparatively restrained opponent with a record of getting things done than wild shouters whose policies have no chance of being put into practice.

Bourguiba is himself quite aware of it and expressed the same opinion quite frankly in his speech of April 21 before the Neo-Destourian students.

All this seems to have thrown the Israeli policymakers into a mood bordering on panic. The weekly meeting of the Cabinet held on Sunday, April 25, was mostly taken up with Bourguiba's move and with the question of what to do about it. To convey the prevailing confusion and disarray here is, in large part, the report that appeared next day in the independent and excellently informed daily *Ha'aretz*:

> The Cabinet yesterday dedicated considerable time in its political discussions to the declarations of Mr. Bourguiba, after Foreign Minister Golda Meir reviewed the latest activities of the Tunisian President and the reactions to them in the West and in the Arabic countries. . . . Among those who took part in the discussion were Prime Minister Levi Eshkol and Deputy Prime Minister Abba Eban.
>
> The Foreign Minister dwelt at length on the importance of the very event of Bourguiba's statements that it is necessary to come to terms with the fact of the existence of Israel; that war will not solve the Palestine problem, and that it is necessary to try to seek a solution by political means. This event in itself, even if it resulted from developments in the inner relationships among the Arab states, is an important watershed, which is susceptible in the distant future of bringing about desirable change in the region. . . .
>
> *However, simultaneously with all this, both the Foreign Minister in her review and the other ministers who participated in the debate expressed the opinion that in the long run there is hidden in Bourguiba's plan a great danger to the very existence of Israel* (Emphasis in the original text).
>
> The various data assembled since Mr. Bourguiba made his first declarations show that the Tunisian President's campaign is *a result of an internal controversy in the Arab world on the subject of how to bring about the liquidation of the State of Israel.* Till now the method of Nasser prevailed which aims at the elimination of Israel by military means through war. But Bourguiba argues in effect that this method has proven for the last 17 years to be ineffectual and would not lead to the elimination of Israel. *As against this Mr. Bourguiba offers a plan of his own, whose principle it is to use against Israel political means (in contrast to military means)—a plan which he terms 'a solution of the Palestine problem by phases.'* . . .
>
> The Arabs would, it is true, recognize Israel, but the scheme is based on the assumption that in the course of time it will be possible to *encroach upon Israel's sovereignty.* Already the sugges-

tions about the return of the refugees and the reversion to the Partition frontiers hint at the nature of the plan which includes the *preparation of the physical means to subvert the very sovereign existence of Israel*. Other data that reached Jerusalem hint also at a plan to integrate Israel within some kind of a regional set-up, and concerning this plan, too, apprehension was voiced. It tends to create conditions *which in the course of time would prepare the ground for encroachment upon Israel's sovereignty.*

As expressed at yesterday's Cabinet meeting, the danger in Mr. Bourguiba's plans is that "they look good" to the outside world and are thus liable to elicit a positive attitude in both the Western countries and Asia and Africa, while Nasser's plan to eliminate the State of Israel by military means does not win sympathetic ear or serious consideration in those countries.*

. . . Other opinions were also expressed at yesterday's Cabinet meeting. These suggested that perhaps there is in Mr. Bourguiba's statement something of a turning point, which will . . . bring about a constructive solution to other problems of the region on the basis of coming to terms with the existence of Israel. Perhaps Mr. Bourguiba represents even other Arab leaders who reason as he does.

Besides these positive and negative considerations aired at the meeting, the Cabinet did not arrive at defining a final stand, but it was agreed that Israel had to be alert to the coming developments around Mr. Bourguiba's declarations; to follow events and counter them with a campaign to make clear Israel's position against a return of the refugees and a revision to the Partition boundaries; nevertheless to make use of the possibilities to advance the basic principle of Mr. Bourguiba's plan that the problems must be settled by means of negotiations, that is, if in the course of time such possibilities appear.

In the last account, the reason for the bewilderment and confusion of the Israelis in the face of Bourguiba's challenge can be summed up: He offered a single package containing two elements. One of the Israelis liked: recognition of Israel and peaceful coexistence. The other, they disliked—they were afraid of even the thought of it: that peace would have to be negotiated on the basis of mutual concessions. They would have liked very much to have the one without the other. Was it possible? Will it eventually be possible? They hope so.

---

* In a speech briefing the members of the Central Committee of the dominant Mapai party, Mrs. Meir expressed the same apprehensions of the inherent dangers of Bourguiba's proposals.

The analysis by the Foreign Minister and members of the Cabinet is not just that of a group of frightened and bewildered people. Their analysis of each aspect, it must be admitted, has merit and is at least partially correct. For Bourguiba's proposals and explanations are usually couched in terms ambiguous and sometimes ominous for Israel.

More baffling is their apparent mental helplessness and lack of initiative or counter-plan. The government's position appears totally negative; or at least passive. Israeli policymakers have tragically revealed themselves to be objects of currents and events, without aspiring to create currents of their own in the struggle for peace.

The Israelis are not unaware of the danger that their position might in the long run prove untenable in the eyes of world public opinion. They argue, however, that it is not *their* policy which is peculiar, but the conditions to which it is a reaction. Israel, they say, finds itself in a condition unparalleled anywhere in the world. It is the only state whose very survival is threatened by its neighbors' passionate determination to push its people "into the sea." That is why Israel can exist and develop only by the strength of its own military power and human resources; and this unflagging strength provides the only deterrent to the Arabs' military adventures. Any sign of compromise by Israel, let alone an actual concession, could prove fatal. This Israeli policy is generally understood, if not always appreciated, by the world under the existing state of affairs. But the Israelis feared Bourguiba might throw the whole structure out of kilter.

Here is an Arab leader who is fundamentally opposed to a policy of "throwing the Jews into the sea"; he, in fact, does not believe it possible. He offers to engage in discussions to bring the conflict to a peaceful settlement. For official Israel, this initiative brought anxiety lest the world be caught in a trap of enchantment by Bourguiba's seeming moderation, good sense, and love for peace. Friendly governments would begin asking questions. It might prove difficult to convince friends and neutrals that Israel must reject Bourguiba's suggestions *a priori*. It would surely be embarrassing if Israel had to refuse even to discuss a scheme which sounded to unsuspecting ears like a peace proposal.

But the Israelis did not have to worry too long. They were rescued (they believe) by—the Arabs. For it soon became clear that

Arab reaction to Bourguiba's initiative was definitely negative, and Israel heaved a sigh of relief.

An Israeli journalist expressed this relief in the most candid terms:

> Once again Israel has been rescued from a delicate situation thanks to lack of political astuteness of the Arab leaders . . . who are most concerned with the Palestine problem and have rejected Bourguiba's proposals. It is good for us to have these proposals rejected by the Arabs and not by Israel. . . . Had the Arabs accepted them they would have appeared as "realists" and "peace-loving" people, . . . and we would have had the onus of scuttling "the peace efforts." This might seem an easy task to those who do not realize that adherence to the Partition resolution and the return of the Arab refugees would be tantamount to Israel's suicide.
>
> The Western enthusiasm for Bourguiba's proposals underscores the bad political predicament in which we would have found ourselves if it suddenly became clear that Israel's refusal to engage in conversations on the basis of Bourguiba's proposals constituted the only stumbling block on the road to peace negotiations. (Ariel Ghinay, *Yedyot Akhronot*, April 26, 1965)

There is plausibility to the argument that Bourguiba's peace campaign might prove more dangerous to Israel than the Arabs' open threats. But the danger is not so much in Bourguiba's cunning as in Israel's own line of thinking that rules out compromise. If Israel's inflexible attitude is taken seriously by world public opinion, it will be interpreted (rightly or wrongly) as Israel's disinterest in achieving peace with her neighbors by mutual concessions.

It was intimated that by May, Prime Minister Eshkol would make a major statement containing a substantive and definitive answer to Bourguiba's proposals. It was also predicted that Eshkol would offer the nation, Arab neighbors, and the world a peace proposal of his own. Such a statement was indeed devilvered at the opening summer session of the Knesset on May 17. Almost all the papers in Israel published it under some such headline as "Israel's Peace Plan." Though the address purported to be a direct answer to the Tunisian President's proposals, it did not mention Bourguiba by name. It referred to him in the plural and anonymously:

Voices have been heard—as is well known—rejecting the idea of war, openly calling for a settlement, for peace, for coexistence.

As far as I am concerned, I believe that these manifestations are not isolated exceptions. . . . We are justified in assuming that among the Arab public, and even among the political leadership, there are still thinking men who accept in their hearts the inevitability of coexistence. . . . If we try to sum up our peace plan . . . let us say first of all that its foundation is full respect for the independence, sovereignty, and territorial integrity of all states in the region. . . .

Peace will be established on the basis of Israel as it is. . . . There may indeed be minor, mutually agreed upon, adjustments at certain points where there are hindrances to the daily life of the population. But this is the rule: peace comes to change relations between states, but not the states themselves. . . .

First of all, this applies to the express obligation to refrain from all aggression. We warn against the aggressiveness of certain Arab rulers, and we can point to threats and planning for aggression on their side. On the other hand, any Arab who proclaims his fear of aggression on our part is only a victim of propaganda. . . . Let there be *mutual* undertaking to refrain from aggression.

Israel lies on the crossroads between Asia and Africa. If the entire region becomes an open area, dedicated to cooperation and mutual assistance, that will be a blessing to the peoples of both continents, and among them, ourselves and the Arab States.

Orderly transport by road and rail; freedom of transit through airports; radio, telephone, and postal communications; access to our ports on the Mediterranean in the form if a free area, under suitable conditions, for the benefit of Jordan, which has no outlet to the sea; facilities for the sale of oil through the revival of the oil pipeline or the building of larger ones; the encouragement of tourism in all countries of the area, free access to the Holy Places, with facilities for religious pilgrimages to centers sacred to all religions—all these are only part of the picture that will take shape as the outcome of the liberation of the Middle East from the oppressive atmosphere that prevails at present.

Orderly processes of trade will be instituted; patterns of economic cooperation will be worked out on the basis of the experience acquired in other parts of the world. There is room for the joint exploitation of raw materials through extraction and marketing, for joint research on the problem of water desalination, which engages some of the countries in the area.

Let us work together for the fructification of the arid areas; let us cooperate in conquering disease, in medical and agricultural research; let us strive side by side for the exploitation of the new sources of energy, for mutual scientific and cultural fertilization, in the broadest terms. . . .

A climate of negotiation for peace will of course enable us to act together to restrain the arms race and cut down armaments in the region.

All the states in the area can only benefit from reliable arrangements for the limitation of armaments under mutual control; all of them will be able to divert tremendous financial and human resources, now exploited for purposes of war, to the development of their economic and scientific potential and the diminution of the need for external aid.

The enormous resources thus liberated will also largely facilitate the completion of the resettlement and absorption of the refugees in their natural national environment, namely, the Arab countries, with their extensive territories and wealth of water resources, which are sorely in need of development, and people who are their brethren in nationality, tongue, customs, outlook, and faith.

Israel is prepared to help financially to her best ability and with the aid of the great powers in this work of resettlement and rehabilitation.

The settlement of the refugees in the Arab countries is the only solution compatible with their true and basic interests, as well as ours.

In a similar way, in a national environment, Israel has absorbed Jewish refugees from Arab countries in numbers not less than the number of Arab refugees who have left our territory. . . .

Such a peace program is no fantasy. I do not imagine that the cooperation which exists today in Western Europe, for example, seemed less fantastic as little as twenty years ago. We are approaching the end of the twenty years since the War of Independence. It can be done here too. . . .

This was not truly a peace plan, but rather a post-peace prospect. The speech contained a fine picture of relations possible among nations that have been at peace for some time. It gave no hint of a program to achieve the climate for such wonderful developments still to be started. For practical purposes, according to the Prime Minister, Israel is ready to do nothing—or at best, very little.

His assertion that Israel had no intention of attacking the Arabs and that their fears were a result of hostile propaganda could not, observers might say, bring them absolute assurance. Premier Eshkol may have been completely sincere, but Arab memories might also recollect that in 1956, a few days before Israel launched the Sinai campaign, Prime Minister David Ben Gurion had expressed from the same Knesset podium similar reassurances in even stronger terms. He had said that only a demented mind could think of attacking the Arabs.*

No thoughtful analyst would criticize the laudable aims expressed in the address, but we can look askance at the innocence of their author, who apparently considered his speech at least a hint at the peace settlement. Yet surely it could not be so understood.

Apparently equally innocent, the body politic in Israel received the Prime Minister's address with approval, if not excitement— with some low-voiced marginal exceptions.

The world press was not highly impressed. The London *Times*, in an editorial on May 19, pointed out that nothing in Mr. Eshkol's speech would advance the argument along new lines. The official Tunisian news agency wryly remarked that his declaration was still a "long way" from accepting Bourguiba's proposals. The Egyptian press used the speech as an excuse to attack Bourguiba once more— the Cairo *Al Akhbar* described it as "the second act of a farce begun by the Tunisian President."

Israeli reactions in general and Eshkol's proposals in particular may have exhibited prudence, but their presentation was often marked by a lack of diplomatic sophistication, psychological insight, tact, or grace of style.

Many Israeli leaders are gifted in many fields and on several levels, but they have much to learn about the art and style of diplomacy. They still appear awkward and crude in this art— which is a severe handicap in the effort to achieve improved relations with their Arab neighbors.

Not that the Arabs are any better. But their irrationality, emotionalism, and rudeness can be, if not justified, at least explained by their humiliation in being what Bourguiba calls "the losers." Israel, which emerged victorious in consecutive military confrontations with the Arabs, could afford to exhibit greater forebearance and understanding without expense to her security.

But even when they are talking peace and conciliation, Israeli spokesmen exhibit an irritating if not offensive attitude of condescension toward the Arabs. Equally guilty of this fault are the left-wing circles which profess to espouse the cause of peace and which work according to their own lights for a rapprochement

---

* True, the reference was to Jordan and not Egypt. It was in answer to a speech by Mr. M. Begin who suggested attacking Jordan.

between Israel and the Arab states. When an Israeli politician preaches the necessity for peace, he concentrates not on the needs of Israel, but on the benefits to the Arabs. He usually portrays a peaceful region where Israelis will put at the disposal of the backward Arabs their know-how, their technology, and their vast international connections, for the development of the whole region.

There are many illustrations of Israel's psychological blundering; but two are connected with Bourguiba's initiative and they both involve statements by highest officials of the Israel government. In an interview with Jon Kimche, editor of the *Jewish Observer* and *Middle East Review,* Eban said that the Arabs' "chief gain from peace, would be peace itself." They would also gain a variety of blessings:

> Liberation from a negative obsession. Freedom from a conflict which has wasted creative Arab energies. Liberation from a constant source of complication in the realities between the Arab world and external powers and interests. The possibility of giving the Arab voice its full international weight. An opportunity to inaugurate a dramatic upsurge of development such as that which Europe began to experience when its nations decided to forget old conflicts and build a continent together.
>
> I do not underestimate the gain which Israel would obtain from peace. But many people underestimate the heavy burden which Arab nationalism has imposed upon itself by an antagonism which is, after all, not crucial to its destiny.

Such an experienced and extremely eloquent diplomat as Mr. Eban should have sensed how unbecoming it is for him to patronize the Arabs, and tell them what they stand to gain from peace with Israel. Such a lecture is a gratuitous irritant; economic and technological cooperation are the last "blessings" which would appeal to the Arabs in the present psychological climate. Indeed it is Israel's economic and technological expansion that they fear most whenever the problem of recognizing Israel is discussed.

It is significant that the Egyptian Foreign Minister, Mahmoud Riad, in a speech in Cairo during the violent anti-Egyptian demonstrations in Tunis, chose precisely this issue as the major point of danger in Bourguiba's initiative. In his vehement indictment of the Tunisian President, Riad barely referred to the Palestine refugee problem. Instead, he detailed the danger of Israel's economic and technological expansionism inherent in Bourguiba's peace proposals.

He argued that Bourguiba's suggestions, if adopted, would pave the way for recognition of Israel and the establishment of economic ties with her. This last, said the Egyptian Foreign Minister, is, in Egypt's opinion, the most dangerous; for the present, "Israel lives on charity, grants, and aid from abroad; and she is anticipating the day when economic relations between her and the Arab states will enable her to flood their markets with her industrial products." This is the greatest danger, he said, to the whole Arab nation, "especially in view of Israel's expansionist plans."

Of course, these accusations are as unsound as Eban's paternalistic preachings, but in the present atmosphere of mistrust, the Arabs are unable to welcome an offer listing the economic blessings of a peace settlement. If they ever agree to peace, it will not be because of these "blessings" but in spite of them.

The second example of Israel's lack of sensitivity was demonstrated by Premier Eshkol, generally considered to be a moderate man of pleasant disposition. Of all unlikely occasions, he chose a religious festival of the Druse community in northern Israel to articulate specifically the rejection of Bourguiba's proposals for return of the Arab refugees. The Arab refugees, he asserted, should remain *"for their own good"* in the Arab states among their own people:

> The benefit of the Arab refugees demands the continuation and support of their resettlement and rehabilitation among their religious cultural and lingual kinfolk in their natural economic and cultural setting.

To the objective analyst, it would seeem inopportune to make such a speech to the Druses who, though non-Moslem, and full-fledged citizens of Israel, are nevertheless a non-Jewish Arab-speaking minority in the state.

Mr. Eshkol clearly meant nothing ulterior, but if his Druse listeners had wished to take offense, they might have misconstrued his statement as an invitation for them, too, to go and live elsewhere, "among their religious, cultural, and lingual kinfolk."

The same disdain for Arab sensibilities is expressed in another explanation of why Israel cannot admit sizable numbers of refugees. Her spokesmen argue that the new state must prepare for the reception and settlement of new Jewish immigrants; often the expectation is expressed that these will be in the hundreds of thousands, if not millions.

Pursuing this line, Prime Minister Eshkol argued sharply in a

Knesset debate against a Mapam (left Labor) favored plan for a Middle Eastern Federation, that such a federation might permit free movement within the confederated states; thus Arab refugees, and for that matter other Arabs attracted by Israel's prosperity, might come and settle in Israel. Don't people understand, asked Mr. Eshkol, that there is no room for this, since Israel's absorptive capacity must be preserved for new Jewish immigrants?

That Israel expects millions of newcomers and therefore cannot house Arab refugees is a deep emotional provocation and a source of outrage to Arabs. *Le Monde's* Eric Rouleau, before whom Mr. Eshkol developed these arguments, remarked: "It is precisely this perspective which arouses in the Arabs the fear of Israeli expansionism. . . ."

In spite of such warning signals, Israeli spokesmen and writers persist in their erroneous psychological approach. Why do they not leave it to the Arabs to decide the virtues of peace for themselves?

Indeed, Israel might do better were she to express sympathy for the Palestinian Arabs, and an honest recognition that the establishment of the State of Israel brought human tragedy to those who are now refugees. Israelis could even afford to undertake some bold, even risky, compensatory action to heal the wounds, and create a condition for peaceful coexistence.

Such an ascription of some possible right to the Arab cause would not minimize the overwhelming need which brought about establishment of the State of Israel. In our complex world, clashes often occur—not between right and wrong, but between conflicting human needs. The solution should therefore be sought through mutual understanding and accommodation.

Perhaps a word should be said, though reluctantly, about the style of some of the Israeli pronouncements. If de Buffon is still right, even in our graceless generation, that the style is the man, then Israel should worry about her best and most eloquent spokesmen. For instance, Eban managed to claim that ". . . our reaction to the Bouguiba initiative was correctly balanced. . . . Our reactions . . . were measured . . . not hasty. . . . What we said was frank and candid and realistic and honest." This self-praise, coupled with the picture of bliss that would await the Arabs if only they accepted Israel's terms of peace, as well as the tears shed for the refugees enforcedly absent from their congenial environment, scarcely seem the style of a gracious man.

One paragraph in Premier Eshkol's "Peace Plan" is of great importance, although the thought had been repeated in different ways for so long by so many that it no longer received attention. Speaking against resettling any refugees in Israel, Eshkol reiterated the benefits to the Arabs if they stopped spending so heavily for armaments:

> The enormous resources thus liberated would also largely facilitate the completion of the resettlement and absorption of the refugees in their natural national environment, namely, the Arab countries . . . which are sorely in need of development and people who are their brethren in nationality, tongue, customs, outlook, and faith.*

Is this not an eloquent plea for pan-Arabism, i.e., one Arab nation, the "uma Arabia"—where all are "brethren in nationality, tongue, customs, outlook, and faith?" Is this what Mr. Eshkol really meant to urge? Did he agree that Nasser is justified in his campaign to unify all Arabs into one "United Arab Republic" and is such a prospect in the vital interests of the State of Israel?

If so, what about the incessant Israeli claim that the Middle East is a pluralistic region of many nations and not one indivisible pan-Arab entity? Did Eshkol intend to side with Nasser against Bourguiba, who declares the existence of one Arab nation is a myth, and that it is imperative for the interests of all the nations, including Egypt, to destroy the myth and liberate the whole region from fears and pathological tensions?

The answer is Eshkol was not thinking of such fundamental problems as the nature and destiny of the region. Often the shapers of Israel's policy consider such broad questions too remote—if not in space, at least in time. The foremost and immediate preoccupation is preservation of the *status quo,* and they prefer to postpone the showdown. Even the danger of pan-Arabism is a matter of the future, whereas one refugee may actually arrive today.

In the frightful "refugee roulette," there is, somehow, a hidden subconscious harmony between the diverse claims of the two antagonists. The Arabs contend that more than a million homeless

---

* Abba Eban expressed the same thought in almost identical terms: Apart from that, if you could get an integration of Arab refugees in countries to which they are akin in language, social outlook, and above all, in national loyalty then this is both preferable, more statesmanlike, and a more human solution than creating the sort of tensions which would exist between Arab refugees and an alien environment. (*Views,* Autumn issue, 1965.)

refugees from Israel, languishing in camps, clamor to go back to their homes; that Israel does not legally exist, and its territory should be given back to its "rightful owners."

Strangely, the Israelis do not rush to contradict these claims and to prove that they are not rooted in reality. They don't bother to challenge the number given. Certainly the million refugees—if such a number could have been mustered—did not all stem from the small part of Palestine which became Israel; nor did the majority reside in camps as homeless exiles from their own country which was Palestine. The greatest number were full-fledged citizens in their own country—Palestine—which now goes by the new name of the Hashemite Kingdom of Jordan.

Here is surely a peculiar situation in which one protagonist distorts the case; the other somehow implicitly acquiesces. Why? Because neither party really has the problem of the refugees at heart.

The Arab states aim *not* at a solution of the refugee problem but at "a final solution" to the existence of Israel. They believe that by inflating the number of the refugees and by distorting all the facts pertaining to their situation they will lend credence to their contention that the very existence of Israel is a "permanent act of agression" and therefore should be ended. The Israelis, on the other hand, believe that by not challenging the facts and figures they can muster world opinion to agree with their contention that the refugee problem is of such a magnitude and so intractable that, short of national suicide, they can do nothing about it.

Were, however, the facts brought out into the light, the problem would appear to be manageable, and a just and practical solution would be in sight. But reducing the problem is not what either party aims at; it would disturb their feeling of "coziness" under the *status quo*.

Psychologically it is easier for both to brand the conflict unmanageable, rather than cope with a soluble problem, which might shatter their world of illusions, fears, and prejudices.

As part of this weird accord, both sides agree there is no halfway solution for the Palestine problem—that it does not lend itself to palliatives, or to a peaceful approach. Both demand all or nothing; when Nasser says that war is inevitable, he echoes Israel's expressed conviction that peace is impossible, (True, the Israelis hope that with time Nasser and the others will convince themselves that Israel cannot be overrun by force, and will surrender to the *status quo*.)

This psychological, though unconscious, collaboration is also discernible in the reaction to Bourguiba's initiative. Each antagonist was secretly happy at the other's rejection of the Tunisian President's proposal; both use every excuse not to be shaken from the *status quo*. Both acknowledge pan-Arabism in principle, and acknowledge Nasser as the indisputable leader, with the concomitant Egyptian hegemony—with which Bourguiba takes such violent issue.

The Israelis explain that Bourguiba's proposals have validity, but Israel's problem is not with Bourguiba (whose North African country is too far away to be a factor in the Middle East) but with Nasser, the as-it-were uncrowned leader of the Arabs, who does not want peace. One sometimes has the impression that Israel, like her Arab neighbors, is somehow fascinated by Nasser. In many circles, especially among the Left, he is spoken of with admiration as a leader almost without peer.

Another aspect of this Israel-Arab inverted collaboration concerns the point that it is "good for the refugees," (or as Eban puts it, "It is . . . a more human solution,") to be absorbed into the Arab countries rather than to live in "an alien environment." Here Israeli leaders corroborate the Arab contention that Israel is an alien enclave in the Arab world. The logical conclusion is that such an enclave ought to be eliminated.

This admission gives Israel a bad certifiicate from human as well as political considerations. Why should her country be "an alien environment"? Why should not some Arab refugees wish to live in the state where the standard of living is the highest in the region; under a democratic regime with freedom of expression and association, where the government is stable, where educational facilities are or will soon be available to all citizens, where, even according to Eshkol and Eban, everything is so congenial? Why is it so much "in the interest" of any people to live under regimes which are more or less totalitarian, where the press is under strict control and censorship, where the governments are either weak or changing in endless *coups d'état,* where there are underdevelopment, limited educational facilities, and very few opportunities for those with higher education; where one must conform, and where the secret police is virtually omnipresent?

Luckily (from the prevailing Israeli point of view), these factors are not likely to influence any considerable number of the refugees. Possibly a small minority would be motivated by such common-sense considerations and wish to return to Israel. But it is both a spurious altruism and a self-libel to argue that Arabs should live only with Arabs, and Israel is alien soil. Of course, Israel can make it uncongenial for the Arabs to live there, by a variety of repressive measures, and the creation of a hostile environment (of which she is already culpable to some extent). But this would be an artificial and arbitrary response, and not an objective reality.

Yet the "alien environment" gambit does not prevent Messrs. Eshkol and Eban from taking other occasions to picture Israel as a natural, loyal, and deeply rooted member of the Middle East. Inconsistency is their handmaiden. On May 17, the Prime Minister used his familiar argument when he opened the debate on foreign policy in the Knesset; but a week later he postulated an opposite point of view, inveighing against admitting any refugees not because Israel is "an alien environment" but because the environment may prove too much of an attraction.

The trouble is that both the Arabs and the Israelis have come to feel comfortable in the prevailing conditions of tension, mutual threats, and fears, despite the obvious dangers inherent in such a situation and the tremendous financial burdens it imposes. This complacency may help account for the negative reaction on both sides to Bourguiba's positive initiative—an unwillingness to be shocked into action. The influential Tunisian weekly *Jeune Afrique* commented editorially:

> It seems that in the eyes of both sides the *status quo* is the lesser of the two evils. True, this situation is abnormal, very costly, and cannot continue for too long, but they have become accustomed to it. . . .

One is tempted to apply the Yiddish saying that to a worm living in horseradish, there is no sweeter thing in the world.

As time wore on, the original tone of the Israeli attitudes softened and mellowed. The sarcasm and belittlement gave way to sober, formal pronouncements and compliments. Bourguiba became a far-sighted leader, a courageous fighter, and a perspicacious statesman—no longer a freak or the lonely swallow which does not presage spring.

Eban, now Foreign Minister, took pains to point out the promising signals in the Tunisian President's initiative. Prime Minister Eshkol, who had feared that an encouraging word might provoke "the Evil Eye," now proclaimed that Bourguiba was the harbinger of a turning point in the Arab attitude toward Israel. He told a study group of the American United Jewish Appeal visiting Israel:

> I think I can say that we are advancing toward a turning-point in the history of the Middle East. . . . For the last year Israel's condition has improved. . . . The Arabs now evince a more realistic policy toward Israel. . . .

And on this occasion he praised the realism of Bourguiba "who came out with his plan for a peaceful settlement of the Israeli Arab conflict," and *"whose views are now shared by other Arab leaders, though they are unwilling to admit it."*

With remarkable forgetfulness (or cheek) characteristic of politicians of all time and all lands, Israeli spokesmen now claimed to have said things they never uttered—in some cases they had said just the reverse. In an interview with the editor of the British quarterly, *Views,* Eban claimed that from the beginning of Bourguiba's initiative it had seemed to him that

> there was the general doctrine that Bourguiba expressed in statements which had a broad international resonance . . . . about Israel's permanence and solidity as an entrenched fact of Middle Eastern history. . . . In our reactions, which were measured, not hasty in terms of their immediacy, we stated . . . that he had performed a revolutionary act on the intellectual plane. This was the first time that an Arab national leader had developed this calm, if reluctant, vision of Israel as a reality. . . .

This is a far cry from the irony about the "swallow that changes its tune daily," and his unwillingness to recommend Bourguiba for the Nobel Prize for Peace. Of course, no one should be criticized merely for emending his views; but in charity, the most we can say is that Mr. Eban changed his manner and modified his style. And he still tries to have it both ways; continuing with some extravagant praise, he abruptly changes course and implies that the Arab is aiming at the destruction of Israel:

> If Israel's choice is to be either peace or the sacrifice of our sovereignty and security, then we would be prepared to go with-

out peace for a longer time until Arab thinking develops further.

If this accusation does not tally with the compliments to Bour-guiba for having "performed a revolutionary act on the intellec-tual plane" by describing a "calm vision of Israel . . . as a solid and entrenched reality with which the Arab nations would have to come to terms," perhaps Israeli policymakers merely find it con-venient, or prudent, to blow hot and cold at once.

It would be rash to espy a change in Israel's attitude; only the rhetoric has changed, and the substance remains exactly what it was ten months—or ten years—earlier.

At the beginning of 1966, *Le Monde's* Eric Rouleau interviewed Mr. Eshkol:

> *Rouleau:* Mr. President, the policy called "the outstretched hand" by Mr. Ben Gurion, which in fact constituted a peace offer based upon the *status quo,* has proven sterile. Do you envisage modifying this attitude and seeking other paths to a settlement?
>
> *Eshkol:* To be frank: On this subject I don't differ from my predecessor (Eshkol never mentioned the name of Ben Gurion). I should be grateful to anybody who would show another way. As far as I am concerned I see none. Of course, there are Mr. Bour-guiba's peace proposals. From our point of view they do not seem, in their present form, to lend themselves to consideration; but we thought they might have, by strict force of circumstances, consti-tuted the starting point of a dialogue. But the reactions in the Arab world were discouraging. The Tunisian President has been abused—banished from the Arab family. Hence, why do you ask us to make a show of greater imagination?
>
> *Rouleau:* The Arab states think that Israel should abide by the resolutions of the United Nations. Wouldn't you think that these offer a basis for negotiations?
>
> *Eshkol:* Absolutely not! . . .

The Israeli leaders persist in misrepresenting (wittingly or un-wittingly) Bourguiba's proposals, implying that he suggested Israelis must agree prior to any peace negotiations to give up parts of their territory and accept the return of all the refugees. It is true Bourguiba originally gave the impression of demanding Israel's acceptance of the United Nations resolutions of 1947 as a pre-condition for any negotiation. The Israelis jumped at this without making a serious effort to arrive at some clarification of his intentions.

Yet Bourguiba gradually, in the course of his campaign, modified his definitions, or perhaps crystallized them in his own mind, and presented more attractive, sophisticated proposals—making the implementation of the UN decisions only one basis for negotiations, and not the exclusive pre-condition. The Israelis continued to ignore this evolution, and have offered no counter-proposals. On the contrary, they repeat that they welcome the principle of negotiation, which in itself is a recognition of Israel; but it must be undertaken without any pre-conditions whatever. The Arabs see this as an Israeli trap to gain Arab recognition in return for nothing, and a strategem to make them lay down their last effective weapon. They have lost nearly everything else on the Palestine front—both politically and militarily.

Some indication by Israel even if vague and only philosophic—that she is willing to offer some *quid pro quo*—would probably evoke a genuine Arab response. This, however, is what Israel seems not yet ready to do.

As at the beginning, Israeli leaders insist they could do little to hasten a settlement, but the Arabs must change their outlook and demands. In the autumn of 1965, Eban declared in an interview:

> . . . . You must achieve two processes within the Arab mind. First eradicate the concept of an Irredentist war which will make Israel disappear from the future of the Middle East. . . . Then you might after a period of time make a transition to a more affirmative relationship in which they think not only of the absence of war but the presence of peace . . .

And again he reiterated that the refugees should be resettled in Arab countries rather than in such an alien environment as Israel.

Eshkol, too, claimed that if concessions were to be made, the Arabs should make them, since the Jews had sacrificed everything possible long ago, before the state was established. In support, he, like other officials and publicists, referred to three consecutive occasions when the British whittled down the original Palestinian territory assigned for the Jewish National Home.* In itself the statement is quite accurate. But from the point of view

---

* The first time, during World War I as a result of the Sykes-Picot secret agreement; the second, when the Churchill White Paper was promulgated (July 24, 1922) ; the last, as a result of the Partition.

of the Arabs this is no argument. Their emphasis in explaining the present situation in Palestine, is not on concessions made by the Jews, but on their own political and military defeats at the hands of the Israelis.

There is no visible evidence that Israel attempted seriously to keep Bourguiba's initiative alive, despite a warning by *Ha'aretz*:

> It is too early, it seems to us, to engage in a public debate with Bourguiba and his supporters on this or that detail of his proposals. Such a thing is likely only to discourage, especially since our basic attitude concerning the refugees and frontiers is well known. Our main task is not to let Bourguiba's initiative fall asleep as a result of our lack of reaction, or from emphasis at this time on the difficulties which lie ahead on the road to a permanent peace with the Arab world.

Inflexibility, and refusal to budge from an entrenched position, are not limited to the case of Bourguiba's proposals, or to the level of high policy. It was exhibited in daily relations with the Arabs in the mixed Israeli-Arab Armistice Commissions. George de Carvalho, a foreign correspondent and authority on Middle East affairs of *Time-Life* whose sympathies lie rather with the Arabs, nevertheless knows the conditions, the leaders, and the people of the area. In an article on Bourguiba's proposal, he tried to set forth the background conditions:

> In Amman, Jordan's Foreign Minister Hasem Nuseibeh, who holds a doctorate in philosophy from Princeton, discussed Israel with me late into the evening. 'Negotiations with the Israelis are absolutely hopeless,' he said. 'They don't give an inch. We have challenged them a hundred times to implement the United Nations resolutions, but they refuse. We have talked ourselves hoarse in the United Nations and achieved nothing. God knows we don't want war and slaughter but I often think of Armageddon. . . .''
> Lt. Col. Mohammed Daoud, the thin, graying Jordanian delegate to the United Nations Mixed Armistice Commissions, says:
> 'Never in my seventeen years' experience have the Israelis ever made a single friendly gesture. They have never agreed to anything except in their own interests. An Israeli would not give an Arab the dirt under his fingernails. If an Arab tries to pick up an orange from his own grove across the armistice line, the Israelis shoot him dead and throw his body back.'

UN officials are scrupulously impartial; unofficially they agree that both sides constantly infringe on the armistice agreements. 'But when the Arabs do something wrong,' one UN observer said, 'it's usually stealing a sheep or picking fruit in Israel. When the Israelis act, it's usually to take over more land, or set up military positions, or clobber the Arabs somewhere.'

Of course, this is a distorted and highly prejudiced view. The Israelis could not equal the Arabs in their haughty intransigence, fanaticism, or rudeness—to say nothing of their vociferous determination to destroy Israel altogether. It must be remembered that it was they who originally defied the United Nations by invading Palestine from all sides, and have ever since violated such United Nations resolutions and armistice agreements as those calling for access to the holy places in Jordan, free passage through the Suez Canal, and restraint from the threat of war.

Their hauteur often takes absurd forms, from spurning innocent social gatherings to ignoring important functions of international organizations. Vital United Nations scientific, technical, or humanitarian commissions have been disrupted by deliberate boycott.

Sick Arab attitudes may explain, but not entirely justify, Israeli retaliation, but the Israelis would do well to try to understand Arab humiliation and frustration resulting from their several defeats on the Palestine front. There were political defeats—in the international councils; in the United Nations; in the mere fact that almost all the world's governments recognized Israel; in the widespread Western assistance to the new country. There have been the successive major military defeats for the Arabs, and Israel's large-scale retaliations for terrorist activities by Arab Fedayin raiding Israel's borders, which the neighboring Arab countries sometimes could not check. Finally, the problem of the Arab refugees still waits for a solution. It is true, the Arab leaders have exploited the situation, but it is unrealistic to expect them to take the initiative or exclusive action.

Instead of exhibiting an understanding of such considerations, Israel's line is that she owes absolutely nothing to that part of the Palestine population which became displaced with the establishment of the State of Israel. This lack of understanding, even in simple, human, and hence moral, terms of the Arab grievances is the more reprehensible since the Israelis are the victors and thus far the stronger party in the protracted conflict. The concept of *noblesse oblige* demands of victory and strength a display of magnanimity. The Israelis are more often than not oblivious to this requirement.

Perhaps Bourguiba's most daring, almost heroic phrase, spoken at the Beirut press conference, called for a settlement in which there would be neither victors nor vanquished. The Israelis could have reciprocated this sentiment without endangering their sovereignty or weakening their security; but they did not choose the line of the strong. Theirs was basically the policy typical of the weak, the frightened, the unimaginative. Such a policy is also one of self-distortion because it might imply that Israel was not deservedly victorious—just lucky—which is not the case.

We must attach utmost importance to signs that the Israelis have begun edging away from inflexibility, and evolving a new policy of understanding and compassion. Possibly a new perspective has pervaded them that this is the only way to alleviate the bitterness and tensions, to break the ice, eventually to sit down and discuss the serious business of peace.

How is it that a people, otherwise so gifted and energetic, could become so immobilized in the face of the first peace offensive they had to face?

Whence does their intransigence stem?

Since time immemorial most governments have stood foursquare for a Great Fallacy: in an international conflict, concede nothing, lest it be interpreted as weakness. It is the "philosophy" embodied in that cliché known as "bargaining from a position of strength." Unfortunately, this concept has often been vindicated —but at what price!

In the case of Palestine, any concrete concession by Israel must contain serious risks. To grant the refugees a free choice might open a Pandora's box of complications of both a political and security nature. Under pan-Arab propaganda, most of the refugees might opt for a "return to their homes"; and any increase of Israel's Arab population (which already makes up about 10 percent of the total) could create a fifth column whose aim would be destruction of the state from within. Since Arabs are reproducing at about twice the rate of Jews, a considerable "return" of the refugees could endanger the numerical preponderance of Jews in the country. Already Israeli statisticians are pointing to this danger.

Then there is the specter of Cyprus, and other countries where communal strife is the daily fare because the population is ethnically heterogeneous. The risks are real, but the question is not whether there is a road to peace without real risks; of course there is not. The greater question asks whether the *status quo,* with its inherent prospects of war, does not involve risks more terrifying.

The dilemma is indeed painful; and the art and secret of life entail making the best choice among alternatives, none of which offers complete safety. The real danger arises when we stop thinking in alternatives; when we ignore option and behave "computer-like" according to an abstract formula, such as a "position of strength."

There is another, perhaps even weightier, reason for Israel's intransigence. Jacques-Francois Simon, whom *Le Monde* sent to Israel to undertake a special survey, reported great outward change there: "in this country, where a few years ago one would hardly see a man wearing a tie, there are now hotel bars where jacket and tie are required." "Yes, outwardly, Israel has grown older, but writes the reporter, "none of its historic, geographic, and political elements, which make of this country an entrenched assembly camp and which compel it 'to be prepared to win the war without losing the peace' has undergone any fundamental change in the last seventeen years." (*Le Monde,* June 2, 1965) Here reside perhaps the only people in the world who live in a permanent state of siege. They are surrounded by enemies who do not limit themselves to outrageous demands; Israel's Arab neighbors seek her total destruction.

These conditions accentuated the Israelis' patterns of reasoning; but they did not create them. Jewish settlers brought their mental habits along, consciously or unconsciously, from the ghettos where they had lived under mandated or self-imposed confinement, but always under heavy pressures from a hostile environment. For centuries the ghetto was literally a walled enclosure, with confinement enforced by armed guards. Though these physical walls had been removed from most ghettos by the nineteenth century, they were again erected in the twentieth under Hitler when they served as an ominous prelude to "total destruction."

Of course, the word "siege" is not wholly applicable either to the traditional ghettos or to the present condition of Israel, for a seige implies an active military investment whose objective is conquest of the besieged by a superior force capable of consummating the conquest. In this case, the besieged Israelis, far from being the weaker, are in a sense the conquerors. But the term siege surely describes their condition of being under constant pressure by a hostile environment. And this feeling is deep, continuing, and atavistic; in the blood, as it were, made the more vivid by ancient memories overloaded by recent tragic experiences.

To Israelis the siege of Jerusalem in the seventh decade of the first century, which ended in national catastrophe, is not just a dim memory of the ancient past. It is a poignant event, still commemorated each year, exemplifying the destiny of the Jews who are attacked and persecuted by enemies for no fault except their passion for freedom. In fact, in their consciousness the ancient siege, the more recent ghetto confinement, and the present-day Arab hostilities somehow blend into one continuous state of malevolent beleaguerment. The effects of the Arab blockade and boycott, and of the closed and heavily guarded frontiers, were felt in the daily life of individuals and the nation.

This history and the resulting mental attitudes gave rise to a policy of merely holding out—of survival until the beseiegers should see that they cannot prevail, and give up. It was a policy of doing nothing else, since there was nothing else to do. There was nothing to offer because the enemy wants only surrender and destruction. What was there to talk about, to initiate? Any offer, any concession, regardless how trivial, would be interpreted by the besiegers as a sign of weakness. It would strengthen the enemy's will to continue the siege.

This mental attitude with time spawns fatalism, belief in miracles, rigidity, inability to think in alternatives. So when a Bourguiba appears and speaks of peace, it does not occur to the besieged that they have perhaps to deal with an act of wise statesmanship. The psychology of the besieged prompts a suspicious reaction: this may be a perfect stratagem to relax the defenses.

In addition, the fear of a peace initiative stems ironically from opposite suspicions: Perhaps it is real, and will bring some peaceful settlement which would change the *status quo*. Would it be good for Israel? Is Israel prepared for peace at this difficult transitional period?

A sympathetic foreign observer defined the enigma:

> The people and government of Israel have performed such prodigies under Arab pressure that any change in the form of the pressure, any reduction of its intensity raises important political

and psychological questions for a country that in many respects
lives in a state of siege.*

Here is a true and deeply perplexing intimation: Israelis are
attuned to threats and attacks; they flourished and solidified
their country in a climate of siege and war. The whole country—
its economy, its social and communal integration processes, its
national coherence, its civil obedience under a most exacting
fiscal and tax system, its sacrifices of all sorts—all are geared to a
situation of emergency.

The Israeli Government is never inhibited in exacting direct
or indirect taxes, imposts, levies, charges, or obligatory loans, in
an ever-spiraling pace. At least 40 per cent of the government
"Ordinary Budget" (as distinct from the "Development Budget")
is spent on military security—on the ground that the defense and
survival of the country demand it. The citizens, though grumbling
about non-essential details, are basically in agreement with their
government's policy, proud of it, and thankful for it.

Hence, when faced with an initiative which may in the course
of time change the imperatives, people experience the same shock
as when any aspect of their routine existence is threatened. In
describing this state of mind Drew Middleton remarked in his
dispatch:

> The traveler is impressed by the manner in which the duel with
> the Arabs had mobilized the energy and emotion of the people.
> The enemy is just over the hill, just across the lake, and the gov-
> ernment asks for, and receives sacrifices comparable to those in
> the Britain of 1940.
> Some fear that if the enemy settles into a state of peaceful co-
> existence, Israel will lose some of the dynamism that has enabled
> her to survive and prosper.

But there is more to it, much more. Having suffered persecution for so long a time in history, the Jews found themselves the
only people who were, in relation to their oppressors, consistently
in the right—not necessarily for any special virtues, but because
their enemies were wrong. The suffering has continued for some
twenty-five centuries; it is clearly not a paranoiac state of mind
but an objective state of reality. Toward the Jews the world has
been wrong and cruel and unjust, and the cruelty was climaxed
by the Nazi extermination.

---

* Drew Middleton in *The New York Times,* May 3, 1965.

It was with this feeling of having been right for so long (and their oppressor wrong) that the Jews came to Palestine. They came with a Messianic vision of a national renaissance—but also as the only solution to their survival. The combination of these and other factors made possible the superhuman exertions, and the acts of heroism and dedication that achieved a miracle: revival of Hebrew sovereignty.

But the same qualities, virtues, and perspectives which were so important in *achieving* a sovereign existence did not prove helpful or creative in *sustaining* it—in dealing with routine problems of national existence in an evolving and troubled world.

Entirely different qualities and outlooks are required for dealing with the Arabs. People who are accustomed always to being right do not excel in diplomatic relations. The Jews had to discover that the line between right and wrong was no longer drawn as distinctly as the one to which they had been accustomed in their history of exile. Suddenly they found themselves in a situation where justice was not all on their side. This can be disconcerting under any circumstances; in this unique situation it complicated matters enormously.

The Jews carried their sense of being right into a new reality and continued to behave as if the Jewish night of the long exile had not yet come to an end. They acted as if they still faced a hostile environment through no fault of their own, as if the Arabs were anti-Semites in the European tradition, or indeed as in Arab countries where the Jews were minorities. Because of the carry-over of the ghetto mentality, they failed to see that regardless of how desperately just the cause of Hebrew national revival was, its realization was achieved at the price of what the Arabs of Palestine regard as gross injustice. The situation cried out for both humanity and statesmanship.

The Arabs, for their part, refused stubbornly to make allowance for the justice of the Hebrew cause, and responded to the instigation of a blind, fanatical, and often corrupt leadership in a narrow-minded and savage way. They behaved as if Palestine had always been an Arab state (which it never was; it had never even been under Arab rule) ; as if Palestine was always densely populated by Arabs (which it never was, but only became so as a corollary to Jewish immigration and development) .

Whatever the reason for the refugees' flight in 1948—whether they were coerced or misled by their leaders or genuinely felt menaced by the Israelis—the fact that they fled does not nullify their birthright. The great failure of both Jews and Arabs was that they were unable to make mutual adjustment through a process of give and take. But Bourgiba, on the Arab side, was the man who came to the conclusion that this is exactly the historic imperative.

This writer, himself an Israeli to whom the welfare and destiny of the Jewish State is of utmost concern, views Israel's rigidity with great apprehension. He is against surrender in any form, under any pretext. But he favors compromise and mutual concession. He is fearful lest a policy of complete inflexibility, whatever its merits when the going is safe, may become a disaster when the pressures become too great. Flexibility permits successful adjustment and greater vitality, and is, in the long run, one of the absolute requirements for Israel's safety, integrity, and future prosperity.

This becomes especially clear if one accepts Ben Gurion's perfectly correct appraisal: "We could defeat the Arabs a dozen times and they would still remain in existence. If we lose once, we are finished."

Are there different voices in Israel?

> The status quo between us and the Arabs is not sacrosanct, as if it were transmitted through Moses from Mount Sinai. It is incumbent upon us to develop a formula for reacting to Bourguiba's statements, and to follow paths which are not necessarily official, in order to advance the cause of negotiations between us and the Arabs. . . . It is necessary to accustom our public to [the necessity] of compromise, which is impossible without mutual concessions.

These are the words of Prof. Shlomo Ghinosar of the Hebrew University of Jerusalem and a former Israeli ambassador. He made this statement on April 27, 1965, at a radio symposium in Jerusalem on the subject of Bourguiba's proposal.

When asked later by an interviewer from *Ha'aretz* to amplify, he said that he spoke as a private citizen who considered that

> the paramount question is to educate the Israeli public to [political] thinking and reacting. We will be asked to react not necessarily by the Arabs but rather by the French, the Americans, and the English. In accepting [in principle] Bourguiba's proposals for direct negotiations, it is worthwhile to emphasize on the one hand that forsooth we do not accept or reject his conditions, but

on the other, we know that negotiations mean mutual concessions.

As near a perfect formula as possible.

How representative is this "other" voice? How many Israelis
think as he does?

Ironically, it is sometimes more difficult to accurately gauge
trends in a democratic society than under an authoritarian
regime. It is quite certain, for instance, that libertarian trends
in Russia or Poland are deep and widespread; but until the
recent explosion of the Vietnam issue it was difficult to assess the
strength of opposition among the American people to any given
policy of the United States Government, especially on foreign
affairs. Democracy in our day has worked out techniques of
voluntary conformity and acquiescence to the prevailing policy of
the government, especially in the press and other mass media. It is
remarkable how in a free country one can pick up almost any
newspaper on a given day, see stereotyped views, and find the
same editorial with little variation in many newspapers in the
country.

In Israel today, the problem is especially complicated by factors
peculiar to that country, most important of which is "partisation":
a barbarism which correctly reflects the nation-wide dominance
of political parties. Many activities which in other democratic
countries fall into the domain of private enterprise or municipal
or national government, are in Israel the main preoccupation
of the political parties and of *Histadrut,* supposedly a trade union
but in fact the leading employer and financial mogul of the
country (there have been strikes against *Histadrut* itself by its
own employees!) .

Thus in "normal" times—between one round of war and another
—Israel's political parties are interested only marginally in foreign
and international relations (preparations for defensive war, regardless how brilliant, are not politics) . Their main performances
are in fields which elsewhere would be closed to them, except
covertly: business enterprises, banking, education (though education is officially a state prerogative, the parties have a decisive voice
in the "trend" of all schools) , building construction, investments,
publishing. Under such a system an individual joins a party (political in the sense that it seeks representation in the Knesset) not
primarily because of political affinity, but to find more suitable or
lucrative employment, acquire an apartment, educate his children

in a better school (or in a school which corresponds to his religious beliefs—or disdain of them), invest his savings, or engage in an industrial enterprise. The newspapers are predominantly party properties. Out of several dozen dailies in Israel, in a variety of languages, only three can be said to be independent. Even the theater and sports are directly or indirectly party-dominated.

So most of a man's activities are to a great extent controlled either by a political party or by *Histadrut,* to which the vast majority of income-earners belong, regardless of whether or not they are workers in the accepted sense. Even wealthy men belong to *Histadrut.*

Under such a system where the parties and the *Histadrut* (which in turn is dominated by a single political party—*Mapai,* and lately by *Ma'arakh**) monopolize so much of the life and activities of the citizenry, politics proper are more often than not only a secondary preoccupation. This party domination, coupled with the prevalent passion for personal economic betterment, has brought about a great indifference concerning vital political matters. Usually the citizens leave it to their leaders to decide upon these issues, ignoring that in the final analysis it is basic political decisions which determine their country's destiny and consequently the course of their lives.

This is background for the assertion that it is difficult to ascertain how strong is the willingness to achieve "peace at a price." (Everyone is for peace at no price.) At all events, since Israel is a democratic country, with full freedom of expression, overt reactions to Bourguiba's proposals ranged from vehement rejection to enthusiastic approval.

At one end of the spectrum of Israeli public opinion stands the ultra-nationalist *Kherut* party. Spokesmen and the official newspaper of that party called the Tunisian President a hypocrite, a conspirator given to intrigues, and flighty. In a sense they were the only ones who did not speak out of both sides of the mouth. Their attitude was unequivocally and consistently negative and hostile. They demanded exposure of Bourguiba as an outright enemy of Israel, more dangerous than Nasser.

At the other end of the spectrum are several small groups: the *Ikhud* Association, founded by the late Rector of the Hebrew University in Jerusalem, Professor Judah L. Magnes. (In the pre-Israel period, Magnes urged a binational state in Palestine.) *Ikhud*

---

* *Ma'arakh* is the alignment but not merger of the two parties *Mapai* and *Akhdut Avoda.*

consists of several renowned personalities, chiefly academicians. It publishes a periodical (about eight times a year), *Ner,* under the editorship of an indefatigable fighter for the cause of peace, Dr. S. Shereshevsky. Then there is the *Hapeula Hashemit* (Semitic Action) which publishes an interesting and intellectual biweekly *Etgar* (Challenge) * edited by Nathan Yalin-Mor, former commander of the underground *Lekhi* (Fighters for the Freedom of Israel, better and scurrilously known as the Stern Group or gang). A prominent personality in the peace camp, is Uri Avneri, publisher and editor of the widely circulated illustrated sensational weekly *Ha'olam Hazeh* (This World). [Avneri in the last election won a seat in the Knesset on behalf of a group newly formed around his weekly called *Ha'olam Hazeh-Koakh Khadash-* (New Force). He is now one of the most active members of parliament.] As against these small groups there is the relatively large left-wing *Mapam* party with a strong base among the *kibutzim* (farm collectives); especially active in the cause of peace is the left wing of *Mapam,* grouped around the English-language monthly *New Outlook,* though some notable outsiders contribute to this serious and responsible magazine.

There are also isolated individuals, journalists, writers and intellectuals, such as Professor Ghinosar whom we have quoted above. They are to be found in almost every party, including Kherut. But what is more encouraging are the many anonymous people in all walks of life, whether belonging to a party or not, who don't share the official policy and its mystical overtones, and who take a more realistic view of Israel's political condition in the Middle East. They are mostly younger people, Sabrahs ("Cactus" —the nickname of the generation born in the country) who are free from many of the attitudes of the older generation. In their native jargon the word "Zionism" means affected, cliché-ridden palaver. Most representative of this generation is Amos Kenan, perhaps the greatest Israeli political satirist. They are a minority in Israel and not yet very articulate. But the wave of the future is theirs.

Of course, it may be imprudent oversimplification to include several different groups in a short and generalized summary. There are shades, and perhaps even more than shades, which distinguish each group from the others; and within each group, as in *Mapam,*

---

* It ceased publication last year, for lack of funds.

must treat all these opposition groups (with the exception of a few non-conformist individuals) as "a family", though they bicker degrees of opinion. But within the framework of this survey we and fight each other. What characterizes these groups is that they are all oriented to the left.

To Bourguiba's initiative the attitude of these groups was favorable, even enthusiastic. On the whole they did not doubt the sincerity of his search for peace; they refused somewhat uncritically, to ascribe to him any deception resembling a trap. These groups were outspoken against official Israeli reticence to welcome the Tunisian's declarations; they criticized the government for not grasping Bourguiba's initiative as a crack to be exploited in the wall of hatred. They demanded that their leaders indicate what Israel is ready to do to advance the cause of peace.

Although somewhat vague in presenting counterproposals, these groups tend to favor a Middle Eastern federation or confederation which would treat the eastern Mediterranean as a "Semitic region" of which both Israel and the Arab states constitute organic parts. They have shown no overwhelming concern for the eventual fate of Israel's independence within such a framework, in which Arabs will outnumber Israelis perhaps 25 to 1. But some individuals of influence in *Mapam* look upon the federation idea as a serious beginning to an "Israeli-Arab dialogue;" they believe it unconscionable to ask for Israeli-Arab negotiations and at the same time reject *a priori* all of the Arabs' claims and demands.

Mapam, left of *Mapai,* took a favorable stand on Bourguiba's initiative, and planned both a propaganda campaign within Israel and international political action. On April 19 an extra-ordinary session of its Central Committee, which had lasted three days, adopted a plan of action after leading party figures pointed out that Israel had already missed at least three major peace opportunities. One leader, H. Schor, declared that "those who minimize the importance of Bourguiba's statements are not qualified to direct Israel's foreign policy."

The April 19 proclamation of the plan embraced the following five points:

1. Opening of immediate negotiations with the Arab states concerning a solution of the refugee problem.
2. Steps to proclaim the Middle East a nuclear-free zone.
3. Allocation of the Jordan River waters without recourse to violence.

4. Immediate abrogation of the military jurisdiction over Arab areas in Israel still subject to martial rule; and

5. Study of a plan to federate Israel with the Arab states. (A first step should explore the possibilities of economic union with Jordan.)

One of the leading Central Committee members, I. Barzilay (Vice President of the Knesset), was sent abroad to contact "progressive Tunisian circles."* Barzilay hoped that these contacts would be facilitated by *Mapam's* left-wing friends in European countries, especially in England and France. The *Mapam* leadership also hoped to develop pressure in Yugoslavia and among Socialist branches in other countries to encourage peace initiatives. There is no evidence that much, if any, activity resulted from these resolutions.

Nevertheless, after the Knesset election in the fall of the year, *Mapam* joined with *Mapai* and other parties it had accused of sabotaging Bourguiba's initiative, to form a coalition government.

Though right-wing *Kherut* is a comparatively large political party, and left-wing *Mapam* is deeply rooted in Israeli life, both are at this time of marginal importance and their influence, though growing, is still slight. The official line of the government is, however, widely representative. Where in the United States the Administration may be enjoying the support of about half the public, as much as 80 per cent to 90 per cent of Israel's population support the government's official line.

A complicating and inhibiting factor in the quest for peace is that the search is almost an exclusive monopoly of leftist groups—the Communists, *Mapam* (mainly its left wing), the Semitic Action and its bi-weekly *Etgar*, Uri Avneri and his magazine *Ha'olam Hazeh*, and the Israeli Arabs associated with these groups. The trouble is not only that the non-leftist groups are amazingly averse to hard thinking about paths to peace, but that those (the left-oriented) who do think are influenced and conditioned by ideologies, transcending the imperative of Israeli-Arab peace per se. Ideologies, by necessity also imply prejudice.

Thus the left-wing leaders and writers treat the problem of

---

* This move was not unanimously approved; some prominent members had reservations, and shared the general suspicion that Bourguiba's plan might have been inspired by evil intentions to liquidate the State of Israel.

peace with the Arab neighbors not only on the merits of the issue and from the exclusive point of view of Israeli interests but also from ideological considerations. They view the Arab world as roughly divided into two camps: a progressive-revolutionary, and a reactionary. The former is symbolized by and incarnated in Nasser. Their attitude to him is ambivalent: as Israelis they hate him—he is an enemy of their country. As socialists they admire him. There is no such ambivalence towards the other camp. Both as Israelis and socialists they have a double aversion toward the "kings, kinglings and potentates." Hence, as they see it, the prospect of peace means primarily trying to achieve a *modus vivendi* with the progressive-revolutionary camp, represented by Nasser. It is not an object of this study to go into an analysis of the merits of these attitudes towards the contending camps in the Arab world, though this writer does not think that the totalitarian, one-party regimes are really progressive nor does he understand exactly in what sense they are revolutionary. But this is, within the context of our discussion, besides the point. What *is* to the point is the fact that the two countries concerned with the Palestine problem which are the most likely candidates for peacemaking are Lebanon and Jordan and neither of them is in the progressive-revolutionary camp. One has a capitalist economy; the other is a monarchy still with some of the traditional trappings of Oriental autocracy. In foreign policy they are, generally speaking, pro-Western. The Israeli leftists therefore tend to minimize their role in any future peace settlement and profess to see in Nasser the only feasible potential partner with whom they can deal. Their reasons? That he is the only stable power in the region; that he alone enjoys enough prestige to force a peace settlement upon Arab public opinion; that the future of Middle East peace in general belongs to the progressives.

Some of these reasons may be valid to one degree or another while others are not valid at all. But one major consideration seems to be ignored altogether, namely which of the Arabs countries stand to lose and which to win from a peace settlement, not according to some generalized ideological characterization but from the point of view of the interests of the respective regimes in all countries which are at war with Israel. Yet, the rather simplistic philosophy of the Israeli left-wingers ignores the complex and pragmatic reasons why such states as Egypt, Syria or Iraq would welcome the disappearance of Israel, while for Jordan and the Lebanon the disappearance of Israel might prove fatal to their own survival. As long as the Palestine question is not solved peaceably pan-Arabism erupts intermittently with such force that it endangers the independence of the smaller and more moderate Arab countries. The disappearance of Israel, as an hypothesis, would certainly enable pan-Arabism to overrun countries like Jordan and the Lebanon and do away with their independence as sovereign states.

For Egypt and Syria the disappearance of Israel would facilitate their competitive drives for pan-Arabic consolidation; Israel is both an enclave—breaking their geographic continuity—and a stumbling block in that drive to unify the region under some kind of pan-Arab military dictatorship under the spurious flag of socialism. For Iraq, Israel constitutes a dangerous example for the fighting and freedom-loving Kurds to imitate and achieve their independence by breaking away from Baghdad. For all these three "revolutionary-progressive" regimes—dominated by military dictatorship, anti-Western and pro-Russian—see in the existence of Israel—democratic, Western oriented, technologically sophisticated —a thorn in the flesh, a nuisance and a reminder to their masses that things can be different under a liberal, forward looking regime. Israel is objectively a living challenge to these countries and may sooner or later infect their populations with the germs of social and economic reform.

The Lebanon and Jordan, despite their asserted animosity, have many interests and views in common with Israel. Both have been more exposed to Western influence than their regional neighbors. In both, Islam has undergone some dilution: Lebanon is half Christian (though the Christians are ethnically Arabs) ; the Christian holy places are in Jordan's jurisdiction. French and British influence have been strong in the two, in recent years, and both grope toward democracy in spite of the difficulties posed by their geography, history, and tradition.

The Lebanon is interested in a pluralistic Middle East with each country free to develop its distinct personality and follow its destiny. The non-Moslem majority would like to see its own unitary bi-communal pattern duplicated in a new Palestine.

Jordan fears *Palestine* nationalist separatism as a real threat to its own existence, for the setting up of a Palestinian State beside a truncated Israel would necessitate dismemberment of Jordan as well. Were such a Palestinian State to emerge concomitantly with the *disappearance* of Israel, the even greater danger would be the new state's complete absorption of Jordan.

It was not, therefore, sheer coincidence that Bourguiba chose these two countries for launching his peace campaign. In them he had the best auspices.

But most Israelis are not very receptive to analytical conjecture about the serious prospect of peace. While it is true the leftist groups welcomed Bourguiba's move, their "commitment" to peace is complicated if not compromised by the fact that to them peace is not an end in itself. It is an aspect—an important one, but only one—of their neutralist, socialist, and often pro-Soviet orientation. Their activities in this field cannot be very effective because they are confused by doctrinaire considerations. Their appeal must by necessity, then, be marginal.

In spite of the grimness of our report thus far, there is a discernible improvement in the public atmosphere in Israel. During the last decade the psychological terror exerted against any attempt to freely express nonconformist views has perceptibly subsided. The tone of the government itself, and of the press, has changed a great deal, at least on the surface. Eshkol, Eban, and other leaders, as well as the organs of the press, find it fashionable now to talk peace, though they utter little more than generalities. The change arises from a combination of factors, chief of which is probably the political failure of the Sinai military triumph.* In addition, governments friendly to Israel—the United States, France, and Great Britain—tactfully advised and sometimes pressured the Israeli government to change the style if not the substance of its policy, and to refrain from military adventures that it might otherwise have undertaken. And then, of course, there was the impact of Bourguiba.

A prominent critic of the official Israeli line is the president of the World Zionist Organization, Dr. Nahum Goldmann. At the height of the Bourguiba controversy, at a press conference in Tel Aviv (May 3) , and another in New York ten days later, he intimated that Israeli leaders had failed in the past to seize opportunities to create a more congenial atmosphere for coming to terms with the Arabs; he cautioned against repeating the same mistakes. He added:

---

* The only direct advantage derived from the Sinai campaign was the opening of the port of Eilat to Israeli navigation. This, of course, is a considerable achievement, but out of any proportion to the original objectives of the campaign which aimed at a final showdown and the imposition of peace on Israel's terms. (This refers to the war of 1956 and was written in 1966.)

I welcomed the courageous stand taken by President Bourguiba of Tunisia, even if the contents of his proposals are not acceptable as they are. But the most important thing is that a recognized Arab leader—one of the most popular in his own country—has dared to come out and tell the Arab world they must accept the *fait accompli* of Israel's existence, and look to political methods to normalize Israel-Arab relations, solve the refugee problem, and not rely on a war of annihilation, which is both immoral and unrealistic.

I am sure many Arab leaders in their hearts think in a similar vein, although they may not have the courage displayed by President Bourguiba to state it publicly.

Of course, peace will be a slow process which will take years, he said, because most of the Arab countries are not yet ripe for peace and because of the bitterness which has accumulated for the last seventeen years. "I am not certain whether Israel did not contribute in the past to these tensions, and my attitude toward the policy of retaliation is known." And then he urged that now, since the wall of Arab unity was cracked, the time had come for Israel to be more active.

Just to sit and wait till a new generation of Arabs grow up who may be ready to accept Israel is not enough, and nobody knows whether time works for a peaceful solution.

Among other activities Dr. Goldmann suggested that:

Israel should get Jewish communities outside Israel interested in [Arab-Israel peace] especially in countries where there is a large Arab diaspora, which for many years lived in good relations with the Jewish communities, primarily in South America. . . . The *rencontre* between the Jewish people and the Arab peoples, historically seen, has been one of the most creative, peaceful rencontres in the history of the Jewish people.

It would be a denial of the past, and a violation of the tradition of Arab-Jewish relations for many centuries, if a violent conflict should develop between the Arabs and the Jewish people, with the Arabs becoming the forefront of neo-Nazi movements.

Naturally, the Jews outside of Israel cannot negotiate on behalf of Israel . . . But the Jewish people, with the help of many non-Jewish liberals of good will, could help create an atmosphere which would facilitate and create a psychological basis for direct Israel-Arab contacts.

It is not our purpose here to dwell upon the Arab minority in Israel. It is enough to say that under the pressure of tragic events they have developed attitudes characteristic of any restricted minority. Their voice is in general neither coherent nor expressive of a healthy state of mind; insofar as it is heard (the great mass prefer to brood within themselves) it betokens either abject surrender (e.g., the Arab deputies elected on the *Mapai* lists) or rank sedition (e.g., the *Al Arad*).

Like other helpless minorities, the Arabs as individuals have learned to pay their way, to beget many children (about twice as many as the Jews), and to live with circumstances they would change if they could. But, as in many other places, their leadership has been severely disappointing. It lacks the balanced recognition that the State of Israel is there to stay, combined with the readiness to fight for the full equality to which they are entitled as citizens of a professed democracy.*)

The response of Israeli Arabs to Bourguiba's statements although not vociferous, was generally favorable. First, at a reception in honor of the newly appointed Chief of Israeli Police, Pinkhas Kopel, the Deputy Mayor of Acre, Muhamed Khabashi said that what the Tunisian President saw as a vision of the future was already a reality in Acre, where Moslems, Jews, and Christians lived side by side with mutual respect. He then "invited" Bourguiba to come and see for himself. The Chief of Police in his answering address said that if Bourguiba, who was then in Beirut, only a two-hour drive from Acre, would accept the invitation, the police would see to it that he entered and left the country safely. Pleasant badinage, but hardly on the policy level.

In a more serious pronouncement, a few days later, the Mayor of Nazareth, Abdul Aziz Z'ubi, recalling that the Israeli Arabs, the majority of whom live along the frontiers, "will be the first to suffer the effects of a new war," asked the Arab heads of state whether they had taken into consideration this tragic perspective.

"As Arabs," he said, "we are proud of our Arabism; the happiness of the Arabs (in the Middle East) is our happiness, and their misfortune is our misfortune. Fate wanted us to become citizens of Israel, and like all the minorities in the world, it is is our duty as citizens to remain faithful to the state under whose flag we live.

---

* The population in September 1965 numbered 2,580,600 persons, of whom roughly 2,250,000 were Jews and 275,000 non-Jews (including Moslem and Christian Arabs as well as Druses).

For seventeen years we have enjoyed exemplary stability and tranquility such as we had not known before."

After having denounced the danger of war "which we hear daily preached on the radio and TV of the Arab countries," Mr. Z'ubi asked: "If by misfortune a war breaks out between the Arabs, our brothers, and Israel which we have come to accept as our state, what will become of us?" The Arabs in Israel who wish to live in peace will never agree to become part of the game "of certain leaders" who dream about destruction. In conclusion, Mr. Z'ubi appealed in the name of Arabism and of Arabs in Israel to all heads of the Arab states to abandon any idea of waging war—"for the sake of us, our women and children, our property, and for the good of the whole Arab world."

This is not a selection, but virtually *all* the Israeli Arab public comment on Bourguiba's campaign.

There is indeed a school of thought which holds, though rarely in public, that considering Israel's vital interests, peace is not necessarily an immediate objective. This reasoning points out the desirability of the *status quo,* that is, the current condition of no-peace, for present purposes. Peace is obviously the ultimate aim; but the new state is not yet prepared for Utopia, regardless whether or not the Arabs could be induced to come to terms.

Israel needs time to approach nearer the primary aim of the state, which is *Mizug Galuyot*—integration of the Jewish communities from some three-score diasporas, from disparate cultures and social orders. In perhaps a generation, these kaleidoscopic communities will have become one nation, and until then nothing may distract the Israeli leaders from this prime task. Peace would not only pose new problems which might divert their energies; it might also disastrously delay the fusing of the Jewish communities into one nation. While there is outside danger from the Arabs, the instinct of self-preservation unites all Hebrew Israelis and sharpens their national self-consciousness. Patriotism and the army are the catalysts of cohesive nationhood. Were peace to replace the ever-present tension heightened by sporadic hostilities, each of the major communities—*Ashkenazim* (Europeans, chiefly Eastern) and *Sephardim* (North Africans, Middle Easterners, etc.) —might strive to retain their separateness rather than submit to assimilation.

Hence we hear that peace is desirable but will come only "in about fifteen years." The "public" explanation is that it will take the Arabs that long to prepare for peace. But the rationalizers were not too happy about the distracting intrusion furnished by Bourguiba: it did not fit Israel's independent timetable. Perhaps the best that can be said about the Tunisian President's campaign is that it was too early. Some critics believe this is also the reason why similar opportunities were previously ignored or actually frustrated.

Actually Israel's professions for peace are sincere. Were the Arabs by a miraculous turn of events willing to come to terms on the basis of the status quo (that is, without demanding substantial concessions) Israel would, no doubt, accept the offer and ignore the danger to *mizug galuyot*. The people would go wild in celebrations, and the leaders would share the popular enthusiasm.

But since settlement with the Arabs is still out of sight, Israeli policy has concluded that the state can prosper and grow without peace. Abba Eban has often reiterated the formulation:

> Peace with the Arabs is an important objective of our policy, but it is not a condition for the existence of the State of Israel.

But the question still stands: why is Israel so deficient in the art of peace? There is a single, simple answer. It is not that Israel prefers a state of conflict and tension to normal relations with her neighbors. It is that the minds of the Israelis are totally preoccupied with the job at hand: to build up the country, absorb new immigrants, integrate the various communities into a self-conscious national entity, overcome economic difficulties, and, above all, constantly strengthen the military deterrent. These immediate tasks are so vital and overriding that anything else is regarded as a distraction.

Israeli policy seemed rooted in a conception of imposing upon the Arabs the *status quo*. In 1956 it was hoped that peace would be imposed by force of arms. Since it did not work, it was hoped that the *status quo* would be imposed by Israel's military deterrent power. The hope was that the Arabs would weary of waiting, and would arrive at the same conclusions as Bourguiba—that they must reach a settlement through negotiations.

In a May 1st speech at Petach Tikvah, Prime Minister Eshkol expressed this attitude in an almost brutally frank manner. He praised Bourguiba for his courage in telling the Arabs that Israel could not be destroyed and hence they must begin thinking of a negotiated settlement. But, he said, certain skeptics were suggesting that Bourguiba actually hoped for the liquidation of Israel by means other than war. Never mind these doubts, said Mr. Eshkol. "We have the army which will continue to defend the borders of Israel as they are today."

This self-confidence, this dependence upon military prowess, this posture of the strong and the victorious, may have had advantages. But in the long run it may prove profitless. For the present it may inspire respect—but little sympathy.* In the eyes of public opinion Bourguiba's formula—"peace without victors or vanquished"—is more appealing.

The greatest if not a fatal weakness of Israel's diplomacy is that it has no blueprint of its own for peace. It treats peace proposals like Bourguiba's as if they were onslaughts instead of overtures. Without a plan of their own, the Israelis can only react to the proposals and ideas of others—whether those are antagonists or friends. It is in the nature of things that any plan evolved from without cannot be in the best interests of the State of Israel. Israel is left exposed to all kinds of external pressures, and the necessity of reacting to suggestions of others. It is not a comfortable position. These pressures will surely increase as time goes by, and Israel will find herself more and more on the defensive. No wonder that even her staunch friends have nothing to go by in putting out "feelers" toward a peaceful solution to the Palestine problem.

The situation will become more embarrassing for Israel when her friends begin as they surely will sooner or later, to evolve ideas of their own. Both the United States and France can be expected to begin thinking of some plan for stabilization of the Middle East. It is of greatest importance for Israel whether such plans are based, even partially, upon Israeli suggestions, or if they will have to be worked out entirely without Israeli participation. In the latter case Israel will unavoidably find itself confronted by plans and suggestions which cannot be expected to give major consideration to Israel's legitimate interests.

---

* The late Moshe Sharet was sometimes doubtful whether it would work. In his book *Traveling in Asia* he disputed those who "believe you can reach peace by force."

11

Contacts

HAVE THERE BEEN ANY CONTACTS BETWEEN ISRAELI REPRESENTA-
tives and Bourguiba? In the second half of April, rumors were
persistent that such contacts were in process or had actually taken
place.

The Beirut *Al Jaryda* published on its front page a story that
"a meeting between President Bourguiba and the Israeli Minister
of Foreign Affairs, Mrs. Golda Meir, was set to take place in one
of the Western capitals." The Jordanian newspaper *Al Manar*
wrote that Mrs. Meir would meet Bourguiba in Teheran. No
other source corroborated the projected meeting; in Jerusalem the
Israeli government said merely that Mrs. Meir would be in Europe
at that time for a short vacation. Such a meeting did not take place
but we do not know if it was ever intended. The Arab newspapers
might have been inspired by a desire to compromise Bourguiba
in the eyes of their public.

For some curious reason, the press in many countries published
reports from Tel Aviv that Mrs. Meir had invited Bourguiba to
come to Israel to discuss peace. These reports seem to have been
based purely on her derisive remark in the Knesset that some
Mapam member might go to Tunisia and bring the President or
his representative to Israel.

The Tunisians seem to have taken the story seriously, and rejected the "invitation." In a televised interview on "Europe 1" the
Tunisian Foreign Minister, Habib Bourguiba, Jr., stated: "Not
only is there no consideration of a visit of the President—but the
President would not even answer the Israeli invitation in the negative, because we do not recognize Israel."

L'Action, the French-language organ of the Socialist Destour party officially denied on April 23 that the Tunisian President had sought contact with Israeli representatives. The paper asserted that such reports emanating from "Zionist circles" were absurd, since no Arab leader could substitute himself for the Palestine Arabs in the choice of a method for their "liberation." But the newspaper did not exclude the possibility that under certain conditions Bourguiba would be willing to mediate. "Once the basis for discussions was found, Tunisia could facilitate contacts between the Israelis and the Palestine Arabs."

Bourguiba himself felt obliged to clarify the matter for his own public opinion without foreclosing all possibilities. In his Carthage speech on April 21, he said he did not believe a visit by him to Israel at that time, or his receiving Israeli emissaries in Tunis, would serve any useful purpose. If he were a Palestinian leader, he would engage in such discussions, even though they might prove sterile, as had his contacts with the French before liberation; they might also prove useful.

For their part, Israelis were far less forthright in scotching rumors. On April 9, Prime Minister Eshkol, speaking before the Tel Aviv Press Club, intimated that contacts had been made with a view of clarifying the intentions and meaning of the Tunisian President's initiative. He also intimated that because of these cautious efforts, he must remain silent.

The New York Times correspondent in Israel, Granger Blair, cabled his newspaper on April 24, that "the impression has been gained in some quarters here that Israel may have made some discreet soundings of the Bourguiba proposals . . . though there is no official confirmation of this."

Reports like these appeared at the time when Central Committee of the *Mapam* party had proclaimed its independent political campaign, which included the delegation of one of its leaders, I. Barzilay, Vice President of the Knesset, to Europe for the purpose of getting in touch with "progressive Tunisian circles." Some interpreted this as an indirect method by the Israel government of sounding out the Tunisian government on the meaning of the Bourguiba proposals.

The Israel government not only did not confirm it, but expressed criticism and suspicion. Especially did "governmental circles" criticize the propaganda campaign that *Mapam* launched in connection with the Barzilay mission; such publicity could only defeat its very purpose, they said. Yet at the same time these anonymous governmental circles hinted at steps undertaken by the government to get in touch with Bourguiba, and gave a half-hearted blessing to Barzilay's mission.

As to the essence, merits, and character of the *Mapam* project, a government spokesman declared it was not obligatory to co-ordinate it with official institutions. Whether such "private" missions really could help the quiet efforts of Israeli governmental factors to make contact with Arab circles, is an open question. In any case, the spokesman said, the government did not see itself authorized to prevent *Mapam* from attempting such contacts, except in matters involving national security.

From this statement by an anonymous government spokesman one may conclude that the Israel government did at that time make efforts to get in touch with Arab circles, which in all probability means Tunisians. And though the government denied any "co-ordination" with the *Mapam* mission, the wording of its denial was vague enough to permit the interpretation that the government did not oppose the mission, and might even have been interested in its outcome.

Actually, Barzilay went to Dublin with other members of the Knesset to participate in an international parliamentary convention. He could have tried there to contact the Tunisian delegation. Whether he did so, and this led him to go somewhere other than Dublin, has been kept a secret. *Mapam,* probably under pressure of the government, issued a denial: meeting with the Tunisian leaders was not on Mr. Barzilay's schedule. This was in outright contradiction of previous announcements made with great fanfare.

The most sensational piece of news came from Nahum Gold-mann, President of both the World Zionist Organization and the World Jewish Congress. At the height of the storm in the Arab world around Bourguiba's initiative, Dr. Goldmann announced at a press conference in Tel Aviv (May 3, 1965) that the World Jewish Congress entertained steady contacts with the Tunisian President through its political secretary, A. L. Easterman, stationed in London. "Mr. Easterman," said Dr. Goldmann, "has known Bourguiba well for the last twelve years; they meet once or twice a year concerning various Jewish problems. These contacts will continue." Dr. Goldmann added that in spite of this, "the Israeli government did not propose that I should establish contacts in connection with Mr. Bourguiba's declarations, though there is room to strengthen activities in this field, to create a propitious climate for peace."

Would he be ready to undertake the task of making direct contacts with Bourguiba about his peace initiative? a journalist asked. Dr. Goldmann would "cross that bridge when he comes to it," implying that this task had not been offered him. He asserted he would be willing at any time to assist the Israeli Prime Minister in any mission, in any capacity whether as president of either organization or "as a Jew, a Zionist, or simply as Dr. Goldmann."

He went on to advise the Israel government then and again later, to utilize world Jewish organizations to counteract Arab propaganda in their countries, and to help plant the seed of peace by contacting Arab leaders. Whether the Israel government gave its blessing to such initiatives cannot be ascertained, but some papers criticized the idea as being "beside the point."

Mr. Easterman's meetings with Bourguiba were, therefore, never more than merely part of the work of a World Jewish Congress employee stationed in London; and the contacts were about "various Jewish problems," not about Palestine. It is difficult to imagine, however, that such regular meetings should never mention the Palestine problem, as if any aspect of "Jewish problems" could help but overlap with those of Israel! We may assume that if Mr. Easterman's contacts were as close as described, he may have heard something from Mr. Bourguiba about the latter's initiative, but for obvious reasons neither he nor Dr. Goldmann made any revelations.

In any event, the advice the president of the world Zionist Organization gave the Israelis in his press conference is significant: "I don't think we should attach great importance to the concrete proposals Bourguiba advanced, nor take too seriously the details of his proposals. What is important is the fact that an Arab leader publicly raised the possibility of bringing the conflict with Israel to arbitration, to find a solution without recourse to war." He added that in his opinion the time had come to embark upon the more dynamic policy of creating an atmosphere which could eventually lead to a dialogue between Israel and the Arabs.

Goldmann's interpretation seems to make perfect sense if we remember that when Bourguiba advanced such proposals as "back to partition," he was speaking not to Israel but to Arabs. In exhorting his people to begin thinking in terms of a negotiated settlement, he had to use terms as palatable to the Arabs as possible. It was not his responsibility to formulate an "Israeli" solution.

Tunisian Ambassador Masmoudi spoke in exactly the same vein

to Uri Avneri, editor of the Israeli *Ha'olam Hazeh,* in a meeting they had in Paris at the beginning of May 1965. In essence, Masmoudi told Avneri the situation required a "division of labor": the Tunisian President would talk about the imperative of peace and prepare the background among the Arabs; someone of influence must do the same among the Israelis.

Were there even indirect contacts on behalf of the Israel government? The record shows some truly strange and incongruous ones. Their grand climax came at the end of April 1965, when a delegation of West German Social Democratic Party leaders spent three days in Tunisia in intensive discussions with Bourguiba and other Neo-Destour personalities concerning problems of a peaceful settlement of the Israeli-Arab conflict.

The wheels had begun turning at an informal meeting of leaders of the Socialist International a few days earlier at British Prime Minister Harold Wilson's official residence at Chequers. Participants included West German Socialists and the secretary general of *Mapai,* Reuben Barkat. Bourguiba's initiative was discussed; it evoked expressions of approval, and even enthusiasm. At that juncture the German socialists suggested to Mr. Barkat that they should try to mediate between Bourguiba and *Mapai* since they were going to Tunisia on other business the next week. Mr. Barkat acquiesced.

When the Germans left for Tunisia they, or their friends, leaked the news. *Mapai* officially denied the story and the spokesman for *Mapai's* central committee, Yossi Sharid, told the press on April 29 that neither he nor any of *Mapai's* hierarchy knew anything about it. "The *Mapai* institutions learned about it from the press," he said. He asserted there was no contact whatsoever between *Mapai* and West German Social Democrats concerning this matter. The denial was probably issued out of apprehension that the truth might jeopardize the mission of the German Social Democrats.

Their final report, though full of contradictions, was, on the whole, rather encouraging. After reporting to their own leadership in Bonn, Hans Dingels, Secretary for International Affairs, accompanied by Hans Jahn, a prominent member of the Bundestag and legal adviser of the party, spent three days in Israel, where they held several sessions with *Mapai* leaders, trying to convey the proceedings and conclusions of their visit with the Tunisians. They also met with Prime Minister Eshkol and Foreign Minister Meir.

In Bonn, official circles of the Social Democratic Party were asserting without reservations that their delegation had carried a message from Mapai to Tunisia's Neo-Destour party. Yet this was denied by Herr Dingels upon his arrival in Tel Aviv. At Lod Airport in Israel when questioned by journalists, he declared that his meeting with Bourguiba and other Neo-Destour leaders were of his own and his colleagues' initiative, and that they had not acted on behalf of *Mapai;* that Israel's problem was only one of the several international issues they had discussed with the Tunisians. He also said he would refrain from revealing details about his conversation with the Tunisian President until he reported to the *Mapai* leadership. But he told reporters:

> I can only say that I was very impressed by what Bourguiba told me, and everything he said was expressed in a responsible manner. He is ready to face the consequences of his views in connection with evolving a plan to liquidate the Israeli-Arab conflict by peaceful means.

But his colleague, Hans Vishnievsky, another Bundestag member who had been at the Tunisian discussions, but who did not come to Israel, was more talkative. On his return to Bonn on May 4th, he told correspondents: "Bourguiba does not want to see tanks in the whole of the Middle East. He prefers to see tractors there." He added that Bourguiba had shown full understanding of Bonn's desire to establish diplomatic relations with Israel. "After all," Vishnievsky quoted the Tunisian President, "eighty-seven countries entertain diplomatic relations with Israel, and there is nothing to prevent West Germany doing the same." Bourguiba then assured him that several Arab leaders agreed with his thinking about relations with Germany and about the imperative need to bring peace to the Middle East; he advanced as proof, among other things, that the suggestion to expel Tunisia from the Arab League had been withdrawn. And the Bundestag member concluded: "Bourguiba can afford to speak out as clearly as he does because of the absolute stability of his regime."

The Mapai leaders did not divulge the substance of these conferences; all Barkat volunteered was that there had been an exchange of views, and that the German Social Democrats dwelt on their party's Middle East policy "and their contacts with the Neo-Destour party and President Bourguiba." *Ha'aretz* reported that Herr Dingels told his hosts in Israel, including Eshkol and Mrs. Meir, that the Tunisian President hated war and had serious intentions of bringing about a peaceful resolution to the Israeli-Arab conflict.

Before taking off for Germany, the Germans held a press conference at Lod Airport. They intimated that if their party were successful at the forthcoming Bundestag elections and became part of the government, they would undertake mediation between Israel and the Arabs. Their present visits to Tunisia and Israel were the beginning of a crystallization of their party's foreign policy in the Middle East, said Herr Jahn. Dingels hinted that the Social Democrats would try to plan an important role in the Middle East, and spark a drive for peace in the area.

"We wish to occupy a position in the Middle East which would permit us to help things to advance in this region," Herr Dingels declared, with Herr Jahn nodding approval.

Regarding an eventual rapprochement between Israel and Tunis, in the light of the mood prevailing in Tunisia, both delegates advised "realism" (whatever that may mean) rather than optimism, and in general intimated it was still too early for conclusions. The cautious reactions in Israel were, therefore, in their view, fully justified. "There is no doubt," Mr. Dingels declared, "that our contacts with the leaders of the Neo-Destour will continue and that we will be in touch with them in the near future. As to *Mapai*, it was decided in principle to arrange regular meetings from time to time, to exchange views and information."

Both Dingels and Jahn took great pains to deny that the German Social Democrats were the bearers of any written message from *Mapai* to Bourguiba. They were so insistent on this point that it aroused some suspicion.

The last of the rumors about contacts was connected with Pierre Mendes-France. It was he who, as French Premier, made the historic declaration in Carthage on July 31, 1954, solemnly recognizing Tunisia's right to independence. He is regarded by many as godfather of sovereign Tunisia—and perhaps more than that. He is a warm personal friend of Habib Bourguiba. He is also a Jew who makes no bones about it, or about his friendship with Israeli leaders.

On June 1, 1965, Tunisia with great pomp began her colorful celebrations of the tenth anniversary of the historic event of Bourguiba's return from exile. Mendes-France attended the fête. Reports immediately became current that the former French Premier, while attending the celebration in Tunis, had discussed with the

Tunisian President, *inter alia,* the "whole complex of Middle Eastern problems."

Before long *Ma'ariv* published a sensational dispatch from its Paris correspondent: Mendes-France was coming to Israel with a message from Bourguiba and would, it was implied, perform the role of mediator between Bourguiba and the Israel government. On the surface it sounded plausible; Mendes-France had the obvious qualifications and connections for such a mission. There was also official confirmation that Mendes-France was indeed coming to Israel. The occasion was an invitation from the president of the Weizmann Institute in Rehovot (who happened to be Vice Premier Eban), to deliver a paper on monetary problems at the third international "Rehovot Conference on Science in the Service of New States."

Ma'ariv's sensational "revelation" proved a monumental embarrassment to all concerned. The Israel government promptly dismissed the report in the most unequivocal terms as "pure fantasy." To M. Mendes-France it was so mortifying that he thought of cancelling his Israel appearance—to which he had agreed eight months earlier, long before Bourguiba set out for his Middle Eastern tour.

He did not forgo his visit, but he broke a rule which he had followed throughout his public career: not to publish denials. He issued a statement branding the dispatch a hoax, and selected a most unlikely medium for disseminating his denial: the Egyptian Middle East News Agency. In a release to that Agency's Paris correspondent, he declared:

> There is absolutely no link between my recent visit to Tunisia and the visit I am to pay to Israel in the middle of August. I will carry no message whatsoever from the Tunisian leader to the Israel government. The only purpose of my visit is to deliver a report on monetary problems at the International Symposium on the Developing Countries, which will take place in Israel between the 9th and the 19th of August. I am on good terms with many African and Arab leaders and I wish to safeguard this relationship.

He emphasized that if he deviated from his custom not to accord interviews to the press, it was uniquely because he wanted to dissipate any uncertainties as to the purpose of his visit to Israel.

Mendes-France delivered a brilliant paper at the symposium. But the advance article in *Ma'ariv,* picked up by many newspapers throughout the world, made everyone inhibited and self-conscious. If there were discussions on other subjects, there was no general knowledge of them.

There was no publicly reported follow-up to this chain of events. Israeli spokesmen, however, began to exhibit an even more serious tone in discussing Bourguiba, paying him greater compliments, though basically they did not change their attitude on the merits of the proposals.

More than a year later, an invitation was sent to President Bourguiba (among others) to attend the cornerstone-laying ceremony of the Harry Truman Center for the Advancement of International Peace, to take place near the Hebrew University in Jerusalem. To the astonishment of everyone, Bourguiba responded with a telegram which read:

> I am thankful to you for your cordial invitation to participate in the ceremony of laying the foundation for the Center for the Advancement of Peace to take place in the City of Jerusalem. Due to previous engagements I am unable to participate in this event, and I wish every success in your enterprise.

He addressed the cable to President Truman; the invitation had come from him. But it is quite unprecedented for an Arab leader to send greetings to an Israeli institution on the occasion of a ceremony taking place in Israeli territory—or even to acknowledge that such a thing exists.

The Israel Foreign Office was so flabbergasted that it ordered *Kol Israel* (Israeli national radio network) not to broadcast the news (after it had already appeared in a routine newscast). When the editor of the news program protested, the Foreign Office information service said that news of Bourguiba's reply would harm him with the Arabs. The editor retorted that the item had been disseminated all over the world; moreover, it was in the spirit of the Tunisian President's larger campaign. The Foreign Office functionary said the cable should not be considered news, having been sent more than six months before. But when the news editor got the original cable he noted that it was dated July 7, 1966, only four days previously.

The spisode developed into a small scandal, with interpellations in the Knesset and critical articles in the press. Foreign Minister Eban "explained" that it was a misunderstanding and that the official in question had been misled by false information.

At his press conference in Beirut on March 11, Bourguiba made the startling declaration that though in the Palestine conflict the Arabs had been the defeated, he considered himself a neutral. Taken at face value, his statement could, of course, mean that since he took no part in the war, and since the Arabs had achieved nothing by their frozen intransigence, he had decided to take a position above the fray. But he was not neutral concerning the essence of the conflict. And although he was, indeed, part of the Arab world, he would not renounce his freedom to express his independent views or his freedom to maneuver and act. It is in these respects that he preferred to be neutral. At the same news conference, and on many other occasions, he declared: "All my life, I have been a man of political action and not of words."

This section of his declaration might have been the most sensational element of his whole campaign. It contained the implication that he offered himself as a mediator to bring the warring sides to the conference table. But he soon abandoned this idea, at least temporarily. Instead he stipulated that if Israel would agree to discuss a settlement on the basis of the United Nations resolutions, he would try to persuade Nasser and other leaders to enter negotiations on neutral territory somewhere in Europe. He refused to contemplate direct contacts with Israel in any form, denying rumors that he was about to meet Israelis in his country or anywhere else. Contacts, he said, must be direct between the Palestinian Arabs and Israel.

Whatever effects these meager indirect contacts may eventually have upon the future Middle East relations, they did no good to Bourguiba's standing with the Arabs, especially in Egypt. The contacts served as an additional excuse for the Egyptian press to denounce Bourguiba as a traitor to the Arab cause. Editorials and columns in the Egyptian press said that these missions "revealed the amazing conspiracy of Bourguiba," and Cairo commentators pointed out that the visits of the German emissaries, coupled with Bourguiba's latest far-reaching pronouncements, showed that the Tunisian President was now ready to enter negotiations with Israel through West German mediation.

On April 20, Radio Cairo commented that the suggestions to bring together Israelis with Tunisian officials were nothing but a provocation directed to all the Arabs. They were aimed at splitting the Arab camp.

12

Reactions in the Western World

TO GET THE FULL MEASURE OF THE IMPACT OF THE TUNISIAN
President's initiative upon Western opinion, it is enough to note
that several important newspapers in various countries proposed
Habib Bourguiba for the 1965 Nobel Peace Prize: the Norwegian
Dagbladet, the *Journal de Geneve*, and the *Washington Daily
News*, among others. On August 4, the *Christian Science Monitor*
wrote:

> President Bourguiba should be awarded the Nobel Prize for the
> efforts he has made in hope of promoting a durable peace be-
> tween Israel and the Arab countries.

In some of the most prestigious newspapers in Europe (and to
a lesser extent in the United States) he was almost daily in the
news, often front page. For weeks leading European newspapers,
magazines and TV networks featured extended interviews, which
sought to clarify his ideas and intentions. In the process, a great
deal of editorial praise and support was expressed.

Next only to the Arab countries and Israel, it was in France
that Bourguiba's initiative aroused greatest interest, for a variety
of reasons. French public opinion is more interested in the affairs
of the Middle East and North Africa than is any other Western
country; serious newspapers give considerable space to Arab and
Israeli affairs, not limited to the conflict between them. *Le Monde*,
for instance, maintains a daily average of a full page of African
and Middle Eastern news and comment, often featured on the
front page. French magazines occasionally give them cover stories.
Thus for several weeks the "Bourguiba spirit" preoccupied the

French press and diplomatic circles, and many larger groups of intellectuals interested in the Middle East; television programs were dedicated to Bourguiba's tour. On one, Arab as well as Israeli leaders appeared, and expressed mutually belligerent views, but the moderator wound up with: "We, too, are of the opinion advocated by Mr. Bourguiba, that everything has to be solved peacefully." French television is an institution of the French government.

Le Monde, in a front-page editorial on April 25–26, 1965 declared:

> One would like to compare Mr. Bourguiba to a child, so great is the temptation to see in him the hero of that fairy tale in which a lone little boy seeing the King with no clothes on, dares to cry out in a loud voice: 'The King is naked. . . .' But to describe this orator we will rather recall St. John of the Golden Mouth who told the mighty and the impostors to their face the truth though this made him out a most ill-behaved person. Likewise, the Tunisian chief of state has said clearly what many other political leaders in the Arab world murmur under their breaths: Since war against Israel is an impossibility one should think of other solutions. . . .

In an editorial under the heading "Very Brave," the *London Observer* (April 26) wrote:

> Tunisia's President Bourguiba has shown great courage. . . . Even though his terms are unacceptable to both sides, he has broken the ice on the Arab side.
>
> This initiative should open the way for the score or so of African states which have cordial relations with both Israel and the Arabs to end this dangerous quarrel which affects Africa as much as the Middle East. African leadership should not let this opportunity pass without at least an attempt to mediate.

The *Manchester Guardian,* in an editorial on April 23, titled "Palestine Viewed from Tunis," wrote:

> President Bourguiba has been saying some revolutionary things about Israel. He thinks that the orthodox Arab line of complete inflexibility is doomed to failure; he does not believe in a military solution 'in present circumstances'; he even wants to see 'a compromise. . . .' Such views . . . inevitably brought much criticism on his head. But . . . he is undeterred. . . .

The details of a possible compromise are at this stage less important than that a responsible Arab leader says openly that a compromise is desirable. . . .

. . . . If Israelis want President Bourguiba's opinions to become really respectable, they ought, of course, to attack them. Whether intentionally or not, by constantly assailing President Nasser as their most dangerous enemy they have helped him to retain sufficient credit among his Arab colleagues to restrain the more hotheaded of them; and thus the crisis feared last summer, when the Israel water scheme started, did not happen. But if President Nasser acts more responsibly than he talks, it is useful to have another Arab President talking responsibly too.

The Italian press widely publicized Bourguiba's declarations. From Rome, Lisa Palmieri-Billig wrote in the *Jerusalem Post* on April 4:

"Bourguiba is seen as a possible bulwark against Nasser's aggressive anti-Western policies and bellicose goal in regard to Israel. . . . The Christian-Democratic *Il Popolo* said . . . 'While one can understand the legitimacy of the Arab world's striving for unity, it becomes impossible to accept the idea that eventual achievement of this aim may or must signify the physical destruction of the state and the people of Israel.' "

The independent center-left *La Stampa* said: "There is no real peace where blackmail reigns in place of justice and where once again a program of genocide is proclaimed with sadistic joy."

In the United States, the great newspapers felt that here at long last was a bold and imaginative attempt, and public opinion, perhaps even more than in France, took an unmistakably friendly attitude. In high governmental circles in Washington Bourguiba was especially admired since he was the only Afro-Asian leader favoring President Johnson's type of negotiated settlement of the Vietnam war without pre-conditions.

Typical of the mood was an editorial in *The New York Times* of April 24, which is of special significance since the paper's editorial policy is pro-Israel.

PRESIDENT BOURGUIBA'S COURAGE

The courage of President Habib Bourguiba . . . can be measured by the denunciations to which he was subjected by his fellow Arabs yesterday. Arab newspapers accused him of "high treason," and declared him to have "become raving mad."

Implicit in this torrent of abuse is the premise that an Arab is a traitor if he is willing to accept anything less than total destruction of the State of Israel. . . .

Against this background the specifics of the Bourguiba suggestions—which are hardly likely to arouse enthusiasm in Israel itself —are unimportant compared to the historic fact that a major Arab leader has dared talk some sense on this most delicate of issues. . . .

. . . Coming at a time of mounting tension over the Arab plans to divert the waters of the Jordan River, the Bourguiba intervention is particularly significant. Fear of war over this issue has been broadly expressed throughout the Middle East for months now, and the actual outbreak of organized fighting could set off a conflagration of major proportions. . . . The courage of this move is exceeded only by its statesmanship, though it would be a mistake to expect any results in the near future from the seed of wisdom that President Bourguiba has now publicly planted.

The Washington Post in an editorial on April 24, wrote:

Tunisian President Habib Bourguiba is a courageous man indeed. . . . The cynics may say that Israel does not intend to comply with the United Nations resolutions [concerning taking back the Arab refugees], and that Bourguiba may only have been impelled to speak out in order to sweeten an American reception for an aid emissary he reportedly is sending this way shortly.

But it is at least refreshing to find one Arab leader daring to publicly face reality, to admit Israel is here to stay. . . .

The United States government greeted Bourguiba's initiative warmly in an official statement. On April 23, the State Department's news director, Robert J. McCloskey, announced at a Washington briefing:

We welcome wholeheartedly any initiative designed to bring about a permanent and peaceful solution of the Arab-Israeli dispute. President Bourguiba has made some suggestions which could form the substance for negotiations.

Now, I should add that while any comment by us on these suggestions at this time would be inappropriate, I would say that the forthright way in which President Bourguiba has broached this subject offers hope that fresh approaches may be made to this difficult problem.

Beyond this, the usually well-informed and responsible *Jeune*

Afrique reported on April 18, that President Johnson had invited President Bourguiba to America to discuss his peace plan. According to the magazine, whose editor is an influential Tunisian, the American President's invitation came as a gesture of the United States' appreciation of the "realism and political courage" his peace initiative evinced. But apparently second thoughts caused the plans to be changed. Instead, it was Habib Bourguiba Jr., the Tunisian President's son and Foreign Minister, who went to Washington. He arrived on April 26 and had extensive discussions with Secretary of State Rusk.

Although informed circles in Washington knew that a main topic discussed by the two Foreign Ministers was the Tunisian President's proposal for a negotiated settlement of the Palestine problem, with Secretary Rusk expressing approval, the State Department found it necessary publicly to play it coy. Even before the meeting, officials in the State Department expressed the private opinion that any additional statements would not be desirable. Too much approval by the United States, they said, could only embarrass rather than strengthen Bourguiba in the Arab world. He might be accused of acting as an American "agent."

The officials also pointed out as "background information" that the Tunisian Foreign Minister's visit was decided upon several weeks earlier, before the Tunisian President had circulated his Palestine proposals. After the meeting, the spokesman declared that Bourguiba Jr.'s visit was arranged to prepare the ground for a loan from the World Bank; that Bourguiba's statements were briefly mentioned, but no conclusions arrived at; and that Rusk expressed approval only in that the United States "supports peace efforts anywhere in the world." At the same time a spokesman for the White House declared that President Johnson was unaware of the item in *Jeune Afrique* to the effect that he had invited Bourguiba to Washington to discuss the Tunisian peace proposals.

American officials went so far as to recommend withholding the announcement about increased American economic assistance to Tunisia. Some observers ascribed this reticence partly to the United States' fears of an adverse effect on relations with the Middle East Arabs and partly to Bourguiba's own apprehensions concerning de Gaulle's reaction: too much enthusiasm in Washington adversely affects the attitude of the French President. In addition, Bourguiba's Minister of the Interior, and chief economic planner, Ahmed ben Sallah, was simultaneously in the United States to discuss with American officials his country's new four-year plan. Any American aid in this connection might look like a "cash" reward for the Tunisians' fine work; hence the Tunisians' visit in Washington must be made to appear unconnected with the problems of the Middle East.

Reference has already been made to the meeting of the Socialist International at Chequers, the official residence of the British Prime Minister. Though the prominent leaders from various countries who participated (among them such former heads of government as Guy Mollet of France) had met to deal with problems of concern to the socialist parties and their stand on the war in Vietnam, the Tunisian's initiative became a major topic. Most participants were enthusiastic; one said: "Bourguiba has revealed himself as a personality of world stature"; another thought he seemed determined to make a bid for rival leadership in the Arab world, to bring it into greater conformity with modern reality.

In April, Bourguiba's personal representative, Mongi Slim, went to the Far East carrying a message from President Bourguiba to the heads of State of India, Pakistan, and Indonesia. In New Delhi he conferred with Prime Minister Shastri, who endorsed Bourguiba's proposals for direct Arab-Israel negotiations and expressed his appreciation of Bourguiba's initiative as an important step toward a possible thaw in the Middle East. The influential *Indian Express* (April 30) dedicated an editorial to Bourguiba's effort, praising it and suggesting that India should at long last follow the example of many other nations which entertain friendly relations with both Israel and the Arabs.

On March 14, an editorial in the major English-language paper *The Sunday Nation* in Nairobi, Kenya, called upon the African states to avoid being drawn by Colonel Nasser into a "quarrel not of their making." It expressed fear that the diplomatic war between West Germany and Egypt would pull in other African states.

> It has always been the policy of President Nasser to make things difficult for brother African countries which deal with Israel. For this reason it is in the best interests of Africa that President Bourguiba's wise words be heeded diligently by Arab states who should refrain from doing anything drastic to the embarrassment of other states [on the African continent].

The newspaper *Express* in Lagos, Nigeria, commented very favorably:

> President Bourguiba having made his wise statements has by this shown his realism and as a true African, expressed what we all think is the only means of bringing about peace in the Middle East. . . . He did not betray the Arab cause but rendered it an invaluable service. It should be the duty of each and every African country to make clear to our Arab friends those basic truths which President Bourguiba has so aptly expressed.

There was little reaction in the Communist countries, and that little was hostile. One of the two Communist newspapers in the Middle East, *Nida* (Lebanon), sharply attacked Bourguiba. And not surprisingly, the *People's Daily* in Peking also came out with a sharp condemnation. By advocating a negotiated settlement in the Palestine conflict, the paper stated, the Tunisian President joined the three-pronged aggression of American imperialism, West German militarism, and Zionism. The Communist organ emphasized that the Chinese people continued unswervingly to support the Arab peoples in their struggle against "imperialism and its instrument, which is Israel."

The only international institution in which Bourguiba's initiative did not create a ripple was the United Nations, though it should have taken up Bourguiba's lead eagerly, since he made the United Nations resolutions the starting point for his solution. Despite Bourguiba's insistence that the crux of the present matter was to bring the Israel-Arab conflict back to the legality of the United Nations, that august institution did not move a finger.

This inaction may provide a measure of its effectiveness. Though it deals directly with very important aspects of the Israel-Arab conflict—through the United Nations Rehabilitation and Works Administration and the peace-keeping force—the fact remains that the United Nations seems more dedicated to perpetuating the status quo than to moving the conflict away from dead center.

Not only did the United Nations do nothing constructive, it was actually a discouraging factor. A *New York Times* dispatch characterized the mood there as "skeptical."

Part Two

Motivations and Purposes

13

Don Quixote or Supreme Realist?

VIEWED SUPERFICIALLY, BOURGUIBA'S ADVENTURE MAKES LITTLE sense. A leader of a small and poor country is confronted with many local economic, social, political, and educational problems. Instead of addressing himself to the problems of his own people and his country, he decides to strike out for a long tour—eight weeks: to visit faraway lands, to tell them to behave in a more civilized manner, to settle their conflicts by peaceful means.

Who is he? He is no direct party to the conflict; Israel has never been at war with Tunisia. They have no common borders; Palestine is at one end of the Mediterranean, Tunisia at the other. Tunisia had not participated in the Arab-Israel war of 1948–1949, because, apart from everything else, it did not exist as a state. And there are no Palestine refugees in his country.

He represents no Great Power; he has neither responsibility nor force to back him up; his national army is not even commensurate with the small size and population of his country. He certainly has no economic or any other inducement to offer—he receives aid from several powers and is constantly knocking on the doors in Paris, Washington, and Bonn to get enough to make ends meet.

Yet he appears on the international scene and with a passion verging almost on obsession tells the Arabs and Israel how to settle their two-decade-long differences. He makes forty major statements in three months—one every second day; keeping his own people in sustained excitement concerning a problem about which they could not care less; about a country which few of them, if any, have ever seen—or would even care to. Without a blink, he tackes *the* most thorny, perplexing, seemingly insoluble international problem—a problem which great powers tried so hard and for so long to eschew. He has not even Don Quixote's restraining Sancho Panza at his side to caution him of the difference between windmills and dragons. Indeed, there is in his initiative something Cervantes sought to portray in his recital of the ancient Knight's grotesque attempts to teach humanity wisdom and chivalry.

Yet many thoughtful heads obviously agree that Bourguiba, though a man of vision, is no Don Quixote. He is an outstanding realist, what an American newsman called "the supreme pragmatist." How, then, explain his fantastic undertaking.

In spite of the public aspects of Bourguiba's tour, it is still surrounded by mystery. Many capitals are still speculating about the questions raised. First there is the unusual, if not unique, length and itinerary. Seldom if ever has a chief of state absented himself from his country for so long, to visit so many foreign countries: eight in eight weeks. Such a protracted and dangerous pilgrimage must have had behind it an overwhelming reason—a reason which is also a great goal. What could it be?

Most of the lands he visited, including the non-Arabic Yugoslavia, Turkey, and Greece, are hardly centers of economic abundance and technological progress, from which he could have sought assistance. Nor does it seem likely his purpose was the strengthening of cultural relations; in this field Bourguiba's aspirations lie elsewhere: he is the champion of a French-speaking community of nations centered in Paris, composed primarily of former French colonies in Africa.

And it does not stand to reason that so responsible a leader as Bourguiba would have left urgent matters of state for eight weeks to pay courtesy visits to eight countries with most of which he had no truly close relations, spending an average of almost a week in each. A day or two would have sufficed for most; and the visits could have been staggered, instead of back-to-back. Also, at courtesy visits it is not customary to deliver explosive statements on controversial issues—to embarrass one's hosts and provoke scandals. So, after ruling out technical and economic aid, cultural exchange, and courtesy calls upon heads of government—the question repeats itself: what was the purpose of his tour? What was his motivation? Let us explore the mystery.

In a long interview, Jean Daniel, editor of *Nouvel Observateur*, (April 15) asked these same questions and quoted some of the most revealing remarks Bourguiba made during his campaign—but remained vague and somewhat confused as to the reason he undertook it in the first place.

Daniel began by saying that he had not come to ask for any further statements.

I would like rather that you reveal for the readers of *Nouvel Observateur* the reasons which impelled you to become the only leader in the Arab world proposing a negotiated solution to the Palestine problem. You have dedicated so many years to reconquering your popularity in the Middle East. Why did you put yourself in a situation which made you lose all over again? Why did you choose precisely this juncture and precisely this moment of your tour?

Replied Bourguiba:

I did not choose anything at all. Before I undertook this tour in the Arab countries I did not think that I should have to express myself publicly concerning a solution to the awful drama of Palestine. Of course, I have had opinions which I often expressed before Arab diplomats in the course of private conversations: I have insisted that one chooses between war and negotiations, and that one ceases rejecting the one and the other by escaping into incendiary speeches. I found that there is a certain flippancy, if not demagoguery, in constantly promising to Palestinian refugees an early return to their country, without having done for the last seventeen years anything really concrete and effective to further the chance of such a return. But I have always refrained from intervening publicly because, after all, it is not directly our business. One will never have said it enough: It is first of all the business of the Palestinians themselves. Apart from that I did not want to introduce a discordant note in the concert of voices which express the desire to unite the Arab world.

I have always profoundly understood the humiliation which was inflicted upon the Arab peoples by the creation of the state of Israel. When the vote was taken in the United Nations which gave birth to this state, I foresaw the tragedies which have accumulated since then; but Tunisia was far from independence, and had to devote all her attention to her own struggle. I voiced protests, together with my brothers the Algerians and the Moroccans. Appreciating fully this humiliation and the wounds which that decision [of the United Nations] inflicted, I also understood that the governments more directly concerned than we with this problem were showing no success in surmounting it. Tunisia did not pretend to give lessons to anybody. . . .

The proof that I had no intention of provoking any incidents? I can give it to you immediately: Before my departure for Cairo I paid a visit, as you know, to my great friend Marshal Tito.* My trip to Yugoslavia was extremely interesting, fruitful, and in the course of our discussions, Marshal Tito and I discovered very many common points between the Tunisian experience and that of Yugoslavia. When we were about to formulate the usual joint communiqué, we agreed to denounce colonial oppression, which still persists in the world. The list which our ministers made up contained such countries as Angola, Mozambique, Portuguese Guinea, etc.

In this inventory, we did not find Palestine, although we, as Tunisians, insisted that it should be included. The Yugoslavs, very reticent, remained unconvinced by our arguments.

In order to emphasize the point that, in our eyes, at any rate, the colonial aspect is at least in principle the same in Palestine as elsewhere, I asked that the list of the countries still under colonial domination be omitted altogether and replaced instead by a sentence denouncing colonialism under all its forms and where it still persists, but without mentioning at this time the name of any country. A list which does not include Palestine might have left the impression that we accept the fact of the existence of Israel as it is. Here is the proof that in principle we are as intransigent as the others. . . .

But this reticence on the part of the Yugoslavs made us think, not concerning the principle of course: for us Israel is a territory which was colonized, and that is all. But each colony has a particular situation of its own and the pecularity of Israel is very obvious, since it arouses an uneasiness with certain unqualified anti-colonialists. After all, there is no doubt that Marshal Tito is a great friend of the Arabs. For a long time he has had a close friendship with Nasser, and he entertains with the Maghreb the most fraternal relations. Yet, there is an Israeli Ambassador in Belgrade; and though Marshal Tito holds that one has to do justice to the cause of the Palestinian refugees, and to restore their rights, he also considers that Israeli colonialism is not exactly the same as anywhere else; that it was born under particular conditions, etc. Why? Is it because he appreciates the agricultural experiments in Israel? Is it because he who succeeded in uniting under his regime

---

* Actually his visit with Tito was two months later, near the end of his tour. This writer failed in his efforts to clarify whether this was the interviewer's error, or whether Bourguiba was confused as to the time table of his tour.

peoples who were divided and torn apart from each other by hundreds of thousands of dead [victims of their bloody conflicts]—believes that Israel-Arab coexistence is perfectly realizable? . . . .

I don't know. But this (attitude of the Yugoslavs) confirmed my own impression (which I had for a long time) that the Arabs as far as the problem of Israel is concerned meet with resistance (to their attitudes) on the part of some of their best friends. In this the Yugoslavs are far from being the only ones. Take for example Cuba: does not Fidel Castro have diplomatic relations with Israel? And Jean-Paul Sartre who, I understand, is a partisan of a negotiated solution of the Arab-Israeli conflict—should he be treated for that as a supporter of colonialism or a lackey of the United States? Either there is something wrong with Arab propaganda, or there is something, some aspect of this Israel colonialism, that one must not ignore. Realism means to analyze all these resistances to see how they were born, from what they stem, why they persist, and how one can overcome them.

It is in this spirit that I came to Cairo and I took care to acquaint Nasser with these conversations I had with Marshal Tito.

It is not easy to analyze this statement, expressed almost in the form of a stream of consciousness. There are in it several contradictory strains; there is confusion and inconsistency, startling for a man who justifiably prides himself on being a champion of common sense.

How is one to believe that a trip of almost two months, involving an entourage of sixty people including his most important advisers, members of his cabinet and Parliament, and journalists, had no purpose? If there was a motive other than the one that subsequently developed, how could it have been abandoned so precipitously, and no word ever whispered? How believe he had no intention of "taking a stand" on the Palestine problem which is the uppermost preoccupation of the Arab world? (Actually he contradicts himself. He says that he had prepared an advance text for the joint communiqués, naming Israel as one of the remaining colonies to be liquidated—as if this were not "taking a stand"!)

As a reason for abandoning his original intention—whatever it was—he gives his visit with Tito. But this did not, in fact, take place until the end of his trip, after he had already created the storm.*

---

* The Tunisian Ambassador to Paris, Mohammed Masmoudi, who was otherwise very cooperative in giving this writer the texts of various documents, has been reticent on this point. When I pointed out to him the conflicting chronology as given by President Bourguiba, and asked him whether Jean Daniel

Then, he implies that he changed his mind; and, of course, whatever he says is supposed to be an explanation of why he changed his mind. At the same time he asserts that he did not change his mind—that basically, and "in principle," he still considers Israel a colonial territory. Whose colonial territory? A colonial territory is subject to an external hegemony. What external power exercises dominion over Israel?

Since his interview with Tito took place only after he made his sensational declarations about solving the Palestine problem peaceably, how can he say that with Tito he was in a state of mind "not less intransigent than the others"? What does he mean by that? How do the two contradictory attitudes tally?

It is said that what he saw and heard during the early part of his tour in the first three countries he visited—Egypt, Saudi Arabia, and Jordan—had a decisive influence upon him, and that their impact was a revelation. In Jordan he saw at close quarters the misery and hopelessness of the refugees; in Saudi Arabia he was given facts, figures, and photographs of how Egyptians behave in the Yemen, where President Nasser's army killed and mutilated thousands of Arabs. In Egypt itself he noticed sharp discrepancies: the ostentatiousness of a regime which pretends to liberate all Arabs socially, economically, and politically, juxtaposed against the miserable everyday existence of the Egyptians themselves.

Perhaps Bourguiba had, as it were, his own "revelation on the way to Damascus": he saw the truth and decided to begin telling the truth that had been revealed to him. This version is sometimes claimed by Bourguiba himself; at least he encourages others to spread it around. But a politician and realist as hard-boiled as Bourguiba does not stake his career or endanger his life for the sake of a "revealed truth."

Curiously enough, competent experts on Arabic affairs, and the leading newspapers in the western world almost universally agreed that Bourguiba had not premeditated the "scandal" when he left for the Middle East. "To assure the success of his tour," wrote Lemine Chatti, an authority on North African affairs, "Bourguiba had originally resolved to keep away from polemics and show a conciliatory, flexible attitude toward his hosts."

misunderstood President Bourguiba, or the Tunisian President perhaps referred to an unreported visit to Marshal Tito *prior* to his tour in the Middle East, I received no response. I do not believe such a visit could have remained secret if it had occurred.

But the crisis in Arab-German relations erupted while he happened to be on his tour, a crisis artificially created by Nasser and exploited for his own political aims in the Machiavellian game between East and West. And Nasser's imperious way, explained the experts, of assuming to speak and decide for all the Arab states without previously consulting them, infuriated Bourguiba. The Tunisian President, thus deeply provoked, decided to challenge Nasser on this issue, to preserve Tunisia's right to independent thought, policy, and action. In a mood of incandescent rage he threw in the Palestine issue as well. As the editorialist of *Le Monde* put it: "Having, almost without willing it, created this crack (in the pan-Arab support of Nasser) he thought he might as well widen it into a window, and he embarked upon a campaign of rationalizing his stand." (April 25–26)

Richard Got, who interviewed Bourguiba for the British quarterly, *Views,* (Autumn Issue 1965) asked him:

Do you think Nasser was annoyed with you over the question of Western Germany or of Palestine?

Answer: Palestine is just a pretext. This is proved by the fact that I held my press conference (in the Old City of Jerusalem) long before the attack he made on me during his Mansurah speech. It was the same day the Arab League was to meet—with heads of state, if I remember well (note the contemptuous irony —S.M.) or possibly foreign affairs representatives—to decide on breaking relations with the Bonn Federal Republic. He said the Palestine problem was very delicate. He said also I was with the Jews, Ben Gurion's man, etc. The funny thing is, when I arrived in Beirut after being in Palestine, the Nasserite newspapers, financed by Nasser, were amazed to see the Cairo papers had nothing against me, that they did not attack Bourguiba (he laughs). But they did attack me when I headed those who did not want to give way (over West Germany).

Mr. Got commented rather ruefully:

. . . It is clear . . . that the failure of his [Bourguiba's] initiative this year was due, not so much to the boldness of his ideas about Israel, but [to] his refusal to follow Egypt in breaking relations with the German Federal Republic. It is ironic that West Germany's decision to establish diplomatic relations with Israel would have led indirectly to the sabotage of the most hopeful public initiative there has yet been in the Arab-Israel cold war.

These assertions by Bourguiba and the commentators unwittingly place Bourguiba in a most unfavorable light, depicting him as a man who acts impetuously, cannot control his temper, confuses issues, and changes his mind—not on the merits but in anger. Some critics, especially in Israel, actually hold these views about him and therefore claim that he should not be taken seriously.

For several reasons this writer does not agree with such an appraisal—either of the man or of the events. First, if Bourguiba spoke impulsively on Palestine and did not seriously mean what he said, he could have dropped the issue immediately after his press conference in Jerusalem. But his "outburst" was the keynote of a long campaign. Second, if the Palestine question was not his central theme, what was? That it could not have been the German issue is clear: when he decided to undertake his tour, this question had not yet reached the crisis stage. Third, are not the two issues—the Arab-Bonn relations and the Palestine problem—interwoven threads in the same fabric?

To follow Nasser on the German issue meant to sabotage Bourguiba's own effort to introduce some sanity into the Israel-Arab conflict. On the other hand, to defy Nasser exclusively on the German issue, separating it from the whole complex of the Palestine conflict and Middle East relations, would have weakened this very defiance and deprived it of its cogency. But the question remains: having challenged Nasser on the German problem, did Bourguiba for good measure throw in the whole Palestine issue, or was it just the other way around? This analyst believes that Bourguiba, having set out for the Middle East determined to challenge the prevailing Arab policy on Palestine, found himself unexpectedly provided with an excellent handle with which to start the motor of his preconceived campaign: the handle was the German issue. Obviously less controversial in nature, it lent itself more easily to recruiting immediate allies.

Bourguiba is first and above all a leader of a people and the head of a state, and as such, is always interested primarily in the welfare and destiny of Tunisia. He plunged into the Palestine dispute, not because the problem of the refugees or even of peace, as such, had become his leading concerns. However sincerely he took up the Middle East issue, he surely did it within the context of Tunisian interests and survival.

Keeping this in mind, it is easier to discern Bourguiba's main theme relentlessly developed with variations during and after his tour that the greatest danger to Tunisia's survival as an independent state lies in pan-Arabism. And the purpose of his tour became crystal clear: to save his country, it was imperative for him openly and dramatically to challenge Nasser's drive to unify the Arab world—both East and West—under Egypt's hegemony and Nasser's leadership. Here, indeed, was a purpose of such magnitude and importance that he decided to stake his career on it, and even to risk his life, not to speak of his popularity in the Arab world.

This decision must be viewed against the background of Bourguiba's political career and the geopolitical situation of his country. Tunisia is a small and practically defenseless land which could not for long withstand strong external pressures from grasping neighbors. Bourguiba is aiming to prevent the start of such hostile overtures and to cause their collapse if they are already in process. What are these pressures? Who is exerting them? Most immediately: Algeria; over the long range: Nasser's pan-Arabism.

Bourguiba had been for years—long before Tunisia's independence—the main propagandist for uniting, federating, or confederating the four countries of North Africa: Tunisia, Morocco, Algeria, and Libya. He had hoped that some form of unification of the Maghreb, by the free choice of the countries involved, would be achieved gradually, beginning with partial economic and cultural agreements.

For this united Maghreb, he envisioned also close cultural and economic cooperation with France on a basis of equality and mutual respect. He saw himself as the initiator of the United Maghreb; he hoped it would be his personal destiny to preside over its materialization to which he dedicated his talents and inexhaustible energy.

We should remember Bourguiba's early and frequent proclamations that he supported the Algerian fight for liberation as an aim worthy not only in itself, but also as a phase in the realization of a united Maghreb. He had reached agreements with the leaders of the Algerian rebellion concerning steps toward the future unification of the Maghreb. But on the very eve of Algeria's independence, Ben Bella was released from detention by the French and succeeded, with the help of Nasser, in seizing power in Algeria. He ousted the provisional Algerian government, which was responsible for the Evian agreements with France (granting independence to Algeria), and exiled its head and some other members. Ben Bella thus became the ruler of the newly independent Algeria. As Nasser's close ally and an extreme spokesman for the Egyptian style of pan-Arabism, he was the Egyptian President's minor partner in blocking the materialization of a United Maghreb.

This was not the first encounter between Bourguiba and the Egyptian President—there had been tensions and conflict between them years before, practically from the moment of Tunisia's independence. But subsequent dramatic events had led Bourguiba to seek an accommodation with Nasser which did not work. Bourguiba was confirmed again in his certainty of Nasser's principal aim: to force all the Arab countries to incorporate themselves into one pan-Arab framework under his leadership. The issue no longer focussed on a clash between pan-Arabism and a hypothetical unified Maghreb; it became a duel between pan-Arabism and the very real Tunisian independence.

Besides practical political matters this clash also involved deep psychological factors: Tunisians resent Egyptian condescension, as if toward an inferior breed. The Tunisianss regard themselves the inheritors of an ancient culture whose origins go as far back as Carthage, with overtones of greatness equal to that of the Egyptians. And they consider Bourguiba a leader of no less stature than Nasser, and no less a fighter for national independence. Nasser was never the leader of a liberation movement fighting against a foreign occupation power as Bourguiba was, and Tunisians miss no opportunity to point out that in the Egyptian's clashes with foreign powers since (but even including) the Palestine war of 1948–49 (he was then an officer in King Farouk's army) he had never scored a military victory. They emphasize that whatever success he had was the result mainly of support from foreign powers—either from "American imperialism" or from "Russian imperialism," in the current vernacular.

Bourguiba has often emphasized that his country, for three thousand years a cultural crossroad connecting the Middle East, Africa, and Europe, is destined to bring about a new synthesis, through cooperation with the West. The greatest obstacle to this national destiny is pan-Arabism, with is totalitarian dynamism, although perhaps an equal danger is that pan-Arabism may trail in its wake Communist infiltration of the most extreme brand— both Russian and Chinese. This, according to Bourguiba, will open the way to suppression and enslavement of the Arab peoples. The fact that Nasser supported and financed Bourguiba's foe,

Salah Ben Youssef, added a personal element to the tense relations between the two Presidents.

The cauldron in which pan-Arabism brews is the Arab League. At the beginning of his country's independence, Bourguiba tried to boycott the League and could not; so he yielded to pressures and joined. At that time, he tried a policy of conciliation with Nasser; again he became convinced he could achieve no reforms there because the League remains an instrument of Nasser's pan-Arabism.

We may assume that in the course of the years Bourguiba has tried to trace the sources of the drive and momentum of pan-Arabism. The usual explanation is that pan-Arabism is animated by nationalism, a desire for unity, based on Arab history, a common language and the Islamic heritage. But none of these encompasses the whole truth, nor does any combination of them. The main source from which Nasser and the pan-Arabists derive their energies is the Israel-Arab conflict, and as long as it is not solved, pan-Arabism will be a force. Palestine is like a generator which constantly supplies new energies and a poisoned atmosphere to nourish the disease.

For years Bourguiba also observed that the whip which Nasser used most effectively to browbeat the governments of the Arab states and force them to toe his line is the same Israel-Arab conflict. Though Nasser and pan-Arabists never tire of claiming that Israel is the greatest stumbling block on the road to Arab unity, the paradoxical fact is that it is the only cement that holds the Arab states precariously together—and the deeper they are divided on everything else, the more they need the Palestine problem; solve it and the structure of pan-Arabism will fall apart. What then will Nasser lead?

Bourguiba is not alone in uncovering this paradox. The widely circulated Beirut newspaper *Al Khayat* formulated it, on the eve of the first Arab summit, in a most succinct way:

> An Arab summit is of no use whatsoever unless it is called to demonstrate Arab unity in the face of Israel. It is a solidarity limited to this single object. It ends there and does not go any further.

Self-righteously Nasser repeats that "Arab unity is vital for Palestine's liberation." And during the crisis in relationship with West Germany: "The German issue is the first step to liberate

Palestine." And this artificially created united front makes Nasser appear uniquely formidable in Arab eyes and in the eyes of public opinion and governments the world over—both East and West.

It became clear to Bourguiba that as long as the myth of Arab unity is perpetuated, other Arab problems cannot be overcome, but only covered up or blurred.

For Bourguiba, pan-Arabism is not merely a possible future threat from some faraway land, but a real and present danger hovering over the threshold of his own country—actually on the Algerian frontier. The Middle East with its unrestrained emotionalism and frenetic arms race lives with the specter of a bloody conflict that may spread to the Maghreb—as indeed it did. Witness the short but fierce border conflict which broke out (in October 1963) on the Sahara frontier between the two Maghrebian neighbors—Algeria and Morocco. Nasser was, as usual manipulating in the background, having sent a contingent of Egyptian troops to assist Algeria. And the border disputes between Tunisia and Algeria may yet come to armed conflict, under one pretext or another, with an attempt by Tunisia's stronger neighbor to swallow her completely.

Ben Bella, Algeria's deposed president, though outwardly a subaltern to Nasser, had ambitions of his own. In order to achieve preponderance and perhaps eventual dominance of all North Africa, the Algerian leader decided to arrogate to himself the Palestinian whip, and in his anti-Israel statements sometimes surpassed his Egyptian mentor, promising hundreds of thousands of volunteers in the battle for the liberation of Palestine. Tunisia is closer and easier to reach than Palestine.

Bourguiba seems to have become convinced that he must fight for his survival as leader of this country, and for the existence of Tunisia as an independent state. Knock the Palestine whip out of Nasser's hand, and Arab politicians in the Middle East could function independently; eventually the facade of Arab unity would crumble. Thus a change in the Arab-Israel conflict might choke off the force that animates pan-Arabism, and in turn weaken Algerian expansionism.

His logical mind reached the logical conclusion that the first line of defense not only of the Maghreb but of Tunisia itself was at the River Jordan. His journey to the Middle East therefore was to open a front against Nasser in Jerusalem, for if he did not win the battle there, his people would be forced sooner or later to fight at Tunisia's own door. Further, for the united Maghreb to take some practical shape in his lifetime, he must destroy the phantom of an Arab nation spreading from the Persian Gulf to the Atlantic, with Nasser presiding in solitary glory.

It may even have occurred to Bourguiba that the surest way to preserve the independence of his own country was to permit the Middle East to develop according to its real structure and composition: a region with various states, of diverse personalities. Though most of these are predominantly Arab, it would be more wholesome if as a built-in safeguard against pan-Arab encroachments, the existence of non-Arabic or not purely Moslem states like the Lebanon, Israel, and eventually an autonomous Kurdistan, should be considered positive factors and not calamities.

The formula of the challenge was simple and pithy. Nasser repeated unceasingly to the Arabs that war with Israel is inevitable; Bourguiba countered that a victorious war with Israel is impossible. The Egyptian said peace with Israel is inconceivable; the Tunisian recalled that Arabs lived in harmony with Jews for many centuries, and concluded that the way to do it again is on the basis of mutual respect. He successfully challenged Nasser on his own ground, for after Bourguiba launched his bombshell on the Palestine problem the Arabs began to quarrel among themselves more vehemently than ever before.

One of the variations of Bourguiba's main strategy, though superficially disguised, is to divorce the Palestine issue from the complex of problems plaguing the Arab world, thus disentangling it from the patronage of pan-Arabism. Hence his contention that Palestine is above all the concern of the Palestinians themselves, and that Tunisia cannot accomplish their struggle—clearly implying that neither can any other Arabic country (even Egypt). He gave more than an implication when, at his Beirut press conference, he explained ruefully that Arabs outside Palestine are more fervent champions of the cause of "liberation" than the Palestinians themselves. A dart aimed deliberately and artfully since it completely serves the needs and aspirations of Tunisia and the Arab countries at the Western edge of the Mediterranean.

All through his tour, he warned the Arab governments to refuse to be Nasser's satellites and to say 'No!' to Cairo when their interests did not coincide with those of Egypt. Hammer, hammer, hammer—he struck the same chord again and again, wherever he spoke.

This seemed to him the most effective formula of challenge. To outbid the others in warmongering against Israel and in threat of "throwing the Jews into the sea," as he had tried for awhile to do, was obviously futile and played straight into Nasser's hand.

Now we can proceed to analyze statements of evaluation by Bourguiba and others concerning the causes of the dramatic rift in the Arab world. The key takes us back to Bourguiba's main theme: the dangers inherent in Nasser's drive for pan-Arab unity.

Bourguiba repeatedly stated that his 1965 clash with the Arabs of the Middle East should be traced neither to his stand on Palestine nor to his refusal to break relations with Germany, but to Nasser's pan-Arab ambitions. All the other complications, internecine conflicts, and crises arise from this and nothing else. He explained:

> All our quarrels with Egypt stem from the fact that we have always refused to become a satellite of Cairo.*

And to the interviewer of the British quarterly, *Views*, he said:

> . . . Nasser feels he can order other Arab countries around like a drill sergeant. Well, as far as I am concerned, he cannot. . . .
> We realized that he [Nasser] was determinedly holding on to his idea of Arab unity. This idea is not for them [the Egyptians] as it is for us [only] an objective an ideal to aim for—no, in their mind, in the mind of certain leaders, it is already an accomplished fact. Egypt is the boss and Cairo is the Arab captial, to such an extent that the Egyptian Republic is now called the United Arab Republic? Why United Arab? They called it United Arab because of the union with Syria. Syria left and it is still called United Arab, with a sort of right of attention, a moral tutelage within its constitution, under the pretext of unity. . . . I say: If it makes them happy, well, I don't mind. But Tunisia is a sovereign state; it wants [none] of it.

Nasser does not challenge Bourguiba's contentions head on. And his entire political career, all his campaigns, most of his speeches, and his little book, *The Philosophy of the Revolution*,

---

* In a speech in the presence of King Faisal of Saudi Arabia, delivered in Kairouan, Tunisia, September 24, 1966.

confirm them. With single-minded persistence, he has made pan-Arabism his life purpose, trying desperately to integrate the whole Arab world, and mobilize its oil riches to help relieve Egypt's extreme poverty and want of resources. With his eyes always on the same goal, he nevertheless advances toward it on a road that is not always straight; he zigzags, using one option and then another.

There was a time when he sought to overthrow the Arab governments whose regimes he considered reactionary, serving only the interests of the privileged classes. For this purpose he started with subversive and conspiratorial methods and assassination attempts. But his most powerful weapon was his propaganda machine, inspiring the intelligentsia and the masses with a vision of a strong unified Arab nation, built on modern technology, industrial development, and socialism.

When innate Arab separatism thwarted this plan and the individual regimes showed remarkable tenacity, he abandoned subversive tactics. Instead he conceived another system to bring him near the goal: he would offer unity instead of division, friendship instead of hostility. He would forsake disruption and try to harmonize Arab interests against the threatening enemy—Israel. For this he initiated the Arab summit conferences of the heads of states. These meetings have shown unique unanimity and harmony, which could not be achieved on any other issue.

But this policy of unanimity is not just a matter of a mood or sentiment. It must involve economic cooperation and mutual help, preliminary to a merger of the whole economies. And there must be gradual integration of the armed forces of all the states. So to begin with, it was necessary to establish a unified command to protect the diversion of the Jordan headwaters.

But such an integration of the armed forces, regardless how modest, requires a uniformity of the weapons at the disposal of the unified command. Egypt is supplied by Russia, Hence the Arab states would have to receive weapons from the Russians for the coordination to be effective—or make sense at all. But most Arab states in the past have avoided Russia as a devout Moslem shrinks from pork. But under the flag of unity against Israel, Nasser was able to bring them into line. Where the Arab governments had previously understandably balked at Nasser's subversion, they acquiesced when the keyword became Israel rather than revolution.

Nasser's feud with West Germany, though originating as a punishment to Bonn for supporting Israel and a warning to other

Western powers to desist from helping Israel, also had a more far-reaching purpose: to begin the process of weaning the Arab states away from Western influence.

Bourguiba's motivations in turn raise several other puzzling questions. If the purpose of his campaign was to challenge Nasser, why did he start his tour in Egypt? In fact, why did he go to Cairo at all? And how reconcile Bourguiba's repeated assertions that when he struck out on his tour he did not look for a quarrel with Nasser; and that he had only peaceful intentions? Most important of all, if Bourguiba's assumption is correct (that an extreme and violent attitude in the Palestine issue is necessary for preserving leadership in the Arab world) why did Nasser agree to Bourguiba's proposals? More than that, why does Nasser sometimes advance the same ideas?

The probable explanation combines the unexpected chain of events at the outset of Bourguiba's tour with a basic misunderstanding between the two leaders as to what Bourguiba meant by his peace initiative.

Upon close examination, the chain of events unfolds as follows:

That the Palestine problem was planned as the central issue of Bourguiba's tour is confirmed by the Cairo press, especially the *Al Ahram,* which hailed him as a champion of the Arab cause and forecast a useful discussion of the Palestine problem with Nasser. So Bourguiba did not catch Nasser by surprise; more likely, the agenda had been discussed before his arrival—which is normal. Palestine is such a central issue in the Arab world that it would be inconceivable for the two nationalist heads of state to meet and omit this subject from their discussion.

We must, therefore, also assume that Bourguiba did not at first intend to open with a frontal attack upon Nasser. He seems to have planned an intensive diplomatic campaign starting in Cairo, to persuade Nasser, King Hussein of Jordan, and President Helou of the Lebanon, of the futility of prolonging the Palestine conflict in its present form, and that the time for a new approach was long overdue. He hoped perhaps to bring about a little summit conference in which he, Nasser, Hussein, Helou, and perhaps King Feisal of Saudi Arabia would participate. He thought that at this conference he might also offer his good offices to settle the bloody war in the Yemen, mediating between Nasser and Feisal. If this were to go over smoothly he might at a later stage try to mediate between Iraq and Syria with a view of bringing about a *modus vivendi* between them.

In addition, Tunisian diplomats in Cairo intimated that Bourguiba would also try to mediate between Egypt and the United States, in view of the growing tension between the two countries. Hence the unusually large group of advisers and experts—more than 60—who accompanied him: he planned for a big deal, and perhaps more than one.

We cannot, of course, know for certain the conversations between the two leaders; but from the sequence of events and the later utterances of both, we can trace the complicating factors which entered the picture. First, it seems obvious that the Egyptian President was annoyed by Bourguiba's presumptuousness in offering to mediate between Nasser and Feisal and between Egypt and the United States, as well as between Syria and Iraq. Who was Bourguiba to assume the stance of an international mediator? Nasser did not need intermediaries, certainly not a potential challenger to pan-Arab leadership; and he probably sensed that this would elevate Bourguiba to a new status of peacemaker-above-the-fray, a prospect he could not under any circumstances tolerate.

But the most important complication was the sudden crisis over relations with West Germany, an event Bourguiba could not have foreseen; and the tense atmosphere spawned mutual misunderstandings over the intent of each other's words.

At the beginning of Bourguiba's week in Egypt, Nasser, though unresponsive to mediation attempts, and preoccupied with other matters, had listened sympathetically to the proposals about Palestine.* He did not at the moment grasp the full implications of what the Tunisian suggested, nor discern his real intentions. He therefore seems to have told Bourguiba that his own views were basically similar to those expressed by his guest.

He was obsessed then with the West German problem and trying to persuade all Arab states to join the campaign against Bonn. At the moment he thought this issue overrode everything else; that if he won this battle, Israel would suffer a possibly decisive blow; that by teaching a lesson to West Germany, he would force the other Western powers to revise their policy of providing Israel with arms; that by humiliating Bonn he could establish an example for others who supported Israel. He might even have thought it a fine gambit to punish Bonn at the same time that another Arab leader was explaining that the solution to Palestine lay not with

---

* Bourguiba later complained, rather contradictorily to his own often repeated assertions, that Nasser was too busy with his electioneering campaign to pay much attention to what his guest had to say. Perhaps there is no contradiction.

providing arms for Israel but forcing her instead to abide by the United Nations resolutions. He may have thought that if he did not disagree with Bourguiba's ambiguous Palestine statement, Bourguiba would reciprocate by going along on the West German issue.

Bourguiba saw the hook in the *quid pro quo*. He insists that had he supported Nasser on Bonn, the Egyptian President would not have incited the Arabs to raise such a hue and cry about his Palestine peace proposals.

The Egyptians have conceded that the Palestine question was, at that stage, only incidental to the developing crisis between the two leaders. Nasser's main spokesman, the editor of *Al Ahram,* hinted at the real issue when he wrote that Bourguiba's campaign affected inter-Arab relations far more seriously than the Israel-Arab conflict. The real issue was awkward for the Egyptians to spell out; hence they had to write and speak with ambiguity. Yet they were clearly aware that Bourguiba did not just advocate a new approach to the Palestine problem; for if this were the case he could have expressed this view privately to the leading officials in the countries he was to visit after leaving Egypt.

> Even though some Egyptians may privately agree with Mr. Bourguiba [reported Hedrick Smith to *The New York Times*] they are almost unanimously stunned and appalled that an Arab President could speak so bluntly about their most tender problem "in front of the world rather than within the Arab family."

Or even if he had intended merely to make his views public, he could have expressed them in constructive and positive terms. Had he done this, perhaps the crisis would not have developed, or it would not have taken on its acrimonious character. But Bourguiba used the Palestine issue as the occasion for a fierce attack upon pan-Arab leadership, which means upon Nasser. This was the issue, though it was never clearly stated by either side, certainly not by Cairo. Hence the violent Egyptian reactions were not necessarily triggered by the essence of the proposals, but by their delivery in the form of a frontal attack on Nasser's leadership; so that this challenge became an integral part of the proposals, and the end result for all the world to see was "a package."

When Nasser finally grasped the nature of Bourguiba's proposals, he realized their far-reaching implications and was stunned. He saw that here was not an innocent trial balloon for a new approach to the Palestine problem, but an assault on him personally. Bourguiba was clearly challenging his leadership in the Arab world. Though Bourguiba denies he had any aspiration for such leadership or toward the pan-Arabism which he opposes, he explains that this was nevertheless the issue as Nasser understood it. News correspondent Martin Agronsky asked Bourguiba on the television program, *Face the Nation* (May 23) :

> Mr. President, your modesty [in not seeking pan-Arab leadership] is doubted in Cairo and in many other countries. They accuse you, in fact, of having proposed this solution for the Palestine problem as a means of furthering your own position of leadership in the Arab world and in effect for your own personal aggrandizement. How would you answer that, sir?
>
> *Bourguiba:* This is evidence that whatever is of interest in the Palestine problem, it is only leadership—keeping and maintaining leadership. And since some Arab countries reacted as people who do not feel any more like satellites of Egypt, the more painful was the shock. And since this country [Tunisia] had enough courage to say no to Cairo on this Palestine problem . . . that was certainly the shock.

But as far as he is concerned, he claims that in his Middle East tour he sought no leadership or co-leadership, but only the good of the Palestine people and their rightful cause.

It so happened that King Hussein of Jordan was in Cairo when Bourguiba arrived, reputedly to try to mediate between Cairo and Bonn. It is quite certain that the Tunisian President and the King met and discussed Bourguiba's proposals, although what occurred at that meeting has not been revealed. However, one is justified in assuming that Bourguiba tried to win Hussein over to his plan, because it fitted so perfectly with Jordan's vital interests. The King was apparently not willing to publicly endorse the plan, but a tacit understanding was probably reached: King Hussein would not object to the idea of Bourguiba expressing his views during his forthcoming visit in Jordan, but would not openly co-sponsor them. Of course, this is pure conjecture, but on the other hand, it is difficult to believe that Bourguiba had put his royal host before a *fait accompli.*

14

Was Bourguiba His Own Man?

ALTHOUGH WE BELIEVE THE PURPOSE OF BOURGUIBA'S CAMPAIGN was to challenge Nasser's leadership and the whole concept and structure of pan-Arabism, we do not intend to say there were no other motivations. Man's motives on all levels of existence, especially in politics, are not simple, or insulated or exclusive, and close analysis sometimes reveals that apparently diverse purposes fit into a general pattern.

What were Bourguiba's other motivations?

For months the air was filled with speculation as to the auspices under which Bourguiba had undertaken his initiative in the Middle East. Commentators argued with some simplicity, if not outright vulgarity, that Bourguiba took an assignment on behalf of one or another of the Western powers, notably the United States. Especially the French semi-official circles and commentators saw behind Bourguiba's initiative the conspiratorial hand of Washington, paying the considerable expenses of Bourguiba's tour, plus a generous promise of increased economic aid to Tunisia. And the Tunisian President, they pointed out, was in a hurry "to cash the promissory note." Scarcely a week after Bourguiba made his Carthage speech his son, Foreign Minister Habib Bourguiba, Jr., and his chief economic planner, Ahmed ben Salah, were already in Washington discussing with the State Department and the World Bank additional aid to Tunisia's new four-year plan.

Even more animated and persistent were speculations as to whether Bourguiba undertook his tour at the initiative of General de Gaulle. Did he desire to pave the way for a French comeback in the Middle East? Was he anticipating an attempt by the French President to mediate between Israel and the Arab states, especially in view of the forthcoming visit to Paris of Lebanese

President Helou and Egyptian Vice President Amer? Or did he act in coordination with some other preconceived French plan?

Such speculations were advanced (but also vehemently denied) by commentators in France, Tunisia, Israel, and other countries. And in this case, too, they pointed out Tunisia's eagerness to present its bill without delay, signalling the fact that almost immediately after Bourguiba made his statements in Jerusalem and Beirut, his Ambassador to France asked and was granted an audience (March 23, 1965) with the French Foreign Minister Couve de Murville. During this interview, the Ambassador asked the French Minister to renew economic assistance to Tunisia which had been withheld after the Bizerte clash and the nationalization of the land belonging to French settlers.

On May 10, Ambassador Masmoudi had also an audience with President de Gaulle and delivered a personal message from President Bourguiba, the theme of which was renewal of close and special relations between France and Tunisia.

At best, these Tunisian *demarches* were interpreted as efforts by Tunisia to get into the good graces of the French President; it was even reported that Bourguiba tried to ascertain whether the French Government would take up his initiative, in one form or another. Tunisian official circles let it be known that the French Ambassador at Tunis, Jean Sauvagharques, one of the most respected experts of the Foreign Ministry on problems related to the area, had been asked to clarify whether the Quai D'Orsay would offer mediation in the Israel-Arab conflict.

The French, through various spokesmen, mostly self-appointed, were suspiciously overeager to deny that France was behind Bourguiba's initiative, and pointed a finger at the Americans. In Washington the finger was pointed back at Paris.

Yet in so many quarters: in France, the United States, Israel, and the Arab countries, people spoke of a "deal." Was there one?

There is no need to pursue such far-fetched notions. International affairs and diplomacy are complex, and the motivations often intentionally blurred. So, although evidence can be adduced pointing to a deal, we know that there was no Bourguiba encounter with either President Johnson or President de Gaulle.

But for Bourguiba to have done what he did, such impetus was not necessary; the Tunisian President knows the objective reality without it. He is fully aware that de Gaulle thinks in global terms; that he has devised solutions to problems of the various parts of the globe: a Europe from the Urals to the Atlantic composed of nation-states as component units, vaguely united, and evermore closely cooperating economically, technologically, and culturally; plus a neutralized Southeast Asia. It is noteworthy, too, that more than any other world leader de Gaulle has established close and cordial relations with former colonies in black Africa. Bourguiba also knows that the French President arrived at his definitions slowly and revealed them even more slowly, often only by hints—in generalizations, sometimes in exalted terms.

There is little doubt then, that in view of de Gaulle's ambition to reestablish France's presence and influence in the Middle East, the French President has been thinking deeply about the problems of the area. France aspires to return to that part of the world where she was present for so long and left such deep imprints, notably in the Lebanon and, to some extent, in Egypt. In both these countries, French is, next to Arabic, the dominant language. French culture has a great appeal to the élite in several Arabic-speaking countries, and France would have a great chance for a dramatic comeback. But in view of her close and friendly relationship with Israel, a real French return to the Middle East is a very difficult prospect.

There are even more urgent considerations—and much closer to home. In the eastern Mediterranean, France's interests and objectives are still limited. But in the western Mediterranean region of North Africa France has great stakes and far-reaching commitments. She is greatly interested to see the Maghreb move toward some sort of stability and progress, but the fever of Nasser's pan-Arabism and the anti-Israeli hysteria are grave and handicapping factors.

Bourguiba also knows that similar (though far from identical) considerations animate other Western powers, especially the United States and West Germany. The United States has serious interests in the Arab countries, both strategic and economic, since American oil companies are the major partners and exploiters of Middle East oil, and there are several American universities in the area. It has poured billions of dollars of economic aid and private investment into the region, and is interested in maintaining—even extending—its presence and position in the Arab world. It is deeply apprehensive of Communist penetration and Russian expansionism. On the other hand, the U.S. has a friendly predisposition toward Israel, and a deep, moral commitment to the survival of the Jewish state. This is accentuated by the existence in

America of about six million Jews whose attachment to Israel is strong and dramatically emotional, perhaps not so much because of the religious as well as cultural attachment, but of what many consider the "miracle" of the rebirth of a Hebrew state after 20 centuries.

In a somewhat similar position, West Germany is ambitious to renew its formerly considerable economic and cultural ties with the Arab East, and hopes under propitious circumstances to expand them vastly. But the government in Bonn feels a historic and moral commitment to help Israel, economically at least, as a partial atonement for the Nazi crimes.

Thus, at least three of the major Western powers (plus England, for other reasons we cannot discuss in the scope of this report) are vitally interested in the Middle East and in keeping friendly relations with both the Arabs and Israel. But the Palestine conflict is in the way, and there is very little maneuverability in the face of it.

More than that, as long as this conflict is perpetuated, it constitutes a danger to the peace of the region, and if inflamed by pan-Arabism as well as Israeli intransigence, it could break out into a war. Although one usually knows where a war starts, no one knows where it might end. Hence, were the Israel-Arab conflict to become manageable, great opportunities would appear for the Western powers to develop friendly relations with all the peoples of the area, and to contribute to a maximum degree toward the economic development of the whole region. Easing of the Middle East conflict would also have a salutary effect upon the East-West rivalry and cold war maneuvers in the area. Above all, a dangerous fuse for an armed conflict, perhaps on a world scale, would be extinguished.

Bourguiba knows all this. He did not have to be explicitly told about it by President Johnson, President de Gaulle, or Chancellor Erhard. He knows that were he to succeed in breaking the spell by introducing some common sense and realism into the Middle East, to move the Palestine conflict from its dead center, he would serve the interests of world peace; and by this very service he could help realize one of the most important objectives of the Western powers as well as of some of the moderate Arab leaders. He could make a great, historic, and perhaps decisive contribution to the vision of Tunisian-French and Tunisian-Western cooperation—as well as to the desired objective of a close association between the Maghreb and the European Common Market.

Bourguiba's initiative represented no bargain, no deal. There was no service rendered by order or invitation, no price paid or received. It happened that in this (as in many other fields) the national interests of Tunisia coincided with the interests of the Western powers. With the very advent of independence more than ten years ago, Bourguiba had arrived at the conclusion that Tunisia's destiny lay in a pro-Western orientation. He also came to understand that such an orientation does not tally too well with the prevailing Arab policy toward Israel. Hence, he once more arrived at the logical decision—to abandon his early stand on this issue and advocate coming to terms with Israel, trying to make these terms as palatable as possible to the Arabs. "Amid these searing prospects [of war in the Middle East], the United States and the West welcomed . . . the first peaceable approach to Israel ever undertaken by an Arab leader," wrote *Life* magazine, June 16, 1965.

If we accept such a conjectural reconstruction, the chain of events becomes quite intelligible. Bourguiba's consecutive statements, some of them obscure, ambiguous, and even contradictory, fall into a meaningful pattern. Otherwise how can we, for instance, understand a statement he made upon his return from his tour in answer to *Le Figaro's* Francois Mennelet? The first question the French journalist asked was: "Mr. President, were you worried when you left for your tour?"

Bourguiba answered:

> Before I left Tunisia there were some who warned me of the possibility of demonstrations in (Tunisia). I told them: Yes, there will be one, the day of my return. Your journalists have seen what took place Friday [during the cheering demonstrations in Tunis upon his return]. In fact, there is between the people of Tunisia and me a bond of confidence.

How else can one interpret this prediction than as confirmation that Bourguiba's initiative was a premeditated plan—which aroused misgivings among some of his collaborators? They feared it might prove unpopular even in Tunis. And it is typical of Bourguiba that he could assure them in advance that they were wrong.

15

A Variety of Motivations

THE ARAB WORLD, IF THERE IS SUCH, IS DIVIDED AGAINST ITSELF IN many respects and on different levels: religious affiliations, social systems, national aspirations, personal rivalries, regional groupings. Pan-Arabism, the movement for Arab unity, is itself in many respects more of a divisive than a unifying factor.

Bourguiba did not create these divisions; he only exposed them. He has been trying as a rational being to sketch some order in the Arab world, by, first of all, realistically acknowledging the true state of things. He must dissipate myths, illusions, paranoiac dreams, and force the Arabs to see themselves as they are; only then will they be able to embark upon enterprises of reform and progress.

One of the truths the Arabs must accept is the non-existence of a viable, unified pan-Arab world. There are various Arab states, each with its own problems and aspirations; there is Nasser, who tries to unify these disparate, often inimical, states by diverse forms of coercion. His objective is unity, not for the ultimate benefit of the parts and the whole, but for the greater glory of Nasser and Egypt, of which the parts would be mere satellites. Bourguiba does not think the Arab states will solve any of their problems by becoming provinces of Egypt; on the contrary, their individual miseries may well be magnified, for Nasser has not succeeded in solving even Egypt's problems.

Bourguiba is experimenting in many ways to counteract Nasser's pan-Arabism, either through consolidating existing groupings, or setting up new constellations rooted in reality. His breadth of view is inspiring; his energy in coping with a broad range of interests is inexhaustible.

Among his efforts are those aimed at creating a more cohesive common policy in the Maghreb—the Arab West. If it can regain a consciousness of its historic traditions and glories, its geographic advantages, and its affinities with French culture, such a regional entity could become to a considerable degree a counterbalance to the more fanatic Eastern Arabs.

A united Maghreb is a vision of a new civilization, a new society —a blend of autochthonous genius and French culture. French is the language of the intellectual classes; the press is predominantly French; and so is the educational system, despite efforts, often artificial, at Arabization. In his vision a united or at least a coherent Maghreb would succeed in establishing firm ties with the European Common Market, hence closer and more organic links with European culture, mental attitudes, technology, and social and political systems. Located geographically so close to France—to Europe—a Maghrebian confederation might herald a harmony between the two regions, which would revolutionize and modernize the peoples of North Africa, and simultaneously add a vital, energizing dimension to Europe.

The Maghreb is, perhaps, Bourguiba's main preoccupation. The Cairo correspondent of *The New York Times,* (April 26) reporting on the refusal of Morocco and Libya to be swept away by the anti-Bourguiba hysteria that broke loose after the Carthage speech, remarked:

> These developments have led some Arab and Western analysts to conclude that Mr. Bourguiba not only [intends] to propose a new Palestine policy for Arabs but is also bent on leading the Maghreb out of Cairo's orbit and is trying to isolate Algeria as the only Maghreb state siding with President Nasser.

Bourguiba decided to make it clear that the Maghreb is not in the orbit of pan-Arabism. He did it by a simple formula: If ever the Arabs are foolhardy enough to wage war against Israel, Tunisia will have no part of it. Editorializing upon this statement by Bourguiba, the Israeli *Ha'aretz* (May 23) commented judiciously:

> Tunisia's participation in a military campaign of the Arab states against Israel is of no particular importance; from a purely military point of view one can say that it does not make much of a difference whether Tunisian soldiers take part in such a campaign or stay home. But from a political point of view there is a great importance to Tunisia's dissociation from all that complex of arms

race, drillings and preparations for the "third round" of the Arab-Israel armed conflict. Bourguiba's vigorous stand against the policy of military adventurism against Israel makes it easier for Morocco and Libya [to adopt a similar course] and makes it more difficult for Algeria (Ben Bella) to follow an opposite course. In fact such a policy on the part of Bourguiba is bound to undermine Nasser's position, in the sense that it threatens to remove from the Arab anti-Israel front the whole of the Western wing. To the extent that the shapers of Egyptian policy tried to make the Arab League a powerful political instrument, which should draw the Arab West into the Egyptian orbit, to that extent must Bourguiba's independent stand inflict great damage to this Egyptian design.

With the accession of Ben Bella to power, the Maghreb ideal suffered a great setback. This Algerian leader drew close to Nasser and the Middle East at the expense of the interests of the North African countries, simultaneously enhancing his personal ambitions to dominate rather than cooperate with his neighboring countries. With Ben Bella's fall, the chances of the Maghreb improved, Bourguiba believed, though his stand was still quite a cautious one. He told the editor of *Views:*

> Perhaps we will be able (now) to look at our common problems, the common interest of the Maghreb. We might even partly join our economies and our culture, and agree on a joint position toward Europe and the Common Market. There are so many factors which might strengthen the ties of solidarity growing between us.

Bourguiba was also trying to bring about a coherence among those Arab governments—Maghrebian and Machreckian (Western and Eastern) —which are moderate in outlook and fearful of Nasser's pan-Arab encroachments. He believes these middle-of-the-road leaders should abandon their timidity, close their ranks in some kind of bloc, and try to counterbalance Nasser.

The notion of a bloc of Arab moderates is not just a product of wishful thinking. Such countries as Tunisia, Lebanon, Jordan, Morocco, Libya, and Saudi Arabia, though divergent in many other respects, have in common their apprehension of the extreme, coerced "socialism" of the revolutionary regimes in Egypt and Syria. Morocco and Libya, like Tunisia, would not like the Maghreb to fall under the sway of Nasser. All of them view with alarm any prospect of his becoming the ruler of some form of Arab Federation, oriented to Russia and the Eastern bloc.

In this respect, too, there are affinities between the moderate Arab states and such Moslem countries as Turkey and, especially, Iran. No doubt Bourguiba discussed this shared apprehension with the heads of state of Jordan, the Lebanon, Saudi Arabia, and even Turkey and Iran, whose guest he was during his Middle Eastern tour; he explored it also with Hassan, King of Morocco, at a later date and, through his representative, with the King of Libya.

Such a grouping of the moderate countries in the Middle East could become the bridgehead for a link between the Arabs at both ends of the Medterranean—the Maghreb and the Machrek. In press reports emanating from Beirut, the Tunisian President discussed such a project at great length with his host, President Helou of the Lebanon, emphasizing the many common interests of the two relatively small but enlightened countries, and their striking affinities. The Lebanon, like Tunisia, was once under French domination; both, far from harboring resentment against the former colonial power, entertain a great affection for France. In both countries the French culture left a lasting impact, and both peoples are French-speaking.

Coordination of policy between the moderate Arab bloc and some of the non-Arabic Moslem countries may not spring from any profound ideological motivation, but such a combination lends itself to interesting, pragmatical possibilities. Turkey and Iran are Middle Eastern countries, *par excellence;* but not being Arab, they are outside the sphere of Nasser's pan-Arab ambitions. Both are pro-Western, close to Europe and the United States in many respects, and trying hard for internal reform and progress on the road toward democracy. The Shah of Iran considers Nasser's aspirations in the Persian Gulf a threat to his own country. Both have relations with Israel. In view of all this Bourguiba seems to have conceived the idea of creating some kind of a united front between moderate Arab states and the non-Arabic Moslem countries in the Middle East.

All these are still vague aspirations rather than well-defined plans, but Bourguiba believes in throwing ideas into the air as one throws seeds into the ground. He thus makes a date with the future, gambling on what time will bring, and on whether the ideas will germinate and bear fruit. Of course, they need to be watered and cultivated with care, but Bourguiba considers himself a man of destiny, well able to nurture new ideas.

16

A Well-Organized Campaign

LOOKING BACK AT THE SEQUENCE OF BOURGUIBA'S STATEMENTS, tactics, and reactions, one does not get the impression of improvisation. In addition to his own prediction, there are other indications that he set out with a carefully-premeditated plan to challenge Nasser on the Palestine issue.

Some newspapers reported that *Jeune Afrique* obtained Bourguiba's approval before it published its plan for a peaceful solution to the Palestine problem through a Middle Eastern Federation of which Israel would be a part. This cooperation cannot be verified, but shortly before Bourguiba left for his tour, he invited the editors of *Jeune Afrique* to Tunis, discussed Bashier ben Yahmed's suggestion of a Middle East Federation, and raised questions about reactions from the Middle Eastern countries. One of the editors, Paul-Marie de la Gorce, remarked in a subsequent interview in Tel Aviv that Bourguiba's first statement in the Old City of Jerusalem sounded like an echo of the discussions held before he left for the Middle East. The Jerusalem statement spoke only of coexistence between Jews and Arabs, and did not mention Israel. As the Tunisian President proceeded, the idea seems to have crystallized that he must go further and suggest a peaceful settlement through direct negotiations between Israel and the Palestinian Arabs.

After each of his statements, even the best-informed observers thought this was the last Bourguiba had to say. But each time "the last of it" turned out to be a prelude. The more ominous the threats to his life and the more vilifying the insults to his country, the more determined became his assertions and the more crystallized his definitions.

For instance, when he announced he would no longer partici-pate in the Arab League unless it was fundamentally reorganized, diplomatic observers thought that this Tunisian boycott meant that President Bourguiba had "said his final word on Palestine. They forecast that Tunisia would refuse to get involved in further polemics," as a Reuter's report had it.

Parallel with his personal appearances in the various countries, the Tunisian President saw to it that *internally* his government endorsed his initiative and that his people gave enthusiastic ap-proval. He also undertook an intensive and ramified diplomatic campaign in Europe, the United States, the Far East, and Africa, to clarify his position before other governments in whose support he was most interested.

Though the meaning of Bourguiba's proposals must have been ambiguous to at least some of his own entourage, the campaign caused no confusion among his immediate colleagues and cabinet members. When the bombshell first exploded, his close collabo-rators did not appear to be caught by surprise. They reacted with assurance and made statements that were in harmony with Bour-guiba's own declarations. Masmoudi's declarations in Paris, Bour-guiba Jr.'s in Washington, Mongi Slim's in the Far East were thoroughly consistent with their chief's. At home, public opinion was kept *au courant,* and the essence of the initiative was explained in Tunisian press organs. The official paper of the Neo-Destour Party, like the Central Committee, gave speedy approval to the stand Bourguiba's initiative took in the Middle East.

After his visit to Jordan and before the press conference in Beirut, he summoned to the Lebanese capital three of his close associates, Mohammed Masmoudi, Ambassador to France; Ahmed Mestiri, Ambassador to Algeria; and Habib Chatti, Ambassador to Morocco. He brought them up to date, and instructed them in the best ways to present his views to the governments and public opinion where they were accredited.

The hub of these diplomatic, political, and public relations activities became Paris, and here they centered on Ambassador Masmoudi, probably the most astute diplomat of Bourguiba's team. He began to organize his campaign as soon as he returned from a briefing from his President in Beirut. For a period of months, the French people kept hearing or reading about Bour-guiba's initiative in the Middle East. Masmoudi gave interviews to all the major periodicals in the French capital. He appeared on television and he took part in public discussions and symposiums. On March 23 he was received by the French Foreign Minister, Maurice Couve de Murville, with whom he consulted on the situation in the Middle East.

The same day, he held a press conference explaining to French and foreign correspondents the meaning and purpose of his President's initiative. The Palestine problem cannot be solved by war, but only by talks and negotiations, he declared. The existence of Israel was a *fait accompli*, attested by its 17-year history. "That country has solved the problem of the victims of Nazism, who enjoyed the sympathy of the world, including the Arabs." But he complained of both the cynicism of Israeli reaction to Bourguiba's enterprise and the lack of understanding by some Arab states. "Emotionalism obscures the Israel-Arab conflict, and it is necessary to throw on it a new light as a prerequisite for its solution." Bourguiba, he said, had sowed some seeds during his Middle Eastern tour which sooner or later would begin to sprout.

From Paris these activities branched out to other capitals of the world. There were reports that before Bourguiba started on his Middle Eastern tour one of his chief advisors on foreign affairs, Professor Cecil Hourani, had spent some time in the United States canvassing academic and governmental opinion on a possible solution to the Israel-Arab conflict. Some reporters thought he had tried to get the United States' advance approval of Bourguiba's forthcoming initiative, but this was denied in Washington.

On April 26, eve of the arrival in the United States of the Tunisian Foreign Minister, Habib Bourguiba Jr., the Tunisian Ambassador, Rashid Driss, was received by Assistant Secretary of State Thomas Mann. Significantly or not, the United States Ambassador to Tunisia, Francis H. Russell, left for Washington the same day, and it was conjectured that his journey, too, was in connection with the Bourguiba initiative.

On April 29, Bourguiba Jr. had his long conference with Secretary of State Dean Rusk. Afterward, he held a press conference in which he confirmed that he discussed with the American Secretary of State his father's undertaking. He expressed his hope that other Arab states would join his father in search of a commonsense solution to the Palestine problem. He reportedly had asked Mr. Rusk for diplomatic support in Tunisia's crisis of relations with Nasser. The next day Rusk privately and non-officially expressed appreciation of Bourguiba's initiative, and said that the American government considered it of great significance.

Secretary of State Mongi Slim, one of Tunisia's best and most universally respected diplomats (President of the 1961 United Nations General Assembly) went to the Far East as Bourguiba's personal representative to the governments of India, Pakistan, and Indonesia. He brought a personal message from Bourguiba.

17

Bourguiba vs. Nasser

THE BACKGROUND OF THE RELATIONSHIP BETWEEN THE TUNISIAN AND Egptian Presidents includes long-standing, bitter feuds. Their rivalry stems equally from political-ideological differences and a deep-rooted mutual dislike. The political-ideological differences are composed of several elements. Though we deal with each in separate chapters, we can summarize them here in three categories: 1) Bourguiba's opposition to Nasser's brand of pan-Arabism; 2) Bourguiba's opposition to Nasser's intervention in the affairs of other Arab nations; and 3) Bourguiba's opposition to Nasser's international policies as they bring Egypt close to the Communist power-bloc.

On the personal plane, among other grievances the Tunisian President has an old unsettled score with Nasser dating from 1956 when Bourguiba's erstwhile friend and collaborator, Salah ben Youssef, at that time Secretary General of the Tunisian Neo-Destour party, rebelled against Bourguiba and his policies. The Tunisian High Court of Justice condemned him to death, but he escaped and found asylum in Cairo. There he continued to plot against the Tunisian regime, reportedly with Nasser's encouragement. He was assassinated under mysterious conditions in Frankfurt on August 21, 1961. Some of his followers are still active in Cairo.

Bourguiba considers Nasser a tyrant of unlimited ambition, who plans to dominate all Arab nations by means of subversion and terror. Bourguiba likens him to Stalin, and considers himself the Tito of the Arab world, comparing his own bravery in defying Nasser when the Egyptian seemed omnipotent in the Arab world with Tito's courageous defiance of the all-powerful Stalin at his zenith. As Tito was proud and jealous of Yugoslavia's sovereignty and independent socialism, so Bourguiba was the guardian and defender of Tunisia's sovereignty, and her own brand of socialism. As Tito is groping for an original synthesis between orthodox Marxism and the economic trends of the free world, so Bourguiba is groping for an original synthesis between Arab nationalism and political practices in the free world. And as Tito broke the hollow monolith of pan-Communism and forced the Kremlin leaders to "go to Canossa" and mollify him on Yugoslav soil, so he, Bourguiba, considers himself the man called by destiny to break the totalitarian mock-monolith of pan-Arabism under Nasser's domination. He took great pleasure in explaining all this to Jean Daniel by a brief anecdote: When he visited Tito, they found in the course of their cordial conversation many an affinity.

> One day when Tito told me how he challenged Stalin, he being the head of a little country braving the huge Russian giant, I remarked that for my part I had done approximately the same thing. I hope you understand me . . . Tito understood me perfectly and burst out laughing. . . .

For his part, Nasser has equally little respect for Bourguiba. He mistrusts his political sincerity and the motivation of his nationalism. Whatever political move the Tunisian President makes, Nasser suspects he is propelled by one or another imperialist power.

When he received him with great pomp in Cairo, he nonetheless suspected that the visit was undertaken mainly on behalf of Washington, to meddle in the Egyptian-Saudi disagreement over Yemen. When it became clear that what Bourguiba had in mind was not Yemen but Palestine, Nasser repeated that this, too, was the work of imperialists.

Nasser has accumulated a rich collection of epithets to characterize the personality of the Tunisian President. He calls him a "criminal" and accuses him of "murder" (in reference to the assassination of ben Youssef). Above all, the Egyptian reproaches him with being venal—"a fifth column that can be bought at any time for five or six million dollars."

Pan-Arabism is a comparatively new historic phenomenon and to some extent, a product of the maneuvers of British imperialism in the period between two world wars. Regardless of how genuine and deep-rooted is the Arab yearning for togetherness, the organizational structure of Arab unity was first evolved by the British. Its putative architect was Anthony Eden—later Lord Avon (but more likely some permanent Colonial official with Eden's tacit approval), and not Nasser or his predecessors. *Jeune Afrique* plainly asserts that the Arab League has never been an independent organism, but was created as an instrument of British imperialism and is today the tool which Nasser uses for his own purposes.

From the very beginning it has been torn among the rival factions in the Middle East, mainly Nuri el Said of Iraq and Nasser of Egypt, the latter labeling the former a British stooge. The North African states, Morocco and Tunisia, which became independent about the same time, did not rush to join the League. Awaiting the outcome of the el Said-Nasser feud, they remained outside the League for more than two years after they achieved independence. In 1958, when the Iraqi revolution took place, sweeping away by the simple means of assassination the royal Hashemite dynasty and its government headed by Nuri el Said, observers speculated that the victory belonged to Nasser. Subsequent events proved, however, that the new leader, Gneral Abdel Karim Kassem, was no less anti-Nasser than his royalist predecessor.

Before long, the new Iraqi Foreign Minister, Dr. Abdul Jabbard Jommard, persuaded Tunisia and Morocco to join the League October 1, 1958 to create a counterbalance to Egypt and her supporters. But the Tunis daily *L'Action,* which represented government opinion, wrote: "Tunisia's accession to the Arab League in no way implies that it will give up its individuality, its traditions, or its own values. Nor does it herald a break in our links with European progress and civilization."

Thus from the beginning the Tunisians were determined to oppose any adventurism in international relations, and to strive for an inter-Arab organization based on equality and mutual respect of all the member states.

On the day his country joined, the Tunisian representative delivered his maiden speech before the Arab League Council, and reproached the League "with serving the interests of only one person and one member country." He left no doubt that that person was Nasser and the country the United Arab Republic.

Nasser could not, of course, ignore such a statement; still less could he overlook such an independent attitude. A fierce clash of wills and words broke out immediately. Bourguiba became the

Number One target of Cairo Radio and was denounced in the hyperbole so characteristic of inter-Arab polemics. Exactly two weeks after admission to the Arab League, Bourguiba broke off diplomatic relations with Egypt.

Le Figaro commented at the time: "Tunis could not forgive Cairo for having given refuge to Ben Youssef. . . . Indeed, Bourguiba accused Nasser of having connived in plots against his regime and his life."

President Nasser denied these accusations and attacked his adversary fiercely. On December 3, he declared:

> *El-Sayed* ('Lord,' 'chief' in Arabic) Bourguiba is one of the last agents of imperialism. We had hoped he would renounce his diversionary activities and back his people, the United Arab Republic, and the other liberated countries in the battle against the enemies of Arabism. Instead, he chooses to make lying accusations against us. . . .

The rift was complete, and Tunisia, contrary to its expectations, found itself in total isolation. Not daring to do otherwise, all the League's members voted for Tunisia's expulsion, though the wording of the order was somewhat oblique. Thus Tunisia's relations with the pan-Arab organization were temporarily ended; but the Bizerte tragedy of July 1961 and other pressing matters brought Bourguiba to reconsideration of his attitude. Through a series of mutual gestures, a kind of reconciliation was effected and the implacable enemies of yesterday became "brothers" again. But as we have seen, the new love proved no more lasting than the old.

Clearly, Bourguiba considers Nasser to be suffering from megalomania and excessive pride; a weak leader who fears the masses, and follows their fanaticism instead of leading and educating them to political maturity. He regards Nasser as lacking in the civil or intellectual courage to speak his opinions openly, a quality which he characterizes as both cowardly and dishonest. For example, Nasser expresses, for foreign export, sentiments very similar to Bourguiba's own ideas, while, for internal consumption, he vilifies him with accusations of pro-Zionism and worse:

> Nasser said [on the Palestine question] the same thing: Let us go back to UN decisions. So I said: Well, we agree. Only I have the courage to express my opinion, and he does not. He says it at the UN in New York, but he does not dare say it to the Arabs— and this is dishonest. (In his interview with *Views*)

Even for foreign consumption, he does not clearly say what *he* thinks about a solution to the Palestine problem, but hides behind resolutions of the Bandung Conference, which met more than ten years ago and was never reactivated.

"All this is not serious. I attach a great deal of importance to the opinions of serious people only," and Bourguiba treats him less than seriously, even when Nasser declares war upon him, for the Egyptian leader may reverse himself completely at any time. At the height of the crisis Bourguiba declared: "It is not a rift, only a tiff."

When the Tunisian press, or the posters carried by student demonstrators, refer to the Egyptian leader as "the king of lies and crimes" they reflect Bourguiba's own judgment.

Bourguiba's interview with the British quarterly, *Views,* brings additional insights into the rivalry and bitter dislike between Bourguiba and Nasser:

> We have had excellent relations with Egypt for a long time. We have always considered Egypt to be a pioneer country. This is why I went secretly to the Middle East in 1945. I settled in Egypt because in those days it was independent and it was helping other countries to free themselves. We greeted the 1952 revolution with much joy and optimism. It happened at the same time as our own revolution. The last crisis between France and ourselves had begun in January, 1952. As a result everyone worried about his own problems, his own difficulties. But we considered the advent of the republic [of Egypt] to be a step forward—a good thing in comparison with Farouk's regime. We offered our good wishes for Egyptian progress and development and the realization of her national aspirations—that is to say, evacuation of the colonial presence and complete independence.
>
> Unfortunately, after 1955, because of friction—I believe for personal reasons—between Nuri el Said and Nasser, between Iraq and Egypt—combined with the pride and megalomania of certain Egyptian leaders, and with the difficulties with America and England, and lastly because of the sale of weapons, the Suez crisis arose. This crisis was considered by the Arab countries to be a gesture of liberation not only economically, *vis-à-vis* the International Suez Canal Company—the seizure of one of the country's greatest assets—but also politically. Then came the Suez aggression which was partly a consequence of the canal crisis, but which actually began with the Israeli aggression, which somewhat complicated matters. But we were particularly happy in October–November, 1956, to be sitting

at the UN for the first time as an independent country, and to witness a unanimous attitude against the Suez aggression, unanimous because the two great powers—the Soviet Union and America—agreed. Things are naturally much easier when they agree, and I thought that America's role was a determining factor on that occasion.* We thought that as a result, Egyptain politics—their vision of foreign relations—would draw closer to ours [that is, pro-Western]. But this was not to be. Problems arose between Egypt and ourselves. Problems in 1955 and 1956, following without any doubt the propaganda made by certain Tunisians—Ben Youssef, etc.—who wanted to flatter Egypt and pan-Arabism. So, the Egyptian regime—Nasser, etc.—followed Ben Youssef's footsteps. They fought against the Tunisian government, against the convention (with France) of internal autonomy which they considered to be treachery. They warned the Algerians against us after Ben Youssef had used his skill to promise the Algerians that Tunisia would join them in their struggle. Then we became the scapegoats of Egyptian propaganda and radio. We were regarded as traitors, people who stabbed in the back the cause of the Arab Maghreb, and Algeria. They attacked us not only on the radio, thus making things difficult for us at a time when our regime was not yet solidly established during a period of transition, but they went so far as to send arms to encourage subversion, and terrorists to create disorders—even to kill the President of the Republic. (I was then Prime Minister.) The situation was very bad. Our differences were tremendous. . . . We caught some terrorists with weapons and forged identity papers issued in Cairo. They were in the habit of doing this with many self-governing countries. Tunisia stood fast and she broke off with Egypt and with the Arab Legaue. In October, 1958, the Arab League aligned itself with Egypt. All the countries, even Morocco, were behind the League although they unanimously complained about intervention and pressures. But [they do it] for internal reasons, reasons concerning the regime [inside their own countries.] Tunisia was the only one to leave the Arab League. She broke off with Egypt, and we remained on this basis for some time. We have progressed on the path of decolonization. . . . Then, during 1961, the Bizerte affair occurred —the battle for Bizerte. On that occasion at the time of the battle, Nasser sent me a cable to congratulate and encourage me. So, after three years we resumed our relations. He sent a delegation. We exchanged ambassadors. I thought that he realized he had made

---

* A hint that it was America which saved Nasser and that his "victory" which he celebrates each year with such fanfare was entirely due to the United States, and not to Russia.

a mistake; he now understood that Bourguiba is not an agent of colonialism, or of French imperialism. We were overjoyed to get back to friendly, normal relations. He invited me to come to Egypt, I invited him to come to Tunisia. He made the gesture of coming first, at the time of the Bizerte celebrations. We thought the problems were over.

But then Bourguiba realized that they were not. This he says he found out during his 1965 visit to Egypt, when Nasser took him for granted and thought he would toe the line on the German issue.

In politics in general and among the Arabs in particular, fighting fiercely over an issue does not necessarily mean that the antagonists basically disagree. We have seen that though Bourguiba seemingly challenged Nasser on the Palestine problem, the two leaders sometimes expressed similar views—almost as if they were attempting to outdo one another in showng, alternately, great belligerence and a monumental love of peace.

But this is not the only case in kind. Now Nasser seems to be dead set against a pan-Islamic bloc, of which King Feisal is the champion. But Nasser preceded the Saudi Arabian king by many years in advocating a similar enterprise. In his little book, *The Philosophy of a Revolutionary*, he spoke of history in search of a hero who would unite large congregations of peoples in three spheres: one a pan-Arab, another a pan-Islamic, a third pan-African. (Historically it may perhaps be proven that the originator of the idea of a Moslem bloc in its *present* phase is not King Feisal but President Bourguiba, who broached it during his visits in Turkey and Iran.) So the question is not always what is to be achieved but who is to achieve it. Such jockeying for power can seem, to the observer, bewildering and confusing. Alfred Max who interviewed Nasser for *Réalitiés* (May 1965, English Edition) confessed this confusion:

> In stating his views he (Nasser) readily uses 'we,' which conveys the royal first person, but also 'we Egyptians,' 'we Arabs, 'we Moslems,' 'we Africans,' 'we Afro-Asians,' 'we the non-aligned'. . . .

Despite the confusion, one can discern a similarity of tendencies and aspirations common to the two Arab leaders. Both reach out for larger spheres of influence, objecting to the narrow limitations of their respective countries. These envisioned spheres are sometimes identical, sometimes different, and sometimes overlapping. Thus, both the Tunisian and Egyptian Presidents are for a larger grouping of Moslem lands. As to Arabism, Bourguiba, though opposing Nasser's brand of aggressive pan-Arabism, hopes for a long-range framework of cooperation first among the four Maghreb countries and eventually linking all the Arab states, and, in addition, he advocates a French-speaking community of African states.

There are the basic differences of degree and approach. In every project, Nasser sees Egypt as the center and leader; Bourguiba understands that while Tunisia can play an important role, it cannot be the predominant one. Nasser uses not only persuasion but also intrigue, subversion, and, on occasion, military intervention—open or disguised. Bourguiba, on the whole, does not resort to force or pressure, but uses his talents to inspire and convince.

Both men wish to influence events beyond the limited borders of their respective countries and the finite boundaries of their own life-spans. Both seem driven furiously to achieve in their lifetime results which will remain after they are gone. The Egyptian President wants to mold the solid framework of a pan-Arab republic stretching from the Persian Gulf with its rich resources of oil to the Atlantic. Whoever possesses that oil, he believes, will be not only independent but able to dictate policy to the Western world. According to him, oil is the most formidable strength of Arab nationalism.

> [Oil is the] sinew of material civilization without which all its machines would cease to function. The great factories, producing every kind of goods; all the instruments of land, sea, and air communications; all the weapons of war from the mechanical bird above the clouds to the submarine beneath the waves—without oil all would turn back to naked metal, covered with rust, incapable of motion or use.*

Egypt lacks that oil and hence, so he seems to reason, is deprived of everything else. Nasser must achieve, therefore, a political structure in the Middle East within which Egypt will be in a position to benefit from this important key commodity. He must do it in his lifetime lest those who come after him lack the will-power and talent to achieve it. If he succeeds, he will leave a durable foundation that will remain even under weaker successors.

---

* Gamal Abdel Nasser, *Egypt's Liberation: the Philosophy of the Revolution,* pp. 106–7.

Bourguiba's furious drive is to achieve the opposite. Despite his enormous energy and good looks, he is reported to be physically not very well, so he is in a hurry. He would like to see an orderly succession during his lifetime, but only after he achieves his main goal—once and for all to break Egypt's hegemony in the Arab world, and thus safeguard Tunisia's independence even after he is retired, or gone. He plans the creation of a constellation in the Arab world in which his successors could not, even if they would, be swallowed up by pan-Arabism ruled directly from Cairo, or indirectly through Algeria. To him this confederation is especially urgent because he is not sure whether or not his successors may fall prey to pan-Arab enticements or be victims of its expansionism. In this as in other aspects he seems to have taken de Gaulle, his adversary of Bizerte, as a model to imitate.

The contest between Bourguiba and Nasser is, therefore, one for time. Its outcome cannot be predicted, since both sides possess solid trump cards. Whoever may prove to be the victor in their lifetime, but in the long run the winner may become the loser and the loser be vindicated after he is gone. There is little chance that pan-Arabism will become an historic reality in the next ten or fifteen years; the Arab nations are more divided than ever before.

Despite the good luck which until now has so steadily accompanied Nasser, there is nonetheless an inherent danger that he may disappear from the scene; then Bourguiba will be certain that his mission has been accomplished. But no crystal ball has yet been invented that can fortell whether the Arab yearnings for unity will triumph in the long run over their centrifugal tendencies.

There is also the question of age: Bourguiba is 64, and Nasser is 16 years younger.*

---

* Though he is reportedly in good health, the pressures and tensions of his office seem to show on Nasser's physique. Alfred Max who interviewed him for *Réalités* in April 1965 related that the Egyptian President appeared to him older, somewhat thinner—quite different from the broad-shouldered tribune of the early years of the revolution. He had about him an air "of slightly disenchanted good faith, with a trace of weariness and tension. What is arresting about him is the contrast between the tall vigorous frame and a slimness verging on frailty."

18

Bourguiba and Arab Unity

IN A SENSE BOURGUIBA REPRESENTS IN THE ARAB WORLD WHAT
de Gaulle stands for in Europe: a vague profession of faith in the
principle of ultimate supra-national unity or confederation. But
such unification must evolve gradually, organically, without coercion, always admitting that the basic contemporary reality is the
individual nation or state, and that it will be so for a long time.

Though a vehement opponent of Nasser's brand of pan-
Arabism, Bourguiba does not reject the *idea* of Arab unity. On the
contrary, unity is mankind's best hope, and worthy of effort on
several levels. The fewer the armed frontiers—the less the number
of small and belligerent nations and of customs barriers—the
better. There is vision in unity and there is grandeur in it.

Bourguiba is the strongest champion of unification of the four
countries of the Maghreb. He espouses the gradual economic
integration of the Maghreb into the economy of the European
Economic Community (the Common Market). He is the most
eloquent spokesman for a commonwealth of the former French
colonies of Africa, to be centered in Paris. It was probably he who
first launched the idea of an Islamic bloc of nations in the Middle
East, North Africa, and Asia. He obviously does not oppose Arab
unity.

But he is dead set against approaching Arab unity with false
assumptions, indulging in Utopian promises and, above all, using
mischievous means for its achievement.

To begin with, he denies the very *existence* of a pan-Arab nation. The fact that several countries speak Arabic does not make
them one nation, just as the world's French-speaking communities
cannot remotely be considered a united French nation. He ac-
knowledges the importance of a common language and other
affinities as unifying factors in a long historical perspective. He

concedes the future possibility of a more or less loose inter-Arab structure. But Arab unity seems to him a nebulous and far-off goal. More realistic and hence urgent is achieving a political and economic association in the Maghreb; but even this limited goal encounters presently insuperable difficulties. In any event, only after the Maghreb has been united can there be even talk of a larger framework for Arab unity. As he visualizes it, this more ambitious goal will consist of the united Maghreb plus the Arab countries in the eastern Mediterranean (the Machrek, in Arabic, *East*, as opposed to Maghreb—*West*.)

The structural and constitutional form of such a cooperation it is too early to ascertain. One thing is fairly clear—it will never be the monolith of which the pan-Arabist dreams. It will, if at all, be a complex of independent nations, each with its own personality and point of view on national and international existence.

Whatever its form, this ideal must not be achieved by force, terror, subversion, or any kind of interference in the affairs of the individual Arab states. It should come about only after consultations, negotiations, and gradual cooperation among the various Arab states on the basis of complete equality. The rights of each state must be scrupulously respected; the only weapon used to gain unity must be persuasion. The only basis of common policy and action must be consent freely expressed by all concerned.

Above all, Bourguiba reproaches Nasser not so much for his dogged insistence on Arab unity, but for his belief that "Arab unity and Egypt are synonymous." It is because of this confusion, holds Bourguiba, that "Nasser gives orders [to the leaders of other independent Arab countries] as if he were a sergeant major."

By the same token, Bourguiba is not against the concept of an Arab League *per se*, but only against that organization as it now functions: an instrument of Nasser through which he tries to dictate to other Arab governments their foreign and even domestic policies.

When Nasser tried to force his will upon the Arab states to break with Bonn, Bourguiba declared:

> What the devil! Arab unity has not been achieved yet. It is still only a wish, a great aspiration which, of course, we are all for but on the condition that the divergences of opinion are accepted, that the sovereignty of each state is respected and that one does not precipitate things.
>
> For the time being the problem is how to create a [larger] Arab

community. But we did not choose a chief over us. Besides, the Arabs recognize more than one. . . . It is not a matter of personalities. In spite of divergences of opinion the friendship between the Tunisian and Egyptian peoples is not endangered at all. On the contrary, it will be strengthened. (Interview with Jean Daniel, *Nouvel Observateur*, April 15, 1965)

CBS news correspondent Winston Burdett asked him on *Face the Nation* (May 23) :

Mr. President, as a realist and a supreme pragmatist, how do you evaluate Nasser's claims to leadership in the Arab world and the slogan of Arab unity that he makes so much use of?

Bourguiba: The truth is that what is called the Arab world, geographically speaking from the Persian Gulf to the Atlantic Ocean, has never been at any time in history a unity, a union. We all feel, and felt—we countries which have just come out from under colonial rule—we felt the need of uniting our strength in order to feel stronger in dealing with our problems. But one should not—and it is impossible to—just disregard and ignore the differences which exist.

We are proposing cooperation, the closest cooperation, but not a systematic union. Not an absolute union. We think it is not realizable because it is not practical.

The fact is that through the use of the Arab League by the Egyptian government, we saw it become an instrument which allowed President Nasser to present himself as the leader of this Arab League. And one should not disregard the fact also that many countries, whether East or West, have done nothing to restrain his feelings of being this leader. And these countries have even helped him by dealing with him as sole [spokesman].

The big change last week [at the Arab League Conference in Cairo] is that the true reality has become evident: the reality of different and independent Arab governments which, though in agreement for a policy of solidarity, of cooperation, and when they agree say yes, would also say no if they are apt to sacrifice their own national interests—just for the sake of the leadership of President Nasser.

So unity is a goal, an ideal. It is not a reality.

On the same program Martin Agronsky asked:

President Nasser seems to be looking more toward Peking and Moscow than he does toward Washington and the West. Do you feel that the future of the Arab world is best served by alignment with the West or with the East in the Communist world?

Bourguiba: I do not agree with the general naming of all that area covered from Iraq to Morocco as the Arab world. I do not agree because the facts are that it is a group of countries, of nations which are independent. [Their] history has been different. Geography imposes upon them [characteristics] which cannot be ignored. So these countries which form what is called the Arab world have different orientations, especially as to the western and eastern blocs. Certain countries feel that it is in their vital interests to lean [toward] the West. Other countries feel that it is in their vital interest to lean [to] the East. The fact that we speak the same language does not impose upon us [an obligation] that we should all follow one of us. They [the Arab countries] should be free to determine their orientation according to their contingencies, taking into account their history, geography, economy, their very interest of survival.

If one Arab country tries to modify—to change—such a normal, natural trend by attempting to impose its policy and to call names those who do not agree to follow—names like traitors, lackeys of imperialism, I mean all these kinds of slogans that you know—such an attempt is to ignore reality. It is weakness. And it is not only illogical but also impractical. One should not—and one cannot—dream even of harmonizing one's interest [with the rest] if one does not take reality into consideration.

The status of the Arab League among its own members is amazingly ambiguous and full of paradox. It is supposed to be the unifying frame for all the Arab states, bringing them nearer to integration as one Arab nation. Yet it is not permitted to open offices in any number of Arab states. Its center is Cairo. And during the Egyptian-West German crisis, when its Secretary General suggested setting up branches in the Arab countries, Lebanon reportedly proposed instead that the League try opening offices in non-Arabic countries. Though there is nominally a "Unified Command of the Arab armed forces," this has remained, so far, a fiction. Egyptian troops are not permitted to be stationed in any Arab country with two exceptions: Nasser's troops have been heavily committed in the Republican "part" of the Yemen, which is no country—as South Vietnam is no country; and some Egyptian troops were stationed in Iraq, probably with the Baghdad government's hope of using them eventually to crush the perennial Kurdish revolt.

The only factor which gives the League coherence is Israel, and this is negative. Although most of the Arab states would like to see Israel disappear from the face of the earth, they have never been able to agree on a "positive" plan to "liberate" Palestine. Jordan strives toward outright annexation (in one form or another); others want to see Palestine a new, independent state—with Jordan giving up all of Jerusalem and all the sections of its territory originally designated by the partition plan.

Bourguiba told an interviewer from *Le Figaro* (April 12):

> To wish to make the Arab League an artificial unit with a common capital and a single chief will run into trouble, of which Egypt has already had a sample. Long centuries have created between the Arab countries of the West (North Africa) and those of the East differences which cannot be ignored. The solidarity of the Arab League cannot be exercised at the expense of the League's member nations. Thus, we could not feel ourselves bound by solidarity to support a sister-state's decision which would recognize the regime of Mr. Ulbricht in East Germany. It was necessary that we destroy certain illusions.

If this is the case, should Arab unity be written off as an illusion? Not necessarily. It depends upon what one means by "Arab unity," what one aspires to achieve, and above all how one proposes to go about it. Bourguiba continued:

> If one takes realities into consideration, one can go forward. This is what we are doing in the Maghreb where progress is first achieved psychologically before the ties become economic. Finally a solution will evolve which the politician must face.

And in another interview (with *Views*) he declared:

> I personally think that the best way to a healthy situation is to return to the sovereignty and independence of all Arab countries. And it is only on this basis that we can create an atmosphere of confidence, of friendship and of normal relations. These relations will become more cordial perhaps, more fraternal, and will evolve toward the coordination of our efforts, the unification of our economies and our cultures before we can even think of political and constitutional unity. This is how I conceive the evolution of the present situation, and I wish all Arab countries would understand it in the same way.

If these ideas and this approach ring familiarly in our ears, it is because de Gaulle has expounded them in Europe. The similarity is striking. Both statesmen warn against illusions of, or premature moves toward, unity; far from advancing the cause, these can only jeopardize the ideal of unity. As de Gaulle advocates a Europe of Nations, so does Bourguiba advocate a Middle East and North Africa of nation-states. Bourguiba, as de Gaulle, is primarily, a guardian of his own country's vital interests. Simultaneously each exercises his personal skills and energies to endow his country with an international influence transcending its material resources, population, and military power. Thus each is, hopefully, building up what is referred to as a "third force." Of course, one must not stretch the analogy too far.*

True to the philosophy that each country must cultivate its own vineyard, Bourguiba welcomed the overthrow of Ahmed Ben Bella in neighboring Algeria—although his attitude was ambivalent because he does not approve of "governments parachuted by 'coups d'état'."

> I personally think the 19th June [1965, when Ben Bella was overthrown]—well, let us say the events which took place on the 19th of June are of course regrettable. We should not encourage these *putsches*, these palace revolutions. But the results are the important issue. The announcements made by the new leaders seem to indicate that Algeria is now really starting to worry about Algeria itself—about Algerian problems. This is very important for us, a guarantee against excesses, megalomania, and the policy of prestige. It is a good thing that each country should give priority to internal problems. I am not saying they should not also care about countries defending themselves, struggling for freedom. I stand for these principles—but I give priority to internal problems, my own people. Well, it is good that the Algerians are moving this way. . . . It is also a good thing to see them move away from Nasser, from Egypt, whose satellite they had just about become. For all these reasons we are very optimistic, we wish the new team lots of luck. Let them succeed in solving the great problems, the immense problems they are facing, the problems of underdevelopment.

---

* This analogy is not lost upon certain minds in the Middle East. Thus the Beirut newspaper *Al Khayat* wrote: "Bourguiba tries to follow (in the Middle East) the work (which de Gaulle started in Europe) to emerge as a third force in the Middle East—with a view of solving the various international problems in the Arab world. In doing this he strives to appear as a de Gaulle of the Middle East."

More than that. Bourguiba believes that it "would be in the best interests" of all the Arab countries to follow the policy which the Algerians proclaimed with the overthrow of Ben Bella. It would be "even in the interests of the Egyptian people" were they to emancipate themselves from their present totalitarian pan-Arabism.

> They [the Egyptians] had enough of bearing the load of this policy of hegemony and its enormous costs, whilst their state of underdevelopment is becoming more pronounced due to the enormous increase of population in their country. Against this, slogans, airy talk and insults [against others] have very little effect. (*Views*, Autumn 1965)

19

Bourguiba vs. Arab Leaders

BOURGUIBA'S CAMPAIGN WAS NOT DIRECTED SOLELY AGAINST NASSER or the extremist regimes of Syria and Iraq, but against practically the entire Arab leadership, even though his purpose was to help the leadership of each country become emancipated from Egyptian tutelage and slowly gain independence of policy and action. It was a thankless task and a complicated one to boot.

The trouble with most Arab leaders is, as Bourguiba sees it, that having been corrupted by Nasser they in turn corrupted their own peoples. In an effort to please Nasser they follow his policy concerning Palestine (since in very little else can they follow him). In the process they learned (or believe they learned) that exactly as Nasser uses the Palestine issue to sustain his leadership in the Arab world, they must use the same tool to preserve their leadership in their own countries.

So the Tunisian President tried through his campaign to persuade his Arab listeners, especially the Palestinians, that they are being misled by demagogic leaders—statesmen, spokesmen, journalists; that these demagogues have at heart not the interests of the refugees, but their own popularity. Most Arab rulers feed their people with lies in order to stay in power, and surely such deception is no solid foundation.

> Because of their belief that they have little credit, that they have been parachuted into the place by *coups* and *putsches*, some leaders think that they must excite the Arab [masses] in order to keep their positions. Well, they will get no positive results. . . .
> (*Views*)

He discerns here a vicious circle: Arab leaders try to maintain

313

power through the Palestine agitation, but, in turn, this agitation makes the foundation of their power shaky. They are no longer free, since by pandering to mob emotions on the Palestine issue, they have become prisoners of their own slogans.

> The trouble is [Bourguiba declared in a televised interview on the French network] that for years the masses have been incited by the Press and Radio. If there are new leaders truly seeking a compromise solution [in the Israel-Arab conflict] they find their capacity for leadership handicapped, since they are prisoners of the masses they have incited all along.

"The Arab leaders," he continued, "all of them know I am right." In private conversations with him they have "shown greater understanding" than is publicly known. But "when facing the mob they castigate me. . . . They are demagogues who appeal to the instincts, stressing the sufferings, poverty, and depression of the people so as vainly to promise them the heights . . . to earn applause and prove their patriotism."

This criticism so often voiced by Bourguiba is mirrored in statements by Nasser himself, to such foreign visitors as U.S. Senators Gale McGee and Albert Gore in 1959, and the former Mayor of Florence, Prof. Giorgio La Pira. Nasser confessed candidly: Even were he willing to make peace with Israel, he could not do so, for if he changed his policy toward Israel, he would risk the survival of his regime and loss of prestige in the whole Arab world.*

In the case of King Hussein and his little kingdom of Jordan, the solution to the Palestine problem along the classic line of Arab propaganda is clearly suicidal. Neither he nor his state could survive the disappearance of Israel or the implementation of the original partition plan, for in either case his territory would be dismembered, and chaos would ensue among his population.

Thus, the perpetuation of the Palestine conflict has become a self-generating and self-propelling movement over which the Arab leadership has no control. The fever around Palestine provides the great escape and artificial substitute for constructive policies, keeping the Arab masses in a paralyzing neurosis, depriving them of any possibility for wholesome development. It is the root of their psychological, political, and social sicknesses. The Palestine problem, Bourguiba told a panel of interviewers of CBS–TV,

---

* From a conversation between this writer and Senator McGee.

(Face the Nation, May 23) "did lots of harm to the Arab countries and it is the origin, and partly the cause, of the instability
and the current *coups d'état* in the Middle East."

The best example of this sick state of affairs is Syria, which
since 1949 has remained for all intents and purposes without a
civilian government. Through a series of nine *putsches,* nine successive army juntas have ruled, and it was during part of the same
eighteen-year period that the abortive union with Egypt occurred.
Today Syria seems to be in greater anarchy than ever before, but
it is in that country that the Palestine fever is at the highest pitch,
reaching an ever higher crescendo. And as long as the Palestine
conflict remains unsolved, those leaders in Syria and elsewhere who
speak more recklessly, will get, or hope they will get, the upper
hand. This inflamed atmosphere of verbal pyrotechnics in turn
increases the instability of each individual state and of the Middle
East as a whole.

In the face of this turbulence and misery, Bourguiba explained,
"the search for peace" was becoming ever more urgent.

It is not easy to be a champion of the weak and subservient,
for such a champion is often exposed to repudiation by those he
tries to liberate. Although Jordan, for instance, exerted a restraining influence, in councils of the League, it could not summon
enough courage to side openly with Bourguiba. More than that,
its spokesman thought it prudent to attack him. After Bourguiba's
speech before the National Council of the Socialist Destour Party,
at which he delivered his forceful attack upon Nasser and the
break with the Arab League was decided, Jordan found it opportune to repudiate the Tunisian President. On the morrow of
that meeting the Jordanian Premier Wasfi el-Tal declared: "Our
attitude to the Zionist robbery will not alter, whatever proposals
are advanced from whatever quarter."

Asked at a press conference in Amman what he had to say about
Bourguiba's prediction that new rifts are likely to emerge between
Jordan and Egypt as a result of Cairo's policy, the Jordanian
Premier answered: "Inter-Arab conflicts are finished, once and
for all."

The newspaper of the Old City of Jerusalem, *Falastin,* commented: "Premier el-Tal's reply was short but complete. 'There
is no need for Jordan to react. Our attitude is crystal clear. We
have but one reply to Bourguiba, as to Eshkol.'" But the Jordanian Premier's statement was rash, and unrealistic, and fruit-

less; his king and country were soon to be reestablished as the main target of Cairo's vilification, abuse, and attempts at massive subversion.

President Bourguiba takes such manifestations in his stride. "Some Arab countries, less stable than others," he told Edward Behr of *Newsweek*, (May 10) "feel they must show loyalty to Nasser by attacking me. But thank God I am strong enough, in my own country, to be able to say 'no' to Nasser." The trouble is, however, that Bourguiba's example does not make their regimes more stable.

20

Bourguiba and the Arabs

TO SAY THAT BOURGUIBA IS ONE OF THE MOST OUTSTANDING ARAB patriots is at once a truism and misleading. Surely he is in many ways the fiercest critic of the Arabs—of their character, their mentality, their complexes, their delusions, their impotence which hides itself in grandiloquent rhetoric, their lack of realism, their isolation from historic trends, their capacity for sterile hatred, their passion for conspiracy, their lack of sincerity.

Jean Lacouture, an astute observer of the North African scene, recounts:

> I can still hear him [Bourguiba] describing a meeting of the Arab League to me, miming the scene with the talent of a great actor. You could picture a circle of people simulating piety, fraternity, and the purest emotions, then suddenly whispering one to another. 'When are we going to get rid of this guy? Who's going to bump him off?' (*New York Times Magazine,* June 6)

The whole ambience of Arab politics in the eastern Mediterranean is foreign and distasteful to him. As he sees it, that milieu is an isolated world, inbred and insular, seething with dissent, intrigue, and reciprocal hatreds. He despises the insincerity that prevails in the relationships among the politicians, all to some degree frightened and corrupted by Nasser's policy of subversion and terror.

Bourguiba is contemptuous of the Arab East's culture and ignorance. "How can one compare," he once exclaimed, "what I have learned in France with the nonsense that the Egyptian educators inculcate in the minds of their people?" A British diplomat, closely acquainted with the Tunisian President, remarked: "I've never seen anyone outside France so near to France, nor anyone in the Arab world so remote from the Arabs."

"Remote" in this instance does not imply indifference or detachment; a more appropriate term would be "estrangement." which is a result not of aloofness, but rather of despair. In his rhetoric there is often something of the wrath of a prophet reproaching his people with harsh truths (though the wounding words are rarely directed against the Tunisians, but against the "other" Arabs, mainly those of the Middle East).

He scorns such character traits of the Arabs as the schizophrenia which splits them between brotherly love on the one hand and murderous hatred on the other. Because of this duality, tremendous devotion and self-sacrifice co-exist with hypocritical courtesy and chivalry. Polished duplicity is an art developed to perfection rarely equalled anywhere else in the world.*

Sometimes his anger is so incandescent that it seems to be directed toward strangers, not his own people. But it is an anger engendered by love and concern, not animosity. He deplores their weaknesses, their fanaticisms, and hatreds, which he sees as negative and destructive, dangerous not to the enemy but to those who harbor those emotions. So obsessed, Arabs substitute curses for deeds, daydreams for performance.

Such gentilitial self-consciousness is not uncommon and Bourguiba is not unique in his tribal hypersensitivity. We know of Russian writers and educators of the pre-revolutionary period who castigated the Russian people for their shortcomings; of Spanish, French, and Italian writers and philosophers who tried to shock their peoples out of deplorable states of mind at various times in history. The United States has had its native critics at every stage in its career, none more vociferous than the protestors of today. Bourguiba is perhaps most reminiscent of the Zionist poets, writers, and leaders of a generation just past who denounced the weaknesses, the pusillanimity, the sterile fanaticism and religious archaism of the Jews just before Israel was established. Their outbursts, whether in poetry, in philosophic-psychological essays, or in speeches, sounded more venomous than those of some of the professional anti-Semites.

In an issue dealing with Arab criticism of Bourguiba's initiative

---

* Another prominent Tunisian, Bashir ben Yahmed, editor of the weekly *Jeune Afrique,* shares Bourguiba's views about the Arabs. He describes, deplores, and denounces their fanaticism, internecine hatreds, extremism, lack of sense of proportion. *Jeune Afrique,* (March 8, 1965.)

(March 28, 1965), the editor of *Jeune Afrique* points out the shocking character of the "custom" of branding as a traitor anyone who dares to deviate from the accepted line. Yesterday's hero becomes the enemy of today, a scoundrel who has sold himself to imperialism. Bashir ben Yahmed wrote that from these hysterical reactions one gets the impression that "the enemy is no longer Israel, the opponent is no longer West Germany, but a small Arab country, Tunisia."

Bourguiba rejects the notion that true patriotism requires one to be Arab first, last, and always. About himself he declares:

> No, I have no fanaticism. . . . Whether Arab or African, I am first of all a man, a human being. I have sympathy and affection, respect also, for my fellow men. Naturally the ties are closer with those who live within my own country, and then with our neighbors [of the Maghreb], those who speak my language, who have my religion. . . .

But then, on another level, he feels closer to those

> who think as I do, who have the same ideas, the same ideology, whether they live in Canada or Australia or in America. And . . . I have no inferiority or superiority complexes. . . . It does not embarrass me to be an Arab, an African, a Mediterranean, or a Tunisian. The most important thing is respecting mankind, respecting this divine spark God has placed within man. (*Views*)

What exasperates Bourguiba most in dealing with vital problems is the Arabs' flight from reality, creating a wide and deep abyss between what they would wish to happen and the reality around them.

Realism, however, demands awareness of one's immediate neighborhood; but also of conditions in the wider world, and their effect upon the local situation. To talk about solving the Palestine conflict simply by war against Israel, even if there were a possibility of vanquishing the Jewish state, is to ignore such world influences as the relations between Russia and the United States; the existence of the United Nations; the sympathy for Israel in Europe, among some African nations, and even in some Communist countries.

Bourguiba is animated by the idea that it is most imperative, in the words of Jean Lacouture writing in *The New York Times Magazine,* (June 6) "to bring the Arabs back from the wasteland of mysticism and eloquence to the domain of reality." Bourguiba told the editor of the Paris *Nouvel Observateur,* (April 15) Jean Daniel (who is, by the way, a North African Jew):

> I always remember the Old-Destour, whose "activists" spent their time hating the French while neglecting to fight them. They were complex-ridden, and did nothing but dream about their liberation. A dream of hatred. I used to tell them that they resemble those characters in an Arab tale who are planted on the shore, who dream of crossing the sea, but who never think of building a ship, of studying the tides and the winds—namely the things necessary for the realization of their dream. In the case of Palestine this hatred leads only to confusing anti-Zionism with anti-Semitism which, in turn, means inculcating—at least among the masses—a fanaticism which will prove dangerous when one will have to begin negotiating.
>
> While in Jordan I visited the refugee camp in Jericho. The sight was indescribable. It forced me to become painfully aware of the responsibilities the Arab people have taken upon themselves these last seventeen years. These refugees are simultaneously fed with chimerical hopes and sterile hatred. If I am not too good at hatred and feel uncomfortable, it is not only because I despise this emotion but also because with the Arabs it hinders any lucid action. It is an alibi for inaction. One yells, one curses, one delivers oneself to voicing insults and abuse; and then one has the feeling of having unburdened oneself; of having done one's task; of being at peace with one's own conscience. At the base of all this is an inferiority complex; one overestimates the adversary.
>
> When [in the Lebanon] I said these things when I spoke of realism, a Lebanese newspaperman retorted that realism consists also of taking into consideration the fanaticism of the masses. This is an answer of despair: if one reasons like this then there is no room for authority, responsibility; and no concrete action is possible. It is as if at each phase of my negotiations with the French I should have been frightened [into action] by the patriotic outbiddings among my own followers; as if the Algerians should not have signed the Evian agreements out of fear that the clauses concerning the French people in Algeria would irritate the fighters of the underground. When one is overrun by one's own propaganda to the point of not being able to keep the narrowest margin for maneuverability, one risks chaos and one runs toward defeat.
>
> All this I found it possible to tell in a courageous and brotherly way, and having said it, it became clear to me that it is possible to do in the Middle East the same educational work of the masses which I have undertaken with the people of Tunisia; to promise

nothing which one is not sure of being able to materialize; not to bind one's own hands by a propaganda which boomerangs; to teach the people first of all to count upon themselves. In this specific case: to teach the Palestinians to organize themselves. I believe that I found an ear with many among them.

In his efforts to move the Arabs from fancy to reality, he exhorts them to give up the "hopeless dream" of crushing Israel. The time has come to wake up and face the fundamental truth that "Israel is, of course, an established fact."

They had also better come to terms with the idea that "you are in no position to start a war," he told the Arabs.

When an interviewer of Réalités asked him in 1965 what he considered "the most urgent problem facing the world today—as seen from Tunis," he answered:

> As chief of the Tunisian state, which is a member of the poor countries, I can tell you that the problem which concerns me most directly is, of course, that of development. But this is most closely tied in with the problem of peace, which I consider of paramount importance. Because if war breaks out, all our efforts will be reduced to nothing. . . . There is no greater problem than that of peace.

In his Carthage speech upon his return from the tumultuous tour in the Middle East, he scornfully pointed out the absurdity of the feverish preparations for war. The Arab leaders, he said, have neither plan nor strategy for conquering Israel as they promise the Palestinians.

He considers armaments a blight for the peoples of the world at large and those of the Middle East in particular. The irrationality, if not the insanity, of an arms race became particularly obvious to him during his visit to Egypt. He saw at first hand the Egyptian masses being fed on visions of "military glory upon the triumphant return to reconquer the plundered fatherland—Palestine." For these mad visions some of the Arab countries were reported to devote 70 per cent of their budgets.

In his Carthage speech Bourguiba derided this folly:

> . . . The armaments race in which [the Middle Eastern countries] are engaged at this moment is perfectly useless. Its immediate result is a waste of resources which, together with the up-

heavals and *coups d'état*, compromise the development of the Arab countries.

Tunisia almost alone among the new nations has chosen to stay out of that mad race for military ostentation. It is the only Arab country that has practically no army except a few small units necessary for internal security. This is the more remarkable, since she is flanked by a powerful neighbor—Algeria, whose population and military strength exceed Tunisia's—with whom she has unsettled territorial differences.

There is no reason to doubt the sincerity of Bourguiba's motives in championing a peaceful settlement to the Israel-Arab conflict. He believes that war or war tensions anywhere in the world are a danger to the whole of humanity—and first and foremost to the underdeveloped countries. Regardless how far away a conflict may seem to be, the danger is still close. War tensions and bellicose attitudes have a disastrous effect on the morale and the healthy development that might otherwise occur in the Arab countries.

Among the things that enrage him most is the lack of common sense in the decision-making of the Arabs—whether by individual leaders or the Arab League.

When he arrived in the Lebanon on March 7, 1965 the Egyptian-German dispute was at its height, and Nasser was trying to create an atmosphere of a holy war, insisting that the future of every single Arab state depended upon the outcome of this issue. At his press conference in Beirut on March 11, Bourguiba reproached Nasser for the hysteria he had created. He, too, had become indignant, he said, about the secret arms deal between Israel and Bonn, and he had agreed that the shipments should stop. But the German surrender should have been celebrated as a great victory for the Arabs; instead they were asked to engage in an unlimited vendetta against Bonn. "What style is this in international relations?" he asked.

It did not make sense to him. "And I," he later told a correspondent of *Le Monde,* "if somebody tells me to do something which does not make sense, I refuse." Here is the essence of his quarrel with Nasser. "To break relations with a country," he told the correspondent, "is a very serious act. It is a declaration of war. I have broken diplomatic relations only once, with France, after Bizerte."* And that was after France had dispatched warships and bombers to Tunisia for the battle of Bizerte where a thousand Tunisians were killed in one day. "And even then I did not ask any other Arab country to follow our decision and break relations with France."

Then why is all the wrath directed against West Germany, he asked, and not also against the United States, though the latter was a major party to the arms deal? Is it because the U.S. is too strong to tangle with? Where then is the principle which alone could save this from being sheer hypocrisy?

The truth is, Bourguiba said at the Beirut press conference, the Arabs are not even strong enough to punish Germany. And, he remarked sarcastically, for the Arabs to retaliate against West Germany was really like disfiguring one's wife to force her to remain faithful. "Have we come together," he asked (referring to the Arab League deliberations in Cairo discussing sanctions against West Germany), "to punish ourselves or to punish Israel?" And since when, he wanted to know, was recognition of Israel considered a casus belli? Three-fourths of the African states are among the 87 countries that have diplomatic ties with Israel,

> To be frank, there was no reason to break relations with Germany, or I should have done the same with all the other countries that recognize Israel. If I broke relations with Bonn I would have hurt only myself and would have done no harm to Germany, and would not by the same token have given any assistance to the Palestinians. This brandishing of the sword against Germany, what does it mean? Perhaps there were some extraordinary reasons for doing it, but they were beyond my comprehension. . . .

He does not deny that his friendly relations with West Germany are motivated by Bonn's economic aid; but his opposition to the German issue "was not based on self-interest [alone], since it is a fact that Bonn extended to Cairo and Damascus more help than she has granted us."

It is Bourguiba's repeated contention that common sense demands a new approach to the Israel-Arab conflict. If a policy has led to a dead end, surely there is something wrong with it and new methods should be sought and applied—that is, if one is serious.

---

* This is incorrect. He also broke relations with Egypt twice: on October 15, 1958 and on October 3, 1966.

"For seventeen years," he declared in a televised interview, "the Palestine problem was at the very center of Arab preoccupation and no results whatever were achieved." For seventeen years the Arab insistence that Israel had to be eradicated by a combined military operation of all the Arab states ("The Arab Nation") did not bring the problem one inch nearer solution. Would it not be reasonable to abandon the old tactics and try a new approach?

21

How Does Bourguibism Apply
to Palestine?

WHAT IS BOURGUIBA'S NEW APPROACH TO THE QUANDARY OF PALEStine? To adopt in the Middle East the philosophy and tactics he applied in his own fight for Tunisia's independence, which became known as "Bourguibism," or "gradualism."

At his press conference in Beirut he asked an angry crowd of journalists why, since seventeen years' experience has proven that the Arabs cannot defeat Israel in a frontal attack, the Arabs should not try his method of "phases"? Solving such a problem as Palestine's gradually is a method which has been tried and found eminently successful.

In his interview on CBS' *Face the Nation,* he declared:

> My optimism [that his campaign will eventually bear fruit] is based on the long experience which I had with the Tunisian people itself. In my struggle I had to deal not only with the French colonial regime but also against certain ideas among the Tunisian people as well. Thirty years ago—after half a century of occupation—Tunisia looked as if it had been already practically swallowed up. And I had to employ this approach, this method of comparison and a step-by-step approach; a method which certainly consisted of recognizing partly the colonial facts which we wanted to fight. And, of course, my method was met with cries and violent and dishonest reactions—the same kind of reaction you can hear now as far as the Middle East is concerned. But I stood by my words and ideas and through my method of cultivating the contacts [with the French] and keeping up my explanations [to the Tunisians], I obtained a great result: the Tunisian people

began to understand the efficiency of my method and the usefulness of this step-by-step policy. If I had not accepted, for instance,
in 1954, internal autonomy, which was strictly limited to home
rule, while leaving external sovereignty to the French—which was
for a nationalist like me, as for any Tunisian, a painful thing—we
would not be independent today. I would not have liberated my
country had I asked for everything or nothing.

From this an Israeli would be fully justified in believing that
Bourguiba's plan aims at the gradual "liberation" of the Israeli
part of Palestine as Tunisia was gradually liberated. True, he also
spoke of peace and justice for both sides, arrived at through a
negotiated settlement; but these contradictory trends have characterized his campaign from the beginning. As we have seen, both
the leadership and public opinion in Israel appraised Bourguiba's
statement as meaning he is aiming at the same thing as the other
Arab leaders: the liquidation of the state of Israel. There is this
difference, perhaps: that he suggests that instead of (or before)
resorting to armed conflict, the Palestinian Arabs should first try
to achieve their objective by political means. These may include
political and economic pressures in the UN, where the great powers will be asked to revert to the original UN partition plan of
1947; to force the issue of readmitting the Arab refugees; to exploit the goodwill of friendly countries, and to mobilize public
opinion everywhere. "We have to act quickly," he said at his press
conference in Jerusalem, "to draw up reasonable plans . . . and
try to win over as many supporters as possible."

But he also suggested that the Palestinians should take their
destiny into their own hands, and fight as the Tunisian or Algerians fought. In such a case the neighboring Arab states would
be in a position to support that fight. In the Old City of Jerusalem
he had declared:

> Imperialism generally stirs up a reaction which leads to coun-
> teraction and provokes a spirit of rebellion. We have seen that all
> the states which were subjected have been liberated, or are on the
> way to liberating themselves. I am convinced that the future will
> lead to freedom and not to imperialism—so long as the oppressed
> people do not lose their enthusiasm.

Bourguiba uses a rich variety of metaphors and parables to illus-
trate his philosophy. Sometimes he tells the Arabs there is no use

bucking one's head against the wall; if there is no opening in the wall it is necessary to skirt it. Sometimes he says: "When I have to get a sideboard through a door too small for it, I prefer to take the sideboard apart rather than pull down the wall." Interesting and suggestive they may be but metaphors, parables, allegories, and especially historic parallels often confound confusion. One cannot illuminate a complex situation with analogies that create more shadows than light.

Unfortunately the "strongest" point in the exposition of his new approach—the parallel with Tunisia's fight for independence—proved to be the weakest. Yet he became a prisoner of it and narcissistically exulted in it, causing confusion and leaving even his sympathetic critics somewhat perplexed. Bourguibism is a philosophy which served a specific problem within a historic contest: achievement of Tunisia's independence from France. Its essence is not to fight for the impossible, but to settle for what the enemy might be willing to concede; the concession is then used as a lever for further pressures to obtain new concessions, until the total objective is attained. But apart from that, Bourguibism also represents the philosophy of moderation, freedom from fanaticism and hatred, a sense of realism, an ability to see the opponent's point of view and, hence, a capacity for compromise and conciliation. This spirit of Bourguibism transcends the particular historic event.

The trouble with the Tunisian President's initiative in the Middle East is that he indiscriminately introduced the two elements of Bourguibism: the historic event—Tunisia's fight for independence—and the spirit of his approach. As a historic precedent it does not apply to the realities of the Israel-Arab conflict; but the "spirit of Bourguibism"—its realism, and, above all, the necessity and the will to compromise—is a constructive method which could be applied to the Palestine problem. Bourguiba, however, did not separate these distinct elements, and compounded the difficulty of those trying to understand his intentions, or the essence of his proposals.

Let us try to disentangle from Bourguiba's analogy two distinct sets of elements—those which do not and cannot apply to Palestine and those which not only do apply but which actually constitute the sole feasible basis for a constructive approach to an eventual just and peaceful settlement of the Palestine conflict.

One important point must be made here. Our procedure will

not consist of rejecting one part of Bourguiba's proposals while accepting another, as both the Israelis and the Arabs tend to do. The Israelis accept with great satisfaction that element in Bourguiba's proposals which calls for a peaceful settlement through direct negotiations, but they reject *a priori* his suggestion of a return to the legality of the United Nations resolutions on partition and the refugees. The Arabs (or some of them) accept Bourguiba's proposals on the application of the U.N. resolutions, but reject direct negotiations with Israel.

We shall analyze the totality of his presentation which is pertinent to the Palestine situation. In doing this, it seems to us, we shall probably come closer to the true meaning of Bourguiba's thought than he himself felt he could under the circumstances. For we cannot free ourselves of the notion that the Tunisian President introduced the historical parallel of his country's struggle for psychological reasons and as a tactical device rather than as a relevant and valid historic precedent.

It is understandable that since his theories in their *ensemble* proved such an international success, he cannot easily disengage himself from the memories of his great historic experience. He therefore cites Tunisia's example as such, probably without realizing the inevitable ambiguities when it is applied in a different historic context. Also, he may have used it to make his own people better appreciate his initiative. Finally, it seemed more effective to offer the Arabs a vivid example of a successful method in its entirety rather than to try to move them by abstract political and philosophic discourse.

Why is Tunisia's fight for independence irrelevant to the Israel-Arab conflict? Why is it impossible to regard it as an historic precedent to be applied to Palestine? Why is Bourguiba's argument that the Palestine Arabs should take their destiny in their own hands and fight like the Tunisians and Algerians, a sheer fallacy, and the main source of confusion engendered by his initiative?

The two situations are fundamentally different. In Algeria and Tunisia the French (or European) population was a small minority—10 per cent or less; in Israel the Jews are a large majority and the Arabs, even including the refugees, a minority. Tunisia (and even Algeria) fought not against the local French (or European) population but against metropolitan France which was occupying Tunisia as a protectorate. In Palestine the conflict is not with some foreign nation whose territory and seat of power are elsewhere, but with a nation which is in part of the same country —Palestine. No matter how that nation was established, the Israeli Jews have no other country outside Palestine and their sovereign and military power is inside that country.

In his speech in the Old City of Jerusalem, Bourguiba declared:

> We fought imperialism, but from the moment that imperialism withdrew, we extend a hand in cooperation, friendship, and fraternity to the people which had subjugated us.

He insisted throughout that in fighting for independence, one must not be animated by hatred and must be free of fanaticism. Then when the struggle is over, one can live in peace and harmony, and even achieve fruitful cooperation with one's erstwhile antagonist. The destiny and survival of France were not contingent upon the outcome of the fight in Tunisia; at stake was prestige, tradition, economic interests, and, of course, the fate of the French colons. So the rebellion, when it was over, did not prevent a resumption of Franco-Arab relations, and a new era of cooperation. Any war between Israel and the Arabs means for Israel a struggle for its very survival, a fight to the end. The attitude of first fight and then make an honorable peace is unrealistic, and so is the concept of successive stages.

Within the context of Palestine realities, Tunisia cannot serve as a cogent analogy. For the analogy can only mean that the aim of the Palestinian minority is to bring about the liquidation of the State of Israel and take over the government. With whom then would the Arabs seek to "cooperate" after a hypothetical victory? Who would be left to "extend a hand in cooperation, friendship and fraternity" to?

There are other, no less fatal inconsistencies in this approach. Bourguiba holds that under present international conditions, war is an impossibility, and that generally wars lead to no constructive solution of international problems. Yet under the Tunisian parallel, he exhorts the Palestinian Arabs to fight. That the fight must be without fanaticism is beside the point; if what arises in heat of battle is not fanaticism, it is close enough to be indistinguishable.

In view of this, how does he differ from the other Arab leaders? In pointing up the difference, he draws a sharp distinction between international war and the national rebellion.* He decries the policies of other Arab leaders who advocate an eradicating war by the Arab states against Israel. In contrast, he advocates, one may assume, a rebellion by the Palestinians themselves, in which case the neighboring Arab states should not participate directly, but only extend various kinds of help. Such a rebellion may not aim at the total destruction of Israel but rather at the exertion of pressures to force her to negotiate an agreement. A struggle needs a positive objective; a negative one will not do. Bourguiba proposes to substitute for the present negative Arab objective of the obliteration of the State of Israel a positive one: implementation of the U.N. resolutions.

This argument is unconvincing as long as it is based upon the Tunisian precedent. Regardless of the objective, it implies that violence and warfare (in whatever form) are not excluded on moral, political, or tactical grounds; on the contrary, they are sanctified to achieve the desired aim—which is to soften up the enemy (Israel) enough to induce negotiations. But then, following the Tunisian analogy, the final "phase" may well be the disappearance of Israel altogether. After all, the Tunisian parallel implies that after a successful first stage, the pressures start all over again—without ruling out a renewal of violence—and so to phase after phase until the ultimate objective is achieved. The trick is, apparently, to avoid trying blindly to achieve the final phase with one assault, which may force the enemy to fight more desperately; such a course contains the danger of self-defeat.

We believe that Bourguiba's reasoning, applied to the Palestine situation, is pregnant with the same dangers as the policy advocated by other Arab leaders. But it is interesting to probe here Bourguiba's version of how he arrived at the formulation.

Having come closer to the Palestinian realities by visiting the refugee camps and talking to their inhabitants, Bourguiba recognized that while a bloody Arab-Israel conflict had developed since the partition of Palestine, the main object of the conflict—the Palestinians themselves—had been forgotten. The quarrel is no longer between the Palestinian Arabs and Jews there; it had be-

---

* The Communists, too, try to make a distinction between international wars and "wars of liberation." They are against the former but encourage the latter. This distinction does not seem to help international peace; on the contrary, it creates situations like Vietnam which imperil the peace of the whole world.

come, long since, a war between the Arab states and the State of Israel, which had further degenerated into a conflict between pan-Arabism and world Judaism, with anti-Semitic undertones. In addition the Middle East became the scene of big-power rivalries—between East and West—which have very little, if anything, to do with the essence of the Palestine conflict.

It thus became clear to him that the Palestinian Arabs were ignored only from a humanitarian point of view; politically, they were useful pawns in an international power struggle. He thereupon decided to remind the world that such people as the Palestinians existed and had needs, dignity and rights. But it was not up to him to fight for recovery of their rights—it was the Palestinians themselves who must take the initiative, give the struggle a national character, and become the masters of their own destiny. Only then were other countries, such as Jordan and the Lebanon, warranted in extending assistance.

Superficially this approach may sound like good sense, but a closer look reveals it to be quite untenable. As we have already pointed out, the *majority* of the Palestinian Arabs are not within Israel's jurisdiction; *they are under the jurisdiction of the neighboring Arab countries,* mainly Jordan.* Was Bourguiba suggesting that the Arabs who live in Israel (who are a *minority* both in Israel and of the Palestinian Arabs in general) should rebel? Or that the Palestinians outside Israel should engage in guerrilla activities? Or that there be some joint military action by the Arabs in Israel plus those at her frontiers?

Such a hypothetical possibility may seem to remind us of the Algerian war that was waged by both the Arabs (and Berbers) inside Algeria, and some from bases in neighboring Tunisia and Morocco. But there are fundamental differences.

In the Algerian rebellion the main burden was borne by the people inside the country who were a vast majority (80 to 90 per cent). The Algerians in Tunisia and Morocco were a quasi-professional army temporarily stationed there, whose aim was to return to their own country. The Arabs outside Israel were *not* an army temporarily stationed abroad; they formed the majority of the Palestinian Arabs, and lived mostly in parts of what was Mandated Palestine—that is, their own country. These parts of their own country were occupied *not* by Israel but by neighboring Arab governments—the Gaza strip by Egypt; and what is

---

* Of course with Israel's victory in June 1967 the situation changed.

called the western part of Jordan, by the Hashemite Kingdom of Jordan. That part of former Mandated Palestine situated west of Jordan was not only occupied by, but was formally annexed to Jordan. The refugees living there were full-fledged citizens of that kingdom; they were Jordanians. Hussein wanted it so.

Now, if the "refugees" who are citizens of a country take up arms against a neighboring state, what does this do to the concept of rebellion? Jordan would inevitably be involved as a state; the Israelis would certainly regard it as a *casus belli*. Israel, of necessity, would not accept any semantic distinction between an "international war" in which states are engaged, and "rebellion" of some kind. Whether it be an attack by regular armies of one or more Arab states, or large-scale guerrilla assaults by Palestinians based in neighboring states to "liberate their country"—the Israelis would treat it as war, and war *à outrance* at that.

Jordan and the Lebanon were also unqualifiedly opposed to guerrilla warfare against Israel for internal and external reasons. These two governments are the only ones which discourage terrorist attempts to organize in their territories or pass their frontiers, and punish those who try. They do not always succeed, as we have seen. These would not seem likely governments for Bourguiba to win over to this part of his proposals.

That he was aware of the roadblocks is shown by his letter of April 27, 1965 to Nasser, in which he pointed out that the Arab governments are disinclined to endorse the idea of guerrilla warfare against Israel; and he endorsed their refusal to do so. Thus there were occasions when Bourguiba himself realized the Tunisian precedent was inapt. Upon maturer consideration he appears to have reached the conclusion that the distinction between war and rebellion does not hold; it contains too many explosive elements and would endanger the stability of the neighboring Arab states as well as international peace. This could become a subversion rather than an espousal of Bourguibism, which is in its essence negotiated peace—neither war, rebellion, nor a fierce fight under any other name. At his press conference in the Old City of Jerusalem he declared—if the Jerusalem daily *Al Difaa* quoted him correctly:

> I regard the Palestine people as responsible for their problem. But nevertheless we are ready to support the people of Palestine when they come to believe in peaceful coexistence with other peoples.

This declaration may mean that he opposed the Palestinians taking up arms or indulging in guerrilla warfare; only in the use of peaceful means could they count upon Tunisia's help, whatever that help might mean. This is also implied by his several statements that if he were a Palestinian he would start negotiations with Israel even without pre-conditions. It was also in consonance with the realities of the Israel-Arab conflict and with the interests of Israel's more moderate and peaceful neighbors—Jordan and the Lebanon. It was above all in line with his main purpose articulated when he started on his tour in the Middle East.

The Tunisian experience as a precedent is no less perplexing from a quite different point of view. If it is, in truth, unacceptable to the Israelis, it is no less intolerable to Jordan and to a lesser degree to the Lebanon. Yet it was in those countries whose guest he was that Bourguiba made his proposals.

In urging the Palestinians to take their destiny into their own hands, was he offering his approval and support to the Palestine Liberation Organization? This organization is dedicated to the proposition that the Palestinian Arabs, themselves, and not the Arab states, must decide their fate and bear the burden of reconquering their homeland. Its leader, Ahmed Shukairy,* and other spokesmen often use the same phraseology as that of Bourguiba: "The Palestine Liberation Organization," declared its representative on April 23 in New York, Dr. Izzat Tannous, "wishes to state that the solution to the Palestine problem lies in the hands of the Palestinian people only." Upon this proposition and argument Shukairy bases his claim to representation and leadership of the Palestinian Arabs, defining his policy and aspirations thus:

> Our new deal policy . . . is one of depending upon ourselves only. We shall draw up a well-conceived plan to liberate the plundered fatherland in stages by recruiting the Arabs' entire financial and economic resources to that end.

Even his criticism of the Arab leadership sounded not unlike that which Bourguiba voiced on so many occasions. In a memorandum submitted after the Arab summit in 1965 to the Secretary General of the Arab League, Shukairy complained bitterly:

> . . . As far as I can see they (the Arab governments) have never

---

* After the Israel-Arab war in June Shukairy was forced to resign his position. *See* Preface.

intended to meet their moral obligations [toward the people of Palestine]. All they have done so far to liberate Palestine is talk, talk, talk. This will neither free Palestine nor provide the refugees with a better future. I am now convinced that the Arab governments have only one desire—to use the Palestine cause and the plight of the wretched refugees just for publicity as they have done for the past 18 years.

Yet to approve of the PLO is to condemn Jordan, because its objectives and the aspirations of its leaders are incompatible with the viability of little Jordan as an independent state. Shukairy publicly proclaims that "the liberation of Palestine must begin with the liberation of Jordan. The destruction of Hashemite rule in Jordan is the first step to the liberation of Palestine from Israeli rule." Therefore, he openly demanded Hussein's assassination. In a speech delivered in Cairo on June 17, 1966, he called King Hussein

> a traitor like his grandfather King Abdullah. . . . A man whose hands should be cut off, [who] has no right to live on Arab soil. . . . He alone, one person and one throne, stands in the path of Arab aspiration.

In another interview on his own radio *The Voice of Palestine* in Egypt, Shukairy declared he does not recognize the existence of Jordan as a political entity, and that "history knows only Palestine. That country still exists and will continue to do so." Transjordan [and later Jordan], he continued, was "'an artificial creation of British imperialism which existed from 1919 to 1948. This British blunder was corrected in the latter year when we Palestinians again treated Trans- and Cis-Jordan as an integral part of the Palestine homeland."

In that interview Shukairy had been asked to comment on complaints that two of the ten persons he had named to the new executive committee of his movement were not Palestinians but "Transjordanians" (Najib Itshidat, dean of the Amman Lawyers Association, and General Ali Hayari, former Chief-of-Staff of the Jordan Army). He replied:

> The boundaries of Palestine extend from the Mediterranean to the Iraqi and Syrian deserts. We regard all Jordanian towns and villages as part of *Palestine*, and therefore the two men referred to are sons of Palestine. . . .
>
> If some inhabitants of this country [Jordan] choose to call it

not Palestine but by the name of one of its rivers it does not worry us. The greatest catastrophe of the Palestine liberation movement lies, however, in the distinction between the two sections of Palestine lying on the western and eastern banks of the Jordan River.*

King Hussein had the same attitude. He, too, considered the two parts of Palestine on either side of the Jordan River as one country and all its inhabitants as one people. That is why he granted full citizenship *en masse* to all the refugees. Some of the refugees achieved the highest rank in the hierarchy of the state— including the premiership and membership in the Cabinet. He usually addressed all his subjects on either side of the Jordan River as "members of the great Jordan family."

In line with this reasoning Hussein seemed to have arrived at a far-reaching conclusion: to completely liquidate the refugee camps as soon as possible. In a sensational speech on June 14, 1966 at the town of Ajlun, transmitted live by Amman radio, he said that the Arab refugees should no longer remain isolated in camps behind barbed wire, dwelling in squalor, and dependent on international charity; they should be enabled to earn their own livelihood and support themselves. And he added:

> We reject the philosophy that through keeping the refugees at starvation level, their feelings of hatred will be nurtured and their desire for revenge strengthened. Only a free and thriving people can have the strength to liberate their country.

As to Shukairy and the Palestine Liberation Organization, King Hussein considers them not just a nuisance but a real danger. He described the objectives of the PLO as an attempt " to split the unity of this country and divide the [Jordanian] Army. . . . That is . . . treason." And in that speech at Ajlun he declared in Shukairy style:

> Every hand stretched out toward our country to spread disunity among us will be cut off as of today. We will scratch the eyes out of any organization attempting to disturb our process of building up [our nation].

He emphasized that "there is no longer any room for coopera-

---

* This is also the position of many Israelis mainly, but not exclusively, the Kherut Party.

tion with the PLO." Indeed, in Jordan, which should be the main field of Shukairy's activities since the majority of the Palestinian refugees were concentrated there, he was, for all purposes, banned, and his men often rounded up and arrested.

Although Cairo exerted great pressure upon Hussein to come to terms with Shukairy, the effort was fruitless.* The PLO leader was not permitted to have his headquarters in Jordan or to train his men—not even to use the radio. King Hussein did not permit him to recruit Palestinians into the "Liberation Army," and when it was done clandestinely, the recruits were arrested—sometimes *en masse*. In the last days of December 1965, more than 400 Palestinians were put in jail. Shukairy had similar difficulties, though less significant, with the Lebanese authorities. Apart from Cairo his best friends are, so far—the Chinese; it is in Peking that he was permitted to open offices. He trained units of the Liberation Army in the Egyptian-controlled Gaza strip and in China, and it was likewise these two countries which were supplying his organization with arms.

Ironically, the formation of the PLO was theoretically inspired in part at least by Bourguiba's addresses at the Arab summit of 1964; yet it is this organization which became the most vehement opponent of the Tunisian President's proposals, and Bourguiba the target of Shukairy's most violent attacks. At a press conference in Cairo, April 23, Shukairy declared:

> There is not one Palestinian who would accept the proposals of President Bourguiba concerning the principle of negotiating with Israel, whatever the suggested basis may be. If the principle of coexistence and negotiations can be accepted in certain cases, they do not come into consideration in the case of Palestine. . . .
>
> The Palestine question can have only one solution: restoration of Arab Palestine without partition, internationalization, or resettlement.

---

* Until the very eve of the outbreak of hostilities in June, when Nasser made war unavoidable, and thus with one sweep created a profound crisis in the area under the impact of which every Arab leader felt himself deeply committed to meet his responsibilities "in the fateful hour of decision," King Hussein resisted the pressures both of Nasser and Shukairy. But in the face of imminent war the Jordanian King thought he had no choice but to patch up relations with the Egyptian ruler. The latter was harsh in his demands. He imposed an Egyptian general to command the troops in Jordan and sent Shukairy as a political commissar in Hussein's country. After the defeat even Nasser considered Shukairy too much of a liability and fired him.

Bourguiba disapproved of the Palestine Liberation Organization with no less vehemence, and, during the mass demonstrations in Tunis on April 27, Shukairy was next only to Nasser as an object of scorn. Posters carried by the demonstrators read: "Shukairy the coward," But it is not only in Tunis that he was unpopular. He is considered a stooge of Nasser in most of the Arab capitals.

Though the authenticity of his dedication to the cause of Palestine cannot be questioned—his whole life record attests it—he is not the ideal man for the job. He parades in military uniform and clamors for blood and battles, sacrifices and conquests, but he is not the stuff revolutionary leaders are made of. He is rather a "professional Arab" of cosmopolitan inclinations and expensive tastes. He has pledged allegiance to and served various governments successively, and his salaries and expenses are said to run into six figures. In the early fifties he represented Syria at the United Nations, but in 1958, after having resigned his Syrian position, he became the Saudi Arabian Minister of State in charge of United Nations Affairs and its delegate to the world organization. When he was dismissed by the Saudis in September 1963, he became a Palestinian again, this time under Nasser's tutelage. He has accepted citizenship in more than one of the countries which he served, and is still in possession of several passports, but claims his "Palestinian nationality," whatever that may mean.

Despite his protestations about the Palestinians' rights to independent action, he is in fact little more than a tool in the interpower game of the Arab states. His base of operations is Cairo, not Amman; and he receives his instructions from Nasser. Though he tries desperately to operate in Jordan, his role is that of an agent rather than a principal. Oddly enough, this makes him and the PLO not less threatening to Jordan and King Hussein, but much more so, because of the identity of objectives of Nasser and Shukairy: to abolish Jordan as an independent state.

The danger of achieving this objective is much more real than the possibility that the PLO will conquer Israel, and the risk is not related to Shukairy's personality. Any "Palestine entity," whose goal is the creation of an independent Palestinian State will clash with the vital interests of Jordan and constitute a threat to its very survival.

How then did King Hussein permit (perhaps even inspire)

Bourguiba to make—in the Old City under Hussein's own auspices —a declaration urging the Palestinians to take their future into their own hands, violating at the same time the accepted policy of the Middle East Arab leaders and the vital interests of Jordan?

There appear to be two clues to this riddle. One is that in the Middle East, even more than elsewhere, leaders often speak in terms so ambiguous as to take on the character of a code or symbol. This is a device, or if one wishes, a trial balloon, for initiating bold ideas and revolutionary proposals. If these appear at first as common and acceptable phenomena, they may have sufficient time to percolate slowly, imperceptibly, into the consciousness of the emotionally charged Middle East without the risk of *a priori* rejection.

Bourguiba used this method throughout his campaign, testing it first in the Old City of Jerusalem at his sensational press conference. It would appear that the agreed code between Bourguiba and Hussein was that "Palestine" is synonymous with "Jordan." When he spoke of "this land" (where Jews and Arabs lived harmoniously in the past and must learn to coexist peaceably in the future) he, of course, implied that Israel is also part of Palestine, which is historically correct. But, he reasoned, that part which is now Israel seceded as a result of world wars, partition, and the Israel-Arab war—a thing which has happened more than once in history. Jordan and Israel are, therefore, only new names which came into being as a result of those historic events—war and partition. Hence, when Bourguiba declared that Palestine is the primary concern of the Palestinians themselves, the agreed meaning was that it was the primary concern of the people of Jordan.

The second clue, appearing at another point in Bourguiba's Jerusalem speech, in spite of its sensational implications went almost unnoticed in the European and the American press: his reference to partition. Though he condemned the original decision of the United Nations of 1947–1948 to partition Palestine, he indicated that since this was a historic fact, it must be considered not as the worst solution, but rather as "the lesser evil." He thus in fact intimated that partition is not such a bad solution after all if one makes the best of it.

From whose point of view is partition not such a bad solution, apart from Israel's? Certainly from the point of view of Jordan. As a result of partition and the ensuing Israel-Arab war, Jordan emerged the only Arabic country undefeated by the Israeli Army.

More than that, as an outcome of the Palestine war of 1948–49, Jordan occupied and annexed territory not previously held by it, nearly tripled its population, and changed from a rickety, scarcely viable political entity to a state with an efficient army, an increased population, and enhanced prestige, and well on the road to economic and social reform. Not bad at all.

Inversely, without partition, the future and the very survival of Jordan looked dim indeed, if not altogether problematical. Jordan exists as a result of partition and the ensuing Palestine war; it was created under highly dubious circumstances by the British, who carved it without authorization out of the Palestine Mandate. Prewar Jordan was far from self-sufficient; it is not interested in the application of the original partition resolution; it is vitally concerned with preservation of the *status quo*.

If Bourguiba's declaration in the Old City does signify that Jordan is the equivalent of Palestine, its people the people of Palestine, and partition fundamentally in its interest, the jigsaw pieces fall into a pattern, and these implications become discernible:

1. If the Palestine problem is primarily the responsibility of Jordan, it is incumbent upon that country to seek a solution. The conflict is no longer between Israel and Nasser's pan-Arabism, but rests primarily between two neighboring states: Jordan and Israel.

2. The Palestine tragedy is a result of "Israel's . . . Zionist aggression," in occupying and annexing *more* territory than it was allotted by the United Nations partition resolution. It is therefore Jordan's task to restore to the "Palestinians" (that is, to Jordan) only the *additional* land which Israel annexed (not to "cast Israel into the sea").

3. If the conflict is between two discrete states, it need not necessarily be resolved by war, but may be susceptible to resolution by a peaceful process of give and take. Now the dispute concerns comparatively minor issues, for in vital matters these two countries share common interests and are greatly interdependent. The Hashemite King is not unaware that Israel provides more of a protection than a danger, and without her presence as a buffer Egypt might already, under one pretext or another, have absorbed the Kingdom of Jordan. It is not without significance that even after the ill-conceived Israeli raid into Jordan of November 13, 1966, King Hussein declared on one occasion that Jordan and Israel face a common enemy to be conquered: the desert. . . .

4. Israel's interest in Jordan's independent survival is even more

understandable. Instead of contending with one huge pan-Arab state surrounding it on all sides, Israel much prefers to deal with several smaller states like Jordan and the Lebanon, with whom the prospects of arriving at a settlement are far brighter*

5. If Israel's existence is not called into question, then war is avoidable and the way can be paved toward negotiations, though before the conference table is reached, non-military, political pressures would be exercised to obtain maximum concessions. King Hussein, like every other Arab leader, feels impelled to bandy pan-Arabic slogans about "reconquering the plundered homeland" for the Palestinian Arabs. But his behavior proves that he is primarily interested in obtaining maximum economic, technical, and military assistance to integrate the Palestinians (including the refugees) securely into the body politic of his country, thus consolidating his kingdom. He may also cherish the hope of striking a bargain and emerging with some additional territory in the final settlement.

6. The immediate problem is not to "liberate" Palestine but to strengthen Jordan. The joint communiqué by King Hussein and President Bourguiba as it was broadcast over Amman radio said in part:

> The two heads-of-state noted *the special responsibility placed on Jordan* in connection with the Palestine issue and its important role in *protecting* the Arab homeland against Israel aggression. *In order that Jordan* may fulfill this task in its entirety, it should be given every possible support. [Italics added.]

In Jordan Bourguiba also warned that to spend 70 per cent of the national budget on armaments, as some Arab states do, is

---

* In Israel an opposite view is widespread. Former Premier David Ben Gurion, and groups more to the left, believe that as long as the Middle East is divided into small states, each must show that it is more anti-Israel than the others, and especially than Nasser himself. If, however, the Middle East were consolidated into a unified framework, this need for outbidding would gradually disappear. A strong unified Arab leadership enjoying the necessary prestige would not be inhibited in negotiating with Israel.

Many Israelis, as well as outside observers of the Middle Eastern scene, also believe that Nasser offers the best chance of coming to terms, even before the pan-Arab dream is achieved. He is the strongest leader in the Arab world, and his influence with the masses is very great. He, more than anyone else, can afford without risk of being overthrown to attempt a peaceful settlement of the Palestine problem. Unfortunately this is based upon the inevitability of pan-Arabism within a foreseeable future. Bourguiba does not believe in it, and this writer fully shares his view.

folly. "Power lies not in armaments." By devotion to economic, scientific and cultural development and by steadily raising the standard of living of the Arabs, rather than by an arms race, one may hope to catch up with Israel: "Only thus we will grow stronger than the enemy."

7. If a peaceful solution is possible, one can visualize a period of reconciliation and cooperation on the basis of mutual respect and for the benefit of both.

Indeed, the original partition plan had suggested "political partition with economic union." Only one phase was carried out with the establishment of the State of Israel: political separation. Peaceful settlement might open the door for implementation of the second phase; economic union or, at least in the early stages, economic cooperation.

8. To make such a dream come true, the final solution to the present conflict must result in neither victor nor vanquished.

That this interpretation is not purely conjectural can be deduced from the fact that King Hussein expressed Bourguiba's views on various occasions long before Bourguiba spoke in the Old City of Jerusalem. In some of his utterances there is a similarity not only in thought but even in expression.

In an interview as far back as January 17, 1960 in Amman, King Hussein criticized Arab leaders for what he called their irresponsible approach to the Palestine problem. He said they were using Palestine Arab refugees as "pawns for selfish political objectives."

He sharply assailed as "dangerous and unrealistic" the proposal to create a Palestine government, and he considered the greatest immediate danger not Israel but communism. "We should form a united Arab front against communism," Hussein said. "We feel there is no future for Jordan or any other Arab country if communism is allowed to take over in Iraq." (There appeared at the time to have been such a danger.)

Both Bourguiba and Hussein were also in agreement that communism may not necessarily come in the form of a direct takeover, but rather operate indirectly through governments so dependent upon Soviet support that they become in fact satellites of Moscow. Syria is one example; eventually Nasser may himself wind up in such a role.

Of course, one cannot be sure this interpretation is correct;

but to this writer it seems, upon thorough analysis and reflection, the only one which makes sense.

"Bourguibism" in Reverse

The shapers of Israel's policy in their anxiety did not perceive that Bourguiba's theory of stages, or gradualism, need not work against them. With more imagination, they could visualize a boldly inventive policy under which gradualism could in the long run work in their favor. For what Israel cannot achieve under present conditions of military entrenchment, Arab threats of annihilation, and Israeli's military power, it could achieve in phases through a peaceful application of Bourguibism in reverse. Such a method of gradualism could be made to work not toward the liquidation of Israeli sovereignty, but toward greater opportunities, influence, self-assertion, spiritual, and economic ascendancy. The most important and probably the decisive example: the Arab refugees. If this problem were to be solved as a first phase, the main point of contention between the Arabs and Israel would disappear. As long as there are Arab refugees, there is "the problem" of granting them the right to self-determination, and to have a territory and a state of their own. When there are no longer any refugees there is nobody for whom to demand self-determination. There would no longer be "a homeless Palestine nation" claiming the reconquest of "its plundered fatherland." The refugees would become rehabilitated and integrated in the two parts of historic Palestine—the vast majority of them within the frontiers of Jordan, a minority in Israel. Some, if given a chance to rebuild their lives constructively, will probably choose to remain in the neighboring Arab countries where they are now—Lebanon, Syria and Iraq. Some would seek opportunity in Kuwait or even overseas.

At all events, the Arabs had more reason to contemplate with apprehension the disappearance of the dream of an independent Palestine nation than the Jews to contemplate the disappearance of the sovereign State of Israel.

Of course, all this was contingent upon an Israeli initiative, an Israeli peace offer based upon an *Israeli solution* of the refugee problem. The Israelis now realize that peace will not be served them on a platter, nor be achieved by decisive military engagement. They will have to offer something tangible—and reasonable —which the Arabs may consider worthy and dignified enough under the circumstances to accept.

There is probably no better—or other—way than to begin with a solution for the refugees, because this is from every angle the crux of the conflict between Israel and the Arabs. Everything else is a superstructure or an excuse. The refugee problem is also the only issue on which Israel can take the initiative and give satisfaction to the Arabs.

The Arabs, when they talk about something other than the destruction of Israel (and this kind of talk will become ever more unlikely), speak of some dramatic compensation of a moral and political nature—what Nasser calls compensation in consonance with the Arabs' sense of justice and dignity. They call for Israel's acknowledgement that an injustice was done the Arabs of Palestine, and that as a consequence they should be granted the right of free choice.

Israel can meet, at least to a substantial degree, these demands of the Arabs. It can recognize the legitimate rights of *bona fide* Palestinians who fled the Israeli sector, and who would pledge to live peaceably in Israel according to the resolution of the United Nations. Israel can recognize that though for one reason or another the Arabs fled during the hostilities of 1948, they did not forfeit their birthright to *all of Palestine—whether in Israel or in Jordan.*

The Israeli fear that a million Arabs will opt to return to Israel is one of those self-generated nightmares. A million Arabs *cannot* opt to "return" to Israel because not all of them came from there. Apart from that, these people are not refugees in foreign lands. Most of them are still in Palestine because the west part of Jordan and Gaza *are* Palestine, no less than is Israel. Hence they are only displaced persons in their own country. There are many more built-in safeguards against a million refugees returning to Israel.

A thorough and impartial census would probably reveal startling facts about the number and composition of the refugees. The people claiming to be refugees fall into a variety of categories, of which only one, though predominant, includes *bona fide* displaced persons who originally lived in that part of Palestine which is now Israel. And even these, if given a genuine and practical choice between returning to Israel or being rehabilitated in Jordan, might not opt for the former. Probably only a minority would. The rest would prefer to become economically integrated in Jordan. Not because of the Israeli-pan-Arabic argument, but first because Jordan, like Israel, is their own country, their native land; second, because many are already integrated, and a return to Israel would merely be a new dislocation.

The tragedy of Israeli policy is that it ignores the refugee problem, and disclaims any responsibility for its creation. In the eyes of the Arabs this is outrageous. The refugees, insofar as one can speak generally about so large a group, are indignant at being thus ignored. They have memories and claims. Many had homes and property in Israel (though only a small percentage had any real properties). They feel that they have rights and grievances. In this isolation their imaginations have magnified their real claims, until subconsciously every Palestinian Arab believes that in the olden days he was a possessor of wealth, land, assets.

And so with every passing year the number of refugees swells, as does the magnitude of their claims. What these people need first and foremost is an end to their neglect as human beings; an awareness that they are being reckoned with—that their grievances and claims will be heard and verified, and if well founded, receive satisfaction. Only in a climate of such recognition of individuals' rights will the problem be reduced to realistic and manageable proportions.*

Of course, Israel must make a genuine offer for repatriation and compensation, but with reasonable safeguards for her own security. That some refugees will choose to return is also clear.

This may to some extent affect the demographic composition of the State of Israel, but there is no compelling reason to view this possible change with alarm. On the contrary, perhaps it is to be welcomed in more than one respect. Direct predictions notwithstanding, a *predominantly* Jewish State may prove more viable than a *purely* Jewish State; and in addition, it may even prove to be closer to the original vision of the Hebrew renaissance as expounded by the greatest Zionist leaders—from Herzl to Jabotinsky. Their vision embraced not just a mere transfer of the ghettos to the shores of the Mediterranean; but rather their transformation into a new society, a sovereignty which would evolve a new pattern to be followed by other nations all over the world. Jewish ethnic isolation, which is now the basic foundation of Israel, is not the most propitious for such a transformation.

Building a new society, a state, though predominantly Hebrew, nonetheless could encompass within its structure a substantial,

---

* It is not possible in this report to treat the refugee problem in its many facets. It is complex, and involves political, international, and economic considerations. We should like to refer to the special study of this crucial subject published by the Institute for Mediterranean Affairs: "The Palestine Refugee Problem—A New Approach and a Plan for a Solution."

free and prosperous ethnic minority (or minorities) fully participating in the creation of the new society. Minorities could be part of all levels of human and creative activities as well as of the state institutions and machinery, including the legislative, executive, and judicial branches, the army, and the diplomatic service.

The activities involved in solving the refugee problem might well create a new psychological and political climate. It stands to reason that a plan involving the repatriation and resettlement of hundreds of thousands of people, both in Israel and Jordan as well as in other neighboring Arab countries, could not be implemented in an atmosphere of frontier incidents, infiltration, *fedayin* raids, retaliatory acts, and blockade. All this would have to cease if a plan for repatriation and resettlement were to be carried out. We can visualize a new cooperation around a problem in which the Arabs and Israelis as well as international organizations and friendly powers would be committed to cooperate.

Limited cooperation in solving the refugee problem might even lead to a more advanced stage of economic and technical joint effort between Israel and the Arab states. For once economic and technical cooperation required by the resettlement were underway, there is no reason to believe it would end there. On the contrary, it could be the beginning of a permanent collaboration transcending the immediate business at hand.

In that new psychological and political climate, with the Israelis and Arabs accustomed to mutual trade, the time might become ripe for a crowning phase in this process of "gradualism": to study the practical possibilities of some kind of economic union or federation with either Jordan or Lebanon, or both.

Does such a "gradualist" approach, as a part of Israeli policy, entail risks? It certainly does—grave risks. But, again, these risks—this staking all on peace—are probably far smaller than those entailed in the present Israeli policy of immobility. In the last analysis, for Israel there is probably no alternative to peace.

22

Back to United Nations Legality

THROUGHOUT HIS CAMPAIGN BOURGUIBA USED A VARIETY OF DIALEC-
tical and rhetorical means to put across his points. He offered
suggestions, historical parallels, philosophical postulations, psychological insights—he even made confessions of faith. He argued
both principles and tactics. Despite many inconsistencies, some
constant trends of thought are nevertheless discernible.

The kingpin of all of these is the proposal to implement the
United Nations resolutions on Palestine. One of the most extreme
aspects of this proposal is the idea of "going back to the original
Partition Plan" as laid out in the UN resolutions of 1947 and
1948.

That even in this cardinal point he is, as in almost everything
else, vague if not confused, may not be entirely his fault. After
all, reality and history have moved so far away from the original
partition plan that it is impossible seriously, let alone precisely,
to refer to it. Nevertheless this is, though not to the exclusion of
other possibilities, the plan that he has constantly put forward,
much to the annoyance of both Israelis and Arabs; Arabs because
it implies recognition of Israel as a state, Israelis because it entails
concessions on their part. The weakness of the thinking of many
Israelis is that they would like their Arab opponents to speak
like Zionists. *Then,* they believe, peace could become a realistic
possibility.

If, as Bourguiba suggests, the Arabs accept the United Nations
partition resolution, they immediately shift their position from
violators of the United Nations Charter to supporters of the law
of the international community. They may confidently expect

world public opinion to veer to their side, while congratulating themselves on their clever and farsighted strategy.

Concrete as this proposal may sound, however, Bourguiba does not seem to have thought through its implications and possible consequences. Yet, as a realist he is aware that any radical cession of territory by Israel is out of the question; Israel could never survive it. Jordan, too, would lose territory under the plan, and Hussein will never agree to the truncation of his kingdom. Perhaps the Tunisian President is actually not interested in this aspect because he does not consider the practical territorial implications of cardinal significance. The principal value of his plan is that it provides an effective gambit for the Arabs as a starting point for negotiations. Occasionally he admits as much.

He knows, he told an interviewer, that the Israelis would not accept implementation of the UN resolutions easily; still it is worthwhile suggesting. Sometimes he speaks about drastic changes in the present frontiers of Israel, and on other occasions he ignores these and intimates that he is really concerned with the United Nations resolution which refers to the right of the Arab refugees to choose freely to return to their homes in Israel or to receive compensation for their abandoned property. Simultaneously, he, and his spokesman in Paris, Ambassador Masmoudi, make it clear that Bourguiba's purpose is chiefly to see the conflict brought within a framework of legal argument instead of war threats.

At best, the United Nations resolutions can serve as a starting point.

In an interview with Philippe Herreman, for *Le Monde* (April 11–12, 1965), he gave an extreme definition:

> One of the solutions can consist of applying the recommendation of the United Nations in 1948, which was never respected, to fix the frontiers as they had been traced at the time. Thus the Israelis would restore those territories occupied beyond that frontier, namely the regions of Jaffa, Acre, and Nazareth, where the refugees could install themselves.
>
> Of course, the Israelis would not agree. . . . But at least the Arabs would find themselves in a better tactical position, and the [erstwhile] commitment of the United Nations would serve them as a serious prop.
>
> Imprisoning oneself within [a policy] of always saying 'no,' of

repeating that the existence of Israel is an injustice, even if it is true, does not serve any purpose.

Changing the emphasis, he made another statement three days later:

> One of the main points of my argumentation is precisely that one has to seek some kind of an international legality within the framework of which one could put up a fight. In this case it is the legality of the United Nations. . . . After all it was the United Nations which created Israel. There is a recommendation of the United Nations dating back to 1948 whose objective was to facilitate the return of the refugees. Why not utilize it? Why not make it into an effective weapon? . . .

It is interesting and extremely important to note that the only mention here concerning the United Nations decisions is the return of the refugees.

Very shortly afterward, speaking to an Arab audience in Sfax, and mainly for Arab consumption in the Middle East, he defined the argument as follows: It is natural that Tunisia's proposals be based on United Nations resolutions. "As a member of the world organization, we recognize its authority and we remain faithful to its principles."

It should not be forgotten that Israel is also a United Nations member and that the United States and the Soviet Union both recognize Israel and maintain relations with her. "But should we enter into a war to defend the United Nations resolutions, we would be sure to find the whole world on our side."

In an exhaustive review of Bourguiba's foreign policy, Tunisian Ambassador to France Masmoudi told a selected audience at the *Théâtre des Ambassadeurs* on December 16, 1965, concerning his President's proposals:

> The Palestinian problem is a drama. Zionism supported by Great Britain has created in Palestine a complex situation with the establishment of the State of Israel and the displacement of more than 800 thousand Palestinians who are today refugees in several Arab countries.
>
> After seventeen years of recrimination and spurious belligerence, the situation has not improved at all for the Arabs. Faithful

to Arab solidarity, but also to its traditional attachments to peace and also out of a sense of realism, the Tunisian diplomacy has proposed accepting the United Nations resolutions as a basis for negotiations, which would permit solving the painful refugee problem and would countenance the restoration of a Palestinian state; it would create a new situation of a different nature and would open new roads leading to a desirable solution in that region.

In taking, on behalf of Tunisia, the well-known stand on the Palestine problem, President Bourguiba has made a rendezvous with history; he is confident of the support and sympathy of all honest men in the Arab world, as elsewhere. It is too bad if in the Arab East, certain fraternal countries which should naturally understand us and help Tunisia in its effort, instead blow the wind of demagoguery and folly which caused the most ardent partisans of a renovating Arabism despair and discouragement.

Three points are clearly in Bourguiba's mind when he speaks of coming back to the United Nations resolutions; each, and all of them combined, are of the greatest significance. One is that these resolutions are suggested not as a *precondition* for negotiations, but merely as a *basis* for negotiations. Second, that what he feels strongest about is the plight of the refugees. Third, that what he hopes, perhaps, from negotiations on the basis of the United Nations resolutions is not to truncate Israel but to restore Palestine as a unitary, a federated or a confederated Jewish-Arab state.*

There was a fairly widespread impression that Bourguiba was groping for a way to capture world attention for the Palestine tragedy, to compel the great powers to act. At times the situation was so stale that nobody seemed interested any longer, not even the Arabs with whom the war with Israel had become a kind of obsessional routine. But their passions and performances had little, if anything, to do with "the forgotten people," the refugees.

As for the world powers, they had been using the Israeli-Arab conflict as an excuse to penetrate the Middle Eastern region by establishing bases and other forms of "presence," as the Russians do; or to obtain oil concessions as the Italians and the French

---

* The last point is, of course, in contradiction to the implications of his speech in Jerusalem, by which he clearly meant to strengthen the hand of King Hussein. But Hussein is dead set against the formation of a new Palestine state, carved out from the West bank.

have lately begun to do. As to the United States, it considers the whole thing a nuisance and an attraction to communist penetration. The end result is a senseless encouragement of the arms race, for all and sundry, with no constructive outcome. In an interview in *Views* (Autumn issue, 1965) Bourguiba declared:

> . . . . I thought it would be better . . . to find a suitable platform which would attract world sympathy and international opinion and would be an improvement as compared with the present situation the Arabs are in. This could lead toward a reasonable and lasting solution—in other words, the construction of peace between the countries in the area. This was my opinion. I said: the first platform we must build on, which would constitute a great advantage and open new perspectives, is a return to United Nations legality, respect for UNO decisions.

The Israelis and some objective observers were not sure of Bourguiba's true intent. Behind these reasonable expressions did there not lurk the hope of doing away with Hebrew sovereignty, with the existence of Israel as an independent state? Jean Daniel, editor of *Le Nouvel Observateur,* asked Bourguiba the big question:

> Mr. President, if I understand you correctly, you propose a different method to achieve the same objective. Your policy of phases should nevertheless bring about the progressive disappearance of the State of Israel, exactly as [inversely] the internal autonomy you accepted [as a phase] from the French led finally to complete independence of Tunisia?

Bourguiba answered:

> It isn't certain. First of all, anything would be better than the present situation. What is necessary is that things begin to move, that there should be proposals, international activities. It is necessary to create a situation which will force new appraisals. I say that one should not declare that one wishes to throw the Jews into the sea if one cannot do it. And the very fact of not saying it could in itself help find a way of coexisting with them. After all, if the French population in Algeria had remained there, in accordance with the rights stipulated in the Evian agreement, there might have been created in the very middle of the Maghreb a new and original situation. And even if the Algerians signed these agreements with the idea in mind that the French population would

depart, still a new situation could have arisen from those negotiations.

The essential, at this moment, is to achieve reparations for the refugees and to see that the recommendations of the United Nations be respected. How is one to go about achieving this? Is it possible to achieve a settlement when for the last seventeen years, alas, as a result of the frozen attitude of the Arabs, the Israelis have become accustomed to having their own flag, a government, and a nation? I just don't know. It is not impossible. What is important at present is to undertake clear diplomatic action. If such action should fail, then we are strengthened by having warned international opinion, by the support of our friends, by the clarity of our attitudes, and above all by a coherent organization of the Palestinians themselves. We will then have to envisage something else.

But even Bourguiba's hint that Israel in its present form may disappear and give way to something new, must not necessarily be understood as fundamentally an anti-Israel attitude. He may think, for instance, that a binational state would be in the interests of both Jews and Arabs; that the form of Hebrew sovereignty should be changed, but not its essence. Though to Israeli official policymakers this proposal is taboo, to the world at large, including some of Israel's friends, it need not be considered a sinister anti-Israel move.

Moreover, the proposal to implement the United Nations resolutions was not invented by Bourguiba. At least once a year, Nasser advances the same suggestion, though not as dramatically, and usually not from an Arab podium or to his own countrymen. In addition, he never dares spell out that implementing the United Nations resolutions means *ipso facto* recognizing Israel as a state; he refuses almost childishly to pronounce the forbidden phrase. An interviewer of the French monthly *Réalités* (May 1965 English edition) asked him to clarify his position if Israel should agree to the implementation of the resolutions; would he accept the existence of Israel in the midst of the Arab world? His answer:

> The Afro-Asian nations at the Bandung Conference said that they would feel satisfied if the resolutions were applied. The Arab states agree on this point.

Bourguiba, for his part, though insisting that his proposition is primarily good tactics, nevertheless denies that he is sponsoring a ruse or stratagem, and insists that this differentiates him from Nasser. When *Le Figaro's* Francois Monnelet asked him to explain the difference he answered:

> President Nasser's statement is quite vague. What I have said was that one has 'to defrost' a situation which seems to have defied a solution for seventeen years. How? By compromise. It is evident that one should apply the texts of the United Nations but it is equally necessary to recognize the decision of the United Nations to create Israel. Everyone would benefit from applying the legality of the United Nations. For the Arab refugees it would mean a possibility of regaining a part of the land from which they were driven out. But even more important it would create a climate of peace and of coexistence, and in this the Jews will be the winners, at least in the sense that the hatred will be suppressed. Mutual concessions and reparations—this is what I wished. (*Figaro*, April 12)

This point, in the long run, may constitute a decisive contribution to the settlement of the dispute, because, in contradistinction to other Arab leaders, Bourguiba makes recognition of Israel's sovereign existence the basis and starting point. If he has anti-Israel feelings, they do not blind him to the realities of history and life.

One should not take Bourguiba's present formula as the last word of the Arabs. An experienced tactician, the Tunisian leader starts with a maximum demand, leaving room for bargaining in the ensuing phases of the negotiations. His primary thrust is that negotiations should begin; to this end he sometimes seems prepared to drop the United Nations resolutions as a precondition, as in his Carthage speech, when he said that if he were a Palestinian he would accept an invitation to go to Tel Aviv without any preliminary conditions.

If negotiations were to revert to "United Nations legality," Israel would not find herself in a disadvantageous position, despite the apprehensions of her leaders. The first, most obvious benefit would be an *a priori* recognition of Israel by the Arabs, to be followed by application of United Nations resolutions, some explicitly in favor of Israel. One, for instance, calls upon Egypt to permit Israeli ships to pass through the Suez Canal. Even more important, if negotiations are based on international legality, the armistice agreements concluded between Israel and her neighbors at the end of the Palestinian war, stipulating that neither party should engage in war or war threats, might cease to be so blatantly violated by the Arab countries.

Israeli policymakers have become so reliant upon their military potential that they often forget that their claims and rights are also explicit in the United Nations resolutions. The world could be reminded that it was the Zionists who accepted, without reservations, the original partition resolution, despite the weird boundaries it delineated; and that it was the Arabs who rejected partition and violated the United Nations decisions by instant invasion. And that this violation brought to naught the United Nations stipulation for the creation of an Arab state in one part of Mandated Palestine, not so much because Israel absorbed areas not originally included in the Jewish state, as because Jordan annexed the territory west of the Jordan River, and Egypt occupied the Gaza strip.*

Discussions on the basis of "back to the United Nations resolutions" would also enable the Israeli negotiators to point out to world public opinion that the United Nations in fact only gave legal sanction to a situation created by a people which in its own country fought for its independence. It was the Hebrew underground armies that brought about the freedom of Palestine; and when these armies were about to liberate the whole of Mandated Palestine with wide support from world public opinion, the British felt compelled to evacuate the entire area—not just a part of it—and dump the problem into the lap of the United Nations. Then in a spirit of compromise, if not surrender, the official Zionist leadership accepted partition. The neighboring Arab states rejected the United Nations decisions, invaded Palestine in a war which they lost.

As a result of this defeat, new conditions, not previously foreseen, arose. Israel not only secured the territory allocated to her by partition but acquired new territory originally allocated to the Arab State in the western part of Palestine. A more complicating factor than territory was the dislocation of many Arabs from both parts of the partitioned Palestine. These are known as the Palestine refugees. Though still in their own country they lost their homes and many their land. This land became since then heavily

---

* It is important to note that while Jordan integrated its acquired territory, Egypt merely administered the Gaza strip by military government, and its residents did not have Egyptian nationality or rights of any kind.

resettled by hundreds of thousands of Jewish immigrants—some of them survivors of Hitler's extermination camps, and some who were squeezed out of Arab countries by the terror that followed the Arab defeat.

Far-reaching political and social changes also took place in the territory annexed by Jordan, where the refugees became full-fledged citizens of the Hashemite Kingdom. Hussein would refuse with as much determination as the Israelis to cede any territory.

In view of the demographic, political, and social changes which have taken place in both parts of Mandated Palestine, to attempt to literally revert to the original partition scheme would be like trying to unscramble an omelet. To dislocate Jewish settlers from parts of Israel and create room for Arabs would solve no problem, but would surely add new ones. To speak of creating a new Palestine Arab state through truncating let alone the erasure of both Israel and Jordan is an exercise in sheer fantasy. A return to the original partition scheme of 1947 is "no more feasible than a return to the condition of 1900 when there were very few Zionist settlers in Palestine; or to the conditions of 1850 when there were between 100,000 and 200,000 people in the whole of Palestine (including Jordan) ;"* or to the conditions of the first century before the destruction by the Romans of the Hebrew commonwealth, when, it is said, there were five or six million Jews in Palestine.

But constructive discussions could lead, not toward far-reaching territorial changes, but toward new solutions in the best interests of all the people, Jews and Arabs—those who fled and those re-settled. Before long, all the parties might be facing the Palestine problem squarely, boldly, and imaginatively.

It must be so, if peace is to be achieved. For just as the Arabs cannot escape the reality of Israel's existence, the Israelis cannot obliterate the existence of the Arab refugees and the grave injustice which waits to be redressed. It no longer matters who was responsible for their flight, or how many there were or are. Exactly as there is world quasi-unanimity as to the right of Israel's existence, so is there general agreement on the moral imperative for solving the refugee problem, as witness the famous United Nations resolution (December 11, 1948 N 194 [iii/9]) affording free choice, with two important qualifications: 1) the peaceful inten-

---

* *Report on the Palestine Refugee Problem,* by the Institute for Mediterranean Affairs, p. 20.

tions of the refugees who wish to return to that part of Palestine which is now Israel, and 2) practicality, as a time element. The consensus is so overwhelming that this resolution is reaffirmed every year over and over again by the United Nations; on one occasion even Israel saw herself morally forced to vote for it.

Bourguiba's cardinal concern was to shift the Palestine conflict from the current state of lawlessness—violence and threats—to the realm of international legality as a pre-condition to any sensible and just settlement. What the settlement might be is too early to forecast. But if the Arabs and Israel learn to coexist in peace if only for a period of time, such coexistence might lead slowly and falteringly to cooperation, which in turn might open up who-knows-what possibilities.

Gilles Anouil of *Réalités* (November 1965) asked Bourguiba, as some observers have suggested, "perhaps in the very long run the best solution would be some kind of confederation or federation in the Middle East, between the Arab states and Israel. Is it, in your view, a desirable and realizable objective?"

Bourguiba replied:

> I don't like to prophesy. And besides, these countries are far away and I am poorly acquainted with them [sic!]. I guess that the best way would be to proceed by phases: the fact of going back to United Nations legality does not constitute an ideal solution, but it would be a "bait" for a solution. Its acceptance by the Jews and the Arabs could unfreeze the problem and perhaps clear the way for peace. Would it be in the form of a federation? A confederation? Perhaps even in the form of coexistence in the same state? I don't know. It's a problem of a psychological climate. Yet, what I suggested could considerably change the psychological climate by curing the complexes of humiliation and frustration from which the Arabs suffer; and as far as the Jews are concerned it would allay their fear engendered by the fact of being surrounded by a hostile world.

Sometimes he thinks that peaceful coexistence (after the refugee problem is solved) may lead to the creation of some kind of a unitary state composed of two nationalities—Arabs and Hebrews. Such an outcome would constitute an interesting and stimulating experiment in statecraft. In this connection he expresses regret at the exodus of the European settlers from Algeria, for had they remained, Algeria's foundation would appear more solid and its future brighter.

In his CBS interview he spoke specifically of a compromise producing "one general state," setting up a system of autonomous cantons for the two nationalities.

Bourguiba has challenged both the Arabs and the Israelis to offer any workable solution, but begs them at all costs to stop the Dance of Death and start talking. A *Mapam* leader, Mr. A. Granot, interpreted Bourguiba's "back to the United Nations resolutions" slogan as "a for-example" proposal and not a "take it or leave it." This is also how some impartial observers understand it.

23

Is Bourguiba Alone in the Arab World?

A CRUCIAL QUESTION IS, OF COURSE, DOES BOURGUIBA REPRESENT AT least the beginning of a new trend in the Middle East, or is he just a lone voice crying in the wilderness? Even Prime Minister Eshkol and Foreign Minister Eban were showing signs of perceptibly beginning to realize that the Tunisian President is not alone in the Arab world.* And Bourguiba, too, has insisted that hysteria was not the only reaction to his initiative, that other reactions were more reasoned, more favorable. In his televised interview on the French network he admitted that the first reaction in the Arab world to his Jerusalem and Beirut statements was one of shock, but this was not universal. In many circles his ideas were received with understanding and sympathy. To his interviewers on *Face the Nation* he declared:

> I believe that the reactions which have been recorded since I made my proposal were not all negative. Many countries of North Africa and the Middle East, many journalists, many politicians, have had the occasion to comment on my proposals and support them. Not all of the polemics, not all the campaign, have been against Tunisia. Part of them are *for* our proposals. And these proposals constitute, in my opinion, a positive step, especially if you see that they have permitted many people who used to be terrorized and felt completely inhibited, to express their real views, in spite of the ways and methods applied [in the Middle East] to those who are not toeing the line. My initiative gave them an opportunity to express their views, to make statements with less inhibitions. . . .

* As early as May 25, 1965, Premier Eshkol declared in the Knesset: "I do not think this [campaign of Bourguiba] is the enterprise of one man."

There is one [decisive] fact [that is, the recognition of Israel as a state]. Now there is a whole press, newspapers in the Middle East which are supporting my proposal—whether in the Lebanon —both the Arabic and the French newspapers—or even in Kuwait. I have read today the paper in Kuwait called *Public Opinion* in which there is an editorial which says that Bourguiba has only made clear and expressed publicly what all Arab leaders have been accepting for quite a few years, by asking the implementation of the United Nations resolutions. A few days ago the newspaper *Al Khayat*, also in an editorial, said that the Arabs have accepted at least 15 or 20 times the partition of Palestine when they have demanded the implementation of the United Nations resolutions, including that of partition itself. Bourguiba has only made public a situation which existed in fact. My conclusion is that there is definitely a gestation, which [my proposal] gave start to. And, too, the atmosphere of terror which has inhibited the people is now, if not fading away, at all events losing its grip upon these people.

In the Arab world decisions of government are rarely seriously submitted to any parliamentary control. Still, there are currents of public opinion, feeble and inarticulate though they may be. Bourguiba seems to have decided to throw the Palestine question, with all its brutally painful implications, into the open so that public opinion in the Arab countries might begin to stir. "I have thrown a big stone into the pond," he said in his Carthage speech.

He knows from his personal contacts and from his ambassadors that there are in Tunisia, Algeria, Morocco, the Lebanon, Jordan, and even Egypt, individuals and groups who are relatively free from the hatreds which seem to dominate current Arab policy on Palestine. He also knows that there are intellectuals, writers, publicists, and political thinkers who recoil at the prospect of an apocalyptic showdown in the Middle East. These intellectuals, though greatly inhibited, are nevertheless concerned to find a way to avoid such a bloody confrontation, and to conceive some kind of plan for a peaceful settlement.

In this connection mention should be made of several discreet meetings which took place in Florence on the initiative of the former Mayor of that city, Professor Giorgio La Pira. Both Israelis and Arabs participated, and some of the Arabs made suggestions similar to those of the Tunisian President.

A *New York Times* correspondent, commenting upon Bourguiba's campaign in the Middle East, reported (April 11):

Informed circles take the line that the controversial views the President expressed were simple logic and that, regardless of the opinion of the journalists whose writings, they say, led to anti-Tunisian demonstrations, a high proportion of ordinary Arabs would be found to agree with him.

It is these ordinary Arabs as well as the intellectuals that Bourguiba has in mind when he expresses hope that in the course of time they may become more articulate and represent a more consolidated factor in Arab public opinion. These may be the fertile ground in which he has sown his seeds.

The governments of the three Maghrebian countries did not join the chorus of Arab condemnation which followed Bourguiba's Carthage speech, despite pressure from Egypt.

The Cairo press was concerned over this silence. The government-owned newspaper *Al Goumhouria* on April 25, 1965 carried a front-page editorial which asked: "Do these [three] capitals support Bourguiba's statement? Does silence imply consent on their part to Bourguiba's proposals?"

According to the Cairo correspondent of *The New York Times,* well-informed Egyptians were convinced that in making his controversial and explosive proposals, Bourguiba expected at least tacit support from some other countries, especially those who, like Morocco and Libya, refused to follow the Arab League in breaking relations with West Germany. There had been persistent reports that King Hassan II of Morocco was increasingly unenthusiastic about the Palestine cause and that King Irdiss of Libya was concerned over what seemed like a Cairo drift to the East.

The quiet endorsement was not confined to the Maghreb. We have seen that Pierre Gemayel, a Lebanese Cabinet member and leader of the country's strongest political party, came out strongly for a peaceful solution to the Palestine problem, even suggesting what that solution should be: a Jewish-Moslem unitary state, on the pattern of the Lebanese Christian-Moslem state. The Phalangist Party also seems to have officially endorsed Bourguiba's proposals.

Other voices for peace were heard in Lebanon. The Beirut newspaper *Al Amal* on March 13 published a laudatory article saying that the Tunisian President appeals to the Arabs "to see the truth as it is, and not as one would wish it to be." Another Lebanese paper, *As Safa,* the same day suggested finding a compromise between Bourguiba's views and those of Nasser. At a later date the Beirut *Al Jaryda* commented that the protests against Bourguiba make no sense, since "all he wants is to get the Palestine question moving again at the level of the United Nations."

Lebanese support for a negotiated peace is not surprising, for the Christians of the country would sigh with relief if the pall of pan-Arabism were dissipated from the Middle Eastern air. With the normalization of relations with Israel, they could derive some comfort from the presence of another non-Moslem population nearby. Other minorities which are either non-Arab or non-Moslem include the Kurds in Iraq and Syria who are not inherently anti-Israel; they, too, would benefit from a Middle East free from the pressures and terrors of pan-Arabism. In a different context and to a different degree the same can be said about the Berbers in Algeria.

What about opinion in Egypt itself? Paul-Marie de la Corce, a French writer and an editor of *Jeune Afrique,* visited Egypt when the Bourguiba controversy was at the height of its fury. He was able to discern a moderate trend represented by the pro-Western middle class, which thinks in terms very close to those expressed by Bourguiba, but speaks only in private discussions. According to de la Corce these bourgeois circles suffer a deep sense of humiliation as a result of Israel's military victories, but they are sensitive to public opinion in the Western world, especially American. But the influence of this group is rather slight in Egypt today; as far as the masses of people are concerned, Israel is synonymous with Satan.

More significant is the French writer's observation that the trend at the left end of the political spectrum in Egypt is also free from extreme emotionalism toward Israel. This far-left group is gaining more and more influence in Egyptian society and in the structure of the state. Its adherents occupy important positions in the mass media and in the administration of Nasser's single legal party. For their purposes, Israel is not a matter of first priority at all, since their main preoccupation is to penetrate and consolidate their positions within the party, ultimately gaining decisive influence and orienting Egypt's destiny toward a course which in their view would lead to progress and independence. To them the question is whether Israel is an instrument wielded by the United States irrevocably tied to the West. The more convinced they become that Israel is allied with the United States, the more they will view her as an enemy. They are not racist, and they do not think that war is the only solution, or that it is necessary to destroy Israel. Therefore, de la Corce concludes, any step Israel took to demonstrate that she is not an American satellite could have a great effect in Egypt and in the Arab world in general. The writer adds, incidentally, that de Gaulle would also view such a step sympathetically.

The Nasserites, however, are sworn foes of Israel, discerning in her an enemy under all circumstances. It may be significant that the issues of *Jeune Afrique* which published articles concerning a peaceful solution to the Palestine problem were permitted to be sold and circulated, though on previous occasions the magazine had been banned. Bourguiba's statements were widely publicized in the Egyptian press, though accompanied with bitter attacks upon him, de la Corce told an interviewer.

24

Bourguiba's Ambiguities: Virtue or Vice

IN REPORTING BOURGUIBA'S INITIATIVE FROM SEVERAL VIEWPOINTS, we have tried to clear up the ambiguities and paradoxes that characterized his utterances. It might be useful here to attempt to summarize these rationalizations. Without offering an apology for Bourguiba, or absolving him of responsibility for the confusion his statements have created, we have tried only to penetrate his hidden intentions, giving him a sympathetic benefit of the doubt, remembering always the sensitive position he was in.

We note first that however definitive his declarations sound within a given context, he is always careful not to state the totality of his thought explicitly. There are far-reaching qualifications and escape clauses; there remains always an air of uncertainty around some essential points. While his criticism of prevailing Arab policies and attitudes was outspoken and often devastating, when he expounded his alternative proposals, he often resorted to ambiguity and outright contradictions. Speaking before the Arabs, he appeared a wrathful chastiser of Arabs; before the Turks and the Iranians, he was the champion of the Arabs. Opinions expressed in press interviews and on TV were soon contradicted either by himself or by members of his entourage; sometimes the opposing expressions occurred in the very same statement, making it possible to quote him on either side of a question. Nor are we dealing with a long span of time during which any human thinking is likely to change. His was a concentrated campaign within the space of a very few months.

We begin with his divergent explanations of the motives behind the campaign. He has claimed that he set out for the Middle East with no preconceived plan to tackle the Palestine problem;

a convergence of circumstances in the course of the tour crystallized his thinking. On another occasion, he intimated that he started out with a clear purpose, fully cognizant in advance that he would stir up trouble abroad, but counting on his own people to approve his initiative and cheer him. Yet strangely enough, before leaving for the Middle East, he asked the Tunisian daily *L'Action* to republish, as background material for his tour, so to speak, his most vehement anti-Israel speech delivered at the Arab summit conference in January 1964. This speech reappeared in the Tunisian newspaper on March 4, 1965—two days before his sensational declaration in the Old City of Jerusalem condemning war with Israel and charging the Arabs to learn to live in harmony with the Jews.

In the course of his tour he declared that Palestine is and is not a classical colonial problem; that he is for and against Palestine guerrillas fighting for the liberation of Palestine; that he is for and against bargaining with Israel; that war is and is not possible; that he would and would not send Tunisian contingents were a war to break out between Israel and the Arabs. In retrospect he even confused the timetable of his tour; he declared that he had visited Yugoslavia before going to Egypt; in reality his visit to Marshal Tito came near the end of his tour.

This behavior not only completely baffled the Israelis and exasperated the Arabs, it confused some experienced political observers and astute journalists. Their appraisal and commentaries often proved faulty, and they had to adjust their views as the campaign progressed.

In general, Bourguiba's is not only a brilliant but a lucid mind; his thought is usually logical; his reasoning is sound and his forensic skills quite admirable. He had no formal training in the stricter disciplines of logic, but he has always known what he wanted, and how to express it. His behavior in the campaign was therefore all the more frustrating to observers and journalists who knew him best.

We must consider that the ambiguities and contradictions, bewildering though they may be, are nonetheless a reflection of a most complex—in fact, unique—situation. Unique because probably nowhere are opposing claims so mutually exclusive yet simultaneously so reasonable and just. Bourguiba's seeming contradictions may actually be manifestations of an attempt to come to grips with a perplexing situation and evaluate it honestly, rather than follow the Arab leaders (or, for that matter, the Israeli leaders) who have reduced it to an abstract oversimplification where all justice is on one side.

Even his attitude toward himself and his position in the dispute was unclear and subject to change without notice. He seemed to consider himself alternately as a protagonist and an arbiter in the Palestine conflict, sometimes even appearing simultaneously as both. The dual role is bewildering to a close observer, but in his own mind he seems to have reconciled the duality: Tunisia was too far away from the Middle East to be immersed in its problems or to take an active part in its struggles. As a man far above the fray he can take a detached view, though he is not a coward and has made his sentiments known. As an arbiter he has no definitive aim to pursue, or plan to offer, but only general suggestions which may lead first to the alleviation of tensions and eventually to peace. In the Old City of Jerusalem he had declared:

> If I were to say that I have a plan to solve the Palestine problem, I should be deceiving you. I am not in a position to draw up a plan. But I could, in spite of the great distance between Tunis and this region, meet Arab leaders [from the Middle East] and discuss with them such a plan. The main responsibility lies with the Palestinian people and with this region—but we for our part are prepared to help.

In his Carthage speech he offered himself as a mediator and declared that he was willing, under certain conditions, to arrange a meeting between Palestinian Arabs and Israeli representatives. "Such contacts," he said, "can be arranged in Rome or in any other country abroad. . . . We could facilitate a getting together . . . to try to arrive at results which would change the physiognomy of the Middle East."

When asked by an interviewer on French TV why his statements aroused so much resentment and bitterness among the Arabs, he gave an answer which may sound either naïve or so ambiguous as to mean a great deal or nothing:

> I declared that one can live on very good terms with the Jews and at the same time I also said that the Palestinian Arabs are struggling for their honor, freedom, and right to self-determination.

Many of his listeners, including correspondents who reported it, understood him to have meant: It is possible for the Arabs to live at peace with the Israelis, on the condition that the Jews recognize the Arabs' rights and have respect for their honor. Thus stated, his short answer sounds like the formulation of a new psychological approach, which may in turn lead to a solution.

Bourguiba seems to have experimented during his campaign in trying to apply his celebrated theory of gradualism to both the Arabs and the Israelis. His proposals were often understood and misunderstood by Arabs and Jews alike, and perhaps this is how he intended it.

The interpretation seemed to Bourgiba at that stage, i.e. during his campaign, to be beside the point. What he tried to do was to alleviate fears and arouse hope in both camps. That results were not immediate was unimportant. If efforts are kept up they may eventually prove effective.

Viewed in the light of such complex realities Bourguiba's ambiguities and contradictions need not necessarily be considered Machiavellian, or lacking in coherent thinking. Rather they appear as a tactical means required by the situation.

But in order to introduce such bold and nonconformist ideas as he did during his campaign, he had to take precautionary measures. He had first of all to reconfirm his "credentials," so to speak, in the Arab world. Hence, his reemphasis of his role as a champion of the Arab cause. Having thus established his record he felt secure and confident enough to indicate that though an injustice was committed, it is nevertheless necessary to understand its historic background: the tragedy of the Jews in Europe. In that light Israel also appears to have some justice on her side. Moreover, whatever the pristine justice or injustice, a new situation has evolved which cannot be unscrambled without inflicting new injustices, perhaps surpassing those originally committed.

Apparently Bourguiba felt that he could not speak the same language, or convey an identical message to all the parties and groups concerned with this conflict. He spoke on different levels to different audiences—to the moderate Arab leaders and the enlightened intelligentsia, to the masses, to Western public opinion, and only lastly, to Israel. Sometimes these messages overlapped, or even contradicted each other, yet the main trend of his thought was never lost: the imperative of arriving at a peaceful settlement. Whatever the inconsistencies in his utterances, they did not seem to alter or bear upon his essential purpose. The

Tunisian Ambassador to France, Mohammed Masmoudi, synopsized the campaign's aims:

> President Bourguiba simply wanted to define the Israeli-Arab problem in political terms. . . . What we are interested in is that the Arab countries begin to think . . . in terms of a peaceful settlement and no longer of war.

Of course, we have not dispelled all doubts engendered by the ambiguities and confusions of Bourguiba's statements. But despite the shortcomings, the totality of his declarations still retain a great amount of good sense, creative imagination, and exceptional courage. From a long-range point of view, his initiative still remains a mighty enterprise of historic significance.

25

A Rendezvous With History:
Bourguiba's Own Appraisal

WHAT WAS BOURGUIBA'S OWN EVALUATION OF HIS CAMPAIGN? WHAT did he think about the reaction he had provoked in the Arab world?

He seemed open and candid in his appraisal, yet his accounts were not necessarily consistent. Sometimes he sounded victorious and optimistic, at others humanly frustrated and resentful, reflecting the stresses of an almost unmanageable situation heightened by a subjective struggle within the man himself. As a realist he rebels against vain illusions; as a man of vision he takes the long optimistic view.

Was he repudiated on all sides? Wasn't this rejection evidence that his initiative had failed? Yes and no. That both parties to the conflict repudiated him is proof of the justice and truth of his proposals, and these carry the seeds of tomorrow's success, he appeared to reason.

But his inner doubts seem to be even deeper, and he wonders how to distinguish between vision and illusion; this is a source of spiritual turmoil. One impulse drives him to champion great ideas and visions against furious opposition, while another inner voice questions, What for? Does he not have enough worries and problems closer to home? But how is one really to determine which problems come truly close to home, and which are far away and irrelevant? Perhaps those which seem far away are essential to the welfare of his own country.

Besides these dichotomous thoughts, he has other doubts. Whom is he going to convert to common sense? Is there anyone in the

Middle East to talk reason to? The minds of the Arab leaders, he told an interviewer from *Le Monde,* "are beclouded . . . Their regimes are not very solid. They do not want to run into trouble with Cairo." They are a bunch of demagogues and afraid of their own shadows. Were they even to appear to agree with him they would no longer be free men. For so many years, he told an interviewer of *Le Figaro,* they have incited their own public and thus have so "created difficulties for themselves that they are no longer free to maneuver."

He is quite clearly torn between two contradictory impulses: At times he seems to make a decision to give up the challenge he has thrown before Nasser and the Arabs and consign the Middle East to status quo while he dedicates himself to "purely Tunisian" affairs. But soon, perhaps within a week, he reverses his decision. Sometimes the two opposing moods are reflected in the same statement.

The measure and nature of his inner conflict come through in his interview in the British quarterly *Views.* Discussing the effect of his campaign upon the Arabs and the Israelis, and whether he foresaw direct negotiations between them, he declared:

> I do not want to take particular responsibility for a very distant country. I look at it on the human plane on the Arab plane. They are brothers who have been chased out. . . . But I cannot forecast what they are going to do. Are they going to discuss or not? All I can ascertain up to the present day is that my ideas have not been accepted by the Jews or the Arabs. This is the most convincing proof, I think, that my ideas are good. They might ripen in the future, on the Arab side as well as the Jewish side. . . . I would rather not fight with people who are still obstinate, people with passionate feelings. I prefer to look after my own country. I am not trying to impose my own solution. I proposed this in all honesty and seriousness. If they [the Arabs] do not like it, if they have better solutions, I don't see anything wrong with that. But they must be good-mannered enough to know that one does not insult a man who spent thirty years of his life fighting colonialism, calling him . . . very unpleasant names, just because he presented an idea which worked in his own country, although it might not work in Palestine. I did it in all good faith, in all honesty, only wishing to solve the problem, to insure a minimum of peace, of coexistence between existing elements, and for which this policy of hatred and bitterness has achieved nothing in seventeen years. That is all. I have no other ambition. I only want to help Tunisia and the Tunisians on the path of progress. That is all.

The interviewer asked him: "Do you think the great powers, or a secondary power, like Britain, can do anything in this instance?" Bourguiba replied:

> I don't know; really I don't know. The unfortunate part is that both parties have refused. This does make it difficult, doesn't it? It could have worked if the Arabs had agreed on this position [with me]. It might have been very interesting: already America was starting to hesitate, to say it was reasonable, that one could start talking; Britain, too, and African countries. . . . It would have been a magnificent platform for the Arabs, and it might have provoked among the Jews a drawing away of the intransigent elements, since my proposal had some advantages for the Jews, too, just as for the Arabs. It would be a true compromise. But I don't know how things will evolve. It depends upon the men and on the way they will react when faced with reality. And the reactions of men will, of course, depend on their leaders. . . . We hope that men and leaders will emerge, who will be conscious of their responsibilities, who will tell the people the truth, even if it hurts them, just as I did, during my whole career, with the Tunisian people. This is why they like me and respect me. . . .

He spoke in the same wistful vein, in his interview on CBS' *Face the Nation.* He was asked by correspondent George Herman:

> Mr. President, you mentioned waiting for one, two, or three years to see what will happen. Do you imply that you are going to wait for one, two, or three years and not take further action yourself, not assist in the gestation, as you call it, or try to push things further yourself by your own words and actions?
> *Bourguiba:* I have always said that as far as I am concerned, I am not seeking for Palestine, which is far away from Tunisia and North Africa, a first role, a first part to play; or to take on special responsibilities; or to seek any leadership in that part of the world. When I went to the Middle East I didn't go there seeking to impose my leadership or co-leadership on anyone. . . . I am modest. I know my possibilities, and I think that the fact that I am the leader of Tunisia is quite enough for me. . . . But being a freedom-loving Arab, I couldn't but feel a kind of solidarity with any of those who are fighting for their freedom, and to recover their dignity and their homeland.
> I felt the sufferings of these people when I visited them in their refugee camps. I proposed a method, an approach which was crowned with success in Tunisia. . . . I have given my opinion. . . . If they don't accept [my proposals], it is their right. I will

only wish them good luck, good work and I will even applaud and congratulate them whenever their efforts are a success.

. . . I have given my opinion. I wish that some serious effort would start there. I will assure by the very fact of taking care of Tunisian development, that I have no intention of continuing this polemic. I made a rendezvous with the future. I wish these countries peace and stability, but I do not intend to push this gestation. It is their own responsibility to grow mature.

But he did not take such an aloof or wistful stand in all his statements appraising his initiative. Nor did he persist in declaring that his campaign must be viewed as having come to an end. On the contrary, in several statements he exihibited exuberant optimism, and promised to continue. To another interviewer, of the French monthly *Réalités,* much later in autumn of that year he said:

I believe that right ideas exert an influence, and that in the long run what is serious and sincere prevails. Sometimes it takes time if they meet with mountains of prejudices. But I am not one of those who despair when success does not appear from one day to the next. In my fight for independence, I wagered on the triumph of good sense—on the part of the French as well as of the Tunisians. But it took 25 years until it showed results. In the final analysis I won. It is in the same spirit that I approached the Palestine problem and the relations between the Arabs and the Jews. I am convinced that my ideas will eventually find their way into the minds and hearts, because time is on their side. Sooner or later one will see that there is just no other solution. Anyhow, they are by now well known—after having been given the honor of front-page in the press of the Middle East. I am certain that many Egyptians, Syrians, Jordanians, and Lebanese think about them. I have noticed that the Jews have studied them, that there are some stirrings in Israel on the subject. It's a good sign. All this reveals an ever growing awareness. People think deeper.

Did he pay too high a price for his effort to enlighten the people on the Palestine issue? Did his campaign prevent the improvement of his relations with the Arabs in the Middle East, or was that not really material to his purpose? He indicated that he did not undertake his tour to improve relations but to challenge Nasser's hegemony; and in this, he claimed to have scored a signal success. In the same interview, he explained:

. . . The fact is that my ideas have been accepted by some and rejected by others. This fact brought to the foreground the problem of inter-Arab relations. This requires an enormous campaign of clarification. You are aware of that desire for hegemony on the part of the United Arab Republic that pretends to be the republic of all the Arabs, facing them with a *fait accompli,* though there has never been accord among them on this subject. Today one sees Arab states beginning to keep their distance, since Bourguiba has shaken the coconut-tree. It is a great accomplishment, since it is only a few months that passed. And *I intend to reaffirm without let-up my position,* because I represent a country which can say what it thinks without being afraid—as the others—of interior complications unleashed from Cairo. [Italics added]

On the same *Face the Nation* he declared:

My hope and my belief is that my ideas will, maybe slowly, but certainly, find their way into the minds of the people of the Middle East, not as a solution—it is only a kind of interim solution—but as a method, an approach to deal with the problem, which was not able to be dealt with by another approach. . . . And this will open the way to the discovery [emergence] of honest political men who will have more courage.

. . . What I consider the real asset [of my proposals] is their common sense. Reason will prevail, and I am sure that the future will vindicate my position. If in one, two, or three years from now nothing has come of the old-fashioned approach—which for the last seventeen years did not bring any results—then it will be proved sterile and the time may be at hand to try a new approach which could cause my ideas to prevail.

26

In the Aftermath of the Six-Day War

AS INDICATED IN THE PREFACE, THIS SURVEY WAS WRITTEN IN 1966. Now, after the dramatic events which shook the world in June 1967, one may ask how does President Bourguiba's campaign look in the light of these subsequent events? To what degree do his philosophy, analyses, as well as his warnings, predictions and admonitions withstand the test of time and history? Were they vindicated or did they become meaningless? A great Hebrew nationalist, the late Vladimir Jabotinsky, used to say that there is, for all intents and purposes, only one kind of political genius: he who knows how trends and events will develop in the decade immediately ahead and makes his knowledge public.

To a very considerable degree this definition certainly applies to the Tunisian President. Basically, he undertook his peace campaign against President Nasser because he saw in his policies a danger both to Tunisia, to all other Arab countries and to Egypt itself. His aim was to challenge the Egyptian leader's striving for hegemony under the banner of pan-Arabism. Though Bourguiba considers pan-Arabism a myth, he also knows that it is precisely under the banner of myths that the most evil movements in modern history have been able to galvanize the masses and ultimately to wreak havoc upon their own peoples as well as upon their neighbors. It is both the destiny and in the nature of pan-Arabism to go the way of all other pan-Nationalist movements: to ultimate disaster. He therefore warned that as long as Nasser is in a position to exploit the Palestine conflict the myth of pan-Arabism will retain a semblance of reality, with all its inherent dangers to the welfare and progress of the peoples in the region. The Palestine conflict is the only issue around which mighty emotions can be unleashed and occasionally, to achieve a seemingly united front—and always around Nasser as the leader and redeemer. Bourguiba went forth to kill the dragon.

Though in this he has not succeeded to this date, his very failure has proven almost fatal to Bourguiba's anatagonist, who suffered defeat and humiliation to a greater degree than Bourguiba himself wished to happen. For Bourguiba, as an Arab nationalist, there is no consolation in the fact that he was proven so awesomely right, though from a long-range point of view the catastrophe which has befallen the Arabs may have a chastising and sobering effect, and may perhaps serve as turning point for new and more hopeful vistas of political consolidation, social stability and economic development. However, as these lines are written, we are still far away from such a revolutionary possibility.

THE SHOCK AND SURPRISE OF BEING PROVEN RIGHT

President Bourguiba never tires of repeating that he is not particularly interested in Palestine. What he is predominantly interested in is his own country. But he holds that so long as the Palestine conflict is not resolved by a peaceful settlement, no Arab state, regardless how far removed from the scene, is safe from external subversion and internal demoralization. This concern was what impelled him to launch his campaign against President Nasser during his tour of the Middle East in the spring of 1965. He saw this campaign as an act of self-preservation on behalf of Tunisia.

Yet he was surprised and shocked when the very truth of his thesis which he so vigorously and lucidly elaborated was tragically demonstrated in the streets and suburbs of his own capital on the day open warfare broke out between Israel and the Arab states.

On that memorable day of June 5, 1967, he suddenly saw himself, for the first time in his long and brilliant career, challenged by a riotous mob, which set fire to the British Embassy and tried to do the same to the American Embassy, but was thrown back by tear gas bombs used by American personnel; the rioters also attacked the offices of the United States Information Center as well as the offices of TWA. Their main furor, however, was directed against Jewish shops, homes and the Synagogue, yelling "death to the Jews!" and "let's burn the Jews!"

Around noon a mob of about 1,000 strong took to the streets in the usually placid city of Tunis—the same streets where two years earlier demonstrators burnt Nasser in effigy, and attacked the Egyptian embassy as a target of their enmity and wrath. And it was in these same streets where the name of Nasser had been anthema that it now became a rallying cry. Tunisian youths yelled such slogans as "Long live Nasser!" "Nasser we are with you!" "Long live Palestine!" And for good measure, "Long live De Gaulle!" For four hours a delirious crowd delivered itself to plunder, arson and vandalism, broke windows of Jewish businesses, tore down doors and set scores of cars on fire. Shops were sacked in the center of town and in the streets with large numbers of Jewish inhabitants, everything was broken or carried off, including property of some Moslems, according to a vivid description in the Tunisian weekly, *Jeune Afrique* (June 18, 1967). The synagogue was partly destroyed. In some cases the rioters even tried to set fire to a home where Jews had taken refuge. This was the first time that Tunisian Jews were molested. Not even in 1956, during the mass demonstrations in connection with the Suez war, had any Jews been attacked either in their person or their property.

The police were on hand but did not seem to have intervened effectively. Even when the Army was called out to help the police, the situation remained chaotic until late in the afternoon when order was restored.

So great was the surprise and so deep the consternation among the Tunisian leadership in the highest echelons, that President Bourguiba called an emergency session of the Council of the Republic for the same afternoon. In the evening Bourguiba appeared on TV and expressed in the strongest terms his condemnation of the rioters, referring to them as "raving maniacs . . . who deserve the gallows." He reminded his listeners that Tunisian Jews participated in the struggle for the country's independence and promised to compensate the victims of the riots and to pay for the rebuilding of the synagogue. Addressing himself to "our Jewish citizens," he explained that Tunisia's stand on the Palestine problem is not dictated by any "religious or racial fanaticism" but only by a profound regard for "justice and liberty." He asked his listeners to believe him when he stated that the vast majority of the Tunisian people declared themselves "outraged" by the excesses perpetrated that afternoon. He also declared that "to make out of the Palestine conflict a racial or religious problem would not only be an injustice, but also a tactical error, which would expose the cause of Palestine to mortal danger."

Mr. Bahi Ladgham, the most important personality in Bourguiba's Cabinet, paid a personal visit to the synagogue the same day, to extend the regrets of the Government and he promised to make available all the funds necessary to rebuild the synagogue and to compensate the individual victims.

Many Tunisian intellectuals expressed horror and indignation at the excesses.

At the same time, Foreign Minister Habib Bourguiba Jr., communicated with the Embassies of the United States and Great Britain expressing the Government's consternation at what had happened and promised full compensation.

By a special Presidential decree, the government appointed a commission on June 21, to assess the losses in property and goods suffered by the victims of the riots with the directive to finish its inquiry as quickly as possible and thus enable the Government to compensate the victims in full.

Apart from that, Chief of Police Mebazza was dismissed and in his place a more responsible public official, Mr. Tahar Belkholdja, was appointed as Director of the Internal Security Forces. It was also announced that the entire Ministry of the Interior would undergo complete reorganization.

More than 200 arrests were made and of these, 114 participants in the riots were promptly brought to trial. At the trial a disturbing fact was revealed: most of them were under twenty years of age, and all except two, unemployed. Sixty youths were tried in correctional court and fifty-four by the criminal court of the military tribunal. The accused were charged with a wide variety of crimes: incitement to violence, directing the riots and vandalism, setting fire to the United States Information Center, and the British Embassy, looting stores which the Socialist Destourian Party had "placed in their charge," burning the synagogue and attacking Jewish enterprises and plunder.

About twenty lawyers defended the accused, who pleaded not guilty. Many witnesses were called who gave, in some cases, contradictory testimony. The prosecutor demanded the death sentence for a 21-year-old student of theology Ben Jannet and for Mohammed Tounsi, a bank employee, who also was the originator of a cultural radio program, Stiff sentences were asked for the others, and for some, life terms.

On August 1, 1967 the court sentenced Jannet to twenty years at hard labor; two others received sentences of fifteen years of hard labor each, and the sentences of the others ranged from two months to ten years.

Many in Tunisia and abroad were stunned by the harshness of the sentences.

These swift and stern measures in the administrative and diplomatic fields as well as the meting out of punishent are very impressive and almost unbelievable if one recognizes that all this happened in an Arab country. In any other Arab country (except Morocco, and there, too, only to a degree) such behavior on the part of the government—to punish anybody for having molested Jews—is plainly inconceivable. Indeed, in most other Arab countries it was the Government itself which, on the day the war broke out in June, undertook the most cruel measures of persecution against the Jewish inhabitants.

Yet, this does not seem to be the whole story. There still remain some mysterious aspects to the riots in Tunis of June 5 which may perhaps never be fully clarified or explained. The main question is whether the demonstrations were spontaneous or organized; had they been encouraged directly, or partially instigated by officials of the Socialist Destour party. If the latter is true, on which policy level were Tunisian officials involved?

It is worthwhile to reproduce the testimony of several eyewitnesses, as published in the Parisian *Le Monde*. One of them wrote a couple of days after the event:

> It is not correct to say that this demonstration was spontaneous and that the police was unable to control it. The Tunisian police disposes of very energetic means, and besides, no demonstration can take place in Tunisia without the permission of the Government or the party . . .
>
> The demonstrators were organized and led by Destourien militants. . . . When the army and police decided, more than 4 hours after the riots started, to intervene, order was restored quite quickly. The general impression which prevailed among the European population was that the demonstration has been under control and limited; that it was therefore, premeditated and organized. By whom and on what level?

Another eyewitness wrote the same day:

> I spent part of the afternoon of June 5 in the streets of Tunis which were taken over by those whom President Bourguiba characterized as "hooligans" who marched behind unfurled Algerian and Tunisian banners, the whole facilitated by the police. They were all youngsters. I happened to witness an attack upon a house

occupied by Jewish inhabitants, who were spared only because one of the youngsters yelled to the others: 'Stop it . . . We were told only the stores, not the homes!'

And a group of Tunisian Jews wrote to *Le Monde:*

We have just left Tunisia and we would like to bring before you our testimony about the anti-Semitic demonstration which took place on June 5th in Tunis and in the suburbs. Indeed we will remain affected forever by this true pogrom. We still retain before our very eyes the scenes of violence, the fires and wholesale pillage and in our ears still ring the hysterical cries of a wild crowd, often aided by the police.

What took place was not at all a "spontaneous demonstration of young hooligans" as the official version tried to present it, but on the contrary, it was a concerted and premeditated affair, meticulously prepared in high quarters and abjectly executed for the most part by "young hooligans". . . .

Now several questions come to mind: How reliable are these reports of the eyewitnesses? And if they are reliable, did President Bourguiba know about the preparations for these demonstrations? And if he did not know, how is it possible for Tunisian officials, whether in the government or in the party, to have undertaken such an affair and to keep their leader in ignorance?

Of course, we cannot answer these questions with any certainty, but we may speculate. This can be done by analyzing the events preceding the outbreak of war in the Middle East and by trying to arrange them in some kind of logical sequence of cause and effect.

Perhaps it is worthwhile to keep in mind that 1967 had been a year of grave danger to Bourguiba both physically and politically. On March 14, 1967 he suffered from a severe heart attack, which almost cost him his life. For many weeks he was in the hospital, most of the time under an oxygen tent. Luckily he recovered, but it was a slow process. In May, though out of the hospital and danger, he still was under strict observation of his doctors. They did not permit him to resume in full, his daily activities.

The shock in the country caused by Bourguiba's illness was tremendous and the confusion and anxiety were universal. The editor-in-chief of *Jeune Afrique,* Beshir Ben Yahmed, an influential Tunisian, wrote in an article (April 30, 1967) titled "Tunisian Suspense," that

> if nothing in Tunis has changed outwardly since President Bourguiba's heart attack . . . yet nothing is as it was before.
>
> Prior to the crisis, Habib Bourguiba was the Father of Independence and President of the Republic; he dominated the scene. Since that time, he has become Father of the Nation, and what was rational support has become passionate attachment. . . . As if the illness has sublimated Bourguiba. Tunisians no longer see any faults and want nothing other than the permanence of his power. . . .

Yet this apotheosis may not have helped matters, since it is not always a good omen for the proper control over the behaviour of mortals. Gods are more often than not worshipped on one level and their injunctions violated on another. And Ben Yashir pointed out that "before, Habib Bourguiba, alone, decided on both administrative and political matters. Now, he reflects more than he acts, observes more than he decides. . . ."

This situation changed radically as we shall see, with his subsequent recovery, to such an extent, that in the months ahead he was to become his old dynamic and domineering self. But in May and in the first days of June 1967, it seemed he did not completely manage the reign of command. His colleagues tried to spare him from the various daily problems. He was consulted and he did indeed direct policy on the highest level, but *only* on the highest level.

And then the crisis in the Middle East came to a head. At first the Tunisians did not take it seriously and considered President Nasser's moves to be a bluff. A Tunisian diplomat at the United Nations is reported to have referred to Nasser as a clown and to his moves as antics. But a few days later, Nasser was to score his initial successes—the removal of the United Nations Emergency Force and the blockade of the Straits of Tiran, as well as the movement of Egyptians troops toward the frontier with Israel. These early inroads unleashed an unprecedented wave of frenzied enthusiasm in the Middle East and the momentum for a showdown with Israel mounted by the hour; the hysteria soon spilled over into the Maghreb. The Tunisians felt they could not remain outsiders to the cause of Palestine when the hour of decision seemed to have struck.

President Bourguiba himself appeared to have been impressed, though not convinced. Immediate decisions had to be made. On May 26, Tunisia decided to patch up, though only on a temporary basis—for the duration of the crisis—its relations with the Arab League, that she had been boycotting for the last two years. Bour-guiba also decided to resume diplomatic relations with Cairo, which Tunisia broke officially on October 3, 1966 and which were practically non-existant since April of that year.

President Bourguiba and various Tunisian officials, among them Foreign Minister Habib Bourguiba, Jr. and Defense Minister Mestiri made statements expressing solidarity with the Arabs in the Middle East and promising support. Thus, on May 26, 1967, the Foreign Minister addressed a message to the General Secre-tary of the Arab League, stating that Tunisia will support any Arab state which might become a victim of aggression on the part of Israel. He also sent messages to the Ambassadors of the mem-ber states of the Arab League in which he declared that "Tunisia is ready to answer any invitation emanating from any Arab coun-try actively to participate in any conference, or meeting, on any level, having as an object to discuss the present crisis in the Middle East."

Of course this is not much of a commitment, nor does it indi-cate that Tunisian cooperation is either unconditional or perma-nent. But before the deputies of the National Assembly he de-clared that though Tunisia is not ready to yield to Nasser's hegemony, in the present state of affairs the differences between the two countries should be considered as secondary in impor-tance, and priority should be given to the Palestine problem.

The Minister of Defense declared on May 26 that "Tunisia will fulfill, when the moment will come, its obligations, all its obliga-tions towards its Arab brothers exposed to threats of Israeli ag-gression. We are serious people. When our President, speaking on behalf of Tunisia at the Summit conference of Arab heads-of-state, committed himself to support our brothers, it was not out of mere courtesy or just in order to make verbal promises. We wish that all Arab leaders take as serious and sincere a stand towards Palestine, as he did."

On May 30, 1967 Bourguiba himself took a stand when he spoke before the Council of the Republic. He declared that "Tunisia is disposed to participate in any common action in the Middle East provided it is well intentioned and serious." He reaffirmed the solidarity of Tunisia with "the struggle of the Palestinians to regain their usurped fatherland" and with all the Arab people who support them. But he also indicated that there are differences between Tunisia and certain other Arab countries on the Palestine question, but "these have no bearing upon the substance of the problem. They only signify that Tunisia is jealous of her sovereignty and would not tolerate any slight to her dignity."

In the last days of May, mass meetings were held by the Socialist Destour party in major cities and towns to explain to the aroused masses the attitude of the Government. The decision was announced that Tunisia would send a contingent of her armed forces to the front in the Middle East in case hostilities broke out. It was also announced that Tunisia joined Libya in permitting the right of passage for Algerian troops ready to depart for the Middle East.

All this shows how much President Nasser was in the ascendancy in those days at the end of May and the beginning of June when the Arabs thought that the Egyptian leader actually had succeeded in inflicting a startling, perhaps mortal, blow to the Jewish State. Hysteria and exaltation swept the masses throughout the Arab world, crossing national frontiers. Tunisians, or at all events, some of them, were swept away by this onslaught of passion that they felt compelled to defy Bourguiba's policy and position—the first time in that nation's history.

More than that, however half-hearted and perfunctory the commitments of support and loyalty voiced by Tunisian leaders in those days, may have been, they nonetheless reflect the momentum of the powerful emotional forces unleashed by President Nasser. These official endorsements were obviously interpreted by some lower echelons of the party and government as sufficient justification to take to the streets. These officials may have initiated, or agreed to have others organize the street demonstrations, basing their action on the decisions of the Tunisian government to side with the Arabs in case an armed conflict broke out. It is also possible that some of these officials were pro-Nasser and thought they had an opportunity to exploit the situation and could with impunity deviate from the official line prescribed by the highest authorities.

Bourguiba himself, and probably most of the members of the Cabinet and the leadership of the party were kept uninformed either as to the whole project, or at any event as to the nature of the demonstration. Perhaps also none of the officials really expected the demonstrations to degenerate to large scale rioting and looting. Otherwise it is difficult to explain the vehemence and ferocity of Bourguiba's reaction as well as that of the Administrative and juridical measures taken by the government on the highest level to punish those who were involved as well as those government officials who should have been responsible for preserving law and order. One may perhaps also assume that when the Government issued statements of support for the Arabs in the cause of Palestine they still did not believe that hostilities would actually break out in the Middle East.

Whatever the background and true causes of the riots, they came both as a surprise and shock to President Bourguiba who forthwith decided to take matters into his own hands.

Before we end our examination of this dismal episode a few remarks are perhaps called for to help place it in proper perspective. In the first days of June 1967 the war hysteria and anti-Jewish outbreaks were not peculiar to Tunisia but swept all of the four countries of the Maghreb. Yet, by comparison, the riots in Tunisia, though serious were actually limited in scope; they were, at all events, not in the nature and magnitude of the events that took place in the neighboring countries. While there were no casualties in Tunisia, only loss to property—dozens of Jewish shops and homes pillaged—in neighboring Morocco and Libya the riots resulted in a considerable loss of life. In Morocco two Jews were killed and in Tripoli, Libya, where the riots lasted an entire week there were, according to reports, more than one hundred dead and many more wounded.

But what is most important to keep in mind is the fact that the Israel-Arab conflict and its aftermath did not shake or endanger the regime in Tunisia, while in Algeria it almost brought about the overthrow of Col. Boumedienne's government. An armed rebellion led by some of the most outstanding officers of the Algerian army and heroes of the resistance movement which fought the French, broke out on December 14, 1967 and the rebels marched on Algiers. The rebellion failed but it shook the regime and widespread reforms were promised to be undertaken after those dramatic events. Boumedienne did as much as confess that the rebellion was the culmination of events that started with Algeria's deep commitment to the Arab side in the war with Israel June last. The opponents of the regime then accused it of meddling too much in external affairs, entering adventures in a far away region while neglecting pressing problems at home.

There is no rationality to the disturbances and upheavals which the Palestine problem provokes in the various Arab countries. In Tunisia the masses rioted seemingly because their Government was not committed enough to the war against Israel, while in Algeria they rebelled because President Boumedienne was too much involved. All this is only a perfect vindication of Bourguiba's thesis, that the Israeli-Arab conflict is a source of endless tensions and internal dangers to all the Arab countries; unless it is resolved peaceably the various Arab states cannot dedicate themselves to the urgent task of internal development and economic improvement.

Whatever the protestations of his doctors and colleagues might have been, it seems that Bourguiba decided on that tumultous and dramatic day in June to take command of the affairs of State, regardless of the risks to his health. And most interestingly, having taken this bold, and yet hazardous decision, he regained his vigour and scored a most spectacular recovery; so much so that everyone —foreign dignitaries, journalists, colleagues and physicians could not but marvel. Shortly he was in complete control, and in every respect his old fighting self.

Once more he became the firebrand of controversy in the Arab world. And in the general disarray and shock resulting from the humiliating defeat the Arabs suffered at the hands of the Israelis, he was the only leader who emerged level-headed, realistic and who tried by direct contact with the leaders of the beaten nations to steer them on to the road to recovery. His efforts have so far met with limited success. Once more he finds himself swimming against the current.

As long as the short war raged in the Middle East Bourguiba felt that he had to suspend his quarrels with the other Arab leaders; now was not the time to challenge, criticize or attack the governments engaged in a life and death struggle. He felt Tunisia could not remain aloof, outside, so to speak, of the Arab family. Under such tragic circumstances there was no other possibility left for an Arab leader than to declare his solidarity and promise help. Such an attitude is natural enough especially if one takes into consideration that even Bourguiba had to reckon with the sensibilities and emotions of his own people, despite his own rational views and attitudes.

Indeed, in the same televised speech to the nation in which he castigated the anti-Jewish rioters and demanded they be sent to the gallows, he was still circumspect enough to appear as an Arab patriot and not a traitor. He declared that the Tunisian army was ready and awaited a request from other Arab nations to send

men and materiel to the front. A token contingent of a few hundred men was in fact ordered "to the front." But it made haste
slowly. The contingent never left Tunisian soil and it took them
four days to travel one hundred miles, from Tunis to Sousse.
When, at the end of these four days, a cease fire was declared on
June 9, they returned quickly to their base. It took them only four
hours to make the return journey. At all events, on June 5, President Bourguiba addressed the following message of support to
President Nasser:

> We have given orders to our army to be in a state of readiness and
> to answer to the request of the Arab nation in these fateful cir-
> cumstances for her future.
>
> At the moment when the people of the United Arab Republic is
> engaged in a war against Israeli aggression, Tunisia takes her
> place at your side in order to support your struggle by putting
> at your disposal her material resources.

Next day, on June 6 Nasser telephoned Bourguiba and thanked
him for his "courageous stand and support." This honeymoon
lasted exactly two days. On June 7 Nasser launched his "canard"
about American and British military participation in the war on
the side of Israel and as a result Egypt and five other Arab countries broke diplomatic relations with the United States and England. Bourguiba, as in March 1965 during the crisis with West
Germany, did not follow suit. On that day the old rift was wide
open again. Bourguiba indicated that he was not going to do things
which were outrageous to common sense and simple honesty,
even during a crisis of emergency. Besides, he could not, even for
the sake of unity, sacrifice Tunisia's national interests. The United
States is a friend and not an enemy of Tunisia, and a most reliable
and helpful friend to boot.

The Tunisians also began to explain that the renewal of relations with the Arab League and with Egypt was not undertaken
solely for the sake of restoring a united front in time of such
trouble. The resumption of relations enabled Tunisian representative to be present in Cairo and to influence President Nasser as
well as the leaders in other Arab countries to follow a more reasonable and realistic course, both toward eventual negotiations with
Israel as well as toward preventing a complete estrangement from
the West.

Special Tunisian representatives were dispatched therefore both to Cairo and Amman. Dr. Sadok Mokaddem, President of the Tunisian National Assembly, arrived in Cairo on June 7, and Minister of Justice, Mongi Slim arrived the same day in Amman to talk to King Hussein.

There was speculation that Mongi Slim tried to persuade the King in two ways. First to disown the hoax about British and American participation in the war against the Arabs; and second, to accept the principle of negotiations with Israel.

We know that to different degrees both Nasser and Hussein have in subsequent appearances expressed many a view originally advocated by Bourguiba, though he did not succeed in selling them on the idea of direct negotiations.

When the disaster of the war in June became apparent Bourguiba immediately offered (as early as June 13) three suggestions: One, directed to the Arabs, argued that it was self-defeating to continue to feed on hatred, resentment and the negative aspiration to wreak vengeance against Israel. The second point was addressed to the Western powers: that it would not serve their best interests "to rub it in" into the wounds of the Arabs by making them swallow a diplomatic defeat after having suffered such a military disaster. And the third, addressed to General de Gaulle, asked him to consider the role of mediator in the dispute.

Bourguiba suggested that the French President might under the circumstances be the most qualified personage for this most difficult job. Tunisian diplomacy made great exertions in this direction, both in Paris and in Tunis. As early as June 12, the Tunisian Ambassador called on the French Foreign Minister, Mr. Couve de Murville, conveying a written message from Bourguiba to de Gaulle. After the audience, Ambassador Massmoudi declared: "Between Israel and the Arab countries, France occupies an excellent position. May the interested parties listen to his advice." He also hinted that as a result of such mediation direct negotiations between the two warring parties might ensue.

Bourguiba also indicated that Massmoudi recommend de Gaulle as a mediator because of all the Western powers France alone had come out of the Middle Eastern war with the least political and moral damage. In his opinion the other Western powers should support his suggestion because it was the only realistic alternative to the Russians playing a dominant role in the present affairs in the Middle East, both directly as well as indirectly through Marshall Tito of Yugoslavia.

De Gaulle seems to have been impressed. The next day, on

June 13, the French President answered Bourguiba as follows:

Dear Mr. President

As you, so I too deplore the cruel damages due to the violence which ravages the Middle East.

Now, since the military operations have ceased and though the respective position of the parties on the ground could have changed, it is evident that the same problems remain, only much more aggravated.

As far as France is concerned she will persevere in her disinterestedness which she has chosen and which appears to be the only one which could one day lead to equilibrium and peace. I have no doubt that this policy meets with that of Tunisia, whose sentiments and interests, under the circumstances are not in opposition to our own.

These were only the immediate reactions while the war was still going on and at the time when the United Nations tried to impose a cease fire. But with the end of hostilities Bourguiba decided to attack the real issues and to make the Arabs see the true causes of their defeat and the lessons to be drawn from their past errors. It was not an easy task, yet he was indomitable. It was his desire that Tunisia play her role in the conclaves of the Arab leaders and to present there his views and offer his suggestions as to the future course of Arab affairs. On June 13 he announced that Tunisia would participate in an Arab Summit conference, if it were seriously prepared and a detailed agenda were drawn up.

But he was soon to discover that the method and spirit prevailing in inter-Arab relationships did not change radically. Bourguiba learned from the newspapers that at a meeting of four chiefs-of-state—Nasser of Egypt, Boumedienne of Algeria, Atassi of Syria and Azhari of Sudan—it had been decided that a meeting of the Arab League Foreign Ministers would be held shortly in Khartoum. Tunisia was not privy to any of these preliminary consultations. Moreover, according to an Egyptian publication the chiefs-of state assembled in Cairo also decided the preliminary conditions each Arab state would have to accept in order to qualify for participation in the conference. These conditions were three:

1. To adopt a policy of reprisals against the West by at least breaking diplomatic relations;

2. To adopt a policy of friendship to Russia and other Communist states for having sided with the Arabs; and

3. To be willing to use all the means at the disposal of the Arabs to fight the enemies of Arabism, that is the Western countries. These would include the withdrawal of accounts from British and American banks, the liquidation of military bases, and halting the flow of oil.

The Tunisians were indignant and announced they would boycott the conference unless their own conditions were accepted. An official spokesman protested at the manner in which the conference had been announced and the agenda determined. "Tunisia will abstain from participating in the conference," he declared, "if it will be held under the conditions previously indicated. . . . It is astonishing that it has been decided upon by a small number of governments without preliminary consultations. . . ."

Pointing out that no official information relative to this project had reached the government in Tunis, the spokesman affirmed that "it is the very problem of the nature of the relationship between the Arab states which is thus being posed and which remains to be clarified. The Tunisian position is quite known, namely, that each Arab country, being a sovereign state, cannot be taken for granted and can be counted upon only if decisions were arrived at by free and preliminary agreement."

The Destourian daily Al Amal severely criticized the behavior of the Arab countries which had decided to call the conference.

"It is intolerable, we say it clearly and explicitly that we will never approve of such a procedure. These Arab governments acted as if the other (governments) were satellites constrained to carry out the instructions which were handed down to them."

Bourguiba used this controversy to fire his first shot at the leadership responsible for the disaster. "The road followed so far has led us three times into an impasse; it's no use to persist . . . and it is a time to change our methods. Now is the time to put our minds together in order to arrive at a common strategy inspired by our respective experiences."

He also used this occasion to castigate those Arab governments which had broken relations with the United States and Great Britain, a step which he thought would be of no avail. The Arabs must learn not to use threats when they are not sure they will be in a position to carry them out.

The Tunisian protest had its effect. The Sudanese President, as host to the conference, sent a special representative to Tunis to deny that the published conditions were authoritative and to work out with the Tunisian government the modalities of their participation in the forthcoming conference.

It is against this background that the first pan-Arab conference took place in the wake of the June disaster. In fact two conferences of Arab Foreign Ministers were held, both in the Sudanese capital Khartoum. One opened on August 1, 1967, the other on August 25. Both were marked by a fierce offensive on the part of Tunisia against Arab leadership and policies.

Selected to represent Tunisia and her views at both meetings was the capable and eloquent Mongi Slim, Minister of Justice. His was the most articulate voice of the moderate Arab governments participating in the Conferences. What the latter did not dare express, for one reason or another, Mongi Slim spelled out in lucid arguments and great forcefulness.

To begin with, he created a commotion when Mr. Shukairy, the then leader of the Palestine Liberation Organization, mounted the podium and took his place among the Arab Foreign Ministers. The Tunisian, it is reported, rose and protested his admission, let alone the participation of Shukairy. "What Government does this gentleman represent?" he asked sarcastically. He reminded his colleagues that Shukairy, perhaps more than anybody else, was responsible for the Arabs having lost the propaganda battle even before they were defeated militarily. He charged that Shukairy continued to make irresponsible statements to the press and on the radio and thus compromises the cause of the Arabs.

He explained that precisely because Tunisia believes it is the Palestinians, themselves, who should assume the main role in the fight for their rights, that it is a calamity to have such a man as Shukairy represent them. As long as such a man represents them, the Arab cause has little chance to make any headway; indeed it is doomed in advance.

Mongi Slim is also reported to have demanded from the Arab leaders an apology to Bourguiba for having been vilified as a traitor and imperialist stooge when two years earlier he had the courage and foresight to predict events and to express ideas which are now accepted by many other Arab leaders.

Egypt's Foreign Minister, Mahmoud Riad, explained that now was no time to settle accounts of the past; that one should concentrate on the urgent problems posed by the present crisis. And as to Shukairy, Mr. Riad explained that one cannot change the Palestinian leadership from one day to another; that anyhow the most urgent problem of the day was not Palestine, but how to proceed to "liquidate the traces of the latest aggression" against the three Arab countries. And inasmuch as the question of Palestine would be discussed the best thing under the circumstances would be to proceed without paying undue attention to Shukairy's opinions and statements. Mr. Shukairy was allowed to keep his seat.

But this was only an incident at the opening of the conference. More important was Mongi Slim's speech on general policy. Though the proceedings of the conference were behind closed doors the contents of his speech, as indeed of those by other participants, "leaked" as is usual in such international gatherings. Mongi Slim is reported to have delivered a sharp indictment of Arab policy concerning Palestine. He spoke of the urgent need to draw lessons from the military disaster as well as from the defeat in the field of propaganda. He outlined Tunisia's proposals for a new policy. Tunisia felt that it could afford to be so outspoken for two reasons: first, because Tunisia's views expressed in the past were completely vindicated by the subsequent tragic events; and second, because during the crisis in May and June, Tunisia ranged itself "body and soul" with the Arab family of nations.

Significantly, Mongi Slim's unmitigated indictment of past Arab performance as well as his appeal to adopt a realistic policy for the future, did not provoke any of the reprobations and condemnations so characteristic in the past.

The second conference which opened on August 26, 1967, was marked by greater controversy and disarray. This was due to a major address delivered by President Bourguiba on August 23 in Kef before the Executive Committee of the Tunisian Students Association, but made public only on the 25th, that is, on the very eve of the opening of the conference. In this speech Bourguiba accused Nasser of having provoked the war in June, and suggested the Arabs abandon their policy, which he characterized as hopeless and one which would lead only to a dead end. He called upon the Arabs to end the state of belligerence against Israel, and to recognize the Jewish State.

These suggestions formulated in the typical Bourguibian eloquence and power threw the conference into disharmony. What many delegates especially resented was not so much the contents of the speech as its timing.

In this address Bourguiba laid down the basic elements for a settlement of the Palestine conflict. Most of the suggestions were not new. He expressed them during his campaign in 1965. But since then, and under the impact of the disastrous war, he developed them, brought them up to date, drew the most logical and courageous conclusions from the new situation. Thus they took on not only new shape but also new and vigorous meaning. He seems to have come to the conclusion that the state of affairs of the Arabs was so sick that one must analyze it with all the necessary ruthlessness and draw the logical conclusions regardless how painful and cruel.

It is significant that once more he chose the student organization (as he had done more than two years earlier) as a platform to voice his daring and revolutionary ideas. On both occasions he seems to have decided to take the bull by the horns, so to speak, since it is the students who are the most recalcitrant element in his country and who are most influenced both by Nasser's pan-Arab and Moscow's pan-Communist propaganda.

The students had just held a conference and had adopted a variety of resolutions on international problems—the Middle East, Vietnam, South Africa, Rhodesia, etc. The resolutions seemed to have annoyed President Bourguiba, though, on the whole they also contained a perfunctory endorsement of the Government's policies. He therefore started his speech with a sarcastic remark that the resolutions reflected the students' concern with what was going on in all the continents of the globe except with the problems concerning the Tunisian students themselves. He would therefore be justified to conclude that they had no problems or difficulties of their own. But he knew that it was not so; that there were problems which had to be studied and dealt with, except that the conference behaved not as one representing a professional-academic organization but rather a political formation " and this is not the way we conceive of the students' role."

After having defined his views concerning the role of the students and the duties they are expected to perform, he explained that only after having studied Tunisia's problems thoroughly and gaining a profound understanding of her needs and of how to cope with them, would they be in a position to understand also the problems in other parts of the world, and not vice versa. Thus, and only thus would they be able "to resist the pressures regardless from where they come and to form their own individual judgment." They would then reject the glibness of foreign demagogues and act according to the dictates of reason. "In a country, such as ours," he said, "where one easily permits oneself to be carried away by passions, it is not easy to practice foresight. Such a virtue demands long training. You know what I am hinting at (the riots on June 5. S.M.) "

After this introduction he tackled the problems arising from the Arab defeat. The Palestine conflict was a complicated problem, he said, and required thorough knowledge of the various elements and aspects of the situation, without which one could not understand what happened, why it happened, or how to remedy the disaster. The trouble with Arab leaders was that they did not act according to the data at hand but according to emotionalism and wishful thinking, thus becoming victims of their own ignorance and miscalculations. Without referring to him by name he used, as an example, President Nasser of Egypt:

> The mistakes of a leader can become fatal for his own people despite the laudable intentions which animate him. This is what happened just recently. Because [the planes] of the aggressor were expected to come from the east and came instead from the west; because one miscalculated the actual balance of forces, and because the moment was inappropriate to modify by force an unjust equilibrium which resulted from a previous defeat, the Arab countries are now subjected to the worst humiliations of a new defeat and the occupation of new parts of their territories.

> Israel was content with her frontiers of 1956 and neither did she claim the entire city of Jerusalem, nor the west bank of the Jordan River, nor half of the Suez Canal, nor the other territories which she now occupies in the Sinai Peninsula. But a series of measures were taken deliberately and without considering the risks involved to bar her access to the Gulf of Aqaba, which constituted one of the elements of this equilibrium that had been tolerated as the lesser evil following the tri-partite aggression of 1956 and which had been embodied in an international agreement.

> One knew very well that the adversary would not fail to react and the Arab press itself made it quite clear. (*Al Ahram,* of May 26, 1967.) This reaction was evidently foreseen. More than that, one awaited Israel's reaction, so as to justify a counter-attack which was supposed "to put an end to the State of Israel."

Since then, the Israeli forces have reached the bank of the Suez Canal and the Arabs after having been subjected to a downpour of fire and napalm are once more on the road to exodus.

As a miscalculation it is truly monumental.

This is how, in good faith, one provokes catastrophe. Also, in politics one always must foresee the various ways in which the adversary may react and one, therefore, must take the necessary measures to meet any eventuality. This is an equation of multiple-unknowns with which a leader is confronted, but which often escapes our understanding.

According to Bourguiba the main reason for these Arab defeats is the obstinacy of their leaders who insist on playing "Don Quixote" and to be qualified, whatever the risk and the price, as "revolutionary" or "progressive." Thus while they go forth to battle wind mills of imperialism they ignore the condition of their own people whose welfare should be their main preoccupation. Instead they let their people sink "in the blackest of miseries. The most elementary freedoms are denied to them." The Palestine problem is an integral aspect of this policy on the part of the Arab leaders, a policy of "dropping the substance for its shadow."

What are the substantive facts of the Palestine problem? And he explained:

> "The State of Israel is recognized both by the United States and Russia. It is a member of the United Nations whose existence is not contested by anybody except the Arab states. Under these circumstances, it is futile adamantly to refuse to recognize this reality. To claim to efface Israel from the map of the globe is to condemn oneself to almost total isolation.

> It is regrettable, unjust, but this is how it is. . . .

> If we want to try putting an end to this injustice, I say that we must take such a fact [Israel's recognition by most states] into account. Instead, the policy which the Arabs have pursued up to now, has resulted in channelling the sympathy of all the peoples, even of the Communist bloc, and of "the Third World" to the side of Israel. It is universally admitted that it is Egypt who created the *casus belli* while from our point of view it is the very existence of Israel which constitutes an aggression. . . .

> After the defeat which has just been inflicted upon them the Arab states should reconsider the policy which they have stub-

bornly pursued for the past 20 years. Whatever the price to pay, the lesser evil would be to put an end to the state of belligerency in order to recover the lands which have been conquered by the Hebrew State, and thus to avert even greater dangers. After that they will have to devote themselves to raise their peoples to the level of strong and highly developed nations, so that one day they may be in a position to prevent any injustice, to deter any aggression and to become the stronger party.

FOR DIRECT PEACE NEGOTIATIONS

This speech caused deep consternation among the assembled Foreign-Ministers at Khartoum and strong protests were voiced.

On the morrow, a spokesman for the Political Bureau of the Socialist Destour party issued a statement that Bourguiba "did not make any recommendation concerning the recognition of Israel. . . . And besides, he does not consider himself qualified at all to make one." In view of the explicit text, officially published, this new statement only increased the confusion.

Yet the Tunisians further explained their explanation. Bourguiba's speech was intended, they said, as food for thought not only for the conference of the Foreign Ministers, but mainly for the Summit Conference of the Arab heads-of-state to take place a few days hence, on August 29. Bourguiba is not going to participate personally in it, but his "second in command" Mr. Bahi Ladgham, will. The statement issued by the Political Bureau should not be understood, they asserted, as a denial or retreat, but rather as a confirmation of a policy thoroughly elaborated by the Tunisian government, a policy which Mr. Ladgham will expose at the Summit. This policy does not entail an *a priori* recognition of Israel, but the beginning of direct peace negotiations with Israel. In such negotiation the Arabs will hold the problem of recognition as their trump card.

In a "private interview" (whatever this may mean) with *Le Monde*'s J. Ben Brahem, President Bourguiba said:

> Let's say it clearly: what we suggest is to cut losses. Let's demand comprehensive negotiations on the whole issue concerning peace in the Middle East without announcing in advance what our position and our arguments will be, as is, by the way, the rule of the game in every negotiating conference. Our point of depar-

ture should in any case be the United Nations resolutions of 1949.* Such a position on our part would provide us with an indisputable legitimacy, especially since Israel has never carried out these resolutions. . . . Starting from this position, everything else is open for discussion. . . .

According to J. Ben Braham, Bourguiba thinks that it is easy to see where such a proposition would lead: Either Israel refuses to negotiate ("and this would be our first diplomatic success"). Or Israel accepts. In that event there is no doubt that pressures will be exerted by all quarters in order to induce both parties to make concessions. As we know, it is in the nature of things, that the vanquished party will profit more than the victor. In this connection Bourguiba counts upon the joint support of the great powers, "who have enough of this firebrand burning in the Middle East" and he thinks that a general peace initiative by the Arabs would contribute to bring about a reversal of world public opinion in their favor. "And besides, as things stand now, what is there to lose?"

The important thing is, therefore, to start negotiations going without in advance making a stumbling block of the problem of recognition. Of course, one might fail. Then, and only then, Tunisia will admit, that since the Arabs have proven their good faith, they will have no other choice but to renew the war, whatever the cost and the duration.

J. Ben Braham asked Bourguiba: Will the Arab chiefs-of-state listen at Khartoum to Bahi Ladgham, when he speaks this kind of language? The President said that he does not hold out much hope. He does not entertain any illusions concerning his chances actually to convince his Arab homologues. Even King Hussein, who had just paid a visit to him, listened to his plan without revealing either agreement or disagreement. So what could he expect from the others?

His pessimism was justified. The Khartoum Summit conference, whatever achievements it may be credited with, rejected both the principle of recognition as well as direct negotiations.

---

* According to *Al Amal*, the official newspaper of the Socialist Destour Party of August 29, 1967: "The Armistice agreements of 1949 stipulate the existence of Israel, and the determination of both parties, signatories of these agreements, to install a durable peace among them."

NASSER MUST STEP DOWN

From this state of affairs Bourguiba drew one more logical conclusion: that the Arabs would not be in a position to change their policy and redeem themselves unless they changed their leadership. From then on he repeatedly voiced the opinion that Nasser must resign. He must do it not only for the sake of Palestine and the Arabs in general, but not less for Egypt's own interests. A statesman must take credit not only for victory but also be held responsible for defeat and draw the consequences. "In a modern state," he declared on September 30, 1967, at a pan-Arab conference of Ministers of Information held in Bizerte "when a leader makes such mistakes and suffers such defeat [as Nasser], he yields his place to somebody else, who will apply a different policy."

In an interview, at the beginning of October 1967 with *Le Figaro*'s correspondent, Ives Cuau, he picked up the same theme, explaining that Nasser's resignation would be of great service to the cause of the Arabs and to his own country. "It would be a worthwhile sacrifice . . . and would facilitate a solution [to the Palestine problem]".

Since this interview constitutes, perhaps, the most comprehensive and far-reaching pronouncement he made in the aftermath of the war in June, it is worthwhile to reproduce extensive portions of it. It is also important to note that Ives Cuau, who knows Bourguiba well, found him in excellent health, when received in his Presidential Palace in Carthage. Despite the recent and severe heart attack Bourguiba did not appear to have changed. His gait was brisk, his manners lively and his deep blue eyes sparkling as ever. But the correspondent also noticed that the President had acquired a majestic serenity when analyzing historic events.

Understandably, the conversation immediately turned upon the crisis in the Middle East and, of course, upon the role President Nasser played in it. Did the Egyptian leader change? Did he after the disaster in June become more realistic? Is one justified to expect him to become a "Bourguibist"?

Bourguiba remarked wittily that Nasser would not cherish such an epithet. Besides it is not a matter of personal relationship.

> The true problem which arises today is in one of leadership. What is the role of a leader? I cannot, for the life of me, perceive how

one can be a leader and be yoked to the masses, instead of guiding them.

During my long career I often had to swim against the current. In the second World War, for instance, the masses were inclined to sympathize with the Axis. I did not follow them. I fight for what appears to me to be the truth. It is a matter of honesty and morality. A statesman should not be swept away by the multitude but always be ahead of it. . . . On certain occasions Nasser appeared before Arab gatherings as a man with a sense of reality and we know that he tried to restrain the bellicose ardor of the Syrian leaders when, for instance, the [former chief-of-state] Hamin El Hafez asked to give him only two hours to split Israel in two and destroy the Jewish state. Yet, in 1967, Nasser indulged in a [reckless] gamble and hoped to get away with it. He organized that great military parade in the streets of Cairo and demanded the withdrawal of the Blue Helmets [U.N. Peace Keeping Force], which, in fact, he probably did not wish to happen. Even today, regardless how hard I try, I cannot understand why he blockaded the Gulf of Aqaba, when without this measure he might have perhaps come out the winner. . . .

We are now going through a difficult period, in which the Arabs are both subject to humiliation and dominated by passion. I know how difficult it is for people to change. It isn't that I personally wish that Nasser resign, and besides it is not my business. He did what he could, and sometimes he has achieved great things for his country. All the Arabs now feel sympathy for him, but at this juncture it would perhaps be better for himself and for his country to quit. Without him it would be easier to arrive at a solution. . . .

It is always difficult for those who made war also to make peace. Had we played the card of peace and even that of cooperation, we could probably, as a compensation, obtain considerable advantages and world opinion would have reversed itself in our favor. For what counts most is effectiveness—the end results.

How did Lenin do it? He was beaten. He immediately accepted the treaty of Brest-Litovsk. The time will come when a new balance of forces may evolve. But to maintain this position of not recognizing Israel, not to negotiate, not even to try to find out what her conditions are, what she would be ready to concede in exchange for a durable peace, all this is, in my mind, just playing Israel's game and falling into her trap. This is to enable the Israelis to remain indefinitely at the present cease fire lines. This is what I call expanding in the role of a victim of aggression. (en qualité d'agresse'). It was necessary on the contrary that the Arabs let Israel retain the character of an aggressor.

Since 1947 Israel has benefited at regular intervals from the errors of the Arabs. Israel proceeded in stages; it is Israel which exercised Bourguibism. Now the Israelis say: the United Nations Resolutions of 1947 are out of date. No, they are not out of date, if by way of compensation we accord Israel the right to live in peace. For her the essential is not to possess Sinai, but a territory within which limits she could live in full security. The Israelis have won a battle but they have not won the war and they risk never winning it. The Arab world is immense, they cannot spread themselves thin in the interior of Egypt or Syria.

The problem of the refugees and that of the guerrillas risk bringing about an endless mess. It is very beautiful to have won such a victory in six days, but Israel, is now, in the last analysis, a ghetto which ever expands, but which remains a ghetto nonetheless in the midst of refugees, hatred and tears.

If we wish to look far ahead we can perhaps perceive the possibility of arriving at a compromise which would lead Israel to withdraw to frontiers which they have themselves previously accepted. But in order to achieve this one will need other leaders.

When I reason like this, I do it as if I were at the head of the people of Palestine. In my fight for independence for the people of Tunisia, I began with putting forward a legal base: the respect for the protectorate. Certain Tunisians held that all this is already old hat, and though I, too, agreed with them, I was in opposition to them and I had to face the beginning of a civil war. The history of Youssefism, was exactly that. I threw all my personal prestige into the balance. But the Parliament in Paris and French public opinion, were not ready to accord us more than what Mendes-France came to give us. One must have a sense of the possible and this is not always easy. There is no question about my going to the Middle East and recreating for myself another career there. But I am nonetheless in a position to offer some advice and to hope that the day will come when a young man of that region will take note. . . .

There is an immense international injustice in the origins of the creation of the State of Israel. But the Israelis are now at the Suez Canal, largely thanks to the errors of certain Arab leaders. After fifteen years of Arab revolutionism this is not a very brilliant balance sheet. The best way to get out of the mess is to face realities. Many of the leaders in the Middle East are forced, in fact, to admit the existence of Israel but they do not draw any benefit from it, when they might as well cash in on it simply by saying it in a loud voice. Alas, politics!

—— You have spoken on several occasions of the possibility of an eventual cooperation between Israel and the Arab states in case the Jewish state accepts a return to United Nations legality, as you put it, asked the interviewer.

—— From the moment that the state of belligerence comes to an end, there will be no possibility not to cooperate. Cooperation will transform the nature of the problem. Cooperation will probably even permit the Arabs to discover that the Jews are people like all other. . . . For us, in order to emancipate ourselves from French tutelage we had to go to France and to impregnate ourselves with her culture and her techniques. Among all the Arab countries, the one which thought it could escape colonization by shutting itself up in complete isolation, was Yemen. The result was not very encouraging. Cooperation is a form of confrontation. Certain among us Arabs, came to a stop at the stage of fantasy, passion, lyricism, and all this is regrettable.

—— When you speak of a return to the United Nations legality, do you think that this would easily be acceptable to King Hussein of Jordan?

—— Yes, I do. And not only to him. But one also has to take into consideration the noxious effect exercised by certain propaganda which rages in the Middle East. The masses were accustomed to the idea of a lightning victory over Israel and of occupying Tel Aviv. This is not exactly what happened. A long campaign of clarification and education will certainly be necessary, but there is no reason to think that an Arab people could not in the long run begin to understand the language of reason. This is the language I used personally in Jericho, in 1965, before the Palestinian refugees, to the great bewilderment of those who accompanied me, who were responsible for my physical safety. But I told them what I would have told Tunisians and they applauded me.

Another interviewer, the renowned author and editor of *Le Monde*, M. André Fontain, asked him if Nasser were to step down who then could take his place? Could Egypt find in this difficult hour a man capable of wielding the same authority as Nasser? Bourguiba's answer sounded as if, in his opinion, almost anybody would be better than the present ruler. The idea that the charismatic ruler is indispensable and irreplaceable is nothing but a fallacy. "Look," he said, "at other instances. Nkrumah, Sukarno, Ben Bella—all these 'indispensable' leaders have fallen. Yet, there is always a Ghana, an Indonesia, an Algeria, and they are not worse off."

In Egypt the need for a change is even more urgent, since we know from history, "that a leader who lost a war is not the proper man to make peace." Who should replace Nasser? "Why not the one whom Nasser himself has designated?"*

He elaborated the same theme before a group of American journalists who accompanied Vice-President Humphrey on his African tour in January 1968. On January 10, he told the assembled American journalists:

> Egypt is politically humiliated and economically bankrupt. The situation in that country is tragic. After having received for 15 years abundant aid from both the United States and Russia, the Egyptians are no longer even in a position to pursue a policy of non-alignment. They are forced to *align* themselves [with Russia] and yet cannot hope to see the Russians helping them to liberate Palestine, since Russia recognizes Israel.
>
> In the Middle East, certain rulers still nourish rancor vis-à-vis the Anglo-Saxons for having helped the creation of the State of Israel, but they persistently forget that the Soviet Union equally participated in that creation. . . .

The Russians, he said, are playing their own game and he expressed concern about the presence of the Russian fleet in the Mediterranean. He regarded this naval and military buildup as an inevitable consequence of the Soviet Union's ambition to dominate the "Third World."

Speaking about the inter-Arab relations he declared:

> Actually, these relations are not good. They are imprinted with duplicity, hypocrisy, fear, humiliation and hegemony.

---

* On June 9, 1967, President Nasser in a broadcast to the nation announced his decision to resign "completely and irrevocably" from every official post and political role. And he designated as his successor one of the Vice-Presidents, Mr. Zakariah Mohieddine. But under the impact of popular demonstrations, the same evening he withdrew his resignation.

In order that Arab policy undergo a change, it is necessary that there is a change in mentality and leadership. For instance, a man who led his people for twenty years without having achieved positive results has to yield his place so that a new policy is given a chance.

It is only then that we could get together and try to discuss and to arrive at a mutual understanding without using subterfuges, traps and kicks under the table.

Bourguiba considers peace in the Middle East imperative from still another angle: the danger of Russia taking over. "Regardless of how one looks at it the Communists are like other totalitarians: when they seize something, they keep it." While with the western powers there is always the prospect that they will eventually withdraw their forces from territories they occupy. As to the Americans they are not even, by nature, imperialists. On the contrary, they have to be given considerable credit for the decolonization process which took place all over the world. He always opposed the totalitarians, he told André Fontain, "and I was always proven right. So today, too, I am on the side of liberty. I cannot do otherwise. It is in this spirit that my outlook was formed."

But the danger is not only one of Russian domination. An even greater menace lies in the prospect that the Middle East may become the scene of a confrontation between the Soviet Union and the United States, since the latter would not permit the global equilibrium of forces to be upset. The mutual attacks, loss of life, and destruction that are taking place in Vietnam, may become the lot of the people in the Middle East with the super-powers taking sides and leaving the cities and the countryside a shambles. We should not forget that in Vietnam, too, what started as a just war of liberation degenerated into wholesale slaughter inflicted by both friends and foes.

It would, therefore, be in the best interests of both the Arabs and the Israelis to arrive at an early accommodation. It seems nonsensical to Bourguiba to make a procedural issue—direct negotiation with Israel—a stumbling block, when on substantive issues the Arabs declared themselves, (at all events behind closed doors at the Khartoum conferences and behind the scenes in the United Nations) willing to yield so many points to the Jewish State. In the Tunisian's view, they have already conceded in advance all they should, but they have derived no advantages from their concessions for the simple reason that they have refused to state them in direct negotiations.

At the same time, he also appeals to the Israelis to renounce their intransigeance, suspicions and fears and show a willingness to understand the Arabs and to strive to reach with them a mutually acceptable settlement.

> Now, after their victory, (he told Leo Bauer, of the German weekly *Stern*) I would advise the Israelis not to overstrain the bow. By doing this, they will only arouse new hatred. For the sake of peace, both parties must offer mutual concessions and sacrifices. I believe that uncompromising attitudes are not in the interest of either side. The Israelis must now prove their maturity and take into consideration the feelings of their Arab neighbors. After all, these Arabs are not responsible for the persecutions the Jews of Europe were unfortunately subject to. These took place in Europe and not in our regions.

According to the *London Economist* (January 20, 1968) he also advised the Israelis to be more forthcoming about what kind of peace terms they have in mind: "They should not require Arab leaders to go on a mystery tour."

Would he consider mediating between the Arab States and Israel?, Leo Bauer asked him in *Stern* (October 15, 1968). He did not rule out the possibility. "To do this," he answered, "I should be asked, and this did not happen yet . . . Mediation is necessary. But this is contingent upon the willingness of both parties. I am under the impression that it is not ripe yet." Then he also remarked that when one speaks about him as a mediator, one should also keep in mind the jealousies prevailing among the Arab leaders . . .

When asked whether his statement about his potential role as a mediator as well as his other opinions expressed during the interview, could be made public, he answered: "Of course. I would even consider it important. I always expressed my opinions openly, and shall continue to do so in the future."

Yet, he is always very careful not to give the impression of a busy body, or of one who is trying to impose himself as a leader in the Arab world. These protestations, he repeatedly expressed on almost every occasion. Ives Cuau of *Le Figaro* asked him:

— Do you intend to meet Nasser?

— No. I have dispatched to him one of my representatives on the morrow of the war, because he has expressed the desire to renew contact with Tunisia. But, for years, he has known my position, which has at least the merit of having never changed.

— Mr. President, you always remained consistent with yourself and events have to a very large extent, proven you right. Don't you think that Tunisia could not play an important role in the framework of the Arab League?

— No. There are geographical imperatives. The Middle East is far from Tunisia, which, by the way, during her fight for independence, had received from the people there, nothing but moral support.

I can only offer advice. I can argue with some of the leaders, but the Palestine problem is before anything else the concern of the Palestinians and the neighboring countries. They have their history, and we ours. I don't intend to play a role beyond my means.

I have absolutely no ambition to play leadership in the Arab world nor anywhere else. My only ambition is to raise the standard of living in my country. And if I achieve this, I'll have scored the only victory I have at heart.

Part Three

The Man
His Life and Philosophy

27

"The Supreme Warrior"

WHO IS THE MAN WHO CREATED THE STORM? WHAT IS HIS BACK-
ground? What are the relevant facts of his life? What motivates
him, and what is his philosophy?

Dynamic and possessed of boundless energy, he has long been
a legend to his own people. He is to them the "father of Tunisia's
independence," "the Supreme Warrior," and "the Beloved,"
which is what "Habib" actually means. Internationally his stature
and influence far transcend the size and power of his little country
—the smallest in territory of all the North African states with a
population of less than five million, and the poorest in national
resources.*

He was born August 3, 1903, the youngest of eight brothers and
sisters. The place of his birth was a village of poor fishermen, but
his father was an army officer. At the age of five, Habib ben Ali
was sent to an elder brother in Tunis to start his education. At 21,
he arrived in Paris to study law and political science; he was a
brilliant student who worked hard for his lawyer's diploma. With
the hard work he managed to enjoy the fun that is the privilege
of a young student in Paris. He was not an ascetic.

When he returned to Tunisia three years later as a lawyer he
brought with him more than a diploma. He had absorbed a great
deal of French literature and philosophy, having been especially
inspired by the history of the French Revolution, which he studied
thoroughly. The ideals of liberty and the rights of man took hold
of him in a way that both shaped and inspired his life.

* Algeria's population is more than 10 million; Morocco's—13 million. Libya,
though an immense and rich country, has a population of less than two million. Algeria and Libya are rich in oil. Tunisia has no natural resources to
speak of.

He subordinated his vocation as a lawyer to higher aspirations: the restoration of Tunisia to a position of liberty and dignity—not as abstractions but as a practical policy to shape the destiny of his people. He became active in the nationalist movement, which at the time was loosely organized and had only a vague program. Actually it was scarcely a movement, but a debating group of intellectual and professional élite. Bourguiba introduced an innovation which is a commonplace of American politics, but at that time and in those circumstances was of revolutionary import: he went out to the people of the towns and villages. He travelled from town to town and to far-flung villages preaching the ideals of national independence and individual freedom.

Already at that early period he discovered the unnerving trait of Arab mentality—of verbal extremism totally unrelated to practical reality. He observed the Old Destour Party whose leaders, indeed, were committed to the ideal of independence from the French, but to whom this ideal was an abstraction; they had no practical program for achieving independence. Yet their slogan was either complete independence or nothing. Therefore, it was nothing.

He lost patience with the old, established Destour ("Constitution") Party which he considered too amateurish and its leaders neither sufficiently serious nor dedicated. They preferred talk of liberty, rather than liberty itself. In 1934, therefore, he founded the Neo-Destour Party, and became its Secretary General. (Early in 1965, it was renamed the Destourian Socialist Party.)

The new party substituted action for empty slogans. And it was early in his political career that he evolved and crystallized his strategy of gradualism, which later became celebrated as "Bourguibism." For the next twenty years he applied this tactic persistently and consistently, seizing every opportunity to push the French further than they were prepared to go. The campaign against the French, as we know, proved effective and in the end was crowned with complete success.

He distinguished himself not only as a political leader and administrator but also as a journalist of flamboyant style, who had great appeal, strangely enough, to both the intellectuals and the masses—the true hallmark of authenticity for a liberator.

During the twenty years between the beginning of his political struggle and the achievement of independence, Bourguiba spent more time in prison than out of it. The successive French governments and their Residents General in Tunis were perplexed over exactly how to deal with the nationalist movement in the Protectorate. The easiest solution was to send Bourguiba to prison, transferring him from one to another and intermittently releasing him.*

When World War II broke out, Bourguiba was in prison (since April 9, 1938) awaiting trial for "conspiracy against the security of the State." After the fall of Paris and French surrender to Germany, Tunisia came under the control of the Pétain regime in Vichy. The Neo-Destour was outlawed and the Tunisian nationalists went underground. Bourguiba was transferred to a prison in Marseilles. He was then transferred to Lyons and finally to Fort Vanica in Ain. But in November 1942 Tunisia was occupied by the Germans (the occupation was short and lasted till May 1943) and the Tunisian nationalists emerged from the underground. The Axis encouraged them to collaborate, vaguely promising them Tunisian independence. Some seem to have been tempted. By the end of 1942 the Axis freed Bourguiba and tried to win him over to their side as the head of their forces in North Africa. He was "invited" to Rome, where he was given a sumptuous reception. Asked to deliver an address on the radio in Rome, he intimated that what the Axis wanted was to substitute one imperialism for another.

"While our country," he declared in his radio address, "is now the theatre of murderous operations, it is at the same time the prey of colonialist cupidity and covetousness of foreign powers." He continued to live in the occupied zone under close surveillance, but warned his comrades not to find themselves on the losing side. Nothing would hurt the cause of Tunisia's independence more, he argued, than to be treated by the victorious Allies as collaborationists. His attitude stemmed partly from principle and his affection for the French people, but also from his conviction that the Axis, despite their seeming invincibility, would inescapably lose the war.†

---

* He was in prison from 1934–1936; 1938–1942; 1952–1955.
† Certain French observers, at the time, did not share this liberal interpretation. They considered it far-fetched. Some even saw in the very fact that he delivered the speech on the Rome Radio, if not an act of outright collaboration, at all events an act of doubtful ambiguity. Bourguiba himself rejected these accusations with vehemence, characterizing them as slander. He repeatedly proclaims that he defied the Axis and takes great pride in it.

With the cessation of hostilities in Tunisia in the spring of 1943 and the restoration of French authority, a military administration was set up in Tunis. In April 1943, Bourguiba, disguised as a woman, escaped from his confinement and returned to Tunis, where he undertook an intensive campaign to prepare Tunisia to join the Allies openly in fighting the Axis. He eluded Italian efforts to capture him. On May 7, 1943, he launched an appeal to the Allied powers for the political and material reconstruction of his country.

This war period of Bourguiba's career is remarkable in several respects. The long imprisonments by the French did not leave a bitterness in his heart, which might have distorted his perspective. A second remarkable thing was his almost prophetic ability to foretell the outcome of the war although he had been cut off from the world for almost five years, and whatever news he was permitted to get was provided to him first by the Vichy government and then by the Axis.

The end of the war did not bring the hoped-for rewards, or even a radical change of attitude by the French toward Tunisia's national aspirations. Bourguiba therefore concluded that what was necessary at the moment was to mobilize international public opinion for the cause of Tunisia's independence. On March 26, 1946 he fled secretly aboard a small boat from a remote Tunisian beach, landed in Libya and went on to Cairo. The journey took a month. He remained in exile for more than three years and visited all the Middle Eastern countries to appeal for support for Tunisia's independence.

September 8, 1949, he returned to Tunis and for seven months crisscrossed the country, organizing the outlawed movement. Then he went to Paris to attempt to mobilize French opinion through sympathetic prominent personalities, and finally reached the government's ear.

A change of direction occurred when Robert Schuman became Foreign Minister, and announced that the aim of French policy was now to direct Tunisia toward independence. Bourguiba welcomed the declaration and agreed that his party would participate in the internal autonomy government designed as a first stage toward freedom.

Taking heart from this first significant achievement, he left for an extended tour of Asia, the United States, and Great Britain. But again there was a change in French policy. The European settlers—about 250,000 strong (mostly French), of whom 100,000 were landowners—exerted tremendous pressure on Paris, which yielded and promulgated repressive measures on the Tunisian nationalist movement.

Bourguiba rushed back to his country and summoned an emergency congress of the Neo-Destour party, but the French government prohibited its convocation, and the congress held its sessions underground. The government outlawed the Neo-Destour and on January 18, 1952 again arrested Bourguiba. For more than two years he was shifted about among various prisons and fortresses and exiled to remote islands, all the while kept in complete isolation. Finally in May 1954 he was taken to Paris and put under house arrest. It was more than a year longer before he was released (on June 1, 1955) and permitted to return home. He left immediately for Tunisia, where he received a tumultuous and triumphal welcome in every town he visited.

Two days later, on June 3, a treaty granting Tunisia formal internal autonomy was signed in Paris. France retained control of defense and foreign affairs. The interests of the French settlers were safeguarded by various stipulations in the treaty.

Bourguiba encountered fierce internal opposition, including accusations of having betrayed the nationalist cause and compromised the aim of independence. Heading the opposition was his rival, the then Secretary General of the Neo-Destour party, Salah ben Youssef. This opponent not only refused any compromise with France, but advocated orienting Tunisia toward Egypt. Bourguiba acted swiftly and with determination. Assuring the people that after internal autonomy, complete independence would follow, he was able to bring about the expulsion of Ben Youssef from the party for advocating violence.

On December 19, 1955 the Tunisian government announced that a convoy of arms, coming from Libya, had been captured in southern Tunisia, apparently destined for Ben Youssef and his adherents. Forty of the latter were arrested and charged with conspiracy, but before a warrant could be issued for Ben Youssef's arrest, he fled the country. He lived for several years in Cairo where he plotted against Bourguiba—with Nasser's blessing. He was finally assassinated in West Germany (on August 12, 1961) under mysterious circumstances—suspicion persists to this day that Tunisian agents were responsible.

It took less than eight months for Bourguiba's hopes to be vindicated. On March 20, 1956, Tunisia gained complete sovereignty.

There is far from unanimous agreement that this success is to be ascribed to the infallibility of the method called "gradualism." Some feel that the method would not work without a leader possessing Bourguiba's attributes as an intrepid fighter and at the same time an accomplished negotiator, and withal an integrity that has made some of his former opponents, like Premier Mendes-France and Edgar Faure, his friends and admirers.

He achieved stability for his regime by a combination of moderation in all things and shrewdness in judging men and events. Avoiding the extremes which are the blight of the post-colonial nations, he judiciously permitted private capital to operate side by side with government-run economic enterprises. He shied away from creating a military Frankenstein monster, and succeeded in obtaining economic assistance from France, the United States, West Germany, and other nations. In his dealings with his benefactors he is dignified, appreciative, and gracious; he often goes out of his way to demonstrate his deep gratitude.

Internally, he is trying to govern by consensus; but he is relentless in educating his people, attempting to raise their political maturity by applying European, rather than Eastern or Arab, standards. He has thus succeeded in maintaining the stability of his regime and increasing his personal popularity.

Despite the President's exalted talk of individual freedom and the rights of every man, Tunisia is not yet what may precisely be called a parliamentary democracy. It still has a one-party regime, with all powers concentrated in the hands of one man—his own. He sees his role primarily as that of educator of the people rather than its elected steward, since the country is still in the initial phases of independence.

The first general elections to a Constituent Assembly in sovereign Tunisia took place five days after formal independence, and the results were typical of one-party regimes. Out of 606,000 votes cast, 599,000 – 98.8 per cent—were for the National Front headed by Bourguiba.

But there were two differences between this election and those in other one-party countries. First, there were 144,000 abstentions —really 20 per cent of the electorate—many of them probably sympathizers of Salah ben Youssef. Second, the National Front was not identical with the Neo-Destour party; it was a coalition. Of the 98 seats won by the National Front, the Neo-Destour kept

86 seats, of which 35 went to labor union leaders and two to representatives of the Jewish community. The other 12 went to "Independent Nationalists."

These elections were the first and last exercise in democracy in newly independent Tunisia. From then on, the political history consisted of consolidating and concentrating all power in the one party—the Neo-Destour—with the President accumulating ever wider prerogatives. On April 13, 1956 a new constitution was adopted by the Constituent Assembly, abolishing the monarchy and divesting the Bey, Sidi Lamine, of "the attributes of sovereignty." All the sovereign power was "vested in the people," which meant for all practical purposes, the party and its leader, Bourguiba. Three days later Bourguiba formed a Neo-Destourian Cabinet (with the exception of the Minister of Health, who was an independent). The Destour members included four labor leaders and one member of the Jewish community.

Pursuant to the new Constitution the Constituent Assembly on July 25, 1957 formally abolished the monarchy and proclaimed Tunisia a republic. Bourguiba was unanimously elected President. The premiership was also abolished and its prerogatives transferred to the President, following the "American system." In consecutive elections the pattern of quasi-unanimity was repeated.

Today Bourguiba is still the leader of the single party in Tunisia, thrice reelected President of the Republic with almost unlimited executive powers, though constitutionally responsible to the National Assembly. A new Constitution promulgated June 1, 1959 regularizes his prerogatives and makes him supreme commander of the armed forces. The election results are invariably close to 100 per cent for the ruling party and Bourguiba personally.

Among the theses advanced by John Stuart Mill in his Essay "On Liberty" is one which holds that autocracy, however benign, and efficient, is abhorrent because it requires of its beneficiaries only obedience. Another point made by Mill is that freedom imposes on people the duty of exercising their judgment—and abiding by the consequences. Mill's direct experience (there was nothing in his wide reading that could serve to affect his views) was gained in England and France, where there was already a relatively advanced political and social sophistication. Yet even in those countries (and later in the United States) where his theses underlie the prevailing systems of democracy, they are ideals which are approached but not attained, and occasionally even lost sight of.

Mill called himself a "utilitarian," which we might today translate into "pragmatist." Pragmatism would undoubtedly dictate that the exercise of political judgment by whose consequences a people must abide, requires a measure of political and social sapience. If the relatively literate peoples of the Western countries are occasionally forced to abide by their misjudgments, how much more often and more destructively is this likely to occur where the people are still politically (as well as literally) illiterate?

The object then is to compare Tunisia not to the Western democracies but to the other countries of the so-called "Third World"—Algeria, Egypt, Ghana. Even such a comparison is not easy to make, for Tunisia is both like and unlike the other countries with one-party regimes. Of course, on the surface there are obvious similarities: only one political party is permitted to function, concentrating all political power of the state. There is thus no official forum for the expression of independent ideas, no free press as we understand it.

Some observers believe that while Bourguiba's centralism has givn his country a stability which no other state in the Arab world enjoys, it has also created and encouraged political apathy in a country which is on the whole more literate and cultured than most other Arab states. This centralism they argue, handicaps free political discussion and hence impedes individual initiative in the various fields of national and social existence. In a country where everything—the good and the bad—comes from the top, the margin for individual creativity is narrowed.

While there is some obvious truth in these observations, they are also misleading. Because despite the similarities there are also basic differences between Tunisia and other one-party regimes. For one, Tunisia's political climate is quite different from the ones of repression and terror which prevail in countries such as Egypt. Public opposition to Bourguiba is not encouraged; yet on the rare occasions when disagreement manifests itself, it does not generate the reaction that occurs in other one-party countries. There have been no political trials in recent years and there are no political prisoners in Tunisia. The judiciary retains a considerable amount of independence; it is no stooge of the party.

If opposition arises from a trade union or independent student organization, the government tries to absorb it into a party-controlled rival organization, usually newly created for the purpose.

If this does not work, pressures are sometimes exerted upon dissenting leaders. If this fails, too, the dissidents show up in Paris or Geneva, but not in a Tunisian prison. Since Paris or Geneva are not far from Tunis, the agitation continues, and the words of the dissenters are heard and debated in their own country. The process of Tunisian authoritarian centralism is comparatively gentle and the door is almost always open for reconciliation—in a true sense of the word. Among Bourguiba's present closest colleagues—both in the government and in the Political Committee of the party—are some who were at one time or other banished because of dissent.*

Bourguiba claims that hatred and vindictiveness are foreign to him on any level; there is a ring of truth in his claim. In the heat of argument he sometimes frankly accepts the designation of dictator; more often he denies it. He still asserts: "I teach the masses, and not vice versa," which is of course a euphemism for dictatorship. Other recent dictatorships have started as benevolent, paternal efforts to lead a nation into economic, social, and political green pastures. The ones that come readily to mind—those of Machado, Batista, Peron, Mussolini, Nasser himself—invariably degenerated into despotic regimes.

Yet most authentic liberals like Mendes-France or journalists like Jean Daniel and Jean Lacouture believe that Bourguiba does not belong in that company, perhaps because Tunisia is permeated with French culture and concepts. French newspapers, books, and magazines are freely circulated and avidly read, and as in France, no subject is taboo; there is frank and free (though private) discussion. In spite of this Gallic influence with its libertarian ideas, the monocratic actuality under which they live does not appear to trouble too many Tunisians.

---

* Since these lines were written the situation seems to have deteriorated. The student rebellions sweeping many a country did not skip over Tunisia. Student demonstrations of a violent nature took place and repression followed. It started on June 5 1967 with the riots in Tunis against the American and British embassies and especially against the Jews. It seems that the harsh sentences against some of the participants exasercated the situation. The center of student unrest was subsequently transferred to the University. As a result a few scores of students and some intellectuals were arrested and will be tried in special courts. Critics in Tunis and abroad, especially French lawyers and professors, accuse the regime in Tunis of brutality and of the denying the accused due process of law.

Bourguiba sees the basic difference between his regime and those in other one-party system countries to be mainly one of diverse aims and aspirations. While other autocrats do not appreciate the ideals of free democracy, he values these virtues but believes his country is not yet ready to adopt them. He seems sincerely to believe that in an underdeveloped country subjugated for many generations by colonial rule, the people are not equipped for the Western type of democracy, although this is his ultimate aim for Tunisia; the present regime is only a transition. And in Tunisia even the period of transition is, in contrast to other new countries, marked primarily by education rather than brute repression. He told the National Assembly in October 1965:

> Contrary to the calumnies . . . democracy is not endangered in Tunisia, and Bourguiba is not a dictator nor is he a despot. We have asked the people for temporary sacrifices during a difficult transition. Democracy is not in question and the limitation of liberty is strictly provisional.

To achieve such lofty aims as freedom and democracy or, for that matter, economic self-sufficiency and peace, is not an easy process, argues Bourguiba. Great things don't just happen without great striving and the affirmative action of people. But how the people perform depends upon their leadership. This is how he puts it:

> It depends upon men and on the way they . . . react when faced with reality. And the reactions of men . . . depend of course on their leaders. Tunisians used to be a little like the Egyptians, or like the Syrians. Simple men are always guided by their passions, rather than by their reason. But the chief, the leader, the guide, must educate them. It is up to him to raise their level, to direct them and make thinking men out of them.

It is sometimes difficult to know for certain whether there is a serious opposition in a one-party country. The certainty is usually revealed only when trouble breaks out, as in Algeria, for instance, when the seemingly popular and widely acclaimed Ahmed ben Bella was deposed and arrested; his removal created barely a ripple. Yet even this kind of coup is not necessarily proof of widespread popular discontent, but rather of the built-in rivalries within such regimes. Thus Ben Bella was removed, as often happens in Arab countries, not by popular rebellious forces but by a close friend and collaborator who was instrumental in his accession in the first place, Col. Houari Boumedienne, head of the Algerian army. (If the new President also has great difficulties, it is not because of the existence of a serious Ben Bella following, but because he has thus far been unable to reverse the policies and problems left by Ben Bella.)

On the other hand in Egypt when assassination attempts against President Nasser were discovered involving a large-scale underground, it became obvious that the charismatic leader was not as universally revered in his own country as had appeared.

But almost everyone, including de Gaulle, seems agreed that Bourguiba's position is different—that he is extremely popular. The many hardships he has imposed on the people in a succession of development plans, their poverty and low wages, do not seem to have diminished their admiration and trust in him. Even after the Bizerte catastrophe which brought humiliation and a thousand dead, he retained his popularity, and his regime remained firm. Bourguiba has been head of his party and later his government for more than thirty years.

By Western standards the Tunisian experiment is not necessarily remarkable as an exercise in democracy, or an assurance of stability, but the comparisons we are constrained to make are with the Arab and other newly liberated countries of Africa. In the past nineteen years Syria, for example, has seen eleven *coups d'état*. The suddenly deposed or deceased heads of Iraq and of African states are too numerous a roster, and still too current, to be detailed here. Nasser's survival may be attributed as much to luck as to vigilance or popularity; but there is no substantial evidence that within Tunisia, Bourguiba is faced with any hidden let alone overt danger of overthrow by rebellion or opposition.

There is still another remarkable aspect of the durability of Bourguiba's regime: the Neo-Destour party which he has headed since its inception more than thirty years ago is the only party in the Arab world which from an outlawed freedom movement under foreign rule became the source of responsible government managing the affairs of a state. The other underground revolutionary movements which arose to challenge colonial rule fell apart, sooner or later, after liberation: the Egyptian *Wafd,* the Syrian *Ba'ath* (now split into warring groups) , the Algerian *FLN* (National Liberation Front) , and the Moroccan *Istiqlal,* were all, to some degree or another, demoralized by internal divisions either before or after they split up into factions. Some were destroyed in the process.

At his press conference in Beirut, Bourguiba proudly stressed the point:

> Once independence has been achieved, few parties escaped disintegration. . . . We have succeeded in overcoming the stumbling block.

It would be specious to say that there is no dissent at all in Tunisia, but the relatively small opposition groups do not seem to represent any popular base; to the extent they can be categorized, they fall into three main groups. The least inchoate is the remnant of the followers of the assassinated ben Youssef, whose main body is a group of exiles in Cairo, headed by Brahim Tobbal. A second group consists of some trade union leaders and their followers, a few of them also in exile (but in Europe) who accuse Bourguiba of trying to "domesticate" the trade unions. A third group is composed of leftist students, centered in Paris. All are marginal and constitute no danger to the regime, only an embarrassment.

Unlike other rulers of newly established nations, Bourguiba does not pursue martial glory. An official publication of the Tunisian government recounting the history of Tunisia and its aspirations for the future has a chapter on the Army. In it we read:

> On June 17, 1956, the first unit of the Tunisian National Army marched into Tunis for the first time. It was then but a nucleus created with the object of providing independent Tunisia with one of the principal symbols of sovereignty.

After more than ten years it is still more of a symbol than a military force commensurate with the size of a nation of more than four million people.* This is the explanation given for not having to rely mainly on the army for its security:

---

* According to the most recent survey (December 1966) the Tunisian army is 20,000 strong. The ground forces count about 13,000 divided in six battalions, and small armored and artillery units, one of which is stationed on the Saharan border. The air force, 1,000 men strong, has about 70 aircraft,

The Tunisian Army and in particular Habib Bourguiba, [then] Minister of National Defense, do not base their country's defense on this modest body of troops alone. They know, and we have said it, that in the world of today Tunisia's security must rest more on a system of alliances and cooperation than on the actual strength of our armed forces.

Though the Tunisian Army is destined to manifest the sovereignty of the State, to maintain the security of its frontiers and law and order within the country, it is above all . . . a method of civic and occupational training: we shall not send unemployable or illiterate men back to civilian life. Every mobilized soldier will have at least a general elementary education and certainly a trade.

Thus the army is at once a symbol, an educational and vocational training institute, and an instrument of internal security and national integrity—all accomplished on a deliberately small budget. For the calendar year 1966, the defense allocation was a little more than eight million dollars—4.3 per cent of the total national expenditure of 191 million dollars. The same budget allotted 25 per cent for education, and 35 per cent for economic development. Some of the other countries in the Middle East and North Africa spend close to 50 per cent of their budget on defense; Bourguiba claims that in some cases it reaches 70 per cent, and scorns his colleagues in the Arab world for spending large sums building up armies while their populations go hungry. In his view they build up strong military establishments not out of need to maintain their integrity but as a matter of prestige.

Because he feels secure at home base, he can confidently make forays into world politics, considering it of the greatest significance that the Tunisian people enthusiastically approve his enterprises. He told an interviewer: "Few chiefs of State can permit themselves to be away from their country for such a long period of time." And referring to the tumultuous demonstration of welcome upon his return, he observed:

> The fact is that between the Tunisian people and me there is a bond of confidence. . . . This regime (of ours) deserves this trust, because it is at the service of the people. We are working for the

---

40 of which are combat planes. Its equipment was all given by the French and Swedes as gifts. The navy is composed of 500 men and possesses 11 small boats assigned exclusively to coast guard duty.

people with devotion and efficacy. My impression is that Tunisia is in good health.

He is careful to emphasize that he is not capitalizing on mass hysteria, or a penchant of the masses to cheer:

> We have surpassed the stage of sentiments and passion. . . . We are converting our élan for national liberation into a movement toward progress for all.

On his Middle East tour Bourguiba lectured in each country on the necesity of internal reforms as a prerequisite for any other aspirations. He preached modernism to backward peoples, and told the Arabs that their leaders must learn to place reform and development above nationalist, pan-Arabic, or even anti-Israel emotionalism.

He is an indefatigable reformer in many fields and on many levels. As far back as August 10, 1956 he announced that polygamy and easy divorce would be abolished. Despite considerable opposition, especially in rural areas, civil registration of marriages became obligatory; marriages before a religious authority alone were no longer recognized, and the marriage ages were raised to twenty years for men and seventeen for women.

An extensive birth-control campaign has been launched by the government in cooperation with Tunisian women's organizations. Family planning centers have been established throughout the country, and loudspeaker trucks drive through the remotest villages to acquaint the rural population with methods of birth control and distribute contraceptives.

Under Bourguiba's leadership women were granted equality of rights; child labor has been abolished; agrarian reforms have been introduced. Daring efforts have been undertaken to re-examine Islamic values and to adjust, and in certain cases abolish, outworm customs. While trying to avoid too hasty and traumatic affront to religious sensibilities, Bourguiba has been trying to secularize Tunisia.

Some of these reforms made Tunisia the first Arab country and the second predominantly Moslem state—Turkey being the first—to pose a legal bar to practices sanctioned by the Koran. Although there has been resistance, he has been able to advance by force of persuasion; he has not had to resort to the brutality of Kemal Ataturk when the Turkish statesman sought to bring Turkey into the twentieth century.

Jean Lacouture vividly describes Bourguiba's challenge to old religious traditions:

> ... Here is a scene that I remember: Bourguiba is watching the crowd massed in a square in Tunis to listen to him. It is midday during the month of Ramadan, a month of rigid daily fasting from dawn to sunset, required by Moslem religion. He takes a glass, pours some orange juice into it and drinks slowly; his magnetic glance still fixed on the wondering people. He knows that he is taking a risk, for conservatives are numerous. But by this gesture of challenge to tradition he wishes to dramatize emancipation. He then delivers a long explanation of the duties of a believer who no longer observes the rites. The duty now, he says, is to be aware of the need to struggle against poverty and build a stable country. "The Holy War is no longer against the infidel, but against underdevelopment," Bourguiba exclaims.

This is how he defines his task:

> Our overriding battle is against poverty. . . . I predict that in four years' time the face of Tunisia will have changed—and not through the totalitarian methods of terror but in a spirit of freedom, regard for efficiency, and amid general enthusiasm.

At the tenth anniversary celebrations of Tunisia's independence, Bourguiba looked proudly at the balance sheet of his country's achievements. Seventy per cent of the country's children are now in school, as against fifteen per cent in 1956; a quarter of the budget is devoted to education, and more than a third to economic development. Tunisia's gross national product has risen to eighty per cent since 1956. Whereas the country used to import almost all its manufactured goods, it soon will be in a position to export fabricated products. New industrial units range from textile factories and canning plants to a steelworks. Significantly, Bourguiba began the anniversary celebrations by opening a new power station to supply electricity for several industrial areas.

This progress, however, exacts a great price. The regime imposes austerity under which the workers, as usual, are affected the most. Economic benefits, as reflected by the standard of living, are still more of a hope than a reality, but the hope appears, fortunately, not to be illusory.

28

Bourguiba and France

BOURGUIBA'S LIFE IS FULL OF STARTLING PARADOXES, ONE OF WHICH is his strained relations with France and President de Gaulle. We know of his great admiration of and devotion to France and French culture, and that he regards himself as almost a Frenchman spiritually and culturally; he boasts many personal friendships among outstanding French political and journalistic personalities. Yet he so succeeded in antagonizing the de Gaulle government that it saw itself compelled to drastically curtail its economic and technical assistance and undertake severe economic sanctions against Tunisia. For example, it embargoed the wine which had made up 25 per cent of Tunisia's exports—an alarming blow to its trade balance. The French action came as retaliation against a series of ill-advised and, in the eyes of Paris, provocative steps by Bourguiba.

The last of these was Tunisia's nationalization of the remaining farm lands owned by Europeans, mostly French citizens. The French were shocked not so much by the act itself as by the provocative form it took. Only a little more than a year after an agreement had been signed setting out the conditions and compensation for purchase by Tunisia of colonial property, an act of the National Assembly nationalized the farmlands outright to "bring about the complete liquidation of agricultural colonialism." Bourguiba with his flair for the dramatic, signed the Land Act on May 12, 1964, on the same day, at the same hour, and on the same table at which 83 years earlier—in 1881—the humiliating Bardo Treaty had been signed, establishing the French Protectorate over Tunisia. "Agricultural evacuation," Bourguiba declared, "must be achieved, as military evacuation has been achieved."

Several explanations have been advanced for Bourguiba's action. One was that other Arab nationalists had gotten away with it: Nasser expropriated the Suez; Ben Bella seized the farmlands in Algeria. In those cases the great powers, including France, had acquiesced, and Bourguiba not only scented success in this gambit, but felt if he neglected it, he would appear a lesser nationalist than other Arab leaders. As we shall see, this was his second miscalculation.

Significantly, some liberal and leftist newspapers and magazines in Paris showed understanding and even a degree of sympathy for the Tunisian nationalization, for sundry reasons. The European settlers had comprised less than four per cent of the population, but had held an inordinately large part of the arable land in the country. They were also, in the nature of things, the most extreme opponents of Tunisia's independence movement. For the most part they remained diehards to the very end, refusing to think in terms of change and adjustment to new conditions.

However, the crisis transcended, the problem of nationalization and compensation. It epitomized the tragic problem of new nations incapable of satisfactorily coexisting with former ruling populations in their midst. In spite of Bourguiba's professed principles of tolerance and moderation, he succeeded no better than other leaders of post-colonial countries in devising a *modus vivendi* with the European population. When Tunisia became independent in March 1956, there were some 250,000 European civilians in Tunisia; of these about 50,000 stayed on.

Bourguiba's other miscalculation involved what the world press came to call the Bizerte crisis or "the stupid war," and it probably left the blackest mark on his career. He achieved his aim; but in those tragic days of July 1961 his actions ran counter to the main tenets of his political philosophy and cast a shadow upon the sincerity of his professions. Tunisia lost a thousand innocent lives in one day, probably more than in the whole of her fight for independence during a quarter of a century. No single aspect of the Bizerte tragedy does any credit to Bourguiba.

When France granted independence to the Tunisians, she retained rights to station troops in Tunisia, especially at the naval and air base in her northernmost Mediterranean city, Bizerte. Bourguiba kept reiterating a demand that the French evacuate *all* troops from Tunisia, including Bizerte. Under subsequent new agreements the French yielded step by step, gradually withdrawing ever larger numbers of troops, making changes in their deployment. At Bizerte alone they maintained a force, although there were indications that eventually this, too, would yield to negotiation.

With de Gaulle's return to power, relations between the two countries appeared to improve considerably. On June 2, 1958, de Gaulle sent messages to President Bourguiba and King Mohammed V of Morocco, calling for normalization of relations and settlement of difficulties. On June 17, after an exchange of letters between the French Chargé d'Affaires in Tunis and the Tunisian Foreign Minister, France agreed to withdraw her troops within four months from all military installations in Tunisia, except Bizerte; in turn Tunisia agreed to negotiate a "provisional status," by which France could continue to maintain forces there. On July 6, evacuation of French troops began after agreements of an economic and cultural nature were signed, including one for the construction of a pipeline from the Algerian oilfields of Edjelah through southern Tunisia to its port of La Skhirra near Gabes.

However, Tunisian relations with France continued to be affected by the Algerian situation. Algerian rebels operated from Tunisian soil (as well as from Moroccan) and this did nothing to promote Franco-Tunisian amity. Bourguiba continued to press for French evacuation of Bizerte, and in January 1960 set a final date: February 8. But this was a time of dramatic upheaval in Algeria, where French conservative extremists in cooperation with the French military undertook armed resistance against the de Gaulle administration for its "policy of surrender." Two days before the February 8 deadline, Bourguiba declared that he shared "the hopes of the world" for de Gaulle's success in "neutralizing the European insurrectional movement in Algeria," and for that reason regarded it as "inopportune to engage in a battle for the evacuation of Bizerte today." This meant in effect that he called off what had threatened to be a showdown on Bizerte. Subsequent relations appeared to improve to an even more marked degree and on February 27, Bourguiba was received by General de Gaulle in an atmosphere of utmost cordiality. At the end of the audience the following joint communiqué was issued:

> All problems of interest to the two countries were reviewed in a spirit of frankness and reciprocal understanding. . . . The two sides noted with satisfaction the improvement which has occurred and which should allow a favorable solution of outstanding problems to be envisaged.

The Algerian question was widely discussed in the light of recent developments and in the perspective of the future of North Africa. General de Gaulle and President Bourguiba were agreed in noting the possibilities and hope which exists from now on for a positive and speedy solution.

International questions of interest to France and Tunisia in various parts of the world were also examined. General de Gaulle and President Bourguiba noted the closeness of their general views.

It was later observed in Tunisian circles that President Bourguiba had told General de Gaulle in that conversation that the French presence at the naval base embarrassed him in his relations with his Algerian "friends," and urged evacuation. Bourguiba went away with the impression that de Gaulle had agreed, but the General's associates assert that he had replied: "Let me finish the Algerian war first." On the whole, there is general consensus in political circles that at that meeting Bourguiba had agreed not to raise the problem of evacuation of Bizerte until the end of the Algerian war. Yet, one month later, the Tunisian President sent a note to the French government demanding immediate negotiations concerning evacuation. He received only a vague answer, and inaugurated a campaign to arouse "popular pressure" against the French government.

In June when the French started to lengthen the Bizerte airstrip, leading the Tunisians to believe that they were reinforcing the base, Bourguiba decided to organize mass demonstrations, and began a campaign of self-intoxicating oratory. In July he told the National Assembly that he was going to drive the French out of Bizerte and out of a part of the Sahara which, he proclaimed, belonged to Tunisia; he further aroused the masses to march on the Bizerte base and "cover it."

This was shortly after the breakdown of peace talks between the French and Algerians at Evian-les-Bains, and Bourguiba seems to have acted under great pressure. Emotions ran high again, and the Tunisian leader obviously felt that a policy of restraint was endangering his prestige at home and in the Afro-Asian world. On July 7, an emissary handed de Gaulle a message from Bourguiba demanding the working out of a timetable for the evacuation of the base, plus revision of Tunisia's southern border with the Sahara. The French government refused to negotiate under threats, and later stated it could not consider giving up the base until the acute Berlin crisis was over; the installation was of primary importance to the security of the North Atlantic alliance.

Bourguiba visited Washington in May of that year and we must assume that President Kennedy discussed this problem with him. Thus the Bizerte question must be viewed within the wider context of the Western alliance, toward which Bourguiba professes friendship and loyalty (at that time the United States was covering something more than 60 per cent of Tunisia's budget—about 80 million dollars in direct aid and technical assistance for that year, plus equipment for Tunisia's little army).

Nevertheless, during the night of July 18-19 roadblocks were set up by the Tunisians at the approaches of the base installations, and on July 19 they opened fire on French planes as they took off, quickly setting off serious fighting. De Gaulle reacted vigorously, as is his wont, transferring several battalions of paratroopers and Foreign Legion units from Algeria to clear the base area and to occupy the city of Bizerte.

The price Bourguiba paid for this inexplicable adventure was extremely high: according to recently revealed figures 12 thousand Tunisians (among whom 4 thousand civilians) were killed; the French lost twenty soldiers.

Bourguiba rejoined the Arab League, whose Council promised him all necessary material, political, and military aid. In the United Nations the Afro-Asian bloc raised a hue and cry and under its sponsorship the Assembly passed a resolution calling on both sides to negotiate the withdrawal of all French forces from Tunisia. De Gaulle remained contemptuously aloof.

By now Bourguiba seems to have recovered his sense of pragmatism; he announced that he was ready to accept French use of the Bizerte base during the international crisis, provided that a time limit was fixed. Two days later both sides exchanged prisoners, and on September 18 it was agreed that the French forces, having achieved their objective, would return to their original positions. The withdrawal of the French troops from the town—not the base —of Bizerte began on October 1. Eventually, after the war in Algeria had ended and the Berlin crisis was over, the French evacuated the base.

In retrospect, Bourguiba may claim, as indeed he seems to by implication, that even in this crisis his theory of "gradualism" was vindicated: Tunisia regained her sovereignty over the whole of her territory, including Bizerte. But there is no reason to doubt that she would have achieved the same end by peaceful means, through negotiations, instead of by tragic confrontation with the

French armed forces—which caused humiliation to him and tragedy to his people. Instead of following "Bourguibism," he sharply deviated from it, and for having done so, was severely punished. This in turn brings us to the conclusion that his theories on the whole are right, but he is sometimes wrong.

The London *Economist,* trying to explain the Bizerte disaster, said that "the simplest hypothesis must be that he (Bourguiba) suffered from a total loss of judgment." This was the general opinion of most of the world press. Jean Lacouture, relating this most disturbing incident in Bourguiba's career, offers what seems a plausible explanation rooted in the Tunisian President's character:

> There are two men within him. First a Mediterranean realist, one of those who founded the Phoenician trade posts, made the laws of the Greek cities, and built the Roman empire. . . . But this realist who knows that Rome was not built in a day is at the same time a tribune who sets the crowds in the forum vibrating. This statesman, whose contribution to contemporary Arab history will probably prove to have been the substitution of politics for prophecy, can transform himself into a prophet—into a muezzin— and declaim in so vibrant a voice that his own eloquence supplants his political end. Sometimes he forgets himself and says things which go too far . . . and he finds himself dragged into an adventure which he has possibly not foreseen. (*New York Times Magazine,* June 6, 1965)

Thus he is sometimes, though rarely, guilty of the same weakness which he criticizes in the Arab leaders of the Middle East. That he survived this disaster gives us the measure of his magnetic grip upon the people.

Though relations between Tunisia and France remained strained and Bourguiba in the French doghouse, the atmosphere between the two countries has gradually relaxed and anti-Tunisian economic sanctions are either eased or removed altogether. With the steady improvement in relations, one may expect that sooner or later close cooperation and friendship will be completely re-established.

Because neither de Gaulle nor Bourguiba lost his sense of history or proportion, a permanent and irreparable break did not result from a momentary aberration. De Gaulle is committed to a French cultural, political and civilizing presence in North Africa and for the sake of this goal in his grand design is willing to show the forbearance which is usually expected from the strong and powerful.

But more remarkable is Bourguiba's patience and long view; having committed the *gaffes* of Bizerte and the Land Act. he tried his best not to envenom the situation, but to prepare the atmosphere for a reconciliation. Though in private he has expressed bitterness and disappointment at the strong French measures against his country, publicly he has voiced his trust in and loyalty to France.

In an interview with Philippe Herreman of *Le Monde* he discussed at length the crisis of relations with France and declared:

> Let us hope that France will one day be among Tunisia's best friends. We, for our part, will always remain faithful to France, whatever General de Gaulle's attitude may be. Together with France we have surmounted difficulties which otherwise have been grave indeed. And think of it, we have finally arrived today at the end of the process of decolonization.

The same day (April 10, 1965) he told an interviewer from *Le Figaro*, with whom he discussed the problem:

> You certainly know it was in all freedom that we opted for our people the culture of France.

Bourguiba has spared no effort to appease France and to return to de Gaulle's good graces. Some time after de Gaulle retaliated for the Land Act he sent a personal message to the French leader assuring him that the Land Act was not meant to offend "either France or her President." He declared at a press conference in Tunis that perhaps he acted "through inexperience," a phrase that de Gaulle had used at one of his press conferences in answer to an embarrassing question. Lately Bourguiba has also tried to justify his nationalization of the farmlands on not so clearly political or philosophical grounds, as on economic expediency: he had to do it because the country was on the brink of bankruptcy. The question of compensation is, in principle at least, open again.

By detour, he hopes, his championing of a French-speaking commonwealth of nations based at Paris will contribute to the establishment of "special" relations between Tunis and Paris. His peace initiative in the Middle East is also said to be a contributing factor.

29

Bourguiba Toward West and East

BOURGUIBA IS NO DOUBT THE MOST WESTERN-ORIENTED LEADER OF a new nation in Asia or Africa, with the exception only of Israel. His most important aim in life is to raise his people to European standards of culture, economy, social amenities, and individual freedom and responsibility.

But he is no enemy of the communist bloc and prides himself on his personal friendship with Marshal Tito. He has cultural and technical assistance agreements with several communist countries, but he believes that the communist regimes will come ever closer to Western standards and social philosophy (rather than the other way around). On the other hand, he also believes that capitalism, in the classical sense, is a thing of the past and that socialism in one form or degree or another will gradually but inevitably be adopted in all Western countries. Each country's foreign policy orientation is a matter of ideological predilections; but it is influenced by what it considers its vital interests. He told his interviewers on CBS' *Face the Nation:*

> It all depends upon the conceptions of the leaders [of each nation]. Some people think, or believe that [one or another] philosophy of life suits them and adopt a policy accordingly. As far as I am concerned— I have always felt that my philosophy of life and myself [as a human being] are much closer to the camp of liberty, to the Western world, rather than to any other. I have felt so even when we thought that the member [governments] of the free world did not themselves act according to their own philosophy. It happens that some members of the free world have been colonial powers, but once the colonial rule is over, we feel that we

have more than a little in common with them. It is our philosophy
of life and our [sense] of values.

Bourguiba stakes his career and the destiny of his country upon
this pro-Western orientation. While he solicits economic, technical, cultural, and even military assistance from the Western
countries, he has so far abstained from asking substantial help
from the Soviet Union. In this respect his record is on the whole
consistent—but no quite. At the height of the Algerian war, Bourguiba announced that his government had rejected a French offer
to sell arms to Tunisia (September 15, 1958) and that he was
seeking arms from Czechoslovakia and Sweden (November 13,
1958) ; but this was an isolated episode. All in all, when Bourguiba criticizes Nasser for playing off the East against the West for
his own nationalistic purposes, he is quite sincere.

An interviewer asked him:

> Isn't the rivalry between the opposing great powers to a certain
> extent a favorable factor and in the interests of the countries of
> the Third World? What do you think, for instance, of the exam-
> ple of Nasser—of his gamble of balancing between East and West?

Bourguiba's answer:

> All this never did Egypt any good, either on the political or
> moral plane. It is fine to be supported by all those who are in a
> position to extend help, and, as far as we are concerned, we have
> excellent relations with both the Russians, or the Bulgarians, for
> instance, and the Americans. But Machiavellianism is not my
> forte and I have no desire whatsoever to make blackmail the basis
> of my policies. The worth of a man in society, as indeed of a peo-
> ple regardless how small in the concert of nations, depends upon
> moral values. (*Réalités*, November 1965, French edition)

Concerning Nasser's threats against West Germany and indirectly other Western countries, for having relations with Israel,
Bourguiba told another interviewer:

> I think this is merely another case of Nasser's political game
> with the power blocs, playing one against the other. I have made
> it clear that I want no part of it. (*Suddeutsche Zeitung*, May 9)

His own policy and attitudes in international relations are based
"on principle and not merely on economic opportunism."

Significantly, twice in his career he broke away from the Arab League; in each case his relations with the West were involved. In 1965 it was over West Germany. As Bourguiba saw it, Nasser's aim was to intimidate not only the Federal Republic, but the other Western powers whose support of Israel by far transcends that of Bonn. In several interviews and statements Bourguiba charged Nasser with "a conspiracy aimed at a break between the Arab states and the West. Perhaps Egypt feels itself obliged to act as an auxiliary for the East, the Soviet Union," but his country would not follow Nasser's line "because this satellite system is to our dislike."

But 1965 was only a repetition of what had happened seven years earlier—in 1958. Bourguiba himself related to the *Views* interviewer the reasons for the background of that first break with the League:

> Our differences [with Egypt] were tremendous. They regarded all European countries and America as virtual enemies, colonialists and imperialists. We believed we could fight against colonialism, as we had been doing much longer than Egypt, without fostering a hatred of people whether it was the French, the American, or the British people—especially since these peoples were in the process of decolonizing little by little. Looking at the situation objectively, I believed that our country's interests lie with the Western world . . . and that it was essential for us to have friendly relations with the Western countries. I said this publicly and it was considered treachery. I say so now and the Tunisian people agree with me. Originally all our difficulties [with Egypt and the Arab League] came from this. We did not follow the same policy whether on the home front or in foreign affairs. Our views differed; in internal affairs, because we believed in decolonization step by step via internal autonomy; and in foreign policy, on the issue of blocs. For all these reasons things were not going well [between us the Egyptians]. . . . We have progressed on the path of decolonization, we always pursued our friendly policy toward the West, without looking at the socialist or communist camp with antagonism. We did not want to encourage anti-communism. We said: they are friends; we want to entertain cordial, fruitful relations with them. But our whole history, our whole past has been linked with the West, with the Mediterranean powers, the Western powers. Because of our ideology of respect for freedom, our duty is to be on their side. Even if they sometimes indulge in colonialism, their principle is nevertheless for human liberty. . . .

Among all the leaders of the newly independent nations he alone has stood firm without any inhibitions against the waves of anti-Americanism which have swept so many countries on all the continents. He upbraids his colleagues in Africa and Asia for shouting themselves hoarse against "American imperialism."

> I have always felt that it is a very curious thing that the United States, which helped so many of the newly emergent nations to achieve their independence, should be branded as "imperialists." Where would a country like Indonesia be, for instance, without the support it got from the United States in its struggle for independence? (Interview in *Newsweek*, May 10, 1965)

The Ford Foundation in September 1965 held its yearly conference on Africa and the Middle East, in Tunis. Bourguiba delivered an address in which he declared:

> The friendship that Tunisia nourished for the United States goes back to the time when we were still engaged in the fight for our freedom, when I was still a prisoner in the fortress of Saint-Nicolas in France during the somber years of 1939–1940. At that time we already believed in the victory of the Allies, which we wished them with all our heart, though we were in the midst of crisis with France.

After reminding his audience how he had been freed by the Germans and then received by Mussolini in Rome, the Tunisian President proudly reminisced:

> We stood firm, because we thought that Tunisia's independence could not be accorded by the Axis powers.

He paid homage to the then American Consul, General Doolittle, who intervened on his behalf with General Juin, and stated:

> Our sympathy for the United States grew in view of the role she played in safeguarding the peace of the world. That the waves of Chinese communists have not yet overrun the world—for this the credit is due to the Americans.
>
> Even after independence we have found the American government understanding; and they extended to us economic assistance.

He stuck his neck out on Vietnam, telling a UPI *interviewer* (September 2):

Many countries see only the American planes in the air, and not the subversion on the ground. The fact is that a legally constituted government in South Vietnam has asked for American aid because there are people in Vietnam who do not want communism for their country.

He is usually moderate in his attitudes toward opposing social regimes competing in the international arena; but he takes rather an extreme stance in his appraisal of Communist China. He considers Peking the greatest single threat to world peace. In November 1965 he declared to *Réalités:*

> . . . You see, the problem of peace is not essentially tied in with the relationship between the United States and Russia. They have achieved an equilibrium and will do everything to preserve the *status quo.* What worries me is China, with her excessive pretensions, her aspirations she believes she can satisfy in the span of one generation. This has been confirmed in declarations by Mr. Malraux upon his return from Peking. I lived between the two World Wars, the *"drole de paix"* (phony peace) between 1919 and 1939, and I have seen how a conflict breaks out in a situation such as that which now exists in the Far East. If one makes concessions, they have no other result than to whet the appetite, to arouse in the ambitious some kind of exaltation, of *"folie de grandeur"* (delusion of grandeur) . . . . It is by madmen that war is waged, and I am afraid that the leaders of China belong to that category.

A smaller replica of what happened during his tour in the Middle East in February and March of 1965, shaped up during Bourguiba's visit to African countries in December of the same year. As he broke the united Arab front during the anti-Bonn hysteria, so at the height of the African anti-British hysteria over Rhodesia he again raised the voice of reason to tell the Africans that for Tunisia to break relations with London was out of the question. Some African leaders (like their counterparts in the Arab world), he asserted, had raised a hue and cry not for the cause of the black majority, but to contest for "the title of an authentic revolutionary."

He considered the threats of war against Rhodesia mere rhetoric, and warned that engaging in such folly would bring "a repetition of the criminal error committed by the Arabs when they attacked Israel in 1948." He pointed out the fallacy of foreign intervention on behalf of a people that does not fight for its own freedom. First the Rhodesian black majority should organize into a liberation movement and prove its mettle; only then would they be entitled to outside help. Great Britain, he believes, should be supported and encouraged in her dealings with the Ian Smith regime in Rhodesia, and not subjected to attempted intimidation by "phony belligerence."

If the African states are truly concerned with international problems, Bourguiba reasons, they must abandon their "revolutionary rivalries" and abstain from the "blackmail" they use in exploiting the tensions between East and West—a policy which dismally failed in the Congo in 1960.

When *Le Monde's* J. Ben Brahem asked a highly placed Tunisian official whether such an attitude does not threaten to isolate Bourguiba in Africa as it did in the Middle East, he answered that Tunisia rejects the idea of preserving at any price a "solidarity of error"; she is willing to be momentarily misunderstood for the sake of being proven right on important issues at the right time.

Bourguiba's attitude toward the Rhodesian crisis is interesting from still another aspect, for here he cannot be suspected of opportunism or self-interest, as in the case of the Middle East conflict. Tunisia gets no economic assistance from Great Britain, and does not expect to; nor would his sympathetic posture toward her affect his relationship with France one way or another.

Bourguiba's attitude toward the Soviet Union is formally correct and even friendly, though he has no sympathy for communism and the totalitarian regime in Russia. An emotional ambivalence permits him to admire the Russians, while criticizing the USSR for being perhaps the last major colonialist country in the world. In the clinches, he clearly sides with Russia against China, as evidenced when he advocated Russia's participation in the ill-fated "Second Bandung Conference" as a counter-balance to China.* He explained to *Réalités:*

One should not forget that more than half of this country

---

* The second Afro-Asian conference was supposed to take place in Algeria in July 1965. Shortly before that, Algerian President Ben Bella was arrested and deposed by the chief of the Army, Colonel Boumedienne. For this and other reasons that conference never took place. China insisted that Russia should not participate.

(USSR) is in Asia—in the region which the Russians have gradually annexed, integrated, Russified, bolshevized, and—let's say the word—colonized.

Question: You mean to say that at the conference of decolonized nations Russia, which is a colonist country, should participate?

Answer: She certainly was just that in the past. To assert that she is still that, one needs to be certain that the Asiatic regions of Russia really still live under a 'foreign' domination. It is however, possible, as the Russians claim, that they have evolved an acceptable *modus vivendi,* and that by having integrated these peoples they have also aroused in them a real enthusiasm; because these peoples participate in the work of development of the USSR. I am under the impression that this might be the case, and I consider the formula valid. Don't forget that even in North Africa the incipient nationalist movements demanded only equality, even integration. For all these reasons, and especially for tactical considerations—in order to avoid a situation in which "a dust" of small nations find themselves face to face with China—it would not be a bad idea to have Russia present at the conference so that the small nations of the Third World could witness the confrontations of the Big Two. They could learn something and prehaps even get some advantage out of it.

30

Bourguiba and the New Nations

BOURGUIBA IS NO GREAT ADMIRER OF THE NEW NATIONS—OR PERHAPS, more precisely, of their leaders who, he believes, resemble the Arabs in their weaknesses and vices. He sometimes seems embarrassed to be counted among them, or to participate in their puerile conferences. Apologetic for having participated in the Bandung Conference in 1955 and in the later Asian-African conferences, he responded to an interviewer of *Réalités* who asked whether the new nations share his opinions about the paramount and transcendent importance of international peace:

> Unfortunately, I am not sure. We touch here upon a grave problem. When the Afro-Asian camp was constituted in Bandung in 1955, I was engaged in the last battle for Tunisia's independence. At that time there were in the United Nations a small number of countries who had been subjected in the past to colonial domination and subsequently were liberated; we counted upon them to help us, in view of their influence, to reconquer our independence. For me that solidarity was essential. It represented the cement which united us through the continents of Asia and Africa. Clearly, this solidarity is still with us. But today, most of the Afro-Asian countries are already independent and since then their attitudes have been a great disappointment to me. They developed complexes of grandeur, of hegemony—a will to power which usually hides a sentiment of inferiority. From this stems all the turmoil in the Afro-Asian camp. This also puts in relief their inexperience and above all the fact that many of the leaders failed to free themselves of the complexes which colonialism engendered in them. They exhibit a sort of rancor toward their former colonizers as well as toward their allies. The cold war encourages them in these attitudes, as does the propaganda of that camp

which poses as an adversary of the former colonial powers. This flatters their vanity. They lend themselves to be impressed by all this. And then they all love to speak louder and stronger than their neighbors; to deliver themselves of insults, to shout so as to prove to themselves they are free and independent.

Thus one hears them incessantly and indiscriminately bandying big words like "revolutionary." These would-be "revolutionaries" are those who rise—in words only, of course—against imperialism and colonialism. But since these latter do not exist any longer, they snap at neo-colonialism. They will always still find some colonialism as long as they remain weak on the plane of their internal affairs. This they do instead of tackling their real and immense problems—those of underdevelopment—and of trying to apply themselves to solve them with the aid of their former colonizers. The latter they are disposed to do, as we know, but without, at the same time, foregoing their antagonistic and insulting attitudes.

The shouts, mass meetings, protests, all give the appearance of youth and dynamism, but lead nowhere.

As far as we are concerned, we in Tunisia are trying to give an example of a country which really decolonizes with the support—even though not disinterested support—of all those who are more advanced than we. But we do it without hatred, attempting to turn the painful page of the past. We have no complexes. I refer particularly to France whom we would like to see as the closest country to us—if it were not for the present difficulties.

Asked his opinion concerning the proposed "Second Bandung Conference" (which failed eventually to materialize) he replied scornfully that it would be "a thieves' market," where everyone would try to cheat everyone else. It would be an unsavory assembly not only because of the confrontation between Russian and Chinese ambitions, but also because the Afro-Asian countries distrust each other.

It is going to be a free-for-all—a wrestling arena where one will see foul punches thrown—all this in order to fortify the revolution in the Third World, particularly in Africa. Here is the beautiful result at which one has arrived!

Who are most responsible for this state of affairs—the Asians or the Africans? At the time of the first Bandung conference in 1955, the Africans were in the minority—six countries among 29 participants. Now, at the conference which was supposed to take place

in Algiers, the Africans would have represented 34 of 58 participants. Would the altered balance make a difference? asked the
interviewer. Bourguiba answered:

> This business of numbers is of very little importance, in my
> opinion. It isn't a question of counting votes. What counts is the
> behavior of the statesmen responsible for the affairs of their coun-
> tries. It is upon this behavior that the success or failure of the
> immense enterprise of Chinese aspiration to hegemony, depends.
> And, besides, there isn't such a thing as a special African posi-
> tion. On this continent we are still too separated from one an-
> other. We are trying, in the framework of the United Nations, to
> come closer, to understand each other, or rather simply to get to
> know each other. But how enormous are the difficulties! Then,
> when a country like Ghana suddenly pretends to form a govern-
> ment for the whole of Africa, well, I say it isn't serious.

Though he does not believe there is imminent danger of Africa
falling prey to Chinese subversion and ultimate conquest, he does
see some hazardous signs:

> If the Africans will not live up to their responsibilities; if they
> do not make at least some progress toward a solution of their
> internal problems, then a sensation of suffocation will grip the
> younger generation, the students, the trade unionists. Then an
> explosion may occur. Anything is possible.

In the same interview, Bourguiba was asked: Is there truth in
the forecast of an emerging anti-white racism? Is there a possibility
that under the leadership of China a strictly Afro-Asian United
Nations will be established?

> *Bourguiba:* The Chinese propaganda tries to utilize the least
> laudable instincts of the countries of the Third World. This is
> part of her arsenal. It would be a crime against humanity to create
> this racism in reverse because it would represent a regression from
> the grand idea which the world is at present in a process of adopt-
> ing, and which constitutes its most glorious title deed: the respect
> for the human person regardless of the color of his skin. It would
> also constitute a grave political error. Because even were all the
> colored people to unite their forces, they still would not be able
> to cause any harm to the white race—even if led by the Chinese.
> The whites are by far the stronger, the more advanced. It is not
> the millions of people who count, as they seem to believe in

Peking, but the means at their disposal. The Chinese masses would not weigh much in the balance if a real confrontation were to take place.

Question: Even if they had at their disposal atomic weapons?

Bourguiba: What Peking possesses isn't much, while the United States advances with a giant's stride. It is something of the magnitude of the Israeli bomb, or the Egyptian, or even that of France. . . . These little atomic bombs are essentially political bombs, window dressing to make an impression. But I doubt whether these countries will be in a position to use them. And if by misfortune they should use them—China or any of the others—they will soon be liquidated by those who possess the real stuff and who are going to have more and more of it.

Question: Doesn't the fact that China has the atomic bomb arouse some kind of pride among the Afro-Asian world? Don't they say to themselves: 'Here is an underdeveloped country which reached the superior level of science and technology?'

Bourguiba: Nonsense! . . . The Russians have shared with them some of their knowledge, then they dropped them when they saw Peking trying to go a little too far. It is not serious. Only this: if one is somewhat deranged, and the heart is eaten up by hatred, then one suffers from inferiority complexes and shouts the miracle of the Chinese bomb. But looking behind all this, one perceives that it isn't much, except for the immense misery, and immense servitude.

Surely there are advantages in establishing working bonds among countries in the process of development, Bourguiba believes, but cooperation must honestly center upon one task only: development. He told the same interviewer of *Réalités*:

> If it's really a matter of studying the means of accelerating development, then all the countries concerned with the problem should unite. But they should do it not as Afro-Asians or as Afro-Asian-South Americans, which means nothing. The important thing is to exchange experiences, to define common objectives, and to mobilize the means to achieve these objectives. It is also important to bear upon the developed nations with a view to bringing them around to cooperate with the Third World—not in a process of haggling, of opposing views and interests, of striving for hegemony, but in a spirit of human duties toward brothers who are still in a state of misery.

What is his role in the Third World? If a new Afro-Asia conference were to take place, would be participate? And if he did, what would he do there?

This is how Bourguiba visualizes his role in the Third World, which may be a proper definition of his destiny in contemporary history:

> If I go, I'll tell them what I have just told you. I intend to raise the voice of reason, the vocie of the Tunisian people . . . which could exert an influence. I'll thus strengthen the camp of serious people who seek peace and efficiency. For this I have at my disposal nothing but my authority, my experience, my past, and my achievements. I'll throw all this into the balance, with the hope that they may be of some weight. I am an optimist. (*Réalités*, November 1965)

31

Bourguiba and the Jews

HOWEVER LOUDLY MOST ARAB LEADERS, ESPECIALLY NASSER, DENY that their enmity to Israel has anything to do with Jews as such, the fact remains that their anti-Israel attitudes are inextricably mixed up with rabid anti-Semitism. Shukairy and his Palestine Liberation Organization openly appeal to international anti-Semitic groups. Nasser's propaganda apparatus is instrumental in diffusing the forged Protocols of the Elders of Zion. In all Arab countries of the Middle East (except Lebanon) the Jewish communities have been nearly destroyed, and those Jews who did not emigrate are subjected to cruel persecutions, imprisonment, often torture.

When Bourguiba made his peace initiative in the Middle East, Nasser and other Arab leaders, the press, and radio presented this initiative to their people as part of a deal among the Tunisian President, imperialism, Israel, and world Jewry. Nasser referred to Bourguiba's "Ben Gurion's man."

According to the Cairo *Al Akhbar* (April 28, 1965) the Tunisian President came out with his declarations after concluding "a dark deal" with the Jewish-owned Rothschild Bank in Paris, which promised a big loan for Tunisia's development plans; similar promises came from the governments of the United States and West Germany. After receiving these pledges, Bourguiba, according to the propaganda, started on his campaign "with the obvious aim to split the united front of the Arabs and pave the way for their recognition of Israel." The same day, Cairo radio accused him of undertaking his campaign "in coordination with Israel." A few weeks later the same *Al Akhbar* went even further and described the Israeli negative reactions to the Tunisian leader's initiative as part of that coordination, and the Prime Minister's speech in the Knesset (of May 17, 1965) as "the second act of the farce begun by President Bourguiba." At the same time, but somewhat inconsistently, the Egyptian press insisted that the Tunisian's present initiative was not something new, but that he had all along entertained contacts with economic and financial institutions which do commerce with Israel; and thus he had been violating the rules of the Arab boycott against that country.

Nasser himself came back to the same theme on several occasions. At a May 1 rally in Cairo, he declaimed, "Bourguiba professes that he is only serving the cause of the Arabs, but I am telling you he is acting in the interests of Israel."

Looking beyond this propaganda and invective Middle Eastern style, we do discern a Bourguiba genuinely untainted by anti-Semitism; he has proven both in Tunisia and in his international stance that he has friendly feelings for the Jews. Perhaps these sentiments are to some extent responsible for his desire to see a peaceful denouement to the Israel-Arab conflict, as they assuredly were for his references to the Golden Age of Jewish-Arab relationship in past historic periods; the common heritage of the two peoples which united them as the "people of the Book (s) ," and the current necessity for coexistence on the basis of mutual respect and understanding.

In his own country Bourguiba's record of dealing with the Jewish population has been consistently friendly and liberal. There has never been a deep-seated anti-Semitism in Tunisia, and the President has exerted himself to discourage any. Tunisian law is the same for all citizens without regard to religion; the Jewish community has never been hampered in the practice of its faith, and cordiality has marked its relations with the dominantly Moslem community. From its inception there were in the Tunisian parliament (National Assembly) Jewish members, as in the present session there is a Jew, Albert Bessis, and there has even been Jewish representation in the Cabinet.

During the years preceding and immediately after Tunisian independence, Bourguiba was so aloof from pan-Arab passions and aspirations that he did not seem concerned that a part of Palestine had become a Jewish state against the fanatical resistance of all the Arab states in the Middle East. People who knew Bourguiba privately and intimately assert that at heart he was a friend of Israel and is interested in how the new state progresses.

Of course, he has not found it politic to voice these sentiments publicly, but has expressed them in private conversations. As far back as January 1955, shortly before his return from Paris to Tunis to assume official leadership of the internal autonomy, he had a long discussion with the Zionist leader, Marc Yarblum (at that time living in Paris and now a citizen of Israel) who, like many other intellectuals and liberals, was a great admirer of Bourguiba and his valiant fight for Tunisia's independence. At that meeting the Zionist leader defended the Israeli cause at length with Bourguiba listening attentively. Mr. Yarblum took down the Tunisian's answering remarks verbatim:

> Were the problem of establishing a Jewish state in Palestine raised today, I would oppose such a project with all my might; instead I would have fought for an independent Palestine, permitting free development to both its peoples. But I am a realist. The State of Israel is already an accomplished fact these last seven years. She is developing at a quick pace, increasing her power and her population. Therefore I do not agree with those Arab statesmen who refuse to recognize this fact and keep proclaiming that as far as they are concerned Israel does not exist at all. To my mind, Israel and the Arab states must seek in common a solution to problems of contention: refugees, political and economic cooperation, etc. Finally, the possibility is not excluded that I may one day be in a position to intervene. But not at the present. It is not possible to do it until Tunisia has gained full independence.

After having made these remarks, Bourguiba took a copy of his recently published book *Tunisia and France* and wrote on the flyleaf: "To Marc Yarblum as a memento of our unforgettable discussion which dissipated much misunderstanding and fortified the eternal and traditional solidarity between Jews and Moslems— affectionately, your Bourguiba."

Yet he was careful to say nothing in public that could jeopardize his future relations with the leaders of the Arab states in the Middle East. A couple of months after the reported conversation with Yarblum, Bourguiba received an Israeli journalist, Philip Ben, who pressed him for a statement about his views concerning the Israel-Arab conflict. Bourguiba told him:

> I can say nothing which is liable to complicate my relations with the Arab states. One cannot exclude the possibility that in the future I'll need their support. I cannot endanger this support. I just cannot afford it.

But he did stipulate that the Israel-Arab conflict would not affect the future government of an independent Tunisia in its treatment of the Jewish community. Apart from that he hinted that his Zionist friends, citing Mr. Yarblum as an example, knew his private views.

Though there never were any official relations between Israel and Tunisia, there were normal postal connections until 1964. Regular mail was sent to and received from Israel. And even today if anyone ventures to send a letter from Israel to Tunisia, the chances are that it will reach its destination. For all these years (until 1964) there have also been normal telephone communications. Even in 1965, after Bourguiba's campaign for a peaceful settlement of the Palestine conflict, there were many and lively communications on this subject between Tunisian Jews living in Israel and their co-religionists who had stayed behind in Tunisia. The Jews in Tunisia who wrote to their friends and relatives in Israel expressed pride and satisfaction that their President had the unique courage to come out with such wise yet revolutionary declarations. They took pains to assure their correspondents in Israel that Bourguiba was sincere in his search for peace and that his words could be taken with confidence.

Again, as late as the beginning of 1964, a Zionist journalist, the late Dr. Haim Shoskess, after having been imprisoned and then expelled from neighboring Libya for alleged Zionist activities, went to Tunis and from there sent an uncensored dispatch to his newspaper in New York about his experiences in Libya, using strong terms of condemnation against the Libyan authorities.

What is more, Tunisian Jews are discreetly permitted to visit Israel and return to their country. Those who wanted to emigrate to Israel were permitted to do so.

Off Tunisia's southeast coast is the 16-square-mile island of Djerba, reputedly Homer's land of the Lotus-Eaters. Here stands one of the world's oldest synagogues, which is also a celebrated place of pilgrimage. The Jews on the island constitute one of the most ancient communities in the world, dating back more than twenty-five centuries and claiming their origin from the exiles who fled Jerusalem after the destruction of the First Temple. Their Torah was reportedly washed ashore in the wreckage of a ship sailing westward from Babylon; its appearance, regarded as a miracle, had spurred the Jews of the island to build the synagogue.

East of the synagogue, into a little grotto that is one of the remaining parts of the original building, barren women descend with lighted candles to pray for offspring. The Jews of Djerba and neighboring villages of Hara-Srira and Hara-Kbirra have preserved their ancient traditions: everyone speaks Hebrew; men wearing long beards and biblical garb cry every year over the destruction of the Temple, and even the most modest artisan is supposed to be an Hebraic Scholar—a Talmudist. Their traditional friendship with their Moslem neighbors has not altered because of conditions elsewhere. But with the establishment of the State of Israel three-fourths of Djerba's total Jewish population (numbering approximately 8,000) emigrated to Israel, where a good number of them became rabbis of Sephardic congregations. Today only some 1,500 or 2,000 remain, the same proportion that remained in Tunisia's Jewish community at large.*

On November 28, 1966, President Bourguiba paid a visit to the Djerba synagogue. According to the *New York Times* and other press reports, this was the first visit to a synagogue by a modern Arab ruler, particularly on his own initiative. The members of the Jewish communities of Tunis and Djerba, led by Tunis' Chief Rabbi, Mordecai Meis Cohen, received him, and at the entrance of the synagogue, a girl in a red and gold wedding dress presented a bouquet to the President; the congregation presented him with a nine-inch gold model of the Torah that reposes in a recess of the synagogue. Bourguiba entered and took a seat in the *tebah,* the little enclosure of latticed wooden walls from which the Torah is read.

The Chief Rabbi in a speech welcoming the President, said that when God made men rulers of nations, He endowed them with wisdom; President Bourguiba had won liberty for the Tunisian people—for *all* the people, regardless of their religion—as Moses had for the Israelites of yore. The Rabbi ended his speech by intoning a prayer that is inscribed in marble on one of the synagogue's walls. It reads in part: "Blessings on President Bourguiba. He who gives victory to kings and authority to leaders of peoples . . . may He bless, guide, protect, and assist the supreme combatant, Habib Bourguiba."

In his reply the President summed up his benevolent policy toward minorities:

---

* There are no exact statistics as of this date. Before independence, there were, perhaps, in Tunisia about 110,000 Jews. Today there are probably no more than 30,000 left.

Our state is one that belongs to all Tunisians without distinction between races and religions. Its preoccupation is to help all its sons and daughters, whatever their faith. The State asks in return only sincerity in words and loyalty in acts.

The question naturally arises: If the condition of the Jews in Tunisia was so satisfactory, why did three-fourths of them migrate? The younger, more Zionist-conscious went to Israel; the others to France. It was not a mass exodus, but a gradual stream.

Did the regime under Bourguiba encourage this process, or try to check it? There are several answers to these questions, some of them overlapping. First, the equality and security of the Jews in Tunisia, though real, is not without some qualifications: two fields of activity are, in the nature of things, "reserved" to Moslems— the army and the foreign service. Although this is a minor restriction and would affect relatively few Jews, there were in Tunisia's evolution other factors which created a psychological undercurrent of apprehension.

Despite Bourguiba's quarrel with Nasser and his crusade against pan-Arabism, Tunisia is still an Arab country and is not entirely immune to anti-Israeli feelings among the population at large and especially the bureaucracy. After the Bizerte tragedy, there was a short period of reconciliation between Bourguiba and Nasser, when the latter visited Tunisia in an atmosphere of great pomp; also, at the first two summit conferences of the Arab heads-of-state, Bourguiba made extreme anti-Israel speeches. These developments could not but affect the self-confidence of the Jews in Tunisia. Conversely, when news spread in 1962 that there had been an attempt on Bourguiba's life, actual panic seems to have spread momentarily among the Jews, who feared that successful removal of Bourguiba might result in a new government with a repressive policy toward Jews.

But this mood of apprehension was transitory and cannot alone explain the massive emigration of the Jews. The decisive reason seems to lie in the country's economic reforms. The Jews who are nearly all merchants and the artisans, were being hurt worst by such measures as import quotas and currency devaluation, and an endless variety of bureaucratic controls and regulations. True, Moslem merchants, shopkeepers, and businessmen are equally affected, but these had not the choice open to the Jews.

It is in the light of these currents and undercurrents that Bourguiba's visit to the Djerba synagogue must be considered. The

President would like to see the stream of Jewish emigration slowed down if not ended altogether, for he is said to see in the Jews a creative element which he would like to preserve for Tunisia's future development; hence the liberalism of the regime and the equality of the Jews before the law. But he cannot shelter any group from either popular prejudices or economic forces.

32

What Fury Drives Him?

WHAT ARE THE MOTIVATIONS WHICH DRIVE THIS MAN WITH SUCH fury and which made him a world figure even though he represents a small, weak, and poor country? The question, in essence, answers itself. Precisely because his country is small and weak, and will never become a power, he wants to compensate by making it an important country. In this he resembles de Gaulle, who intimated that since he represented a prostrated, humiliated, and betrayed country he had to compensate for its weaknesses by the strength of his own conceptions of a glorious France. It is for the same reason that the French leader felt he had to be tough, unbending, and grandiloquent even in his dealings with his allies and protectors—because he had no other power to lean on.

Of course, Tunisia is not France and Bourguiba is not de Gaulle. But in his own way, and in an ever-widening sphere of initiative, he is a man of considerable parts. No megalo-maniac, he too is aware of the relative insignificance of his country and of his own limitations as its leader. But in his lucid thinking he also understands that because his is a weak and poor country, the worst course for him to follow would be to behave in like manner. His fate would then be either to become a vassal of Nasser or be absorbed by Algeria. To retain Tunisia's independence and assure its future progress, he must follow an independent policy and endow it with a distinct style and personality. To emphasize the individuality of his country and of himself as a leader, he must evolve original ideas and shape a school of thought of his own.

In fairness, he also believes that small countries *have* a function to perform in history, not only for themselves but for humanity at large. Since a small country, not involved in dubious affairs of big-power politics, is not expected to use its military or economic power for the solution of international problems, it can afford instead to use its moral assets and its common sense. In an interview with the Paris *Combat* he said:

> In all epochs, moral values had their weight. Great powers have been destroyed because their leaders acted contrary to human nature. . . . History has shown that small countries served as an example for states much greater and much more powerful.

Bourguiba also believes that by building Tunisia's prestige and making it a keystone of new para-national political groupings, he will enable it to contribute to international peace and progress. Such a strategy will benefit his own country politically, morally, economically, and technologically. To bring it down to cases, he hopes to gain for Tunisia the status of a "special and privileged relationship" first with France and then perhaps with the European Common Market.

The Tunisian President may take pride in the fact that to a considerable degree his policies have already paid off. He has endowed his country with international prestige, and has himself emerged as a leader of world renown.

The contention that a similar policy and methods have been followed by other African leaders—Nasser; the deposed Nkrumah of Ghana; Ben Bella of Algeria, and others—is fallacious. Their activities and aspirations were usually animated by negative and often destructive emotions: hatred, defiance, resentment, arrogance, meddling in the complicated relationships between Moscow and Washington, exaggerating out of any proportion the persistence of the imperialist and colonialist tradition. They also neglected the internal stability, economic development and wholesome administration of their own countries. Bourguiba ascribes these vices to the inferiority complexes of most of the leaders of the post-colonial peoples. But the cardinal difference is that those leaders who have not yet been deposed by their own armies are in constant dread of a coup. Bourguiba's regime is stable; he is not even threatened.

Jean Lacouture summarizes:

> Bourguiba's supporters insist . . . that his rationalism gives his country the role of a pilot nation in the search for an Arab-Moslem civilization adapted to the modern world; and that, thanks to

the foundation and progressive consolidation of the Neo-Destour Party, Tunisia possesses the cadres and discipline which make it the best-governed country in the Third World.

He will never make a great power of Tunisia. But an outsider may observe that his patriotism and his talent, summed up in the one word "Bourguibism"—which will remain a synonym for realism—have made Tunisia one of the laboratories where the men of the second half of the 20th century are seeking the solution to a major problem—the relations between great industrial powers and peoples in the process of development.

Some international observers, while conceding to Bourguiba skills and attributes of "a courageous strategist" think however that he "is often a poor tactician . . . and tactless in his choice of words." In our era, when we are accustomed to statesmen who speak in worn-out and tired clichés written for them by ghosts, we may be startled when one of them speaks in vivid language, in a style all his own, advancing ideas which are fresh—and often spontaneous.

His message and the main ideas of his peace initiative were stated in their essence in two press conferences—in the Old City of Jerusalem and in Beirut. His subsequent declarations were mostly elaborations and amplifications; but the breadth of his views and his manner of presenting them covered up their repetitiveness, and they always sounded fresh and interesting. This vitality explains their appeal to the press and TV again and again, not only in the Middle East but also in Europe and in the United States. His style and spontaneity reflect a stormy temperament and a flair for the dramatic in history; these combine to make him a unique phenomenon in the world of international politics—exasperating to his opponents and fascinating to the rest.

ENVOI

It is hardly possible to overestimate the significance of the Tunisian President's initiative. What he said, the way he said it, and the platform he chose created a sensation not only because no other Arab leader had ever dared voice such views, but because even the great Western powers had not dared to. The great powers tried on various occasions to exert a pacifying influence on both sides, but mostly through discreet diplomacy, and only when there was immediate danger of hostilities on a large scale, as in the case of the diversion of the headwaters of the Jordan River in 1965, or in the days preceding the War in June. In general they seemed to view the situation in the Middle East as so hopeless as to despair of the possibility of any solution at all. They came to believe that the Palestine problem is beyond redemption. They, therefore assumed a fatalistic attitude, tacitly resigned to the extremely dangerous status quo. None of these nations had the imagination or the will to lift the problem from a level of despair to a level of the imperative of peace. (At all events, this was so prior to the outbreak of the war in June). Only one statesman did; and he was an Arab nationalist.

President Bourguiba challenged two of the most deeply and widely inculcated tenets in popular Arab opinion: a) that under no circumstances should one accept the existence of a sovereign State of Israel or to enter direct negotiations with it, and b) there is ultimately no other solution to the Palestine problem except war.

Is Peace Possible?

There are pessimists who are just unable to visualize a peaceful denouement to the Palestine drama. They view the claims, aspirations, and vital interests of the opposing parties as intrinsically irreconcilable. There is no lack of substantiating evidence for this somber view. In the course of reporting and analyzing the case history of President Bourguiba's initiative we have tried to bring into relief the claims and counterclaims, the attitudes, the prejudices, the fanaticism, the dogmatism, the intransigences of both sides. Taken at their face values they may lead one to skeptical conclusions.

Yet upon deeper probing and maturer reflection such conclusions would be found unwarranted, because the evidence, though solid, is nonetheless also somewhat selective and impressionistic. The assumptions of the pessimistic view are not always in accord with the deeper realities underlying the Palestine conflict. Oversimplification, whether inspired by pessimism or optimism, is, however, dangerous in so complex a situation.

Certain key questions are meaningless when posed in isolation, that is, not within their proper context. To ask: Will the Arabs agree to make peace with Israel? is such a question. It implies that peace depends entirely upon the Arabs, which is not the case. A more meaningful question would be: Will the Arabs agree to make peace with Israel if the latter were willing to offer some concessions? Or: On what conditions would the Arabs agree to peace? What price would Israel have to pay? and, what price could Israel be willing to pay? What price would Israel *be able* to pay without endangering its security and sovereignty? But in the last account the decisive question is whether the destruction of Israel is the only, exclusive, and all-absorbing aim of all Arab leaders? Or do they think—privately and publicly—in terms of options and alternatives?

The fascinating significance of Bourguiba's initiative is that it was revolutionary, while at the same time it reflected trends latent in Arab thought. How can this paradox be reconciled? By understanding that Bourguiba challenged the extreme postulates of Arab policy and brought into the open those moderate options buried in the consciousness of some of the Arab leaders. Even Nasser, as we have seen, thinks periodically in terms of a peaceful solutions to the Palestine conflict, as do Kings Hussein and Hassan and the leaders of the Lebanon; but frequently the peaceful option is latent and inhibited.

Projections in the Arab World

Bourguiba's dramatic challenge to Arab policy on the Palestine issue captured the attention and the imagination of world opinion. But no less daring was his challenge to an even more firmly lodged tenet: the reality of a pan-Arab nation. While some Arab leaders, and indeed Nasser himself, have deviated on occasion from the accepted line on the Palestine question, the concept of pan-Arabism has for years been considered sacrosanct. Bourguiba alone dared to question this dogma.

His relentless challenge to Nasser is a logical counterpart of his myth-wrecking drive in the Arab world: If there is no such a thing as a monolithic Arabia, then anyone who purports to be its anointed prophet is an impostor.

This projection must be considered as the most formidable extension of Bourguiba's initiative. Whatever else happens as a result of his campaign, one thing is clear: in challenging Nasser's hegemony and exposing its vices and weaknesses, Bourguiba undermined the Egyptian's leadership claim to an irreparable degree.

As part of the crusade against pan-Arabism Bourguiba demanded that the Arab League be reorganized on a completely new basis. He heaped scorn upon it as the handmaiden of Nasser in his scheme to convert the Arab countries into provinces of Egypt. He demanded that the League's headquarters no longer be in Cairo, its meetings no longer held in Egypt, and that its deliberations be conducted on the principle of strict and unqualified respect for the sovereignty and independence of each member state, not just in theory but in practice, with each member having the indisputable right to dissent. Most of these demands have since been accepted by other Arab leaders, and, paradoxically, the most severe critic today of the Arab league is no other than Egypt, though not for the same reasons. It is, therefore, safe to assume that the League will sooner or later make changes demanded by Bourguiba or disintegrate.

Bourguiba is proud of having launched the debunking drive. He told the *Views'* interviewer: "Since (I undertook this campaign) the mystique of unity (based on) terror and fear has been crumbling faster and faster." (Autumn, 1965)

The furor he aroused not only did not destroy him politically —he emerged with heightened stature and influence. He is the only leader who dares to speak out and whose words and ideas, next only to those of Nasser, affect the trends of history in the Middle East. There is no doubt that many of the Arab rulers admire his courage and wisdom and wish they dared emulate him.

One may presume to predict that after some years of fever and upheavals, the Middle East will enter a calmer phase of normal development and stabilization, provided the Russians check their present recklessness in that part of the world. There will, probably, be two or more groupings, with their centers competing for influence; Cairo will certainly be one of them—perhaps, in view of its population, size, and strategic location—the more important but not the only one. The other centers will, probably, be Baghdad and of course the Maghreb.

Whether or not he set out on his tour with that intention, the Tunisian President became aware of the increasing implications of his campaign, and consequently of his developing role of leadership in the Arab world. The awareness seems to have brought greater clarity and forthrightness to his words and acts. This may perhaps explain his relentless pursuit of the campaign, despite repeated predictions that each of his declarations would be the last heard from him.

He has disclaimed ambition, but his behavior and the course of his actions do not entirely support his protestations.

This is not the first time an Arab leader has clashed with Gamal Abdel Nasser. Despite his eminence, and his seeming success in dealing with the great powers (at all events until the last war in June), Nasser has actually scored very few successes in the Arab world. Whenever he has tried to seduce or force an Arab country into his special sphere of influence, he has failed.

Although the Sudan was part of the Egyptian-Sudanese condominium under British rule, it refused to become federated with Egypt. The union with Syria born in 1958 broke up in rebellion against Cairo in 1961. The Hashemite dynasty in Iraq was overthrown July 14, 1958 by rebellious army officers who slew the King and his Prime Minister Nuri el Said—Nasser's chief opponent at the time. But to everyone's astonishment (including Nasser's), the new ruler, General Abdel Karim Kassem, showed himself no less an opponent to the Egyptian ruler than his royalist predecessor. Nasser's protegé (some said rival), former Algerian President Ahmed Ben Bella, has been deposed and arrested. Saudi Arabia's King Faisal emerged as a strong and astute opponent who impeded Nasser's costly efforts to install a satellite republican regime in the whole of the Yemen. Nasser's drive to penetrate into the Persian Gulf area was checked. One of the nationalist leaders in that area told a *New York Times* correspondent in November 1966:

> We can get rid of the British easily enough. The whole world is against imperialism; but the Egyptians will come in the name of brotherhood and stay forever.

In a sense, and despite what happened in June 1967, the most spectacular example of resistance, through the years, is of course that of the young and plucky King Hussein of Jordan.

But there is a fundamental difference between the resistance offered by these other Arab leaders to Nasser, and Bourguiba's challenge. In the enumerated instances there was in each case an immediate and emergency situation. The resistance to Nasser was a reflexive reaction to an immediate threat or onslaught; his intended victims had to fight for their physical or political survival.

For Bourguiba there was no overt, immediate threat to his regime or his person: Nasser has long ago given up active attempts to subvert the regime in Tunisia; it had proven so stable that efforts to overthrow it were futile. But Bourguiba, on his own initiative, attacked Nasser taking the offensive at a time and a place of his own choosing—a distinct advantage in political as well as in military strategy.

This is not the only distinction to be made. Nuri el Said, King Faisal, even Hussein, represent a conservative tradition already regarded even by many Arabs as belonging to a bygone age. Bourguiba represents the modern and progressive trend of our time. He is no imperialist puppet, like Nuri el Said was; his record is not blemished by collaboration with Nazism and Fascism, as is that of the former Grand Mufti of Jerusalem, Haj Amin el Husseini, who has since 1948 been head of the Palestine Higher Committee. Though engaged in a bitter struggle with the French for Tunisia's independence, Bourguiba spurned all the allurements offered him by the Axis. He is a nationalist hero who more than anyone else in the Arab world fought for the independence of his country, carrying on much of the fight from jail or exile. After independence was achieved he fought on relentlessly to remove the last vestiges of colonial rule. His record in this respect is not only impeccable but glorious. The cities of his country are not bazaars of the slave trade, and he is no feudal overlord. He is a socialist, sponsoring a moderate and eclectic brand of socialism peculiar to his humanist philosophy. He did not inherit a throne, as did Hussein of Jordan, Hassan of Morocco, or Faisal of Saudi Arabia. Nor did he come to power by way of a putsch, as did Nasser, Boumedienne of Algeria, or most others in the volatile world of Arab politics.

He was thrice chosen in popular elections and his regime is, despite occasional tensions and dissensions, one of the most solid of any in the African and Arab countries. He has been cautious enough to refrain from building up an army strong and autonomous enough to pose a threat, as has happened in so many of the new nations. And he believes in the destiny of Arabism, if it can throw off its backward-looking, negative and destructive forces; he sees it as a progressive, humanistic vision, blended with and conditioned by Western civilization.

Projections in the West

In the Western world the repercussions of Bourguiba's initiative are immense and far-reaching, regardless of the absence so far of any visible breakthrough in the Palestine conflict. In challenging Arab leadership Bourguiba has challenged also the attitude and behavior of the West, chiefly the United States. Before his initiative, the lines were neatly drawn: concerning Palestine there were two camps of sworn, irreconcilable enemies, successfully preventing attempts to deal with the problem on its merits. The only course was neutrality in one form or another, coping only with such marginal matters as the United Nations Relief and Works Agency for Palestine Refugees, the United Nations Emergency Force, and economic and technical assistance to almost everyone. The latter encompassed as well periodic military assistance to both Israel and some Arab countries, for the purpose of "preserving the balance." The essence of such a policy is to maintain the *status quo,* which is to say to perpetuate the state of war. Bourguiba, argues that it was necessary to unfreeze the *status quo* by peaceful means, by negotiation.

This challenge to the great powers is fundamental and of historic import. The western powers are no longer faced with two irreconcilable camps; they can now choose, not between one intransigence and another, but between intransigence and reason.

Great powers are usually slow to unlearn concepts which they have long entertained. Nevertheless, Bourguiba may have succeeded in jarring the Western powers out of their mesmerized belief in the pan-Arab myth of "one nation" stretching from the Persian Gulf to the Atlantic, whose capital is Cairo and whose only leader and spokesman is Gamal Abdel Nasser. If these powers were to begin looking at the Middle East and North Africa through clearer lenses, they may perceive that there is not much more justification for considering the Arab world as "a nation" than there is, let's say, Latin America, or the Anglo-Saxons on both sides of the Atlantic. They would on the contrary discover (or rediscover) that the Middle East is a centrifugal region, ill-defined geographically or politically, with dissimilar states having disparate interests and which, far from being united, compete with one another for influence and leadership. As long as the distorted vision persisted, no effective measures could have been taken to defuse the live bomb that ticks away at civilization's crossroad.

It must be remembered that the myth of a supposedly monolithic Arab world was fostered, if not invented, not exactly by the Arabs themselves, but rather by Great Britain as a means of maintaining her stranglehold on that crossroad—the Middle East. Political revolution and technical evolution have altered the alignments of the cosmic struggle for power; but though the *dramatis personae* have changed, the motivation remains the same. Pan-Arabism is one of those pan-myths like pan-Africanism, pan-socialism, or pan-communism, pan-Slavism, or pan-Germanism, which though they invariably fail of their avowed aims, generally succeed in creating a climate of international tension, political upheaval, and social strife. They are without exception inspired by expansionist and totalitarian ambitions. These pan-movements, based upon the tenets of race, religion, or ideology, have betrayed a pattern which has invariably proven negative: divisive rather than unifying; restraining peoples rather than liberating them; seking to rejuvenate a dying past rather than nurturing a nascent future.

Not that Bourguiba scorns the ideal of unity. We have seen that he never tires of extolling this ideal as worthy of great sacrifices. But in *his* search for unity, he seeks out built-in safeguards of checks and balances, to prevent the concentration of power in one center or one leader. He stipulates that whatever the structure and source of unity may be, it must be based upon the sovereignty of states freely cooperating within larger para-national frameworks. He also seems to believe it a good thing for such para-national groupings to overlap, another check on unhealthy centripetalism. We have seen his interest in constructive experimentation toward unity not only among the Arabs, but also among the French-speaking nations, and the moderate Moslem countries in both Asia and Africa. And there is reason to expect that some of these projects may evolve into imaginative new experiments in international statecraft. An editorialist of *Le Monde* commented: "Many of those who condemn him today may very well express their thanks the day after tomorrow."

As a result of his campaign, Habib Bourguiba grew in stature. His superior qualities—his enlightenment, his culture, his superb style, his pragmatism, his diplomatic skills, his moderation and common sense, his lack of fanaticism or dogmatism, his analytical astuteness, his warm rapport with his own people, his gift for surprise and original strategy, came out in relief. Beyond this, his vision of historical trends and his many initiatives to affect these trends make him one of the most interesting figures on the modern international scene. He revealed himself a leader of international stature and a champion of peace who must yet be reckoned with.

His offer, in principle, of his good offices to bring together representatives of Israel and the Palestinian Arabs for peace negotiations has so far not been heeded. But the day may not be far off when both parties will avail themselves of this opportunity. They can offord to ignore this offer much longer only at their own risk and peril. The latest series of tragedies, war, bloodshed and destruction make this opportunity most appropriate.

Selective Chronology of Events
in the Middle East

THE HISTORY OF THE COUNTRY WHICH IS NOW TUNISIA STRETCHES back into deep antiquity when Phoenician settlers arrived there probably in the ninth century B. C. According to legend these emigrants under the leadership of Elissar, the daughter of the King of Tyre on the eastern Shore of the Mediterranean, fled their native country because of the tyranny of her brother Pygmalion. The arrivals built a "new city" *Karthadshat* (Carthage). Queen Elissar was subsequently called Dido, i.e., "the fugitive." Carthage developed into an empire, and achieved a position of commercial and naval supremacy in the Mediterranean. It reached its zenith in the fourth century. B. C.

146 B. C.: Romans capture Carthage; Tunisia becomes a Roman province.

648–669 A. D.: Arabs conquer Tunisia.

1574–1881: Tunisia becomes part of the Turkish empire. In 1705 Hussein Ben Ali (probably a native of Crete) makes himself master of the country, though acknowledging Turkish suzerainty. He founds the dynasty which is to rule Tunisia until July 25, 1957 when its last descendent Sidi Mohammed el Amin, the Bey of Tunis, was deposed by the Tunisian National Assembly, and Tunisia is proclaimed a republic.

May 12, 1881: France establishes protectorate over Tunisia.

August 3, 1903: Habib Bourguiba is born.

November 2, 1917: The Balfour Declaration is published, in which the British Government declared that it views "with favor the establishment in Palestine of a national home for the Jewish people, and will use their best endeavors to facilitate the achievement of this object, it being clearly understood that nothing shall be done which may prejudice the civil and religious rights of the existing non-Jewish communities in Palestine, or the rights and political status enjoyed by Jews in any other country."

Jerusalem, the capital of the last Hebrew commonwealth of Palestine succumbed to the assault of the Roman legions on September 26, 70 A. D. The city was destroyed. Its people were severely punished. Thousands were put to death, many more sold as slaves.

The political revival of Hebrew statehood launched by Theodore Herzl, who published on February 14, 1896, in Vienna, his *Judenstaat* (The Jewish State). In August, 1897 was held, in Basel, Switzerland, the First Zionist Congress, which adopted the program of the Zionist movement.

April 24, 1920: At the peace conference, at San Remo, the Mandate over Palestine is entrusted to Great Britain. In 1922 the League of Nations ratified the decision and the document.

1920: The *Destour* (Constitution) movement came into being under the leadership of Shaik al-Thalibi. Its program called for a selfgoverning constitutional regime with a legislative assembly.

1924–1927: Bourguiba studies law and political science in Paris. After completing his studies he returns to Tunisia and begins to practice law.

1930: Bourguiba embarks upon his political career by joining *La Voix Tunisien,* the organ of the Destour party.

1932: Bourguiba creates an independent organ *l'Action Tunisien.*

1934: Bourguiba, impatient with and in opposition to the old leadership of the nationalist movement, creates the Neo-Destour party. At its first congress he is elected Secretary General.

September 1934: Bourguiba is arrested by the French Resident-General in Tunis.

1942: Bourguiba is liberated by the Axis powers.

April 1943: Bourguiba returns to Tunis from exile.

May 7, 1943: Bourguiba launches a manifesto in favor of the Allies and calls for the economic and spiritual reconstruction of the world and of Tunis.

March 22, 1945: Arab League founded in Cairo. Seven heads-of-state were present at the signing of the pact: Egypt, Yemen, Trans-Jordan, Iraq, Saudi Arabia, Lebanon and Syria. Since then six more Arab states joined: Lybia, Sudan, Tunisia, Morocco, Kuwait and Algeria.

March 26, 1946: Bourguiba secretly leaves Tunis for the Middle East. Arrives in Cairo April 26. Visits all the countries in the area to mobilize support for the cause of Tunisia's independence. He is back in Tunis September 8, 1949.

November 1947: The United Nations adopts the Resolution according to which Mandated Palestine should be partitioned into an Arab and a Jewish State, with Jerusalem and Bethlehem internationalized.

Hostilities break out between the two communities in Palestine.

May 14, 1948: The British Mandate came officially to an end and the British High Commissioner departs. The Union Jack is removed from the last official building.

A Provisional Council of State, under the chairmanship of Ben Gurion, proclaims the establishment of the State of Israel.

May 15, 1948: The armies of six Arab states invade Israel. The same day President Truman recognizes Israel *de facto*.

Since then, the vast majority of the nations of the world have extended recognition, and so did Communist China, Pakistan, Indonesia and some others. India entertains consular but not diplomatic relations with Israel.

After the war in June 1967, Russia and her allies, except Roumania, broke relations with Israel. So did Yugoslavia.

December 11, 1948: The General Assembly adopted the resolution recognizing the right of the Palestine refugees to return to their homes if they wish to live in peace with their neighbors; or receive compensation for property left behind. This resolution was adopted in all the consecutive sessions of the Assembly.

February 1949: Armistice agreements are signed at Rhodes between Israel and the governments of Jordan, Egypt, Lebanon and Syria.

Israel emerged victorious from the war with her Arab neighbors and substantially expanded the territory allocated to her by the U.N. Partition resolution. That part of the Resolution which stipulated the creation of an independent Palestine Arab State and tied in economic union with the Jewish State, was abandoned. The territories envisioned for the Arab State (except those conquered by Israel) were incorporated into the State of Jordan. The Gaza Strip fell under Egyptian jurisdiction.

May 11, 1949: Israel is admitted, as a member, to the United Nations.

April 12, 1950: Bourguiba arrives in Paris to gain public support for the cause of Tunisia's independence. Next year he visits the United Kingdom, the United States and several countries in Asia.

February 18, 1951: French government grants greater internal autonomy to Tunisia under a system of "Franco-Tunisian co-sovereignty."

Tunisian nationalists will accuse the French government of failing to implement the provisions of this system.

September 1951: The Security Council of the U.N. condemns Egypt for depriving Israel of her right to free passage through the Suez Canal.

December 15, 1951: Bourguiba returns to Tunisia and convokes an emergency session of the Congress of the Neo-Destour Party in defiance of a French prohibition.

January 18, 1952: Bourguiba is arrested. Anti-French armed resistance breaks out.

July 1952: King Farouk of Egypt is deposed by a group of "Free Officers" led by Lieutenant-Colonel Nasser.

May 2, 1953: Hussein is proclaimed King of Jordan.

October 1953: U.S. Special Representative, Mr. Eric Johnston proposes plan of coordinated utilization of the Jordan River waters between the Arab States and Israel. The latter accepted the plan but the Arabs ultimately rejected it.

July 31, 1954: French Premier Mendes-France offers Tunisia complete internal autonomy. The previous plan of "co-sovereignty" is abandoned.

June 1, 1955: After three-and-a-half years of imprisonment, banishment and house arrest Bourguiba is released by the French authorities and returns to Tunisia, where he is given a hero's welcome by the people.

June 3, 1955: Franco-Tunisian agreement on internal autonomy is signed. France retains control of defense and foreign affairs.

September 17, 1955: First all-Tunisian Government is formed by Tahar Ben Ammar as Premier. Half of the 12 Ministers are members of the Neo-Destour Party. Bourguiba himself is not in the Cabinet.

September 24, 1955: Arms deal is concluded between Nasser and Moscow (officially between Cairo and Prague).

November 17, 1955: Congress of the Neo-Destour Party expels its former Secretary General, Salah ben Youssef, on the grounds that he advocates complete independence by violent means. Bourguiba seeks to achieve the same aim through negotiations.

Four weeks later, on December 18, 40 followers of Ben Youssef are arrested in connection with the interception of a convoy of arms, apparently coming from Libya. They are accused of an anti-Government conspiracy. On January 28, 1956 a warrant is issued for the arrest of Salah ben Youssef, who in the meantime fled the country. He subsequently lived in Cairo and plotted against Bourguiba. On January 24, 1957 he is sentenced to death *in absentia*. On August 12, 1961 he is assassinated in a hotel room in Frankfurt, Germany, under mysterious circumstances, which, up to this day, remain unresolved.

December 19, 1955. U.S. Government offers loan to Egypt to build High Aswan Dam.

March 20, 1956: A new French-Tunisian "protocol of agreement" is signed in Paris, according to which the French promised eventually to grant Tunisia complete sovereignty, including the take-over of defense and foreign affairs.

March 25, 1956: First general elections held in independent Tunisia for a Constitutional Assembly.

April 13, 1956: New Constitution is adopted.

April 14, 1956: Bourguiba forms a new all-Neo-Destour Cabinet.

June 15, 1956: French and Tunisian Governments sign agreement confirming the complete independence of Tunisia in foreign affairs.

July 19, 1956: Dulles rescinds offer of Aswan Dam loan.

July 26, 1956: Nasser nationalizes Suez Canal Company, with physical seizure of installations.

August 10, 1956: Bourguiba announces that polygamy and easy divorce will be abolished.

October 23, 1956: Cairo announces joint Arab command of Egyptian and Syrian forces under an Egyptian commander-in-chief.

October 29, 1956: Israeli forces launch Sinai campaign as part of a secret agreement with France and Great Britain.

After about 100 hours the Israelis achieve a spectacular victory occupying the Sinai peninsula.

October 31, 1956: Britain and France join in an assault on Suez.

November 2, 1956: General Assembly of the United Nations orders an immediate cease-fire.

November 4, 1956: U.N. votes to station an Emergency Force on the Egyptian-Israeli border, in Sinai, and at the Gulf of Aqaba.

November 5, 1956: Moscow threatens intervention in Suez conflict with atomic bombs, rockets and "volunteers."

November 6, 1956: Britain, France and Israel accept cease-fire.

November 12, 1956: Tunisia is admitted to the United Nations.

November 24, 1956: U.N. votes "forthwith" withdrawal of the invading French, British and Israeli troops from Egypt.

December 22, 1956: British and French troops complete their evacuation from Suez.

March 8, 1957: Israel withdraws all her troops from Sinai and Gaza Strip.

July 25, 1957: National Constituent Assembly deposes the Bey and proclaims Tunisia a Republic.

September 14, 1957: Tunisia votes in the U.N. Assembly in favor of a resolution condemning the Soviet Union for the "continued defiance of the resolutions of the Assembly" on Hungary and for its actions in that country.

February 22, 1958: Union of Egypt and Syria proclaimed as the United Arab Republic.

May 12–13, 1958: Armed insurrection breaks out in Lebanon.

July 14, 1958: Iraqi Government overthrown by a military junta headed by General Abdel Karim el-Kassem. The King and his Prime Minister and others are killed.

July 20, 1958: At the request of the Lebanese Government the United States lands about 1000 marines. On August 18, the United States made a formal commitment to withdraw the marines. They were subsequently evacuated following a resolution of the U.N. Assembly, which provided for the evacuation under the auspices of the U.N. and the Arab League.

October 1, 1958: Tunisia joins the Arab League.

October 15, 1958: Tunisia breaks off diplomatic relations with Egypt, accusing Cairo of conniving with Bourguiba's foe, ben Youssef, to subvert his regime.

October 28, 1958: Soviet Union offers to "participate" in the construction of the Aswan High Dam in Egypt.

December 3, 1958: Nasser, in a speech, accuses Bourguiba of being an "agent of imperialism."

Shortly afterwards Tunisia is expelled from the Arab League.

December 27, 1958: Soviet Union and Egypt sign agreement for implementation of the first stage of the Aswan High Dam.

February 4, 1960: Bourguiba attacks Ramadan, the Moslem month of fasting and one of the five religious obligations of Islam. Before a mass rally he demonstrated his opposition to the fast by drinking a glass of orange juice.

January 30, 1961: Tunisia ends its boycott of Arab League and attends Arab League meeting of Foreign Ministers.

February 27, 1961: Bourguiba holds lengthy discussion with President de Gaulle, which lasted the whole day. During these discussions Bourguiba brought up the question of Bizerte, which was still under French control. De Gaulle is reported to have said that his first priority is to bring the Algerian war to an end, and everything else has to wait. Bourguiba got the impression that de Gaulle reacted favorably to his suggestion of an early evacuation of the naval base.

July 7, 1961: Message from Bourguiba to de Gaulle demanding the formulation of a time table for the evacuation of Bizerte.

July 17, 1961: Bourguiba declares in the National Assembly that he will give France 24 hours to evacuate Bizerte; otherwise he will order a blockade of the French naval and air forces in the base.

July 18, 1961: Note from the French Government tells the Tunisians that the problem cannot be solved under threats and that the French troops will resist any attempt to take over the base by force.

July 19, 1961: Tunisian troops and civilians besiege the French at Bizerte. Fire is opened against French planes bringing supplies and paratroop reinforcements. French forces return fire.

July 20–21, 1961: French troops break the blockade and occupy the whole city of Bizerte (not only the base) after heavy fighting. According to a later Tunisian estimate 1,300 Tunisians were killed, including civilians, women and children.

An even greater number was wounded. The French casualties were 25 dead and about 100 wounded.

July 22, 1961: U.N. Security Council adopts a resolution calling for an immediate cease-fire. Both France and Tunisia inform the Council on the same day that their forces stopped fighting.

August 3, 1961: Tunisia announces it will reestablish diplomatic relations with Egypt.

August 25, 1961: U.N. General Assembly's Special Session adopts a resolution condemning the French presence on Tunisian territory. France boycotts the entire debate.

September 5, 1961: De Gaulle says at a press conference that France has never contested the principle of Tunisian sovereignty over Bizerte and that one day it will be necessary to negotiate the withdrawal of French troops. But he adds that this is important now because of the critical world situation.

September 6, 1961: Bourguiba declares in a broadcast: "It appears that General de Gaulle has finally recognized the principle of evacuation of Bizerte. . . . Thus it is possible for us to come to an understanding on the evacuation time table. We have never asked for evacuation today or tomorrow."

September 8, 1961: Bourguiba proposes an agreement allowing France to retain her base "during the present world crisis."

September 29, 1961: Syria breaks away from the Union with Egypt and proclaims its independence.

September 27, 1962: A military coup overthrows the Yemen Monarchy. Egypt accords economic and military aid to the newly-proclaimed Republic.

February 8, 1963: A military coup overthrows the regime of General Kassem in Iraq. Kassem is captured and shot.

March 2, 1963: France and Tunis sign agreement of transfer to Tunis of French-owned farm land which provides for compensation to the French owners, both for the land and the equipment.

October 4, 1963: Bourguiba announces before the National Assembly that France will evacuate Bizerte by October 15.

December 13, 1963: Celebrations are held in Tunis of the French evacuation of Bizerte. Among the foreign dignitaries attending the ceremonies is President Nasser.

January 13–16, 1964: First "Summit" conference of Arab heads of state is held in Cairo. The communique announces the decisions a) to create a unified command of the Arab military forces; b) to create a Palestine Arab political entity in the framework of the Palestine Liberation Organization and c) to divert the headwaters of the River Jordan. All these resolutions are directed against Israel.

May 5, 1964: Israeli Government announces that water has begun to flow through pipelines from the Sea of Galilee to the Negev.

May 11, 1964: Tunisian National Assembly approves legislation authorizing immediate expropriation of foreign-owned land (mostly French-owned). This legislation was in violation of previously signed agreements with the French Government, which stipulated a time-table and compensation.

May 12, 1964: France retaliates. Paris announces as a "first measure" the cancellation of all economic aid to Tunisia, because of its failure to "respect agreements."

September 5–11, 1964: Second "Summit" conference of Arab heads of state in Alexandria.

Conference spokesman announces that the delegates have reached unanimous agreement on military measures to counter Israel's diversion of the Jordan River waters into the Negev.

October 5–10, 1964: Second Conference of non-aligned nations is held in Cairo.

West Germany's Arms Deal with Israel

January–March 1965

Press reports in the United States, West Germany and in other countries revealed that West Germany committed itself to supply arms to Israel in the amount of $80 million. This was either initiated by, or, at all events, received the blessing of the U.S. Government. Nasser made it a political *casus belli* and declared that if West Germany doesn't stop arms shipments to Israel he will break off diplomatic relations with Bonn. He further threatened to recognize East Germany if Bonn recognizes Israel. He tried to mobilize all the member states of the Arab League to act in unison with him. Chansellor Erhard, under the impact of these threats, announced that arms deliveries to Israel stopped. But this step didn't appease Nasser and he invited the head of the East German State Ulbricht on an official visit. Thereupon, Bonn decided to enter negotiations with Israel about compensation for the arms still undelivered and about establishing normal diplomatic relations with Tel Aviv.

January 12, 1965: Thirteen Arab Premiers, at the end of a four-day Arab League meeting, issue a joint communiqué, announcing their agreements to pursue a unified policy against any foreign nation which will either establish new relations with Israel or "consolidate Israel's aggressive military efforts." This statement was a warning to West Germany.

January 16, 1965: Premier Eshkol declares that Israel will consider any Arab attempt to divert the headwaters of the Jordan River as "an encroachment on our soil" and that if the Arabs put their plan into operation "a military confrontation would become inevitable."

February 15, 1965: Chancellor Ehrard, in a letter to Eshkol says that West Germany strives to find a way to fulfill remainder of the arms obligation to Israel. Eshkol, in a speech in the Knesset, demands that Germany honor its commitments in full and rejects monetary or other compensation. The Knesset adopts a resolution embodying the Premier's statement.

Bourguiba's Tour in the Middle East and Southeast Europe

February 16–April 9, 1965

February 16, 1965: Bourguiba undertakes a tour of 10 countries in the Middle East and Southeast Europe.

February 16–22. In the United Arab Republic
February 22–27. In Saudi Arabia
February 27–March 6. In Jordan
March 7–11. In Lebanon
March 12–14. In Kuwait
March 14–21. In Iran
March 16. Cancels visit to Iraq. Remains in Iran unofficially till March 25.
March 26–29. In Turkey
March 30–April 5. In Yugoslavia
April 5–9. In Greece

February 17, 1965: Syrians and Israelis exchange fire for eighty minutes north of the Sea of Galilee. United Nations observers arrange for a cease fire.

February 21, 1965: Ulbricht leaves for Cairo.

February 23, 1965: In an interview for Cairo radio and newspapers, Ulbricht charges that the "undercover deal" between

West Germany and Israel included "joint preparations to produce atomic weapons."

February 24, 1965: Ulbricht arrives in Egypt where he is given a welcome usually reserved for a visiting head-of-state. Receives 21-gun salutes in Alexandria and Cairo.

February 28, 1965: Egypt calls up some reserves. Military maneuvers are held in the Gaza strip. Cairo reports tell about test mobilization of reserves in Israel.

Infiltrators damage two buildings at Kfar Hess.

March 1, 1965: Israel complains to U. N. Security Council, blaming Jordan for three recent incidents of sabotage.

A $100 million aid package is signed in Cairo during Ulbricht's visit.

Cairo announces it will open a Consulate General in East Berlin. Nasser accepts invitation to visit East Germany.

March 3, 1965: Israeli Army reports Egyptian planes intruded over the Negev.

March 6, 1965: Bourguiba holds press conference in the Old City of Jerusalem where he launches his campaign for a peaceful solution to the Palestine conflict.

March 7, 1965: West German government decides to establish diplomatic relations with Israel.

Israelis and Syrians clash with machine-gun and tank fire north of the Sea of Galilee.

March 8, 1965: Syrians and Israelis exchange fire in fourth tank and gun battle in six days.

March 9–10, 1965: Arab League envoys meet in Cairo on the West German question. Nasser declares that the Arabs must win the "showdown" with West Germany as "last step to liberate Palestine." He threatens Egypt will recognize East Germany if Bonn establishes diplomatic ties with Israel.

The conference of the Arab League envoys decides that final measures against West Germany should be referred to a meeting of the Arab League Foreign Ministers.

March 10, 1965: Arab infiltrators blow up water lines to the Negev.

March 11, 1965: Bourguiba's press conference in Beirut.

March 13, 1965: An atmosphere of war sweeps the Middle East. Egypt has cancelled some military leaves and puts some forces on modified alert.

March 14, 1965: Israeli Cabinet approves "immediate establishment" of diplomatic relations with Bonn.

Conference of Arab League Foreign Ministers by a majority vote (10 to 3) decides to break off diplomatic relations with West Germany. Morocco, Tunisia and Libya did not vote for the resolution.

March 15, 1965: Nasser reelected President. Receives 99.999% of the vote.

March 16, 1965: Anti-Bourguiba demonstrations break out in Beirut and Damascus.

Bourguiba cancels his visit to Iraq because the Iraqi Government informed him it cannot guarantee his personal safety.

Knesset approves by majority vote (66 against 29, with 10 abstentions) Cabinet decision to establish diplomatic relations with West Germany.

One Israeli killed, four wounded in artillery exchanges with Syrian forces north of the Sea of Galilee.

Jordan complains to U. N. Security Council of Israeli "provocation" in the Jerusalem area.

March 17, 1965: Israel charges Syrians have attacked Israeli patrol in the Tel Dan area north of the Sea of Galilee; complains to Security Council of recent attacks on civilian population.

Damascus reports Israeli troops and tanks have attacked Syrian installations for the diversion of the Jordan River project in the Dan Doka area, destroying two bulldozers and killing one driver.

March 18, 1965: Cairo students demonstrate against Bourguiba.

Central Committee of the Neo-Destour party meets and adopts resolution supporting its leader's policy.

The Lebanese Christian Phalangist party comes out in favor of Bourguiba's policies.

March 19, 1965: Syria complains to Security Council of Israel's "aggressive activities."

Lebanon takes "precautionary measures" following reports that Israeli forces have attacked Syrian diversion projects.

March 21, 1965: Israel reports new clashes with the Syrians.

March 22, 1965: U. S. military and intelligence circles disclose they have evidence that Egyptian troops in the Yemen use chemical warfare against royalist villages.

March 23, 1965: Arab Oil Congress approves a boycott resolution aimed principally against West Germany.

Cairo denies its troops use poison gas in the Yemen.

March 25, 1965: King Hussein, in an interview, declares he expects Israel to launch a preventive war against the Arab countries.

March 26, 1965: Levi Eshkol, at a news-conference in London, declares that the peace chances in the Middle East "are not very promising."

March 28, 1965: Anti-Bourguiba demonstration in Cairo.

March 30, 1965: Golda Meir, Israeli Foreign Minister, threatens preventive war in connection with the diversion of the headwaters of the River Jordan.

April 1, 1965: Chinese Premier Chou En-lai in Cairo. Confers with Nasser and other officials. Pledges support to the Arabs in their fight to regain Palestine.

April 10, 1965: Bourguiba returns to Tunis. Received the greatest and most enthusiastic welcome of his career.

April 15, 1965: Tunisian Parliament endorses Bourguiba's Palestine policy.

April 21, 1965: Delivers speech in Carthage before the National Federation of the Neo-Destourian students in which he elaborates on his plan for a negotiated settlement of the Israel-Arab conflict.

April 23, 1965: Violent press and radio attacks in the Arab press against Bourguiba in reaction to his speech in Carthage. Articles of fierce condemnation appear in Egypt, the Lebanon, Syria and Iraq.

U.S. State Department in a statement by Press Secretary Robert McClosky praises Bourguiba's initiative.

Favorable editorials appear in the Western press—in England, France, Belgium, Switzerland. In the U. S. Bourguiba's initiative is praised editorially in the *New York Times* and the *Washington Post*. Among the European newspapers which praised Bourguiba editorially were *Le Monde* (Paris) ; *The London Observer; The Manchester Guardian.*

April 24, 1965: Anti-Bourguiba demonstrations in Cairo. Students attack Tunisian Embassy. Central Committee of the Neo-Destour Party endorses Bourguiba's peace plan.

April 27, 1965: Anti-Egyptian demonstrations in Tunis. Egyptian Embassy attacked.

Nasser retaliates: withdraws Ambassador Radwan from Tunis. Denounces any Bourguiba attempt to mediate Arab-Israeli dispute. Foreign Minister Mahamoud Riad rejects idea of negotiations or compromise in speech at U. A. R. National Assembly which condemns Bourguiba.

Chairman of Assembly for Arab Affairs Committee says Tunisian presence in Arab League causes more harm than good.

Tunisian Ambassador Mahomed Badra arrives in Cairo to participate in Arab League conference of representatives of heads of state, carrying a personal message from Bourguiba to Nasser.

April 28, 1965: Meeting of personal envoys of Arab heads-of-state opens in Cairo.

Weighs proposal that Bourguiba be banned from the League conferences and that a special meeting be called to consider Tunisia's ouster.

Nasser refuses to see Badra. The Ambassador confers with Arab League Secretary General, Hassouna.

Violent anti-Bourguiba demonstrations. Set Badra's residence on fire. Badra claims rioters tried to assassinate him.

Badra boycotts Arab League meeting.

Ambassador Badra and his staff ordered back to Tunisia along with the Ambassadors to Syria, Jordan and Iraq, following violent anti-Bourguiba demonstrations in those countries.

April 29, 1965: Arab League Conference indirectly censures Bourguiba but rejects Shukairy's demand to recommend Tunisia's ouster.

Morocco, Libya and Saudi Arabia oppose extreme action against Tunisia.

Tunisia boycotts meeting.

Ambassador Badra back in Tunis.

Most Egyptian diplomatic personnel have left Tunisia.

President Bourguiba, in a letter to Nasser, offers to meet him to discuss Arab policy towards Israel.

April 30, 1965: Bourguiba's message to Nasser made public.

President Tito and Nasser issue communiqué in Cairo condemning "imperialist powers" for "stepping up arming of Israel" in communiqué.

May 1, 1965: Bourguiba's speech in Sfax.

Nasser answers Bourguiba; attacks him on various grounds.

Lebanese President Helou in Cairo for a four-day visit.

May 12, 1965: Israel and West Germany establish diplomatic relations.

May 12–16, 1965: Simultaneously ten Arab nations (Algeria, Iraq,

Jordan, Kuwait, Lebanon, Saudi Arabia, Sudan, Syria and the United Arab Republic and Republican Yemen sever diplomatic relations with West Germany. Tunis, Morocco and Libya do not follow suit.

May 17, 1965: Premier Eshkol, in the Knesset, calls for peace negotiations between Israel and the Arab States, but rejects Bourguiba's proposals as a basis for discussions.

Tunisian Planning and Economic Minister Ahmed ben Salah in Washington. U. S. Government reaffirmed its willingness to extend "major support" for Tunisia's economic development.

May 21, 1965: National Council of Neo-Destour Party proclaims break with the Arab League.

May 23, 1965: Formal notification of Tunisia's break with the League delivered in Cairo to Secretary General Hassouna shortly before conference of heads of government convened.

May 23, 1965: Bourguiba interviewed by CBS on Face the Nation. Rejects Nasser's leadership of the Arab world and declares him an imperialist who seeks to dominate all Arab nations. Declares Tunisia will not return to the Arab League as long as it is dominated by Cairo or meets on Egyptian soil.

May 25, 1965: Nasser and President Aref of Iraq after discussions in Cairo issue joint communiqués denouncing Bourguiba.

May 26, 1965: Arab League Conference of heads of governments assembled in Cairo (referred to as "the Little Summit").

May 27, 1965: Israeli large scale retaliatory raid into Jordan.

May 28, 1965: Israel announces its army carried out three retaliatory raids into Jordan following recent "acts of sabotage" by infiltrators coming from Jordan.

May 30, 1965: A five day conference of twelve Arab heads of government ends in Cairo. Tunisia boycotts the sessions. It is officially announced that the Arab leaders agreed to consolidate action to liberate Palestine, to strengthen military unity and to continue implementation of the diversion projects on Jordan River tributaries.

May 31, 1965: Two civilians are killed and four wounded in the Israeli sector of Jerusalem by gunfire coming from the Jordanian sector.

Nasser, in a speech inaugurating the second Palestine National Congress, declares that Arab League states are in no position to Liberate Palestine, nor go to war to implement the diversion of headwaters of the River Jordan. He calls to postpone the implementation of all these projects.

June 11, 1965: Arab saboteurs from Jordan raid two Israeli settlements.

Syrian President General Amin el-Hafez criticizes Nasser for his speech before the Palestine Liberation Congress and declares that Syria will accept no solution of the Palestine issue short of the elimination of Israel.

June 19, 1965: Military coup in Algeria. President Ben Bella is overthrown and arrested. Defense Minister Colonel Houari Boumedienne who leads the coup promises stern punishment of the overthrown leader.

July 4, 1965: Habib ben Achur, Secretary General of the General Union of Tunisian Workers (UGTT) is dismissed from his post after having been stripped of his parliamentary immunity from criminal persecution and arrested.

September 13–17, 1965: Third "Summit" Conference of Arab heads of state opens in Casablanca, Morocco. Tunisia boycotts the conference. Bourguiba, in a broadcast a few hours before the opening of the conference accuses Nasser of trying to exercise "hegemony" over all Arab nations and declares that Tunisia will not participate in any further League conferences, unless the League is thoroughly reorganized and free of any Egyptian pressures.

At the end of their deliberations the conference participants adopted a "solidarity" pact which was meant to satisfy Bourguiba's demands. The Arab leaders have agreed to end radio and press attacks on one another and "to ease the way to unity on the Palestine problem."

November 13, 1966: Israeli troops in brigade strength (4,000) supported by tanks, artillery and aircraft, penetrate Jordanian territory and reach the town of Samu, where they destroy houses, claimed by the Israelis to have harbored saboteurs.

On November 25, the Security Council by a vote of 14 to 0, with only New Zealand abstaining, censured Israel for this military act.

November 15 – December 15: Bourguiba on a tour in nine African states. Promotes idea of a French-speaking commonwealth of nations centered in Paris.

February 23, 1966: Military coup in Syria ousts Major General

Amin el-Hafez and places him under arrest. On February 25, the ruling military junta appoints Nuredin Attassi as chief of state.

October 3, 1966: Tunisia breaks diplomatic relations with Egypt.

November 28, 1966: Bourguiba visits the synagogue on the island of Djerba.

February 10, 1967: Tunisia breaks off diplomatic relations with Republican Yemen.

March 15, 1967: Bourguiba suffers a severe heart attack.

May 14, 1967: Egypt begins, with great public display, mobilization of its armed forces against Israel.

May 16, 1967: Egypt asks commander of the U.N. Emergency Force to withdraw from the armistice line between Egypt and Israel.

May 18, 1967: Secretary General of the U.N. U. Thant announces that he has decided to withdraw UNEF.

May 23, 1967: Nasser announces closing of the Straits of Tiran and the Gulf of Aqaba to Israeli shipping and to Israeli-bound shipping carrying "strategic material." Premier Eshkol declares that Israel will insist on free maritime passage to Eilat and calls for support of the maritime powers.

May 30, 1967: King Hussein signs military pact with Nasser in Cairo, placing Jordanian forces under Egyptian command.

Iraqi forces move into Syria, Jordan and Egypt; Kuwaiti and Sudanese forces move into Egypt. Algeria announces it is sending troops and planes to Egypt.

Bourguiba, at a meeting of the Council of the Republic, declares that "Tunisia is ready to participate in any joint action in the Middle East, provided it is well-intentioned."

June 5, 1967: Full-scale war erupts between Israel and its Arab neighbors.

Violent anti-Israel, anti-British and anti-American demonstrations break out in Tunis. Rioters sack the U.S. Embassy, set fire to the British Embassy and to the main synagogue in the capital. Jewish homes and stores are attacked and property is damaged. The mob shouts "Death to the Jews!"

The same evening, Bourguiba, in a televised speech, condemns the riots, his wrath especially directed against those who attacked the Jewish citizens. He calls for severe punishment of the perpetrators of the crimes; declaring: "These hoodlums deserve the gallows."

On July 31 a military tribunal of Tunis sentences 54 persons to forced labor for terms of 1 to 20 years on charges of participating in the anti-Jewish riots.

June 8, 1967: Israel announces its troops have reached the Suez Canal.

Egypt and Syria accept the cease-fire decided by the Security Council.

June 9, 1967: Israel announces that its forces have occupied the Golan Hights in Syria.

Nasser announces his resignation. Next day he withdrew resignation.

June 10, 1967: Russia breaks off diplomatic relations with Israel, followed by other East European Communist countries, except Roumania.

June 12, 1967: Tunisia and Egypt resume diplomatic relations.

June 28, 1967: Israeli Parliament votes the annexation of the Jordanian sector of Jerusalem.

July 5, 1967: Bourguiba resumes his campaign against Arab intransigence, and blames Nasser for all the misfortunes which have befallen the Arabs, especially those of Palestine. In subsequent utterences he demands Nasser's resignation as a prerequisite for peace in the Middle East.

Index

Abdullah, King, 109, 334
Aden, 145
Africa, 34, 54, 94, 96–97, 141, 175, 185, 194, 212, 261, 266, 286, 294, 306, 369, *passim;* Conference for African Unity (July 1946), 63, 97, 184; Organization for African Unity, 97, 184
Agong, King Yang di-Pertuan, 113
Agronsky, Martin, 283, 308
Aljun College, 49
Akbat Jather (refugee camp), 30
Akhbar el-Yom, 109, 111, 152, 214, 439
Akhdut Avoda, 189, 234n
Al Ahram, 22, 65, 69, 72, 107, 110–111, 127, 151, 280, 282, 390
Al Ahrar, 70, 111, 160
Al Aksa Mosque, 30
Al Amal, 74, 117, 121, 131, 142, 359, 386, 393n
Al Arad, 242
Al Assiffa, 51
Al-Azhar University, 120
Al Azhari, 166n
Al-Ba'ath, 112, 159, 160
Al Difaa, 332
Al Fatah, 51, 149
Algeria, 84, 114, 127, 133, 151, 163, 166n, 184–185, 273, 276, 290–291, 294, 302, 305, 311, 320, 328, 331, 350, 356, 358, 360, 380–381, 398, 405, 412, 446
Al Goumhouria, 110, 359
Al-Jaryda, 42, 106, 147, 246, 360
Al Jihad, 112
Al-Khayat, 41–42, 45, 88, 115, 275, 311n, 358
Al Manar, 30, 47, 246
Al Moharrer, 111, 130
Al-Nahar, 41

Al Sabah, 70, 131
al-Sabah, Emir Abdallah al-Salem, 166n
Al-Safa, 41, 359
Al Yaum, 62, 185
Amer, Lt. General Ali, Ali, 146, 149, 168–169
Amer, Field Marshall Mohamed Abdul Hakim, 285
Amman, 30, 32, 40, 50, 125, 225, 335, 384
Angola, 268
Ankara, 60, 74, 79
Anouil, Gilles, 355
Arab boycott, 26, 226
Arab-Israel Federation, 42, 87, 198, 217, 236–237, 293, 355–356, 359
Arab-Israeli conflict, see Israeli-Arab conflict
Arab League, 19, 71, 81, 87, 104, 109, 115, 124–125, 127, 129, 131–132, 136–138, 141, 145, 151–152, 155–156, 159–160, 162, 164, 167, 169, 309–310, 359; Unified Military Command, 20, 23, 29, 35, 53, 110, 119, 129, 135, 146–149, 153–154, 160, 168n–169, 172, 279, 309; Conference of envoys (March 9–10, 1965, in Cairo), 71; Conference of Foreign Ministers (March 14, 1965, in Cairo), 72, 127, 179; Conference of Representatives of Heads-of-State (April 28, 1965, in Cairo), 115, 121–126, 132, 138, 179; council 125; adopts resolution against Bourguiba, 119; Conference of Heads-of-Government (May 26, 1965, in Cairo, often referred to as "Little Summit"), 128–129, 138, 143–153, 159–161, 179–180; against recognizing exist-

475